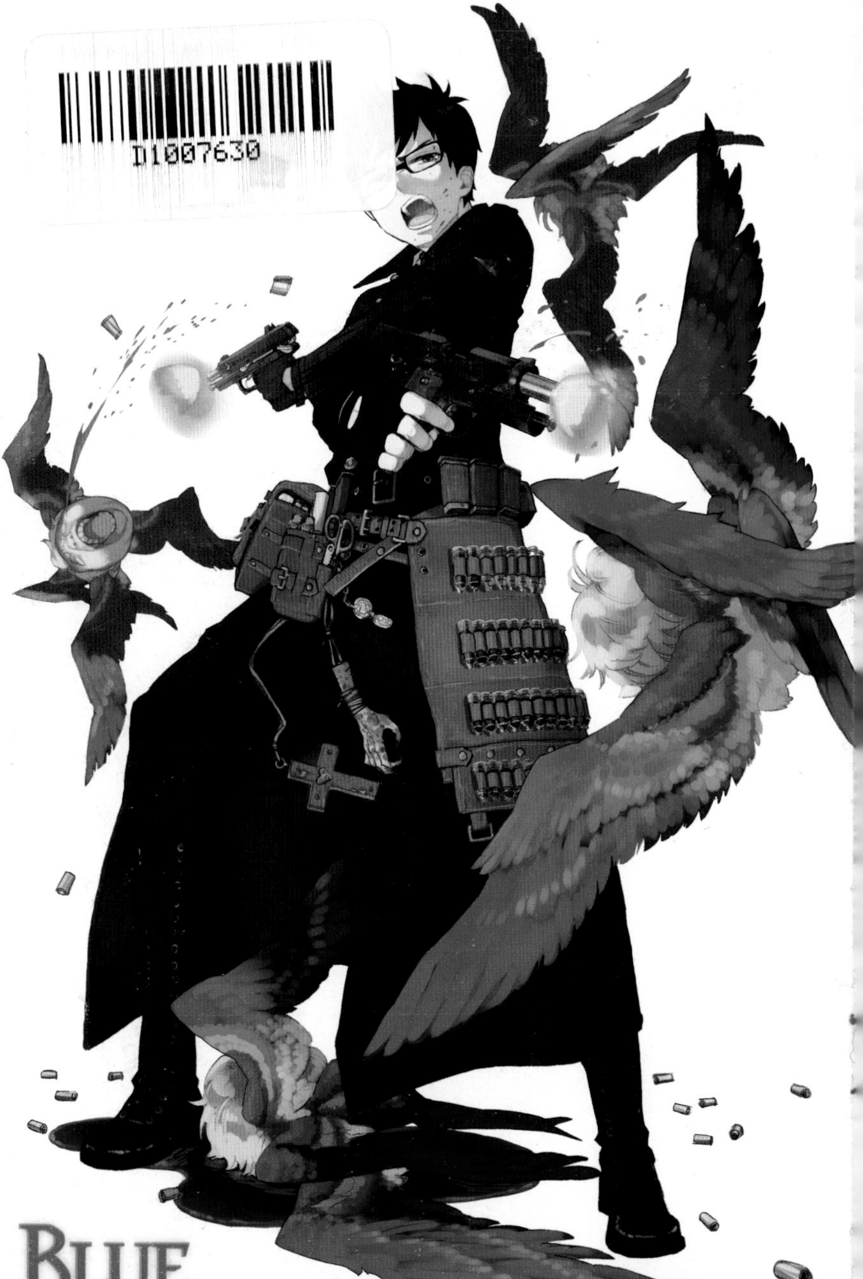

BLUE EXORCIST 15

KAZUE KATO

BLUE EXORCIST

Contents 15

CAST OF CHARACTERS

RIN OKUMURA

Born of a human mother and Satan, the God of Demons, Rin Okumura has powers he can barely control. After Satan kills Father Fujimoto, Rin's foster father, Rin decides to become an Exorcist so he can someday defeat Satan. Now a first-year student at True Cross Academy and an Exwire at the Exorcism Cram School, he hopes to someday become a Knight. When he draws the Koma Sword, he manifests his infernal power in the form of blue flames. He succeeded in defeating the Impure King and affirmed his determination to live with his flame.

YUKIO OKUMURA

Rin's brother. Hoping to become a doctor, he's a genius who is the youngest student ever to become an instructor at the Exorcism Cram School. An instructor in Demon Pharmaceuticals, he possesses the titles of Doctor and Dragoon. Todo told him that his true nature is that of a demon.

SHIEMI MORIYAMA

Daughter of the owner of Futsumaya, an Exorcist supply shop. She possesses the ability to become a Tamer and can summon a baby Greenman named Nee. She passed the high school entrance exam, so now she is a classmate of Rin and the others.

RYUJI SUGURO

Heir to the venerable Buddhist sect known as Myodha in Kyoto. He is an Exwire who hopes to become an Exorcist someday so he can reestablish his family's temple, which fell on hard times after the Blue Night. He wants to achieve the titles of Dragoon and Aria.

KONEKOMARU MIWA

He was once a pupil of Suguro's father and is now Suguro's friend. He's an Exwire who hopes to become an Exorcist someday. He is small in size and has a quiet and composed personality.

KURO

A Cat Sidhe who was once Shiro's familiar. After Shiro's death, he began turning back into a demon. Rin saved him, and now the two are practically inseparable. His favorite drink is the catnip wine Shiro used to make.

BLUE EXORCIST

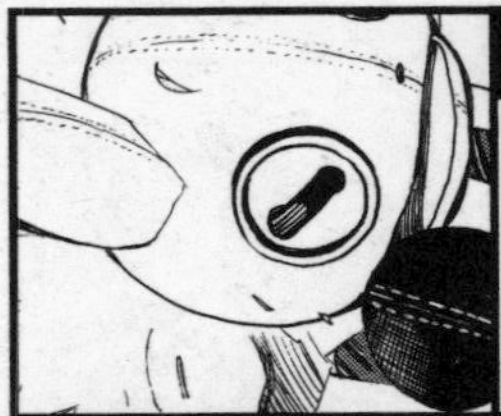

NEMU TAKARA

A student at the Exorcism Cram School. He is a puppet master who can summon and control dolls. Mephisto employed him from outside to serve as supervisor. He is equal in ability to a Senior Exorcist First Class.

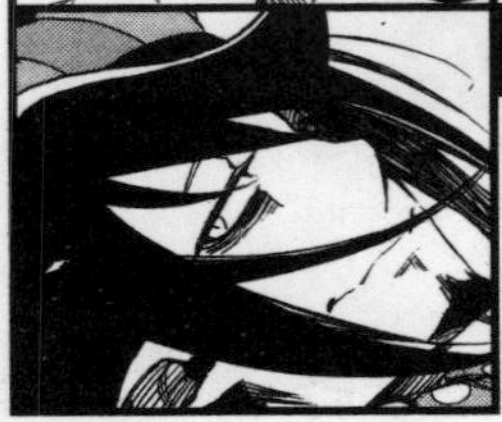

MEPHISTO PHELES

President of True Cross Academy and head of the Exorcism Cram School. He was Father Fujimoto's friend, and now he is Rin and Yukio's guardian. He is the second power in Gehenna and known as Samael, King of Time.

THE KAMIKI FAMILY

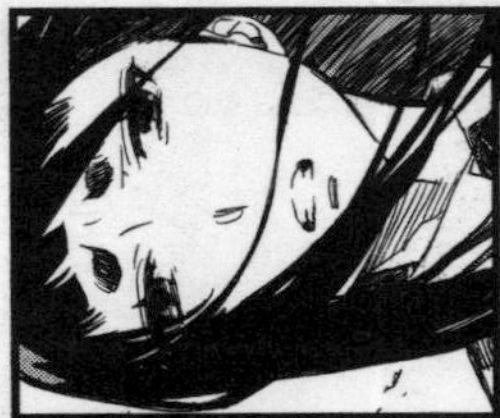

IZUMO KAMIKI

An Exwire with the blood of shrine maidens. She has the ability to become a Tamer and can summon two white foxes. The Illuminati has taken her captive. With help from Rin and the others, she settled her grudge against Gedoin.

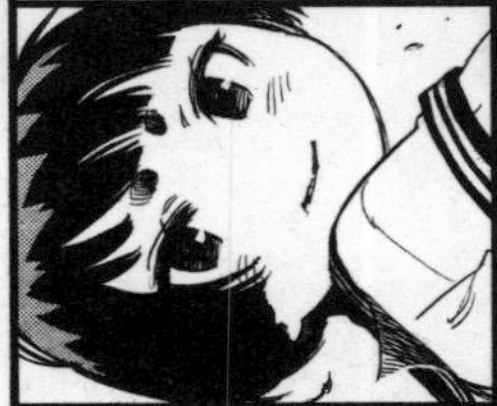

TSUKUMO KAMIKI

Izumo's younger sister. She has the power of a shrine maiden. As the person dearest to Izumo, she is her older sister's biggest weakness. Another family possibly adopted her, but her safety remains unconfirmed.

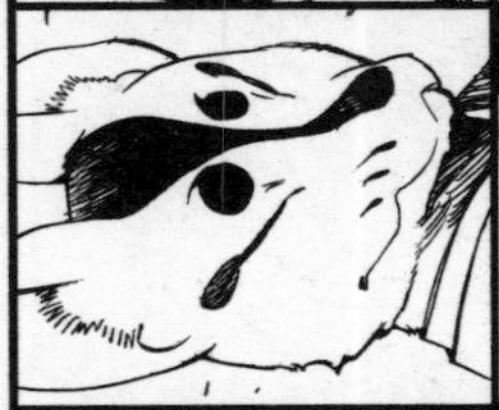

UKEMOCHI

Izumo's familiar and a fox servant of the god Uka-no-Mitama. Destroyed by Shima's familiar Yamantaka, but appeared again when Izumo called.

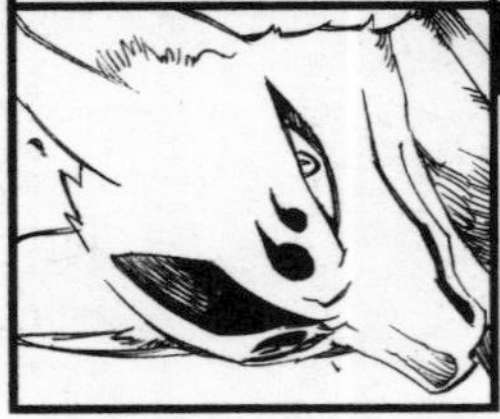

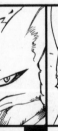

MIKETSU

Izumo's familiar and a fox servant of the god Uka-no-Mitama. Destroyed by Shima's familiar Yamantaka, but appeared again when Izumo called.

TAMAMO KAMIKI

Izumo's mother. She is the 64th chief priestess of the Kamiki family and possesses great spiritual power. As the bearer of the demon fox, aka Nine Tails, her dancing suppressed the Killing Stone. However, when her relationship with her lover Soji turned sour, she lost control and the power of Nine Tails consumed her. When Gedoin transferred Nine Tails to Izumo, Tamamo lost her life saving her daughter.

❀ THE ILLUMINATI ❀

LUCIFER

Commander-in-chief of the Illuminati and known as the King of Light. He is the highest power in Gehenna and plans to resurrect Satan and merge Assiah and Gehenna into one.

MICHAEL GEDOIN

An Illuminati researcher infatuated with Lucifer. He forced a demon to possess him and attacked Izumo!!

???

Lucifer's bodyguard and Shima's direct superior. Her rank is higher than adeptus minor.

LUND & STRÖM

Lucifer's bodyguards.

RENZO SHIMA

Once a pupil of Suguro's father and now Suguro's friend. He trained as an Exwire to become an Aria alongside the other students, but he was a spy for the Illuminati!!

❁ THE STORY SO FAR ❁

UNKNOWN TO RIN OKUMURA, BOTH HUMAN AND DEMON BLOOD RUNS IN HIS VEINS. IN AN ARGUMENT WITH HIS FOSTER FATHER, FATHER FUJIMOTO, RIN LEARNS THAT SATAN IS HIS TRUE FATHER. SATAN SUDDENLY APPEARS AND TRIES TO DRAG RIN DOWN TO GEHENNA BECAUSE RIN HAS INHERITED HIS POWER. FATHER FUJIMOTO FIGHTS TO DEFEND RIN, BUT DIES IN THE PROCESS. RIN DECIDES TO BECOME AN EXORCIST SO HE CAN SOMEDAY DEFEAT SATAN AND BEGINS STUDYING AT THE EXORCISM CRAM SCHOOL UNDER THE INSTRUCTION OF HIS TWIN BROTHER YUKIO, WHO IS ALREADY AN EXORCIST.

RIN AND THE OTHERS SUCCEED IN DEFEATING THE IMPURE KING, AWAKENED BY THE FORMER EXORCIST, TODO. MEANWHILE, YUKIO FIGHTS TODO, AND AS THE BATTLE RAGES, HE SENSES THE SAME FLAME IN HIS OWN EYES AS HIS BROTHER. AFRAID, HE KEEPS IT A SECRET.

LATER, MYSTERIOUS EVENTS BEGIN OCCURRING AROUND THE GLOBE. A SECRET SOCIETY KNOWN AS THE ILLUMINATI IS BEHIND THESE INCIDENTS, AND SHIMA IS THEIR SPY.

WHEN THE ILLUMINATI KIDNAPS IZUMO FOR EXPERIMENTS, RIN AND HIS FRIENDS HEAD FOR INARI, IN SHIMANE PREFECTURE, TO RESCUE HER. THEY FIND IZUMO WITHIN A RESEARCH FACILITY, BUT SHIMA BLOCKS THE WAY. WHEN IZUMO BECOMES HOST TO NINE TAILS, IZUMO'S MOTHER TAMAMO, WHOM IZUMO HAS HATED FOR A LONG TIME, SAVES HER.

WHEN IZUMO SEES HER MOTHER RISK HER LIFE FOR HER, SHE RECOGNIZES THAT THE WAY SHE HAS BEEN LIVING WAS MISTAKEN AND DECIDES TO START TRUSTING OTHER PEOPLE. IN ORDER TO CLEANSE HER PAST, SHE USES THE REPOSE SPIRIT INCANTATION TO EXORCISE GEDOIN, THE SOURCE OF ALL THE TROUBLE!!

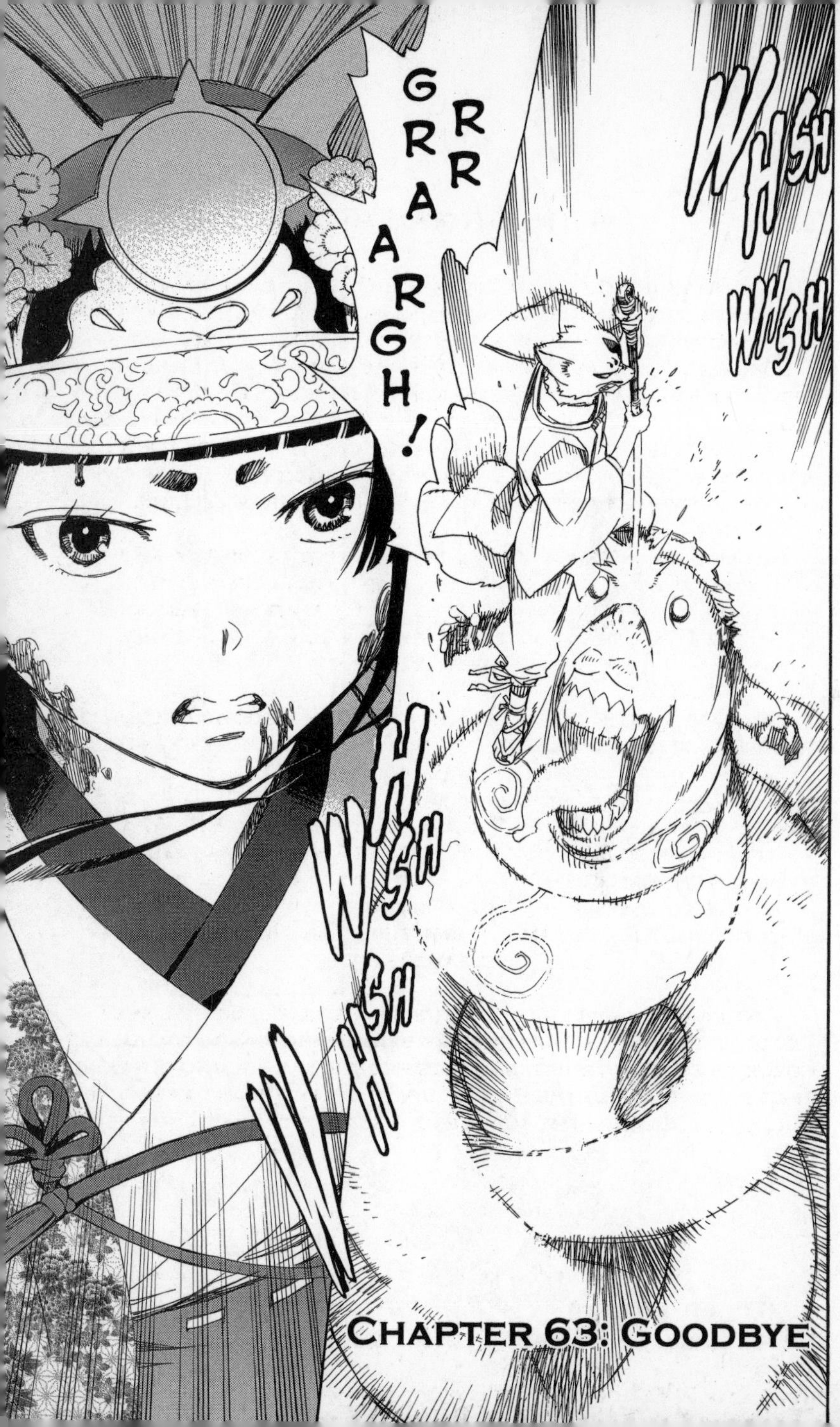
WHSH
WHSH
GRRRAARGH!
WHSH
WHSH
WHSH

Chapter 63: Goodbye

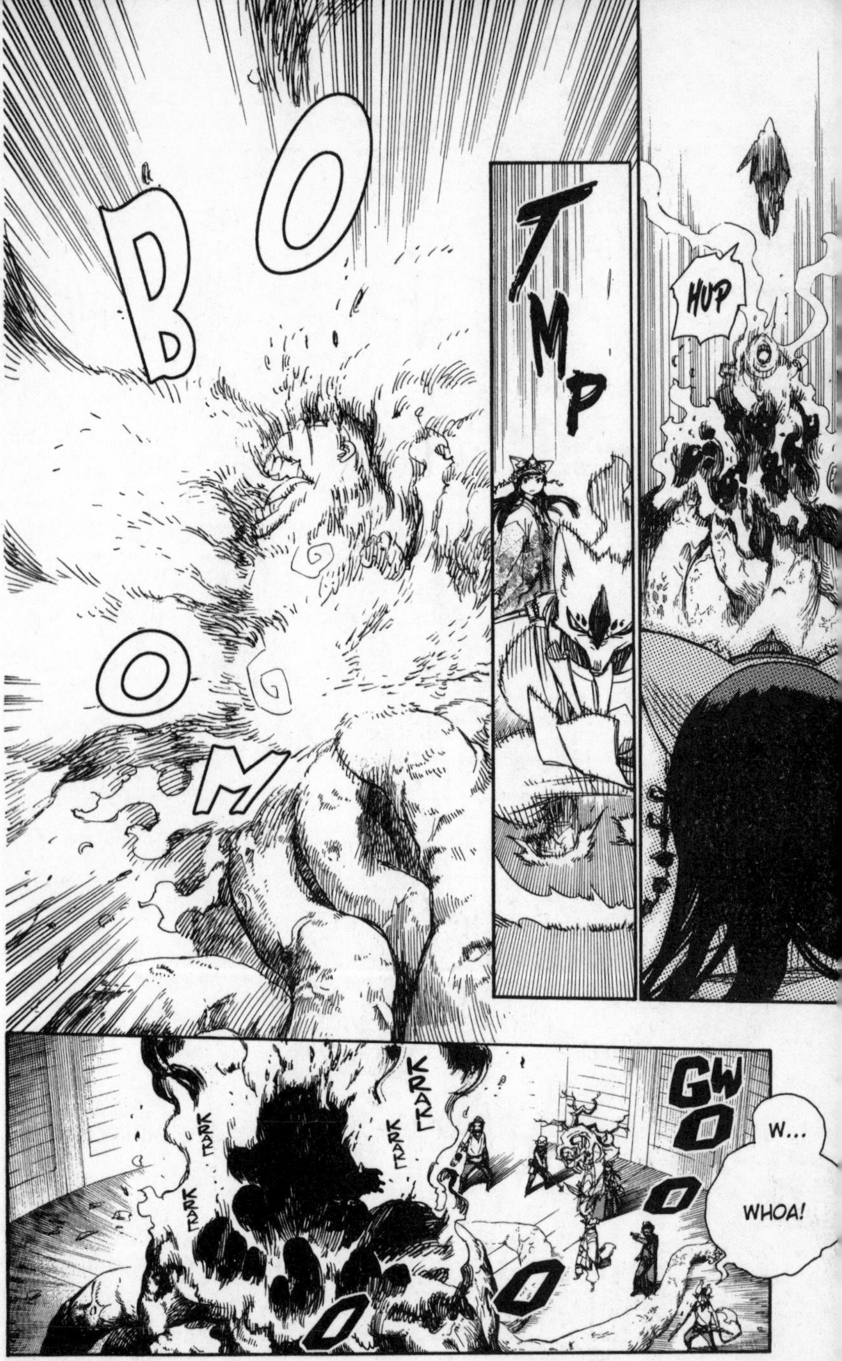

HUP
TMP
BOGOGM
GWOOOOOO
W...
WHOA!
KRAKL
KRAKL
KRAKL
KRAKL

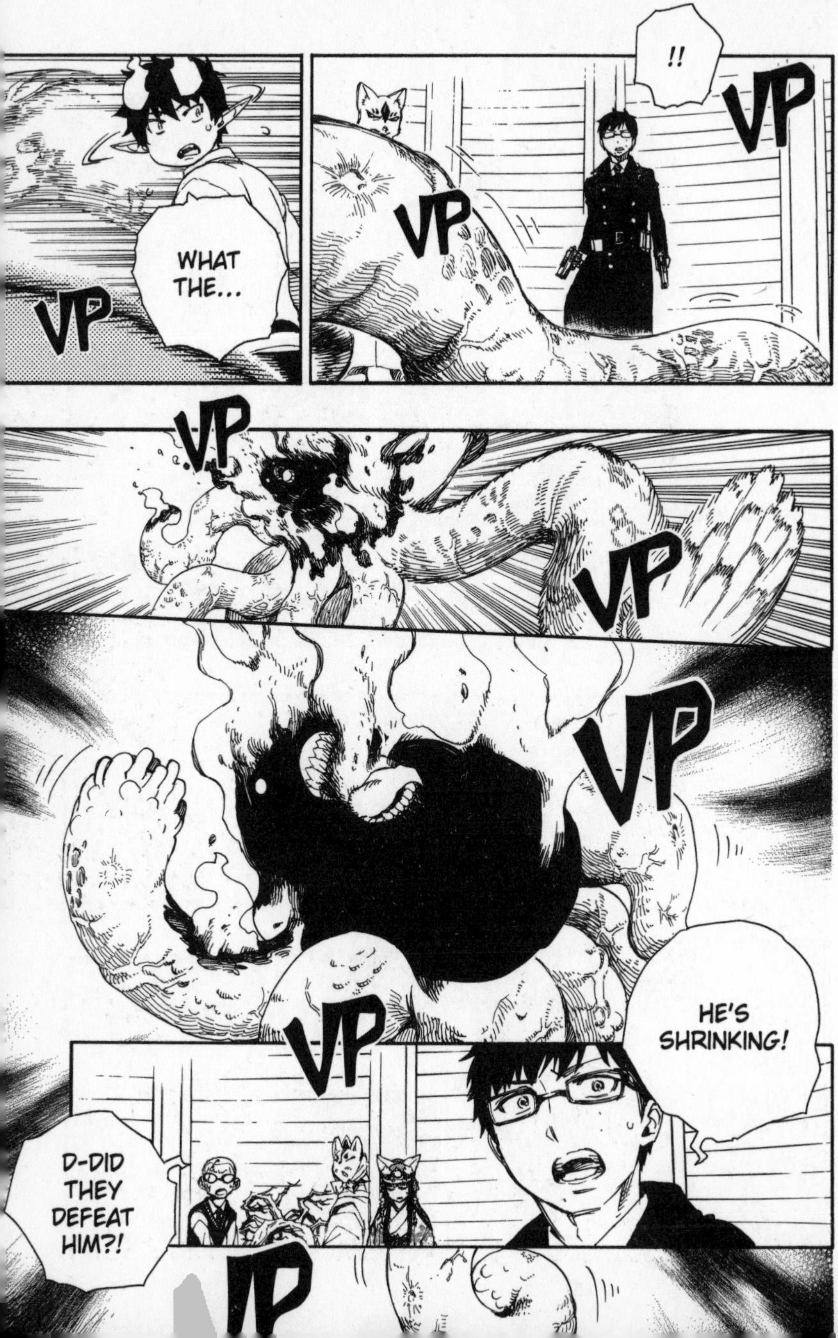
!!
VP
VP
WHAT THE...
VP
VP
VP
VP
VP
HE'S SHRINKING!
VP
D-DID THEY DEFEAT HIM?!
VP

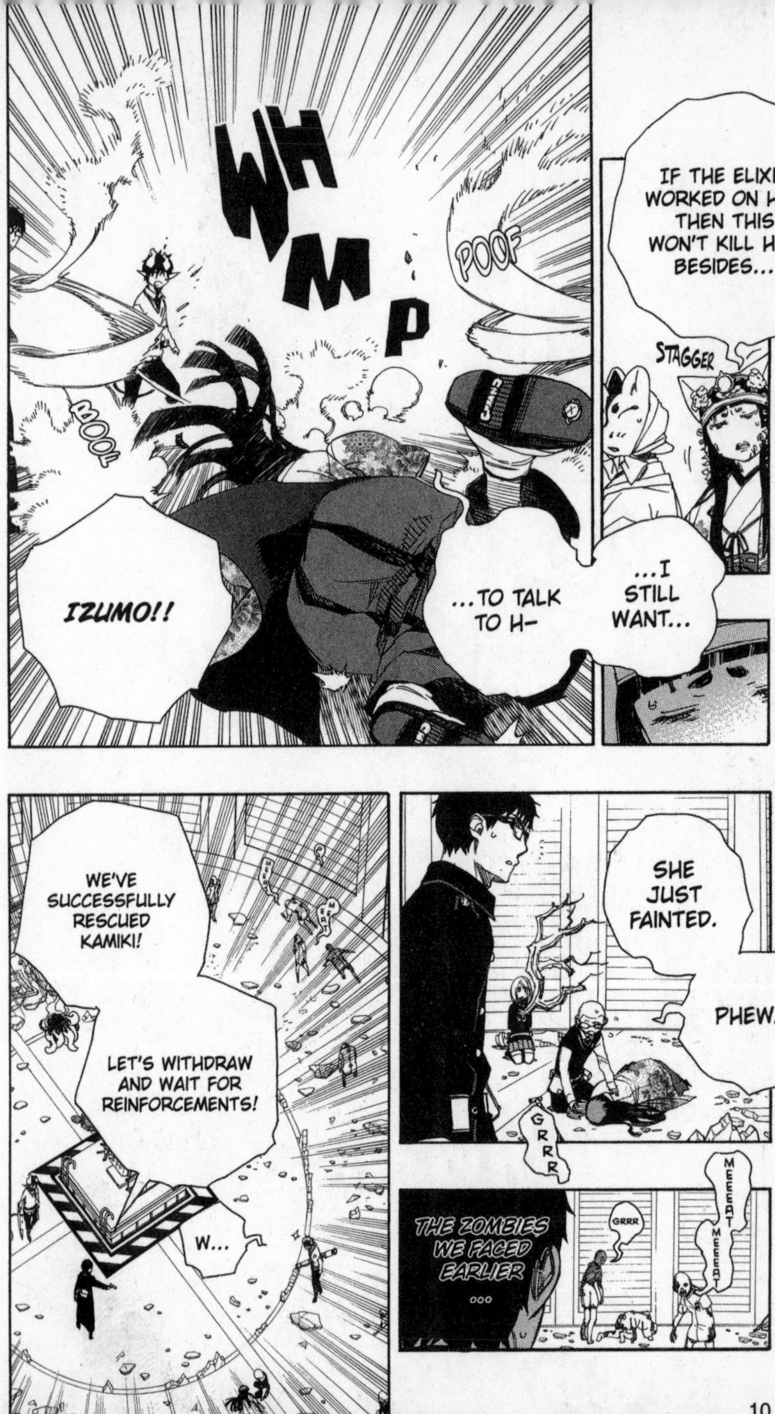
IF THE ELIXIR WORKED ON HIM, THEN THIS WON'T KILL HIM. BESIDES...
STAGGER
...I STILL WANT...
...TO TALK TO H-
WHUMP
POOF
BOOF
IZUMO!!
SHE JUST FAINTED.
PHEW...
GRRR
THE ZOMBIES WE FACED EARLIER ...
GRRR
MEEEAT
MEEEAT
WE'VE SUCCESSFULLY RESCUED KAMIKI!
LET'S WITHDRAW AND WAIT FOR REINFORCEMENTS!
W...

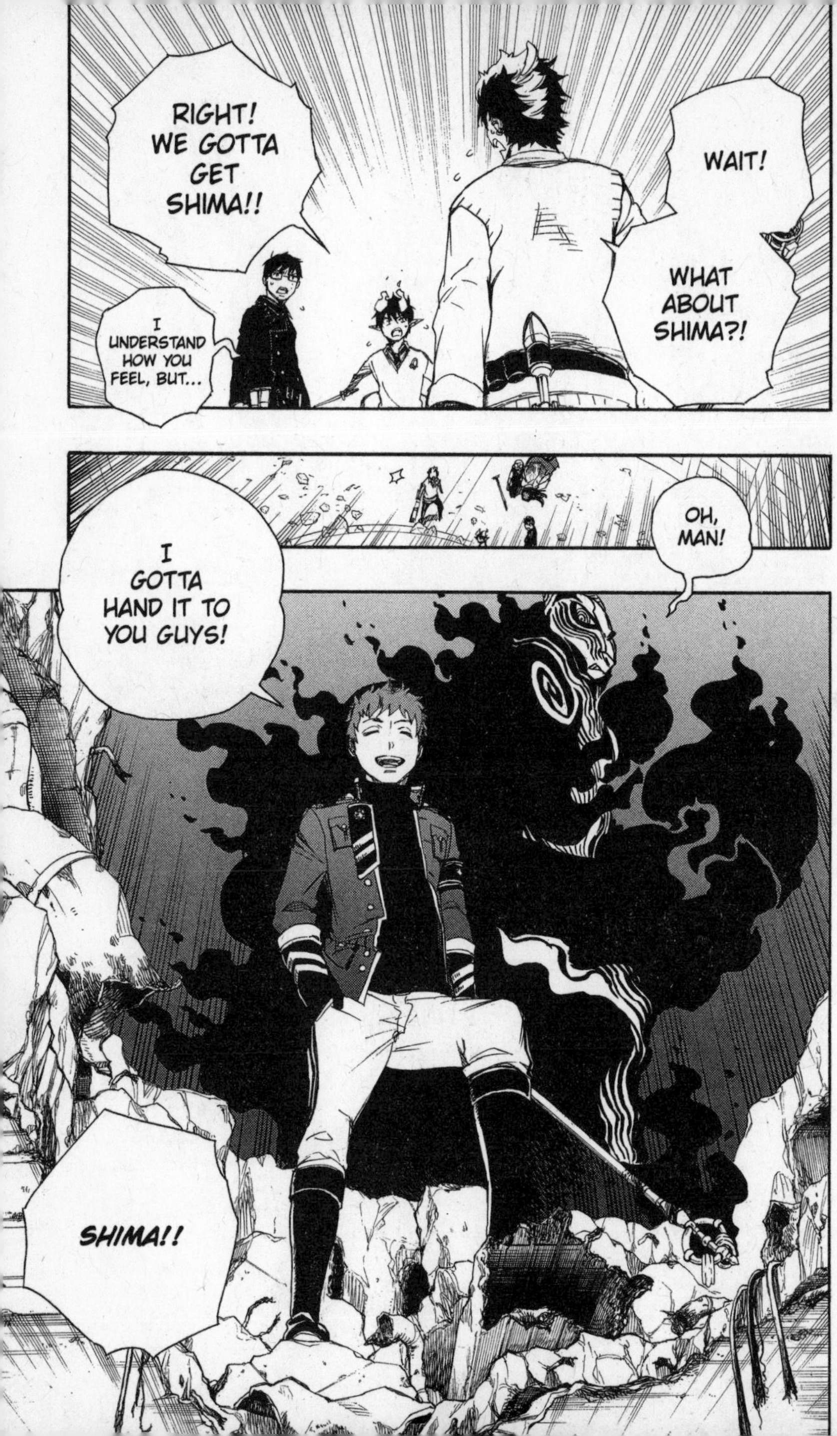
WAIT!
WHAT ABOUT SHIMA?!
RIGHT! WE GOTTA GET SHIMA!!
I UNDERSTAND HOW YOU FEEL, BUT...
OH, MAN!
I GOTTA HAND IT TO YOU GUYS!
SHIMA!!

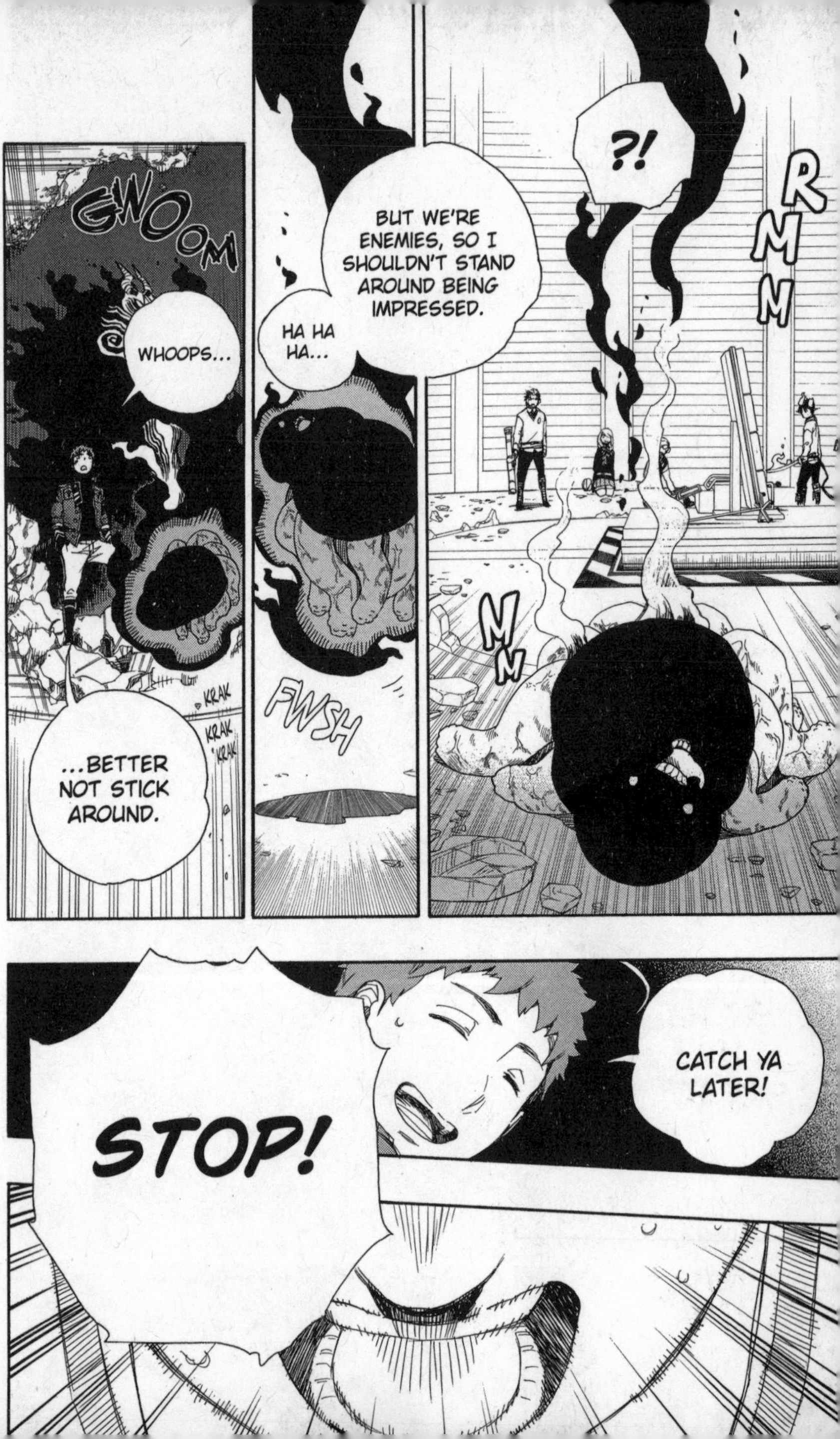
?!
RMMM
MMM
BUT WE'RE ENEMIES, SO I SHOULDN'T STAND AROUND BEING IMPRESSED.
HA HA HA...
FWSH
GWOOM
WHOOPS...
KRAK
KRAK
KRAK
...BETTER NOT STICK AROUND.
CATCH YA LATER!
STOP!

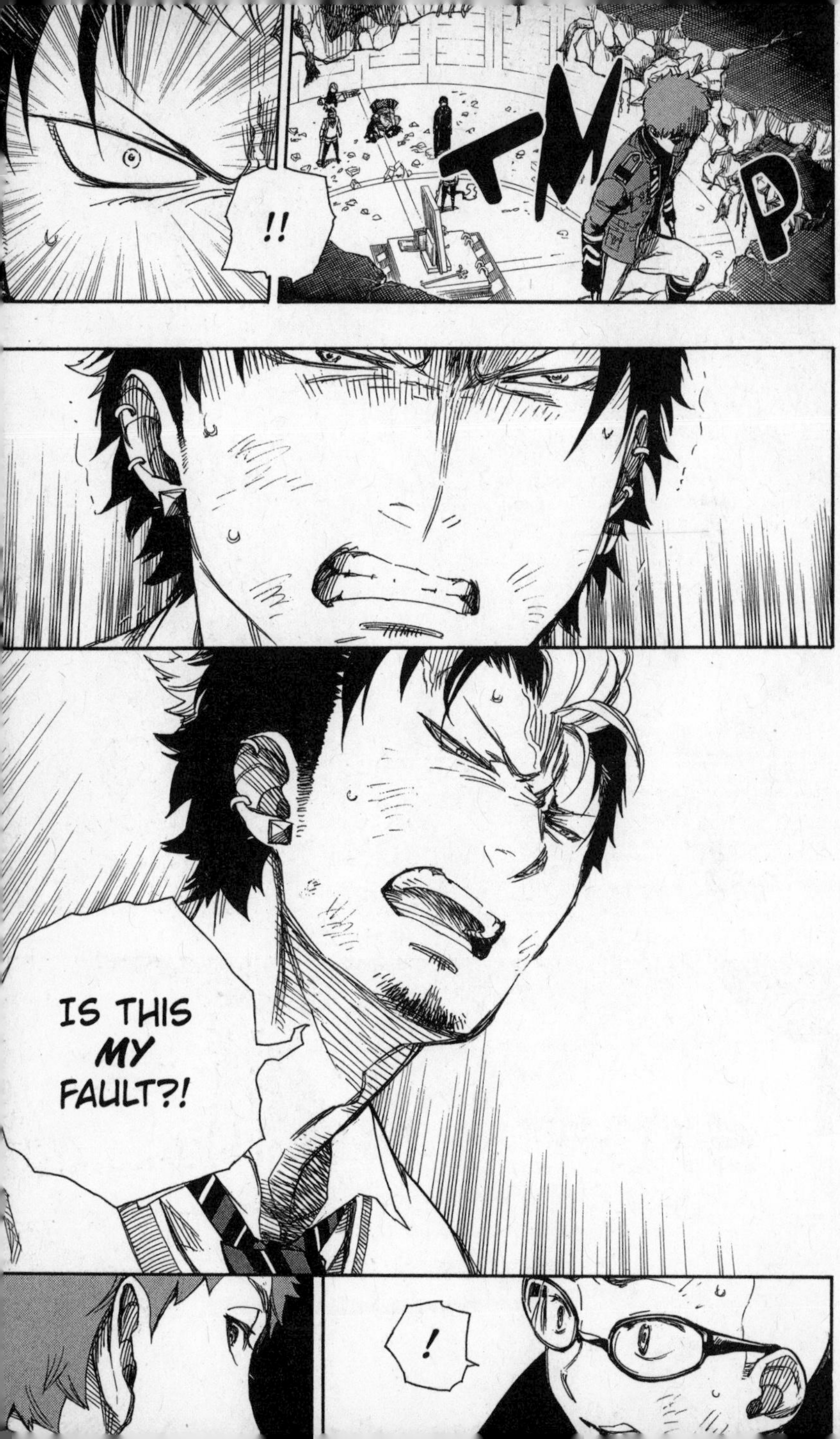
TMP
!!
IS THIS MY FAULT?!
!

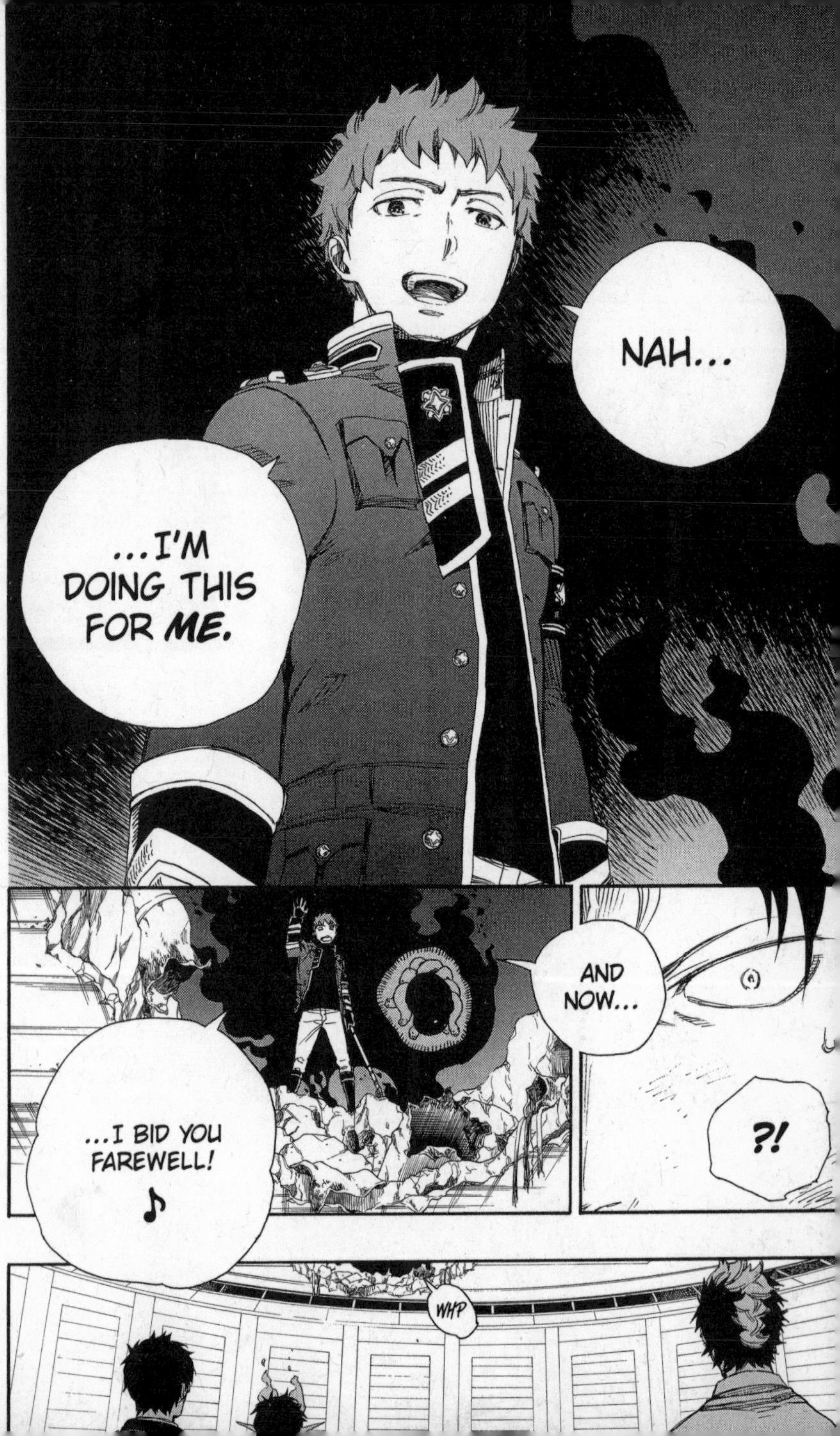
NAH...
...I'M DOING THIS FOR ME.
?!
AND NOW...
...I BID YOU FAREWELL! ♪
WHP

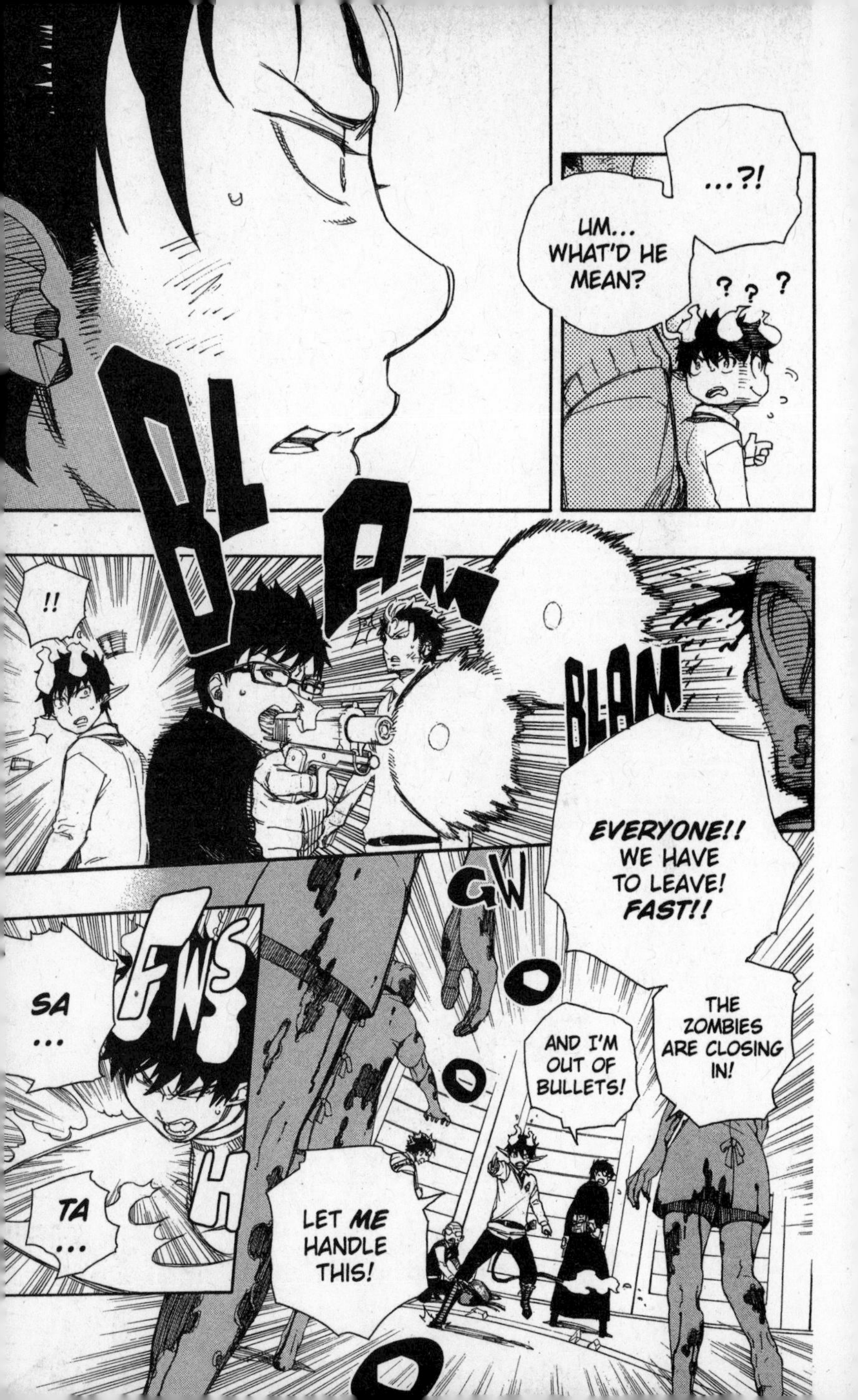
...?!
UM... WHAT'D HE MEAN?
? ? ?
BLAM
BLAM
!!
EVERYONE!! WE HAVE TO LEAVE! FAST!!
THE ZOMBIES ARE CLOSING IN!
AND I'M OUT OF BULLETS!
GWOOO
LET *ME* HANDLE THIS!
SA...
FWSH
TA...

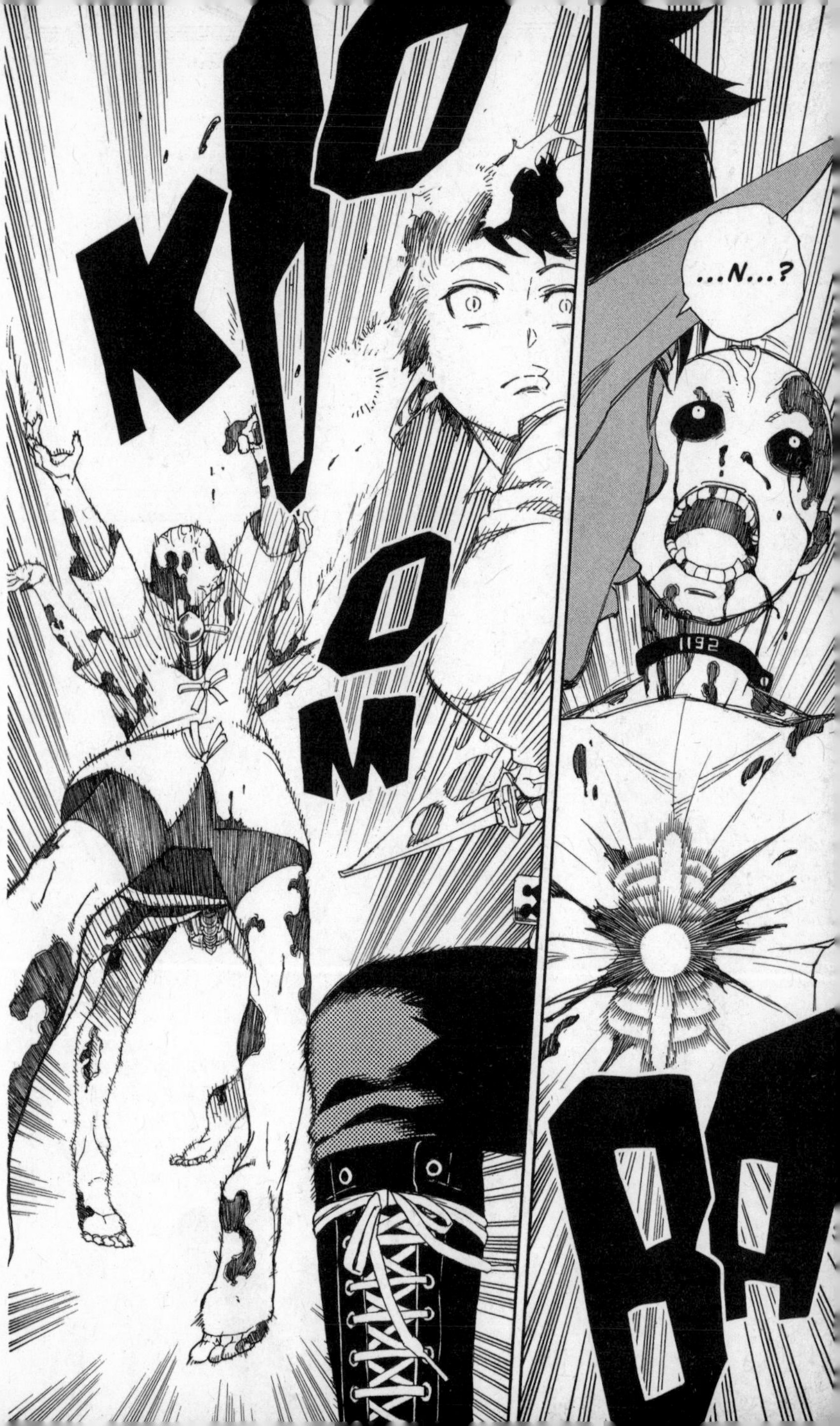
...N...?

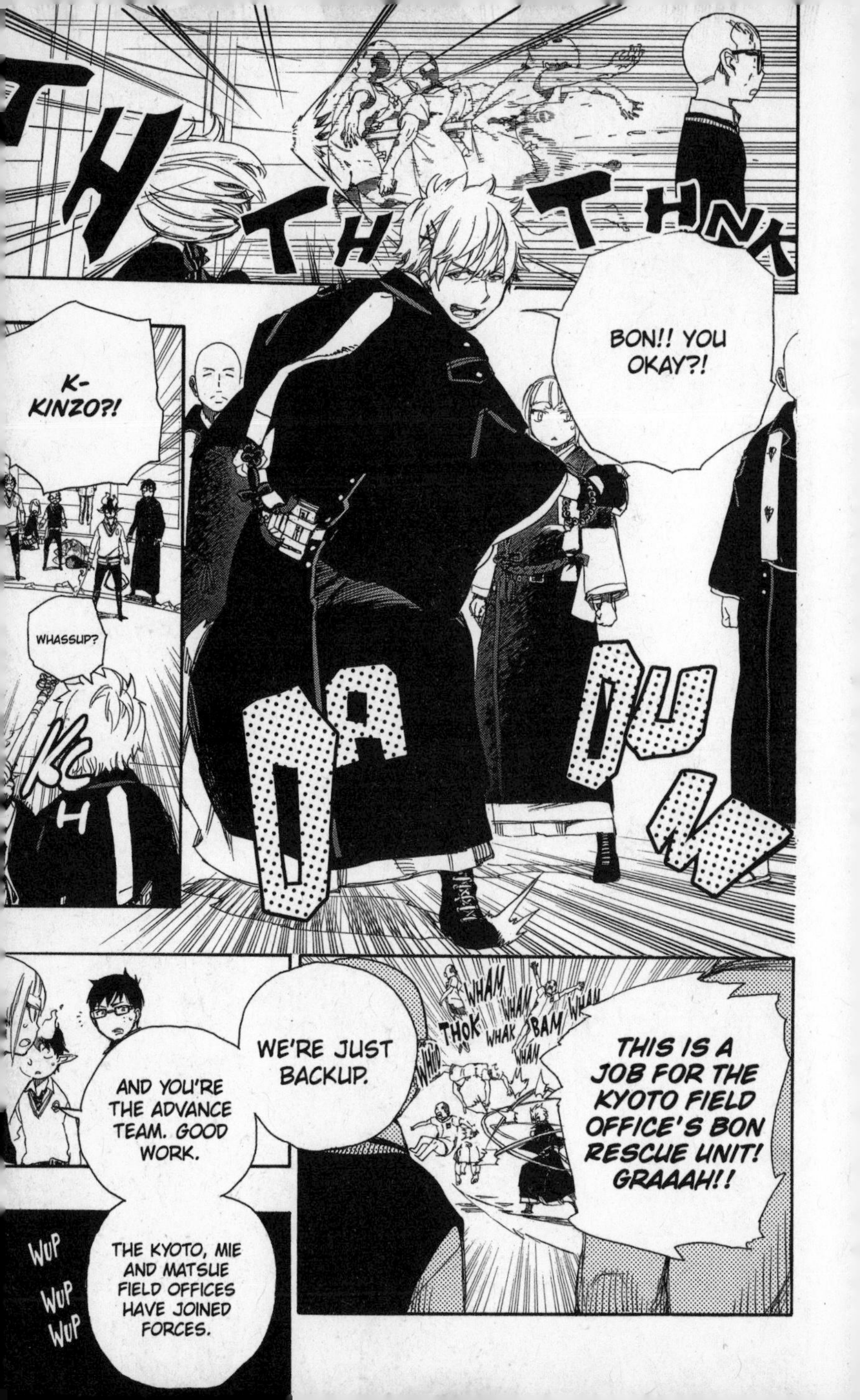
TH
TH
THNK
BON!! YOU OKAY?!
DA
DUM
K-KINZO?!
WHASSUP?
WHAM
WHAM
WHAN
BAM
THOK
WHAK
WHAM
THIS IS A JOB FOR THE KYOTO FIELD OFFICE'S BON RESCUE UNIT! GRAAAH!!
WE'RE JUST BACKUP.
AND YOU'RE THE ADVANCE TEAM. GOOD WORK.
THE KYOTO, MIE AND MATSUE FIELD OFFICES HAVE JOINED FORCES.
WUP
WUP
WUP

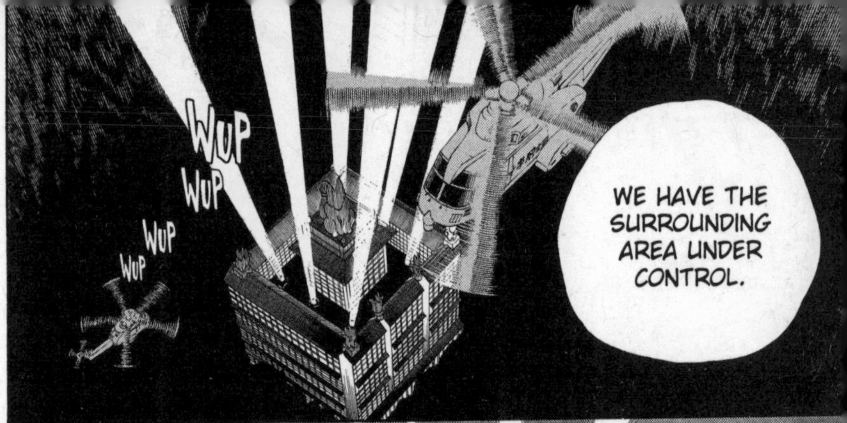
WE HAVE THE SURROUNDING AREA UNDER CONTROL.
WUP
WUP
WUP
WUP

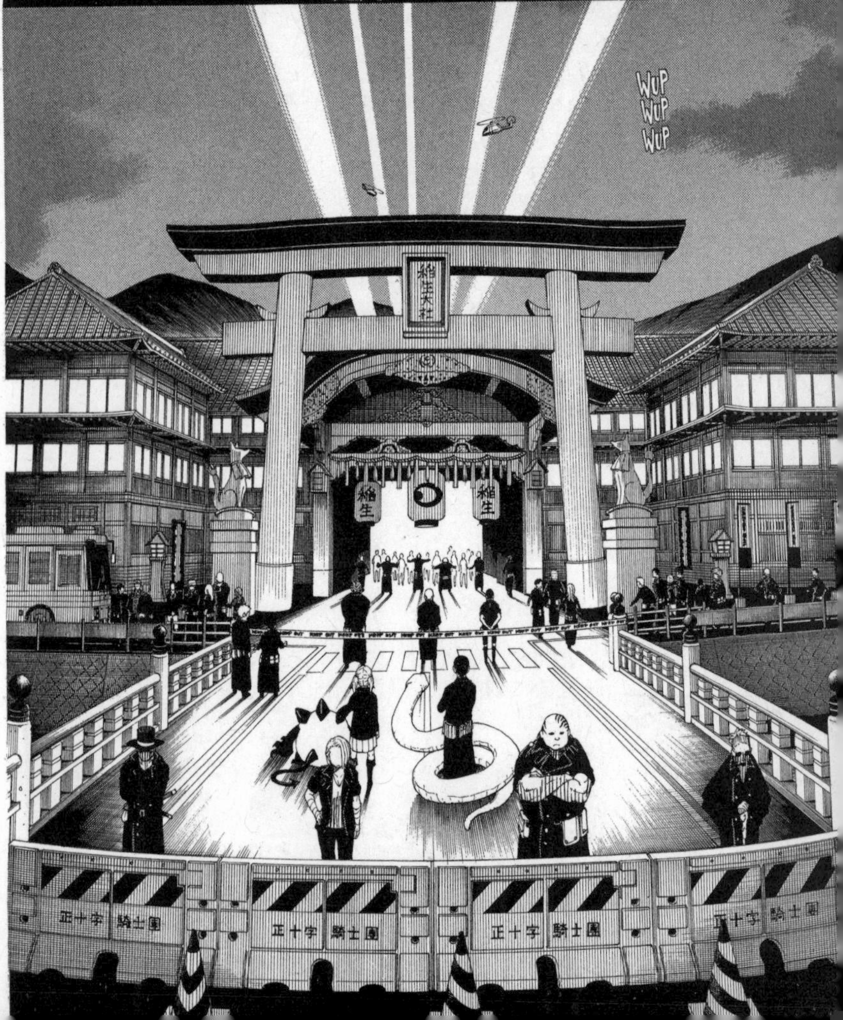
WUP
WUP
WUP
稲生
稲生
正十字 騎士團
正十字 騎士團
正十字 騎士團
正十字 騎士團

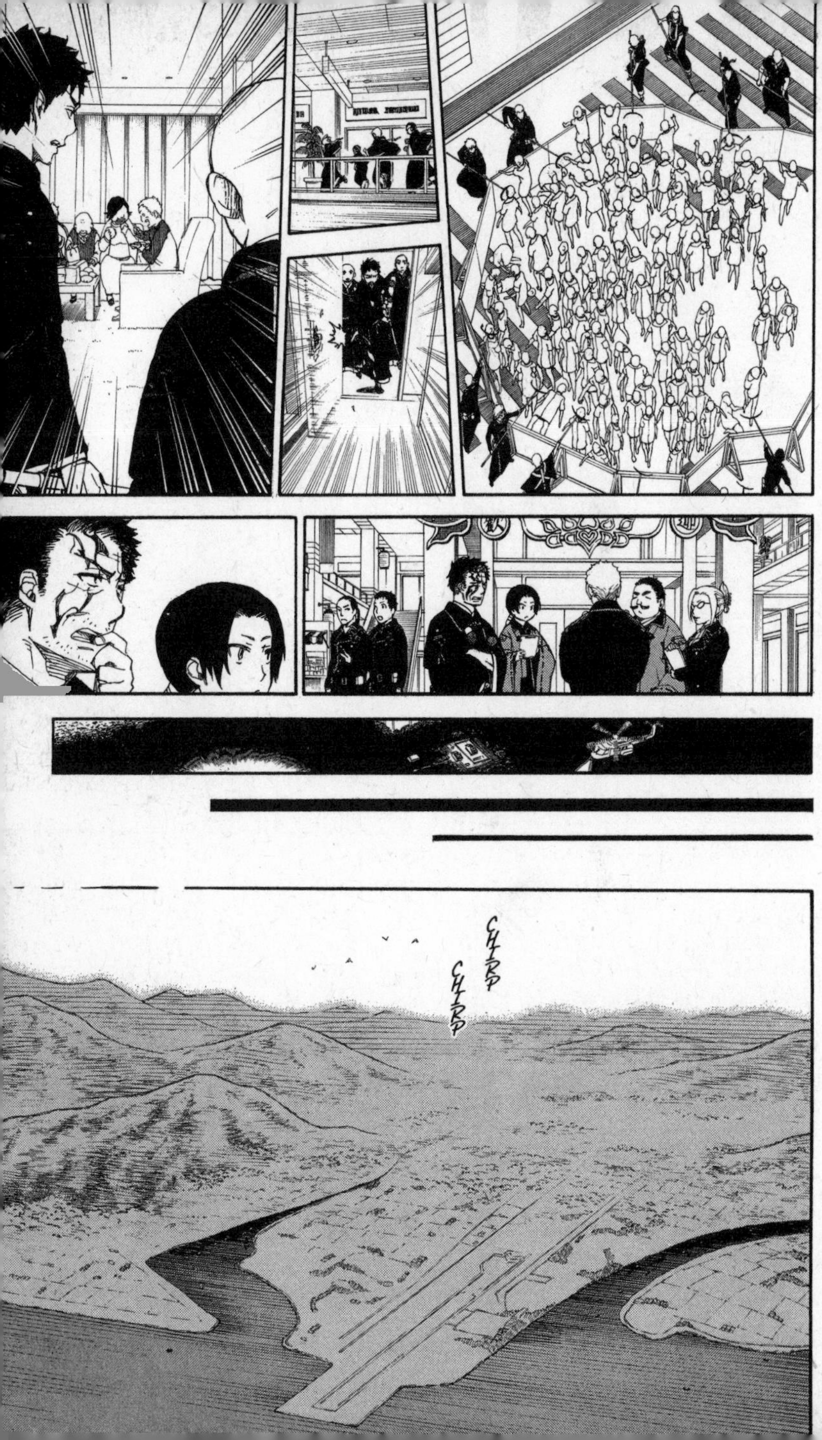
CHIRP
CHIRP

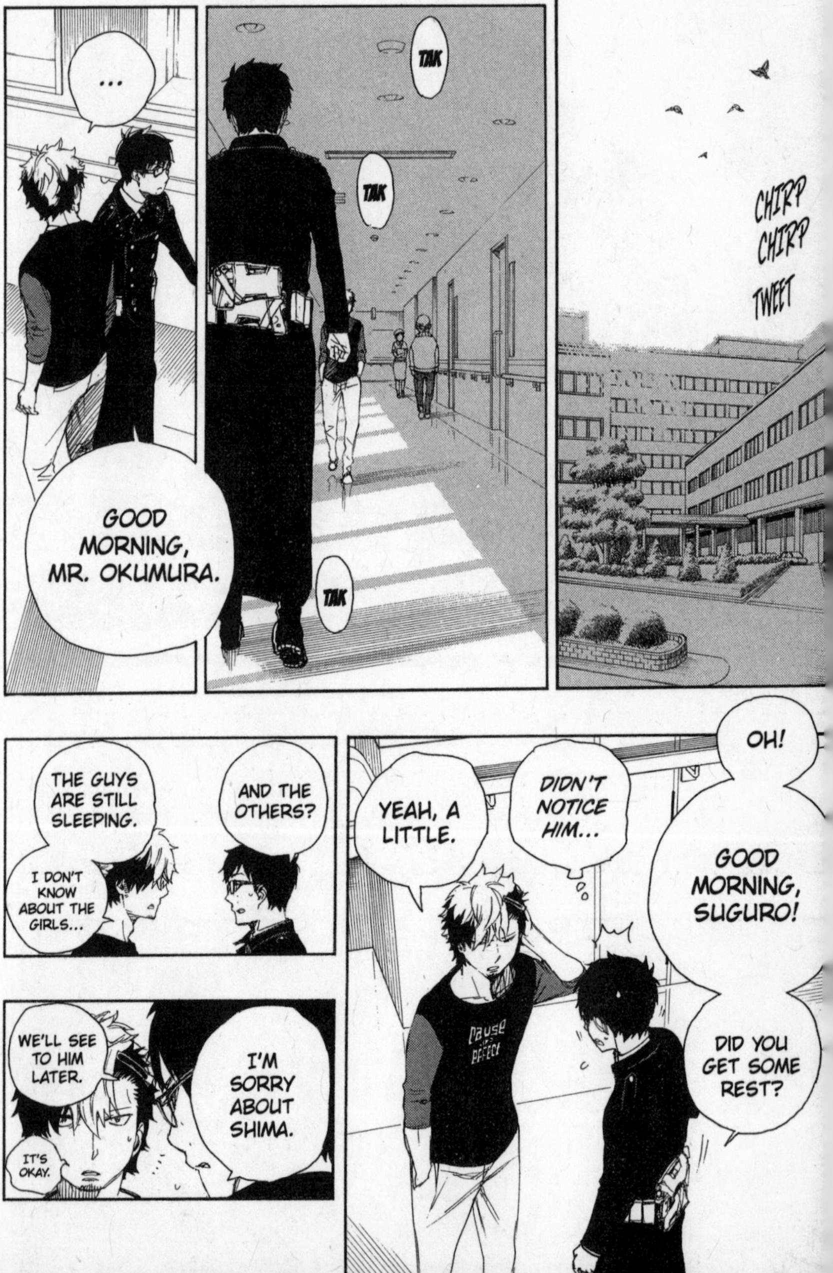
CHIRP
CHIRP
TWEET
TAK
TAK
TAK
...
GOOD MORNING, MR. OKUMURA.
OH!
GOOD MORNING, SUGURO!
DID YOU GET SOME REST?
DIDN'T NOTICE HIM...
YEAH, A LITTLE.
AND THE OTHERS?
THE GUYS ARE STILL SLEEPING.
I DON'T KNOW ABOUT THE GIRLS...
I'M SORRY ABOUT SHIMA.
WE'LL SEE TO HIM LATER.
IT'S OKAY.

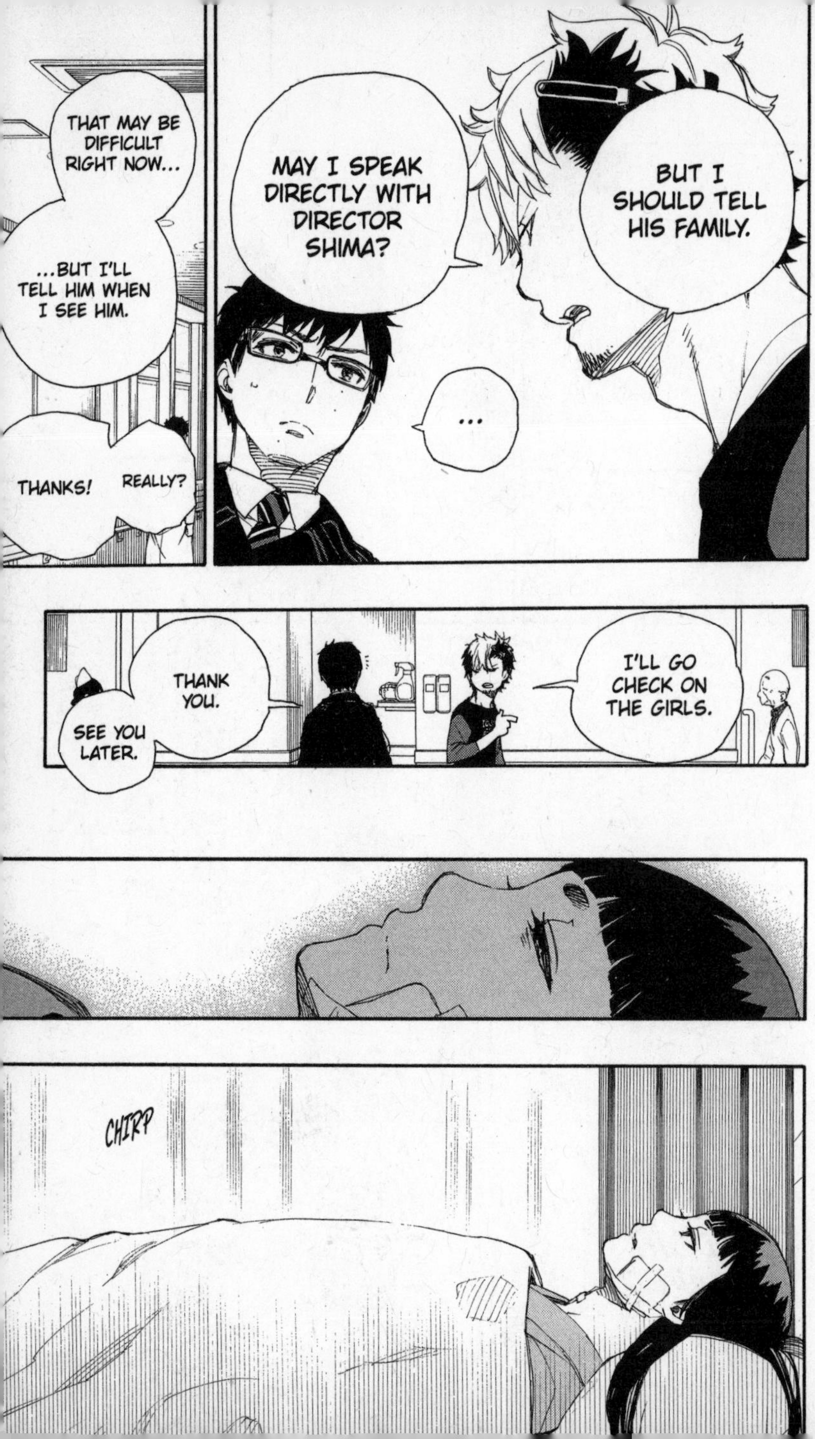
BUT I SHOULD TELL HIS FAMILY.
MAY I SPEAK DIRECTLY WITH DIRECTOR SHIMA?
...
THAT MAY BE DIFFICULT RIGHT NOW...
...BUT I'LL TELL HIM WHEN I SEE HIM.
REALLY?
THANKS!
I'LL GO CHECK ON THE GIRLS.
THANK YOU.
SEE YOU LATER.
CHIRP

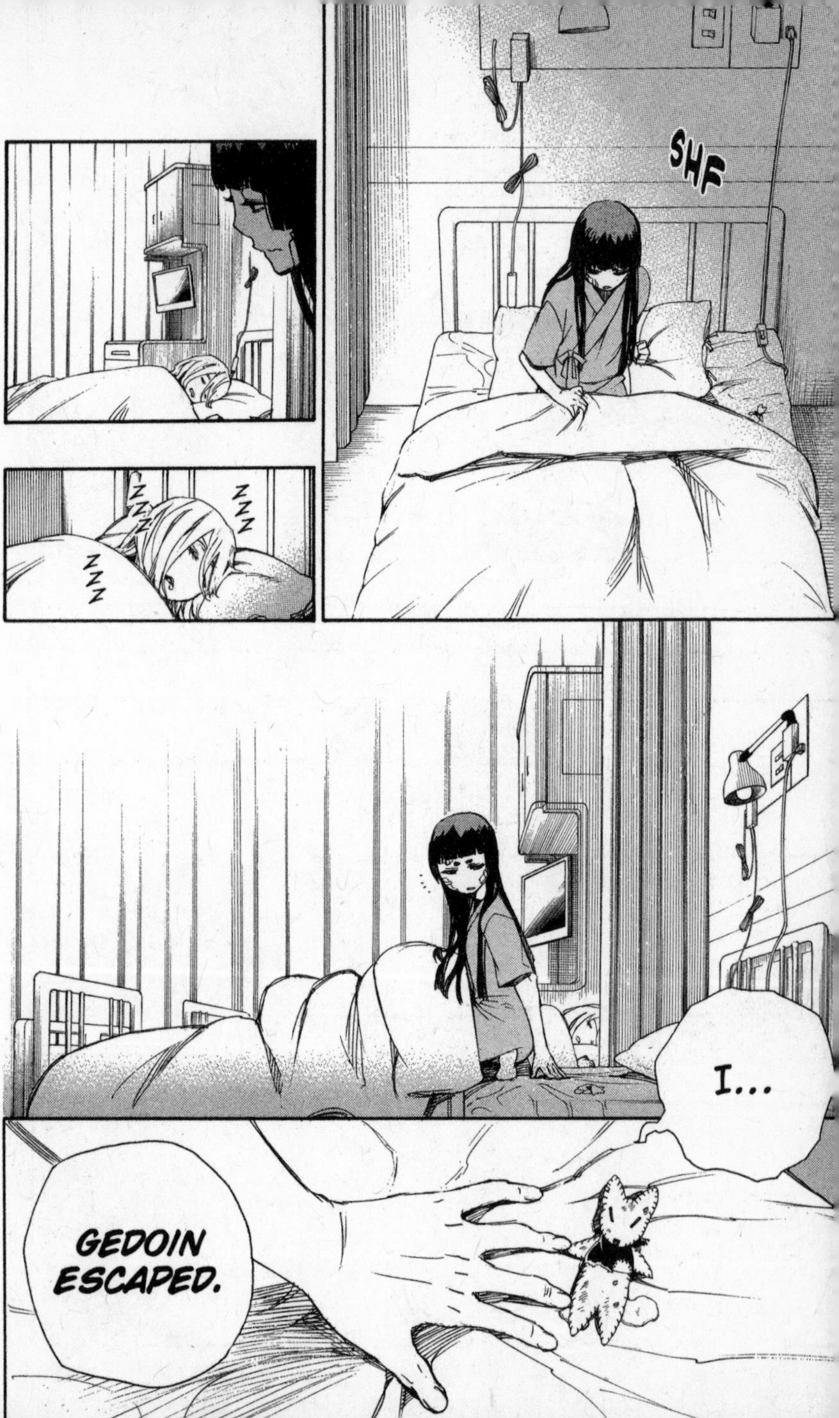
SHF
ZZZ
ZZZ
ZZZ
I...
GEDOIN ESCAPED.

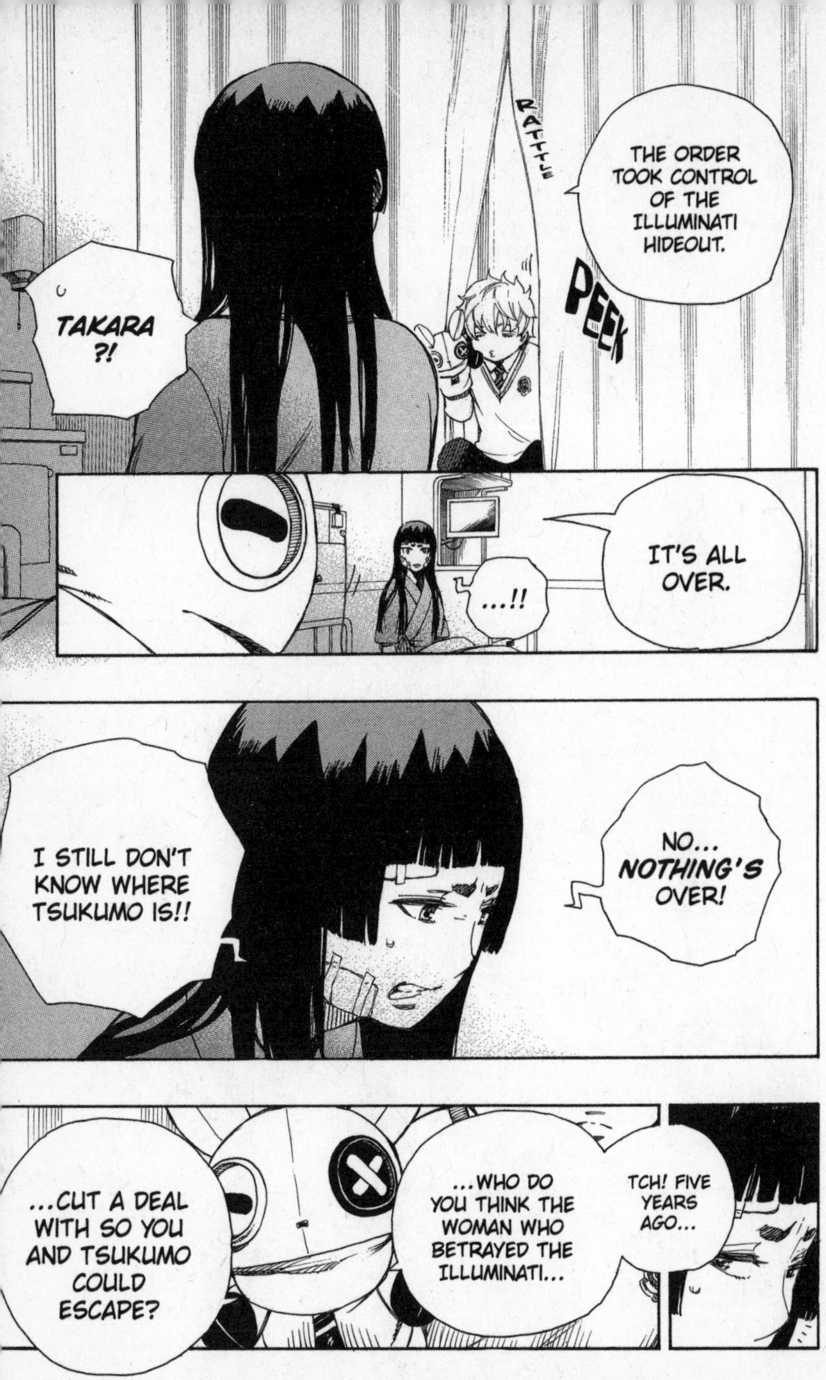
RATTTLE
THE ORDER TOOK CONTROL OF THE ILLUMINATI HIDEOUT.
PEEK
TAKARA ?!
IT'S ALL OVER.
...!!
NO... NOTHING'S OVER!
I STILL DON'T KNOW WHERE TSUKUMO IS!!
TCH! FIVE YEARS AGO...
...WHO DO YOU THINK THE WOMAN WHO BETRAYED THE ILLUMINATI...
...CUT A DEAL WITH SO YOU AND TSUKUMO COULD ESCAPE?

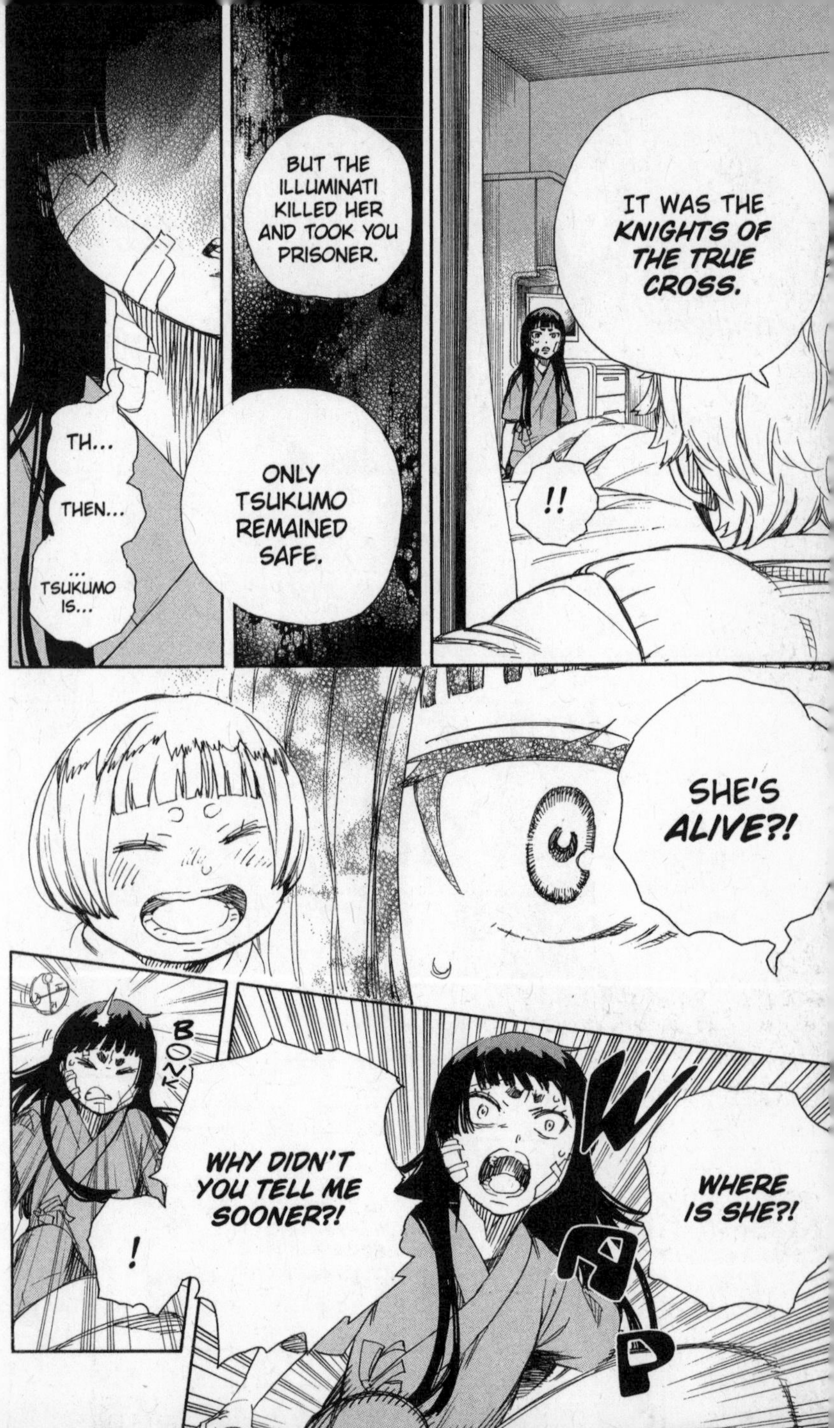
IT WAS THE KNIGHTS OF THE TRUE CROSS.
!!
BUT THE ILLUMINATI KILLED HER AND TOOK YOU PRISONER.
ONLY TSUKUMO REMAINED SAFE.
TH...
THEN...
...TSUKUMO IS...
SHE'S ALIVE?!
WHERE IS SHE?!
WAP
WHY DIDN'T YOU TELL ME SOONER?!
BONK
!

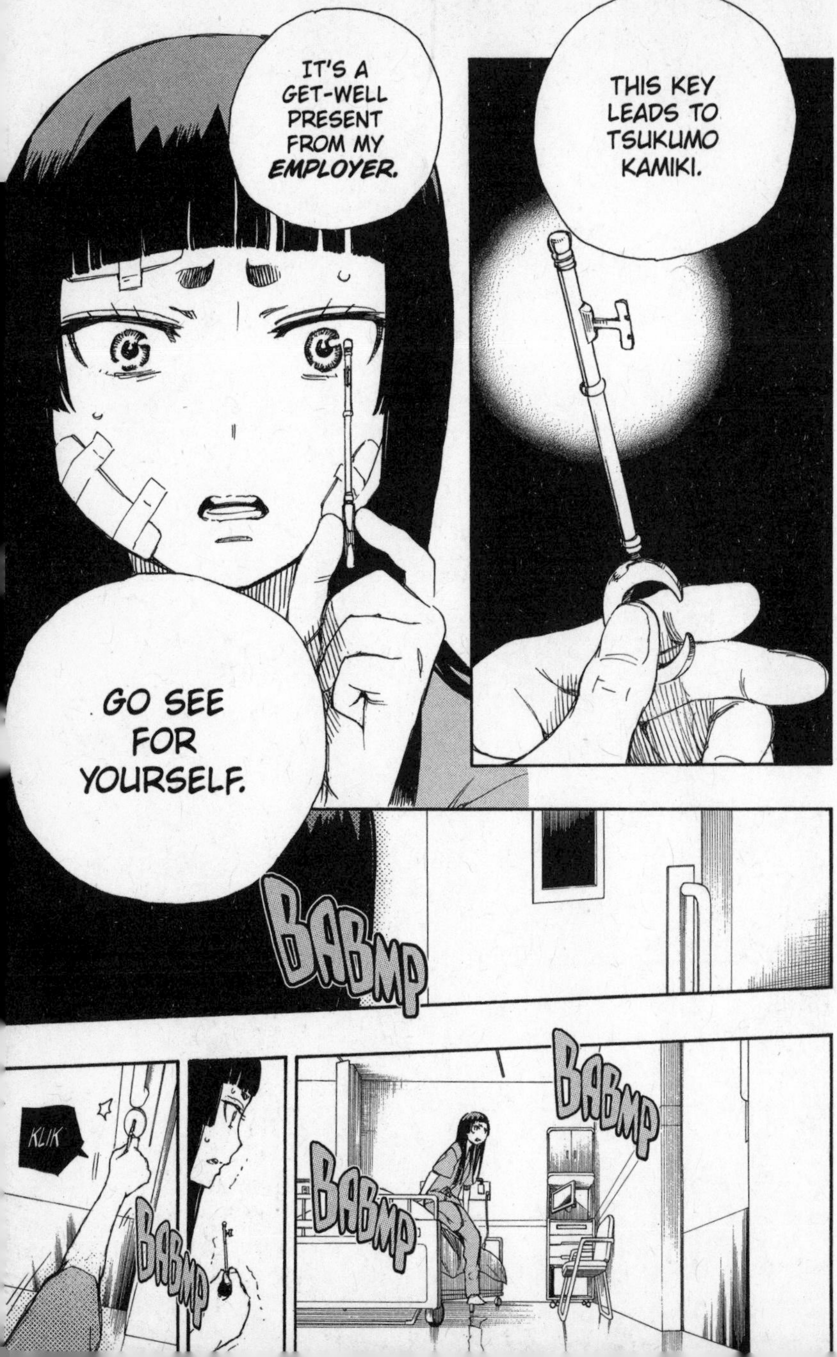
THIS KEY LEADS TO TSUKUMO KAMIKI.
IT'S A GET-WELL PRESENT FROM MY EMPLOYER.
GO SEE FOR YOURSELF.
BABMP
BABMP
BABMP
KLIK
BABMP

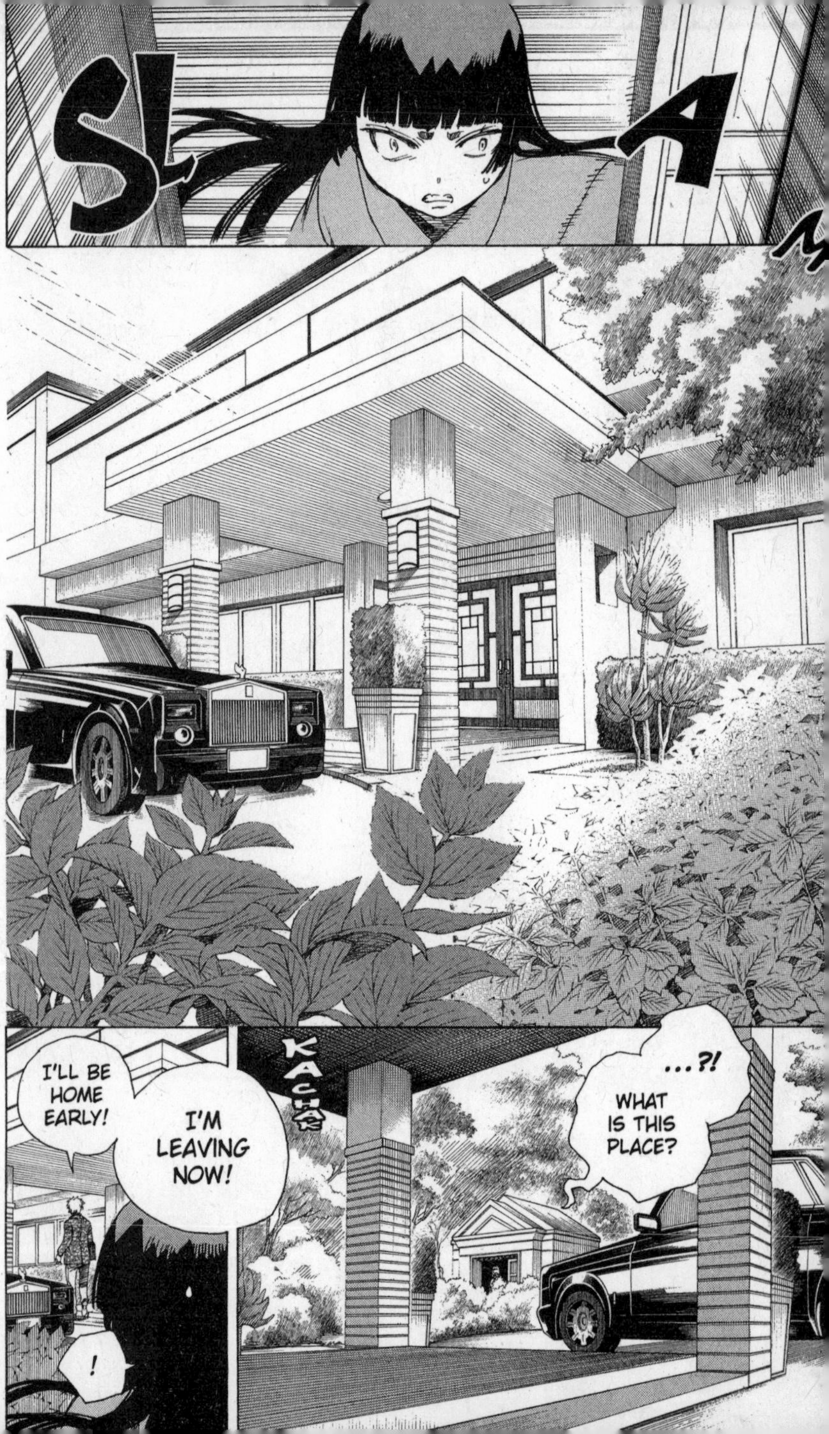
SL
A
M
...?!
WHAT IS THIS PLACE?
KACHAK
I'M LEAVING NOW!
I'LL BE HOME EARLY!
!

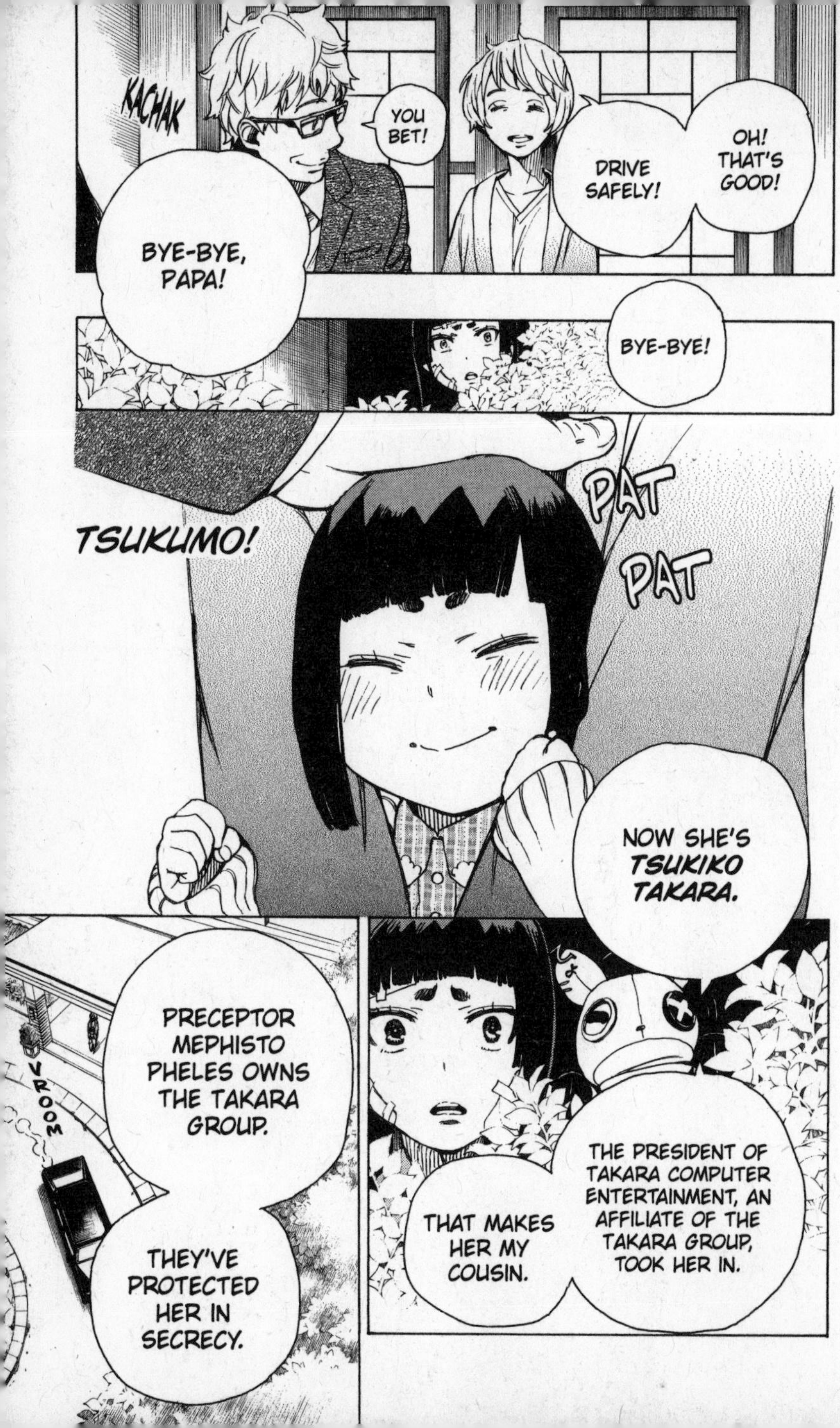
OH! THAT'S GOOD!
DRIVE SAFELY!
YOU BET!
KACHAK
BYE-BYE, PAPA!
BYE-BYE!
PAT
PAT
TSUKUMO!
NOW SHE'S *TSUKIKO TAKARA.*
THE PRESIDENT OF TAKARA COMPUTER ENTERTAINMENT, AN AFFILIATE OF THE TAKARA GROUP, TOOK HER IN.
THAT MAKES HER MY COUSIN.
VROOM
PRECEPTOR MEPHISTO PHELES OWNS THE TAKARA GROUP.
THEY'VE PROTECTED HER IN SECRECY.

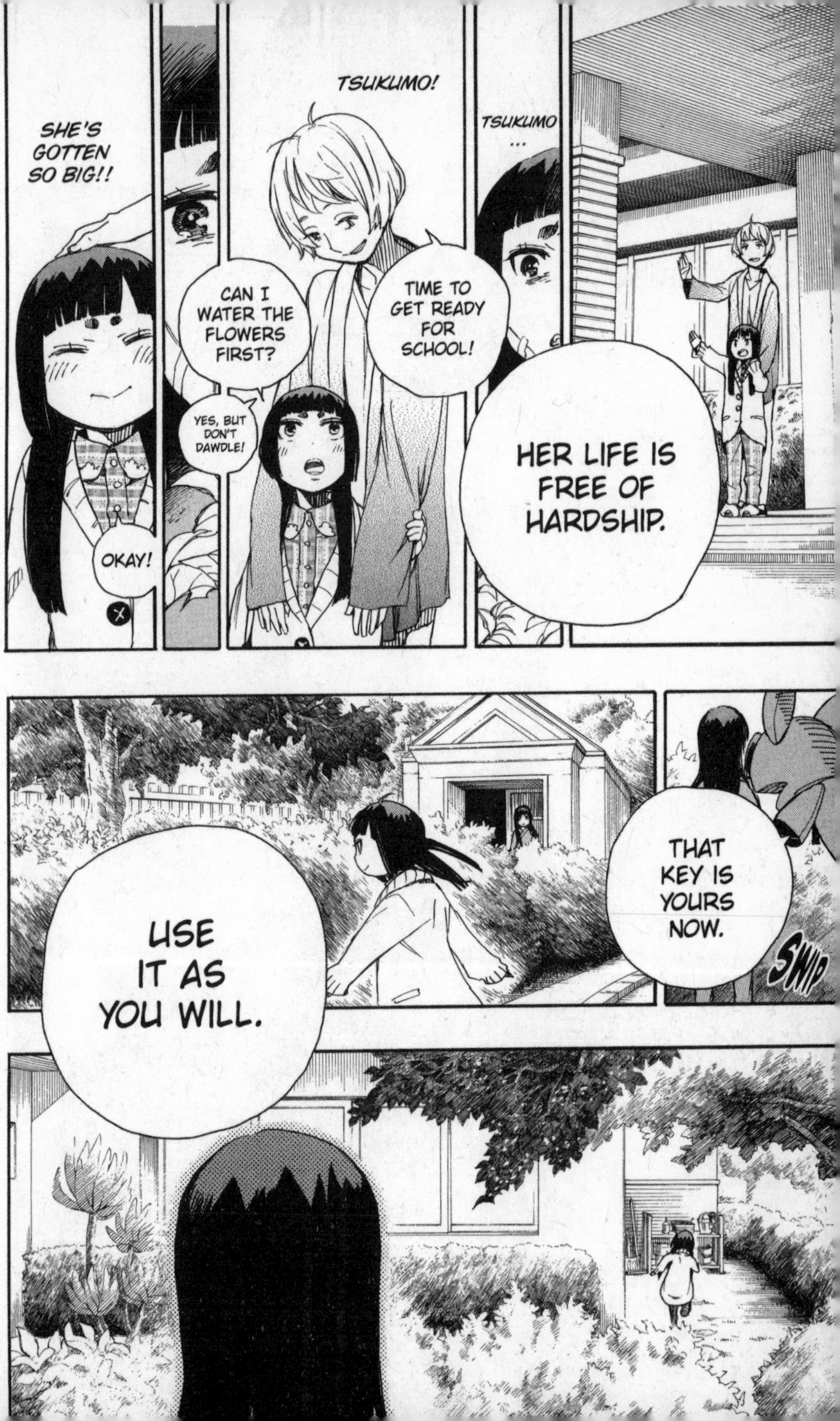
TSUKUMO ...
HER LIFE IS FREE OF HARDSHIP.
TSUKUMO!
TIME TO GET READY FOR SCHOOL!
CAN I WATER THE FLOWERS FIRST?
YES, BUT DON'T DAWDLE!
SHE'S GOTTEN SO BIG!!
OKAY!
THAT KEY IS YOURS NOW.
SWIP
USE IT AS YOU WILL.

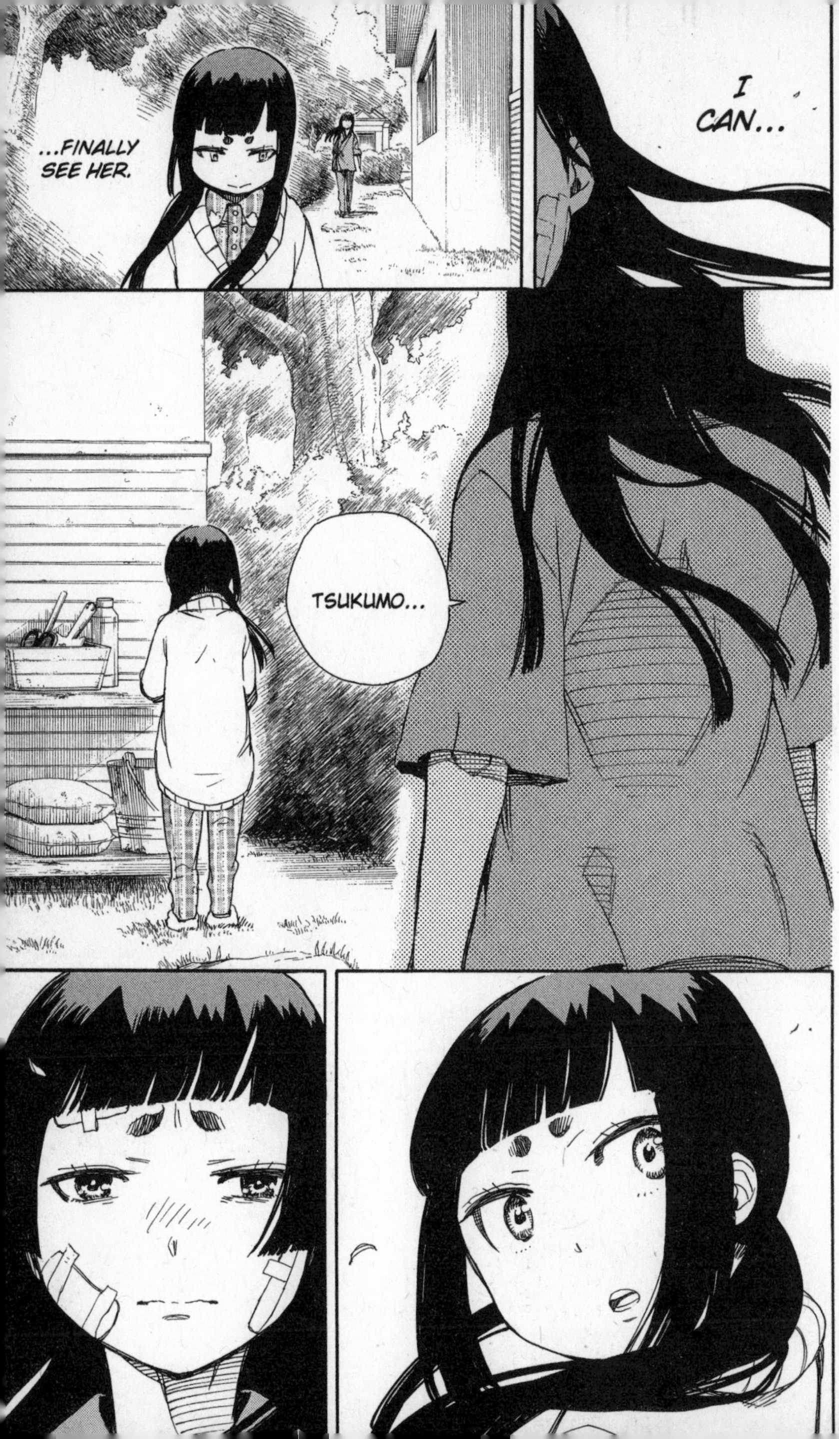
I CAN...
...FINALLY SEE HER.
TSUKUMO...

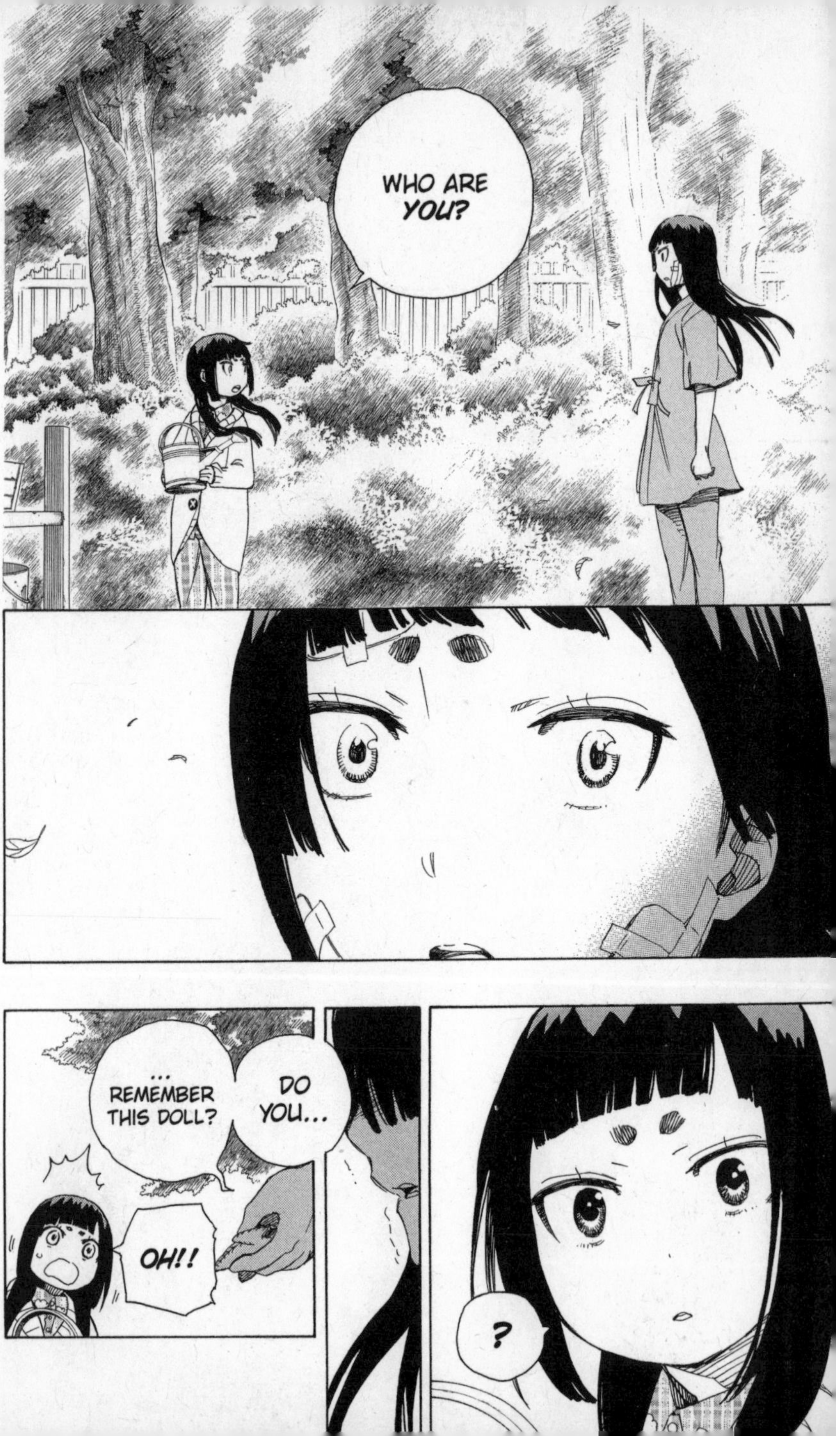
WHO ARE YOU?
?
DO YOU...
...REMEMBER THIS DOLL?
OH!!

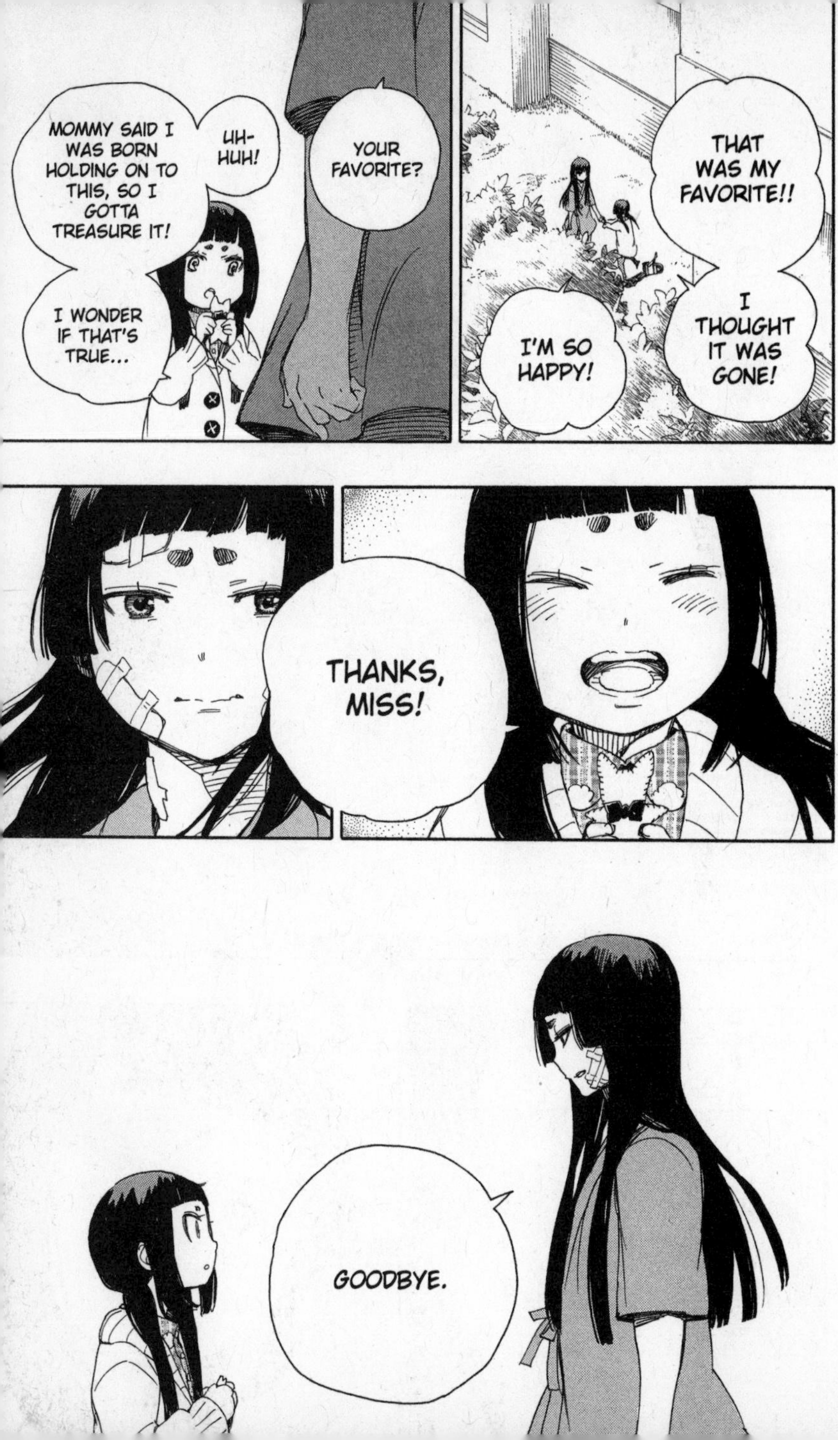
THAT WAS MY FAVORITE!!
I THOUGHT IT WAS GONE!
I'M SO HAPPY!
YOUR FAVORITE?
UH-HUH!
MOMMY SAID I WAS BORN HOLDING ON TO THIS, SO I GOTTA TREASURE IT!
I WONDER IF THAT'S TRUE...
THANKS, MISS!
GOODBYE.

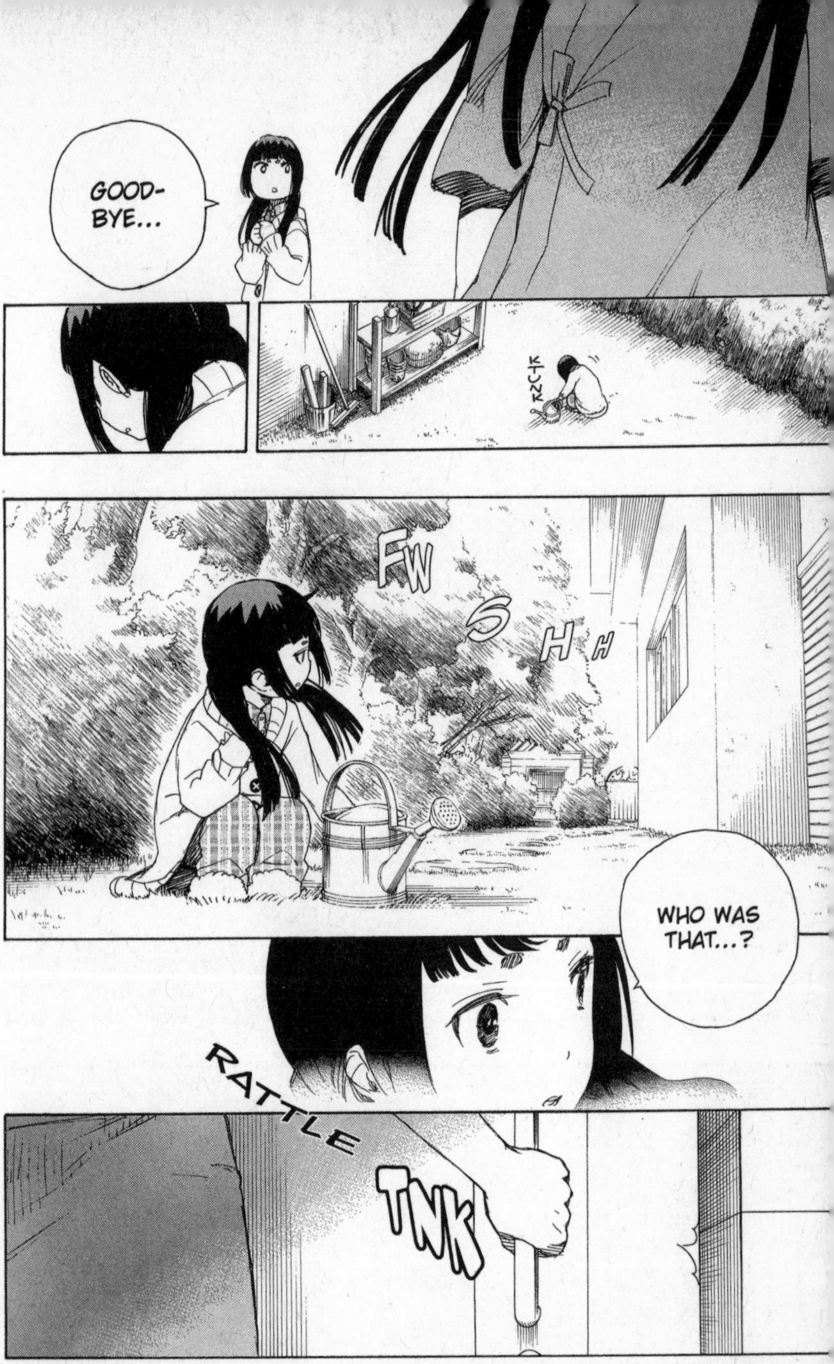
GOOD-BYE...
KTUNK
FWSHH
WHO WAS THAT...?
RATTLE
TNK

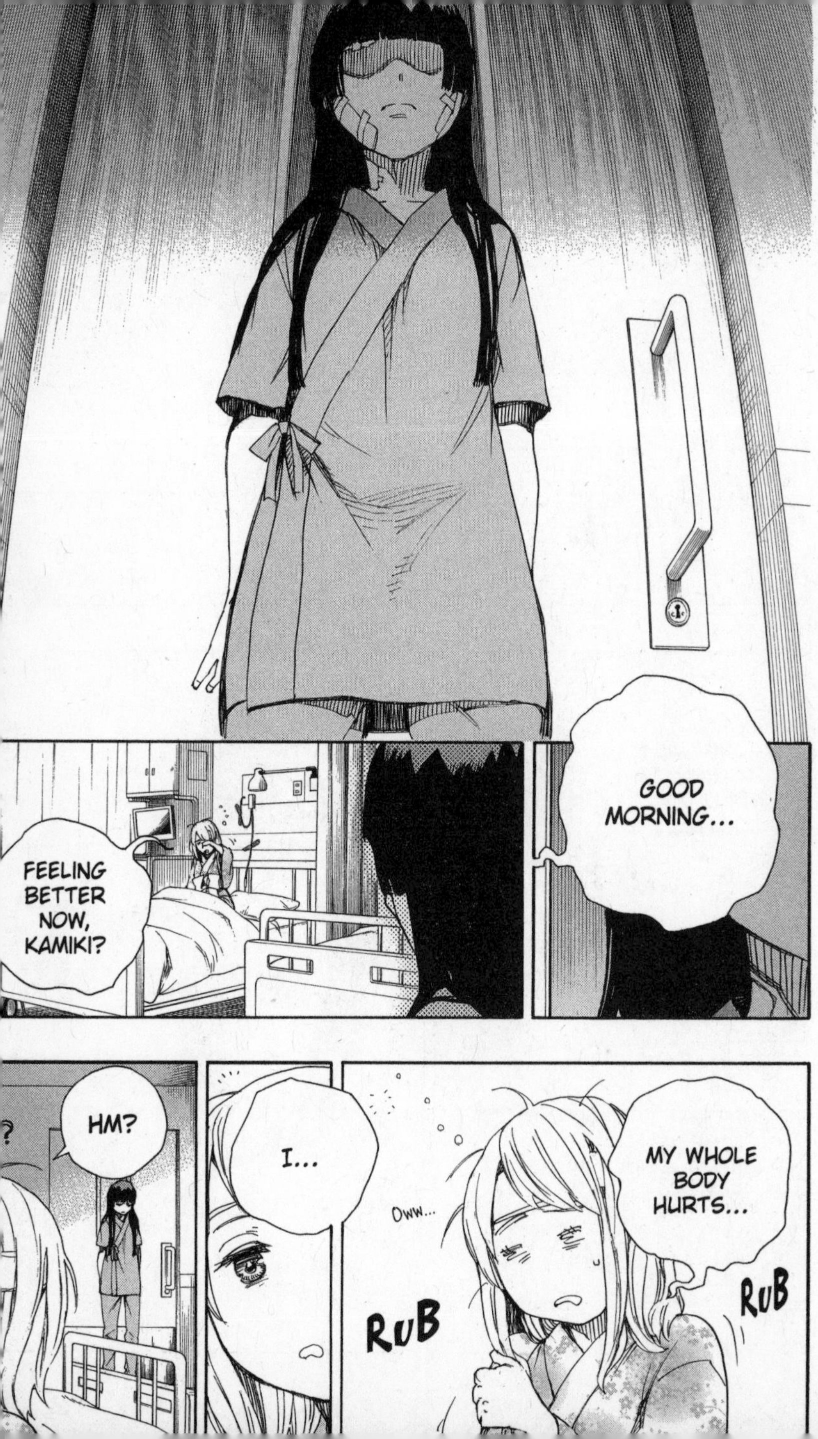
GOOD MORNING...
FEELING BETTER NOW, KAMIKI?
MY WHOLE BODY HURTS...
RUB
OWW...
RUB
I...
HM?
?

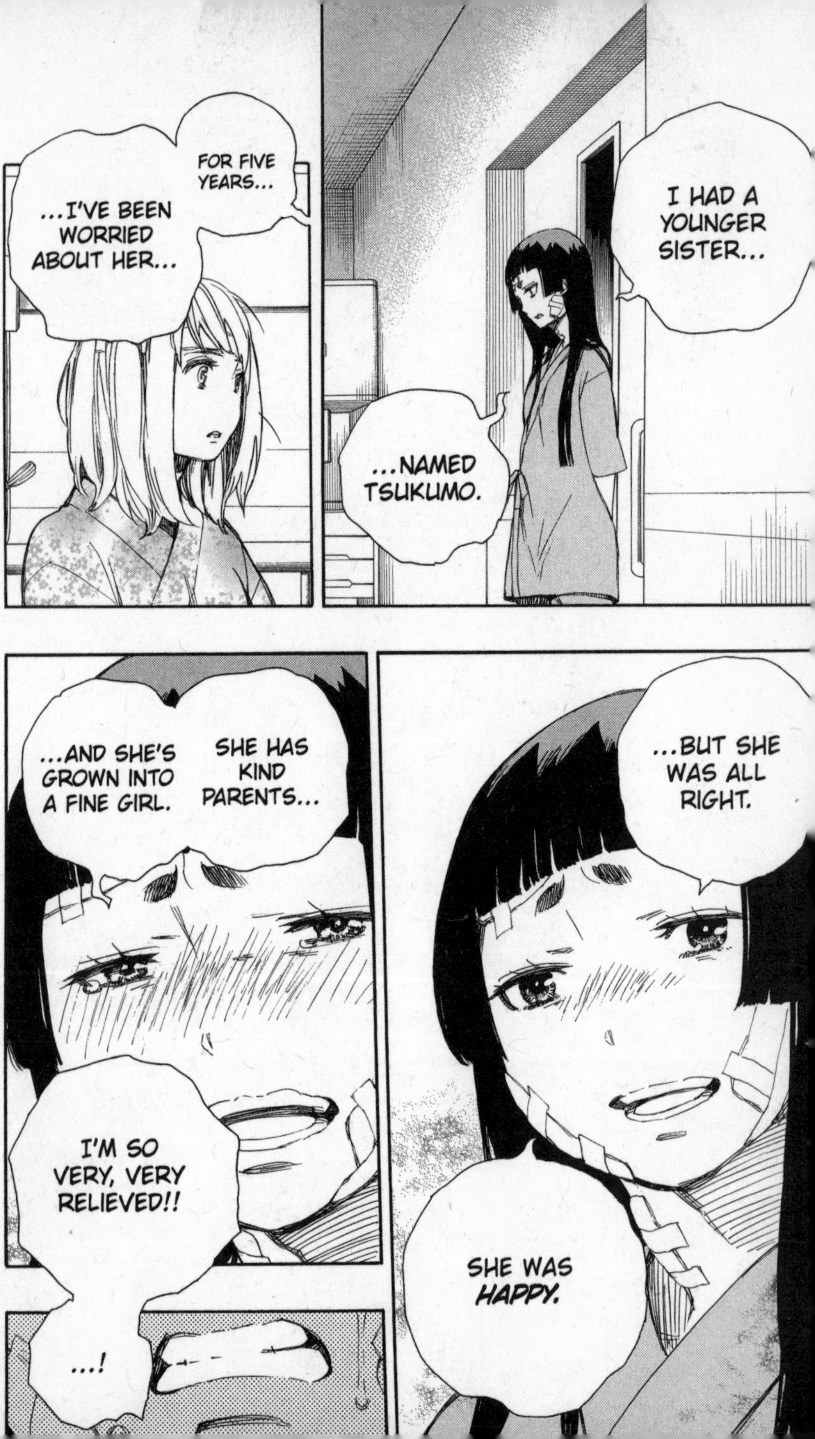
I HAD A YOUNGER SISTER...
...NAMED TSUKUMO.
FOR FIVE YEARS...
...I'VE BEEN WORRIED ABOUT HER...
...BUT SHE WAS ALL RIGHT.
SHE WAS *HAPPY.*
SHE HAS KIND PARENTS...
...AND SHE'S GROWN INTO A FINE GIRL.
I'M SO VERY, VERY RELIEVED!!
...!

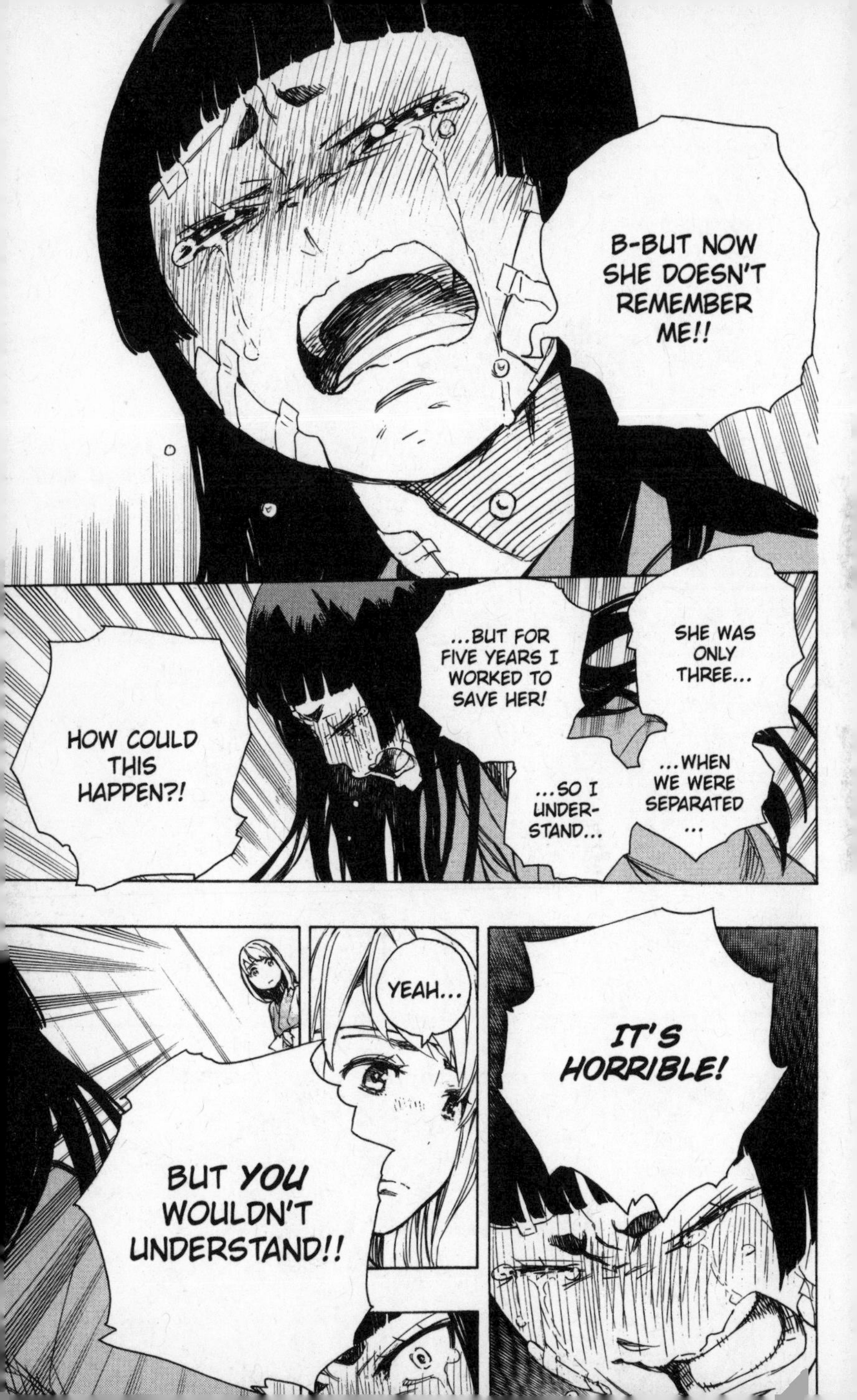

B-BUT NOW SHE DOESN'T REMEMBER ME!!
SHE WAS ONLY THREE...
...WHEN WE WERE SEPARATED...
...BUT FOR FIVE YEARS I WORKED TO SAVE HER!
...SO I UNDERSTAND...
HOW COULD THIS HAPPEN?!
IT'S HORRIBLE!
YEAH...
BUT YOU WOULDN'T UNDERSTAND!!

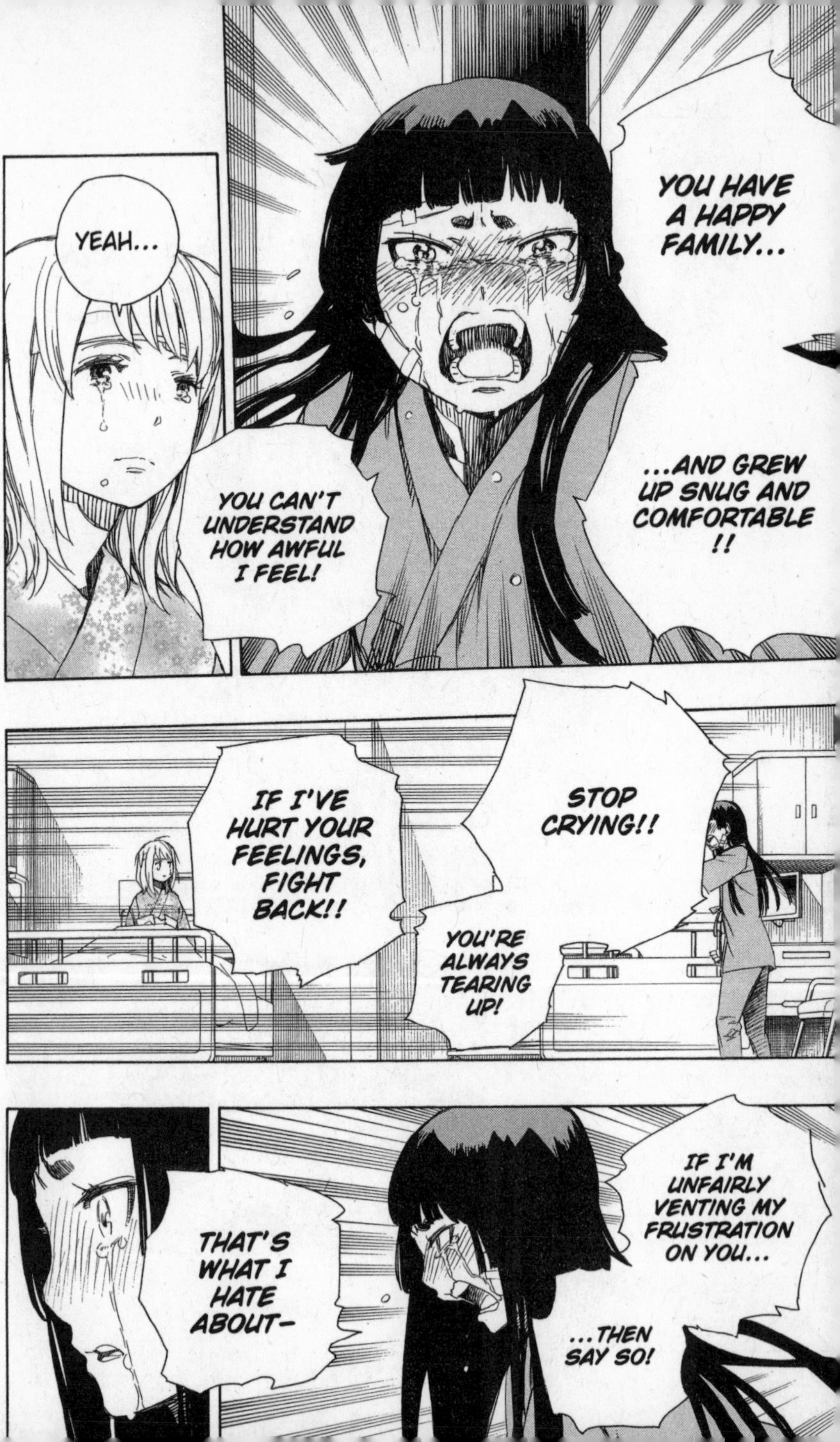
YOU HAVE A HAPPY FAMILY...
...AND GREW UP SNUG AND COMFORTABLE!!
YOU CAN'T UNDERSTAND HOW AWFUL I FEEL!
YEAH...
STOP CRYING!!
YOU'RE ALWAYS TEARING UP!
IF I'VE HURT YOUR FEELINGS, FIGHT BACK!!
IF I'M UNFAIRLY VENTING MY FRUSTRATION ON YOU...
...THEN SAY SO!
THAT'S WHAT I HATE ABOUT-

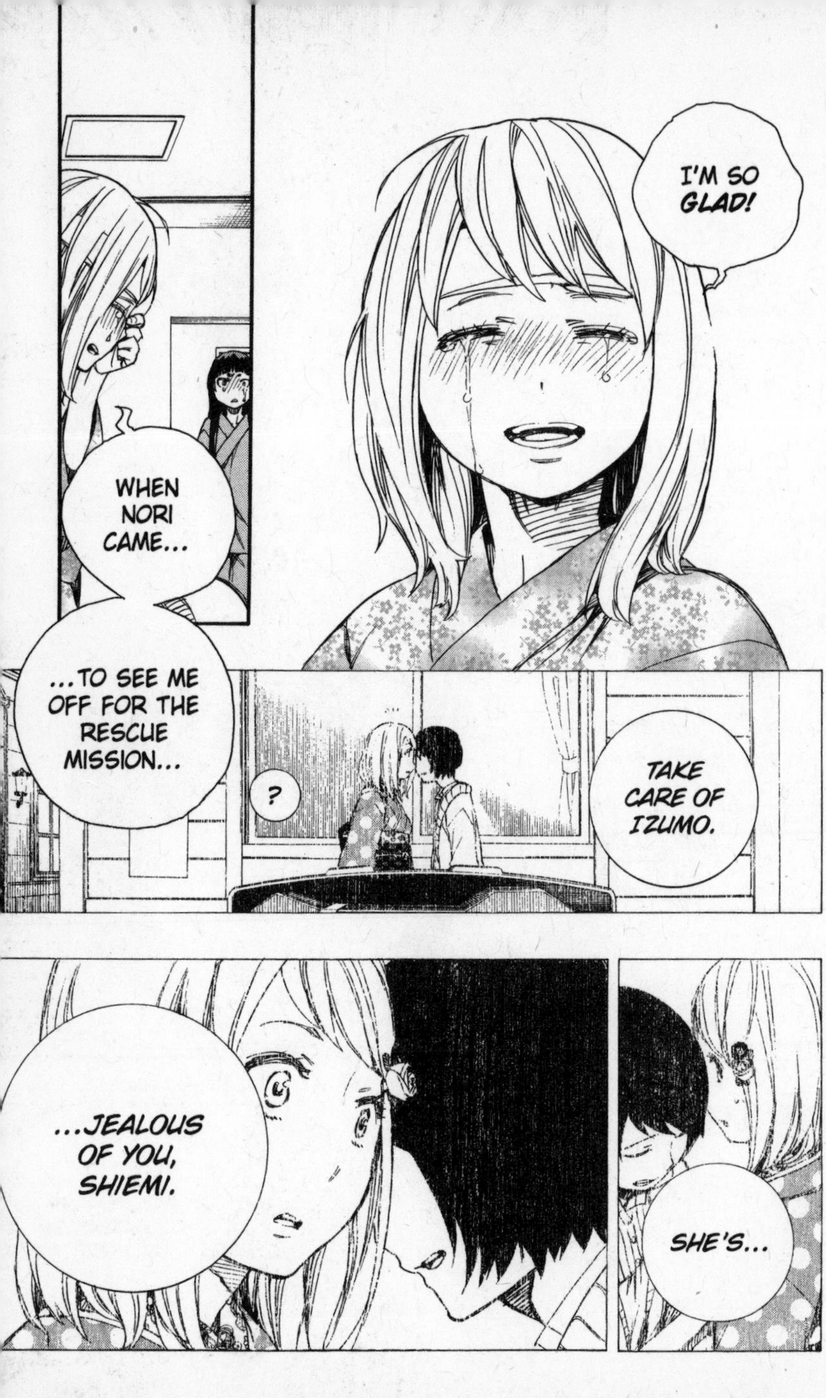
I'M SO GLAD!
WHEN NORI CAME...
...TO SEE ME OFF FOR THE RESCUE MISSION...
TAKE CARE OF IZUMO.
?
SHE'S...
...JEALOUS OF YOU, SHIEMI.

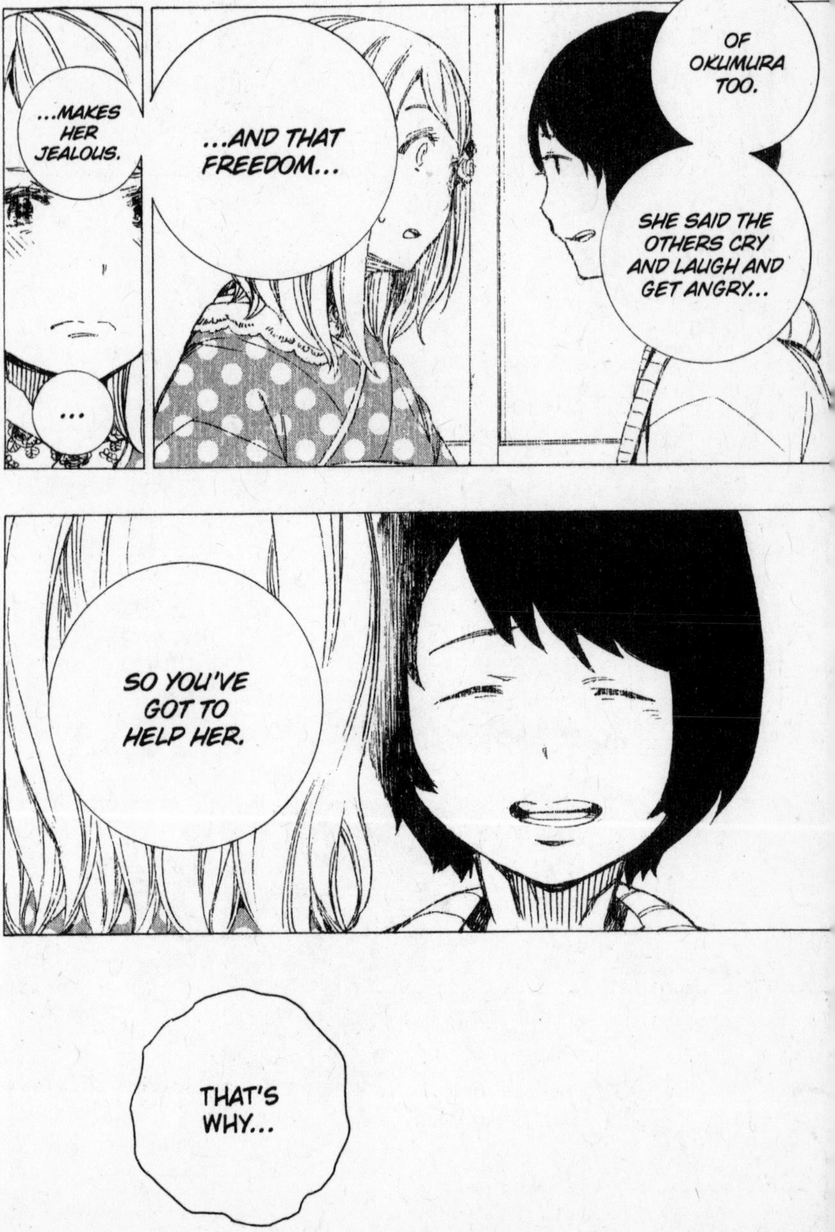
OF OKUMURA TOO.
SHE SAID THE OTHERS CRY AND LAUGH AND GET ANGRY...
...AND THAT FREEDOM...
...MAKES HER JEALOUS.
...
SO YOU'VE GOT TO HELP HER.
THAT'S WHY...

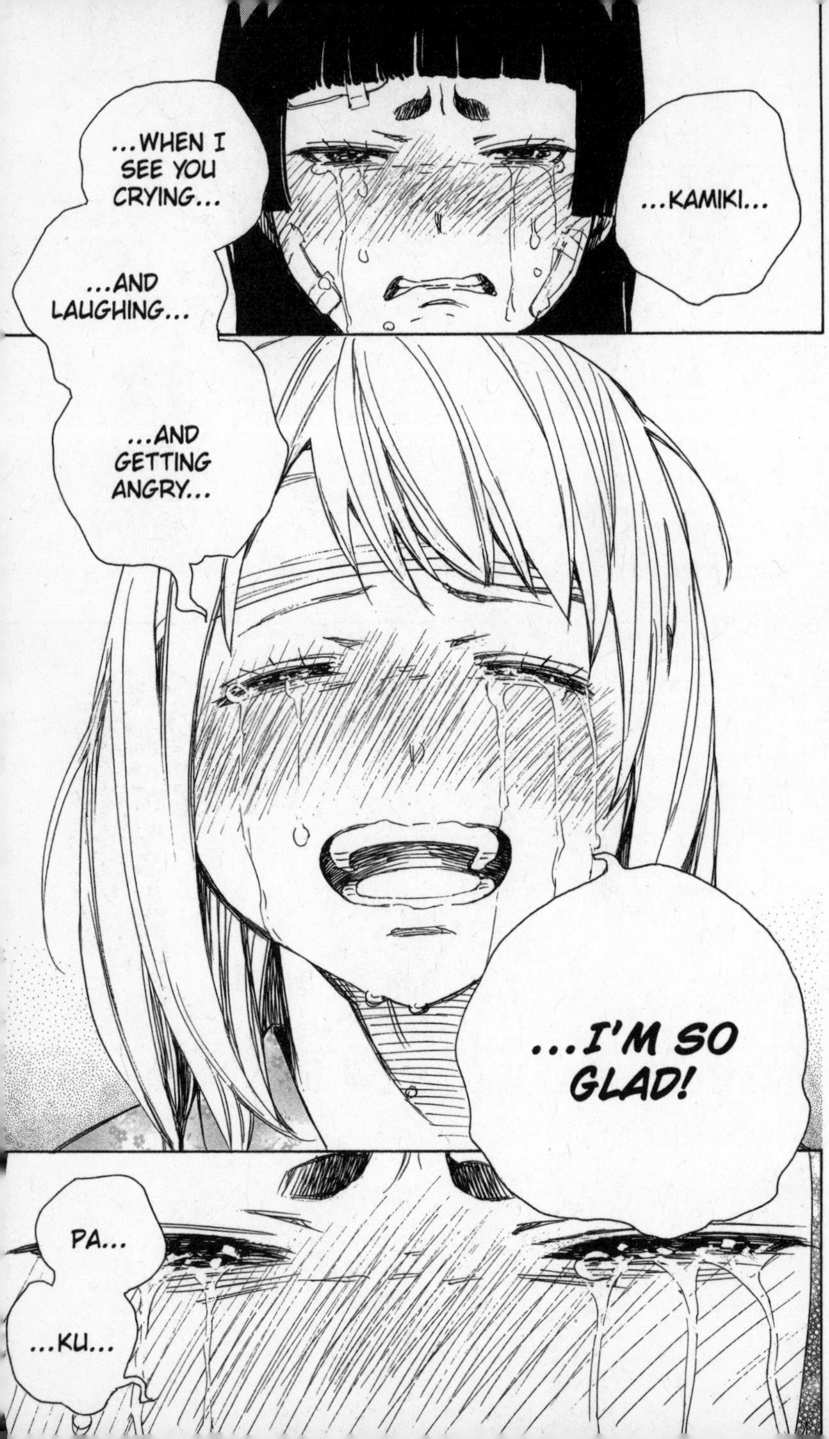
...KAMIKI...
...WHEN I SEE YOU CRYING...
...AND LAUGHING...
...AND GETTING ANGRY...
...I'M SO GLAD!
PA...
...KU...

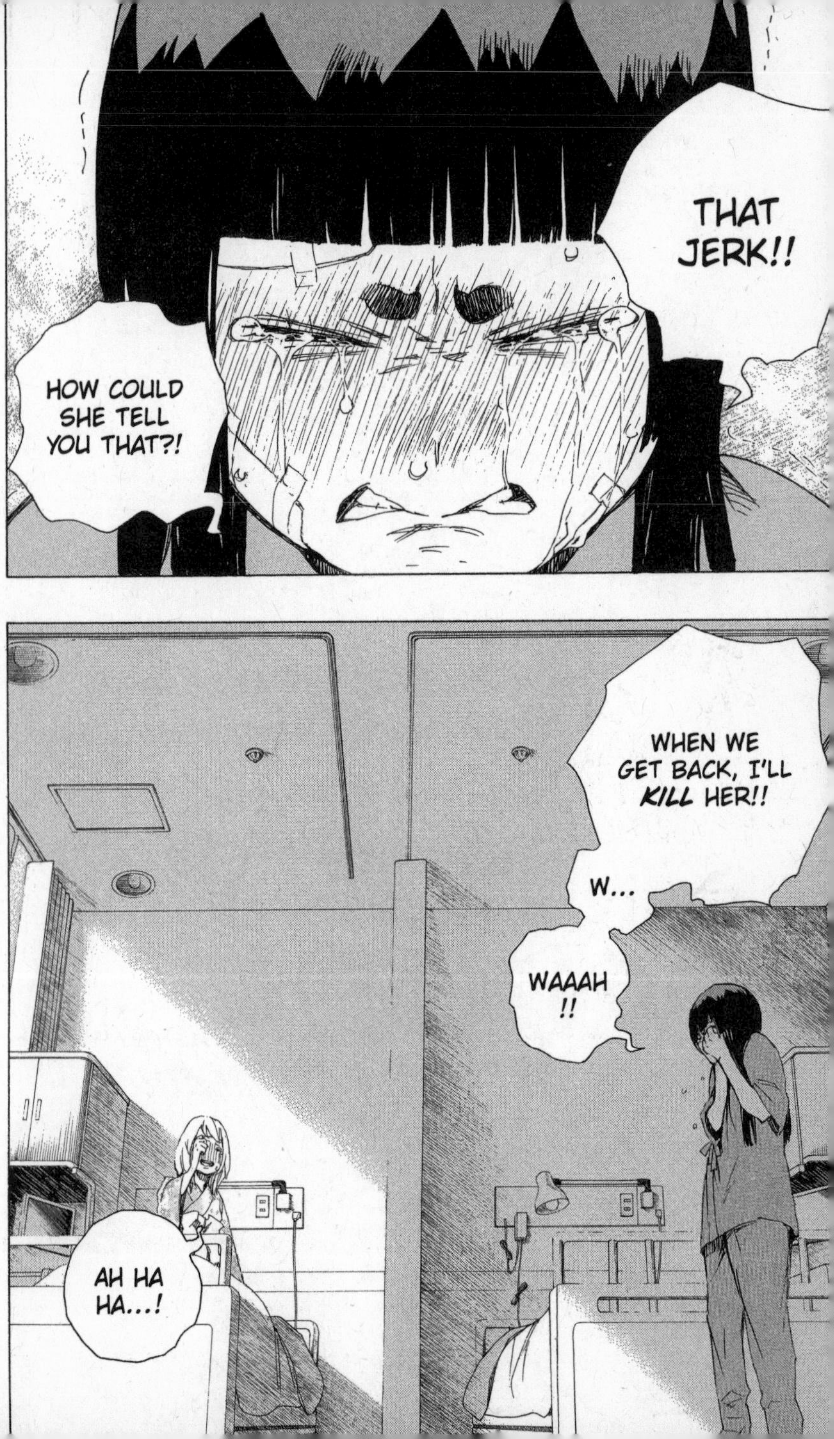
THAT JERK!!
HOW COULD SHE TELL YOU THAT?!
WHEN WE GET BACK, I'LL KILL HER!!
W...
WAAAH !!
AH HA HA...!

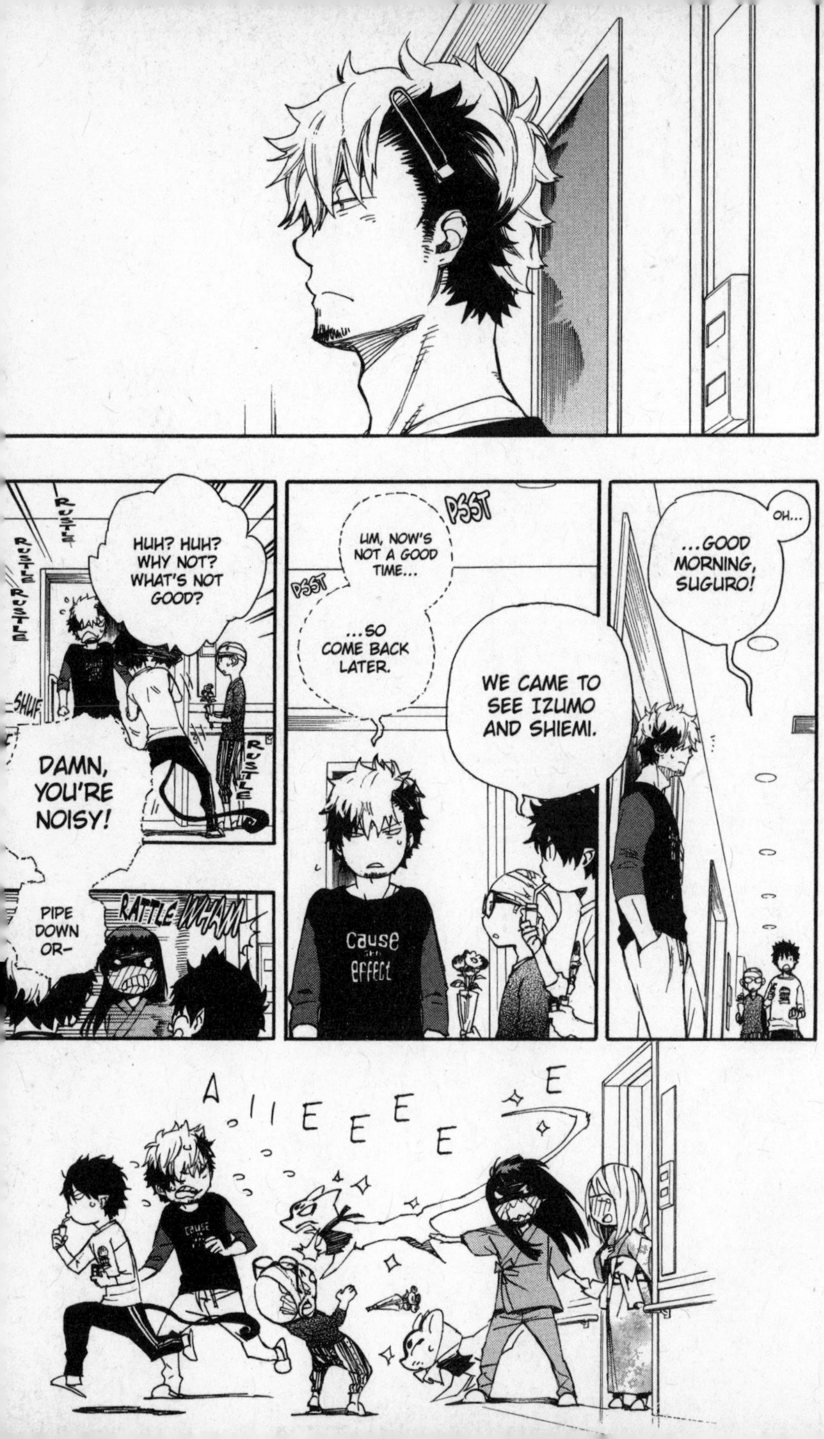
OH...
...GOOD MORNING, SUGURO!
WE CAME TO SEE IZUMO AND SHIEMI.
PSST
UM, NOW'S NOT A GOOD TIME...
PSST
...SO COME BACK LATER.
RUSTLE
RUSTLE
RUSTLE
HUH? HUH? WHY NOT? WHAT'S NOT GOOD?
RUSTLE
SHUF
DAMN, YOU'RE NOISY!
RATTLE WHAM
PIPE DOWN OR-
AIIEEEEE

BLUE EXORCIST CHAPTER 63: GOODBYE

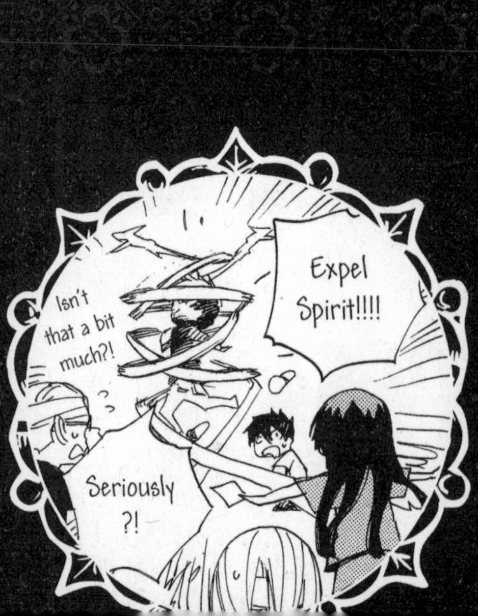
Expel Spirit!!!!
Isn't that a bit much?!
Seriously ?!

Chapter 64: I'll Come Again

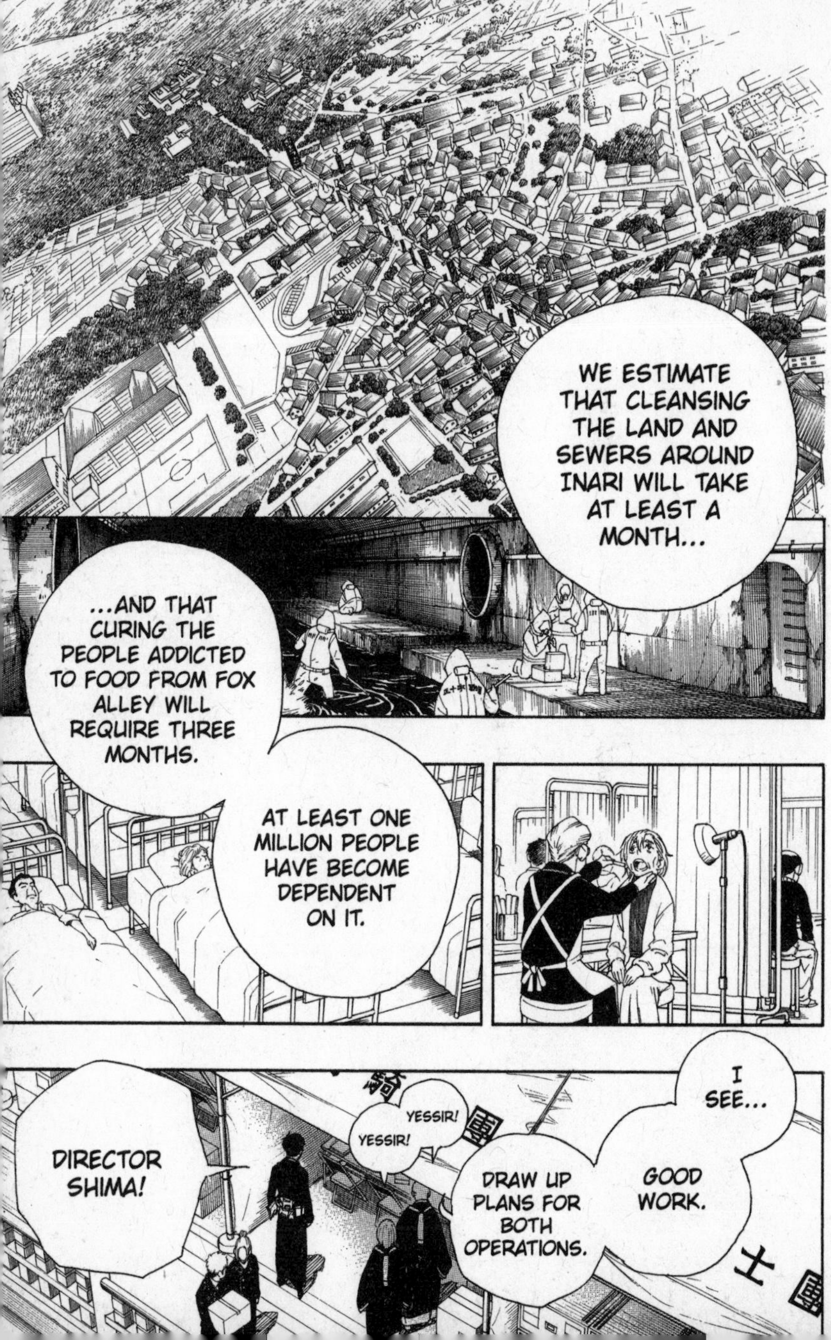
WE ESTIMATE THAT CLEANSING THE LAND AND SEWERS AROUND INARI WILL TAKE AT LEAST A MONTH...
...AND THAT CURING THE PEOPLE ADDICTED TO FOOD FROM FOX ALLEY WILL REQUIRE THREE MONTHS.
AT LEAST ONE MILLION PEOPLE HAVE BECOME DEPENDENT ON IT.
I SEE...
GOOD WORK.
DRAW UP PLANS FOR BOTH OPERATIONS.
YESSIR!
YESSIR!
DIRECTOR SHIMA!

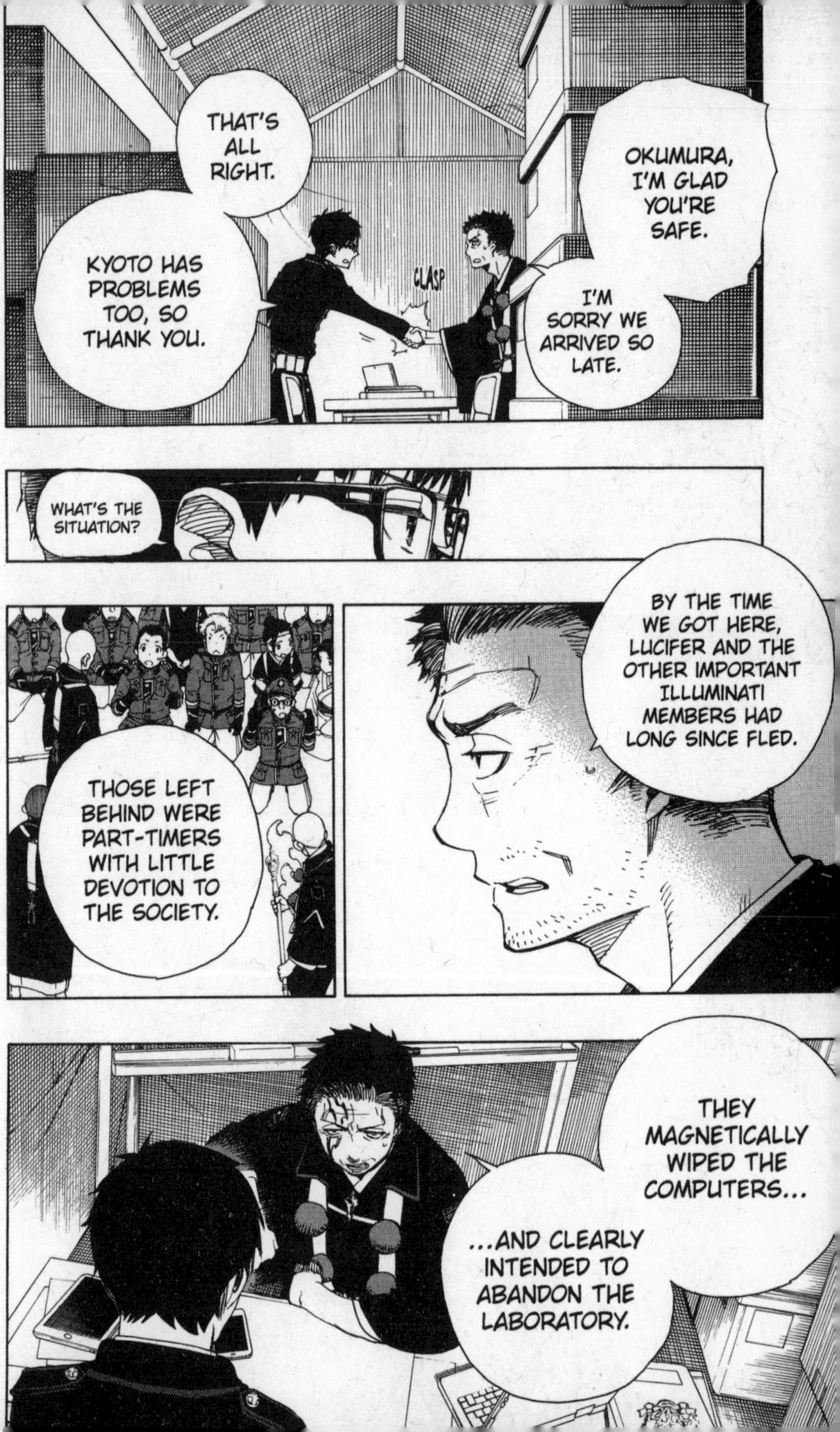
OKUMURA, I'M GLAD YOU'RE SAFE.
I'M SORRY WE ARRIVED SO LATE.
CLASP
THAT'S ALL RIGHT.
KYOTO HAS PROBLEMS TOO, SO THANK YOU.
WHAT'S THE SITUATION?
BY THE TIME WE GOT HERE, LUCIFER AND THE OTHER IMPORTANT ILLUMINATI MEMBERS HAD LONG SINCE FLED.
THOSE LEFT BEHIND WERE PART-TIMERS WITH LITTLE DEVOTION TO THE SOCIETY.
THEY MAGNETICALLY WIPED THE COMPUTERS...
...AND CLEARLY INTENDED TO ABANDON THE LABORATORY.

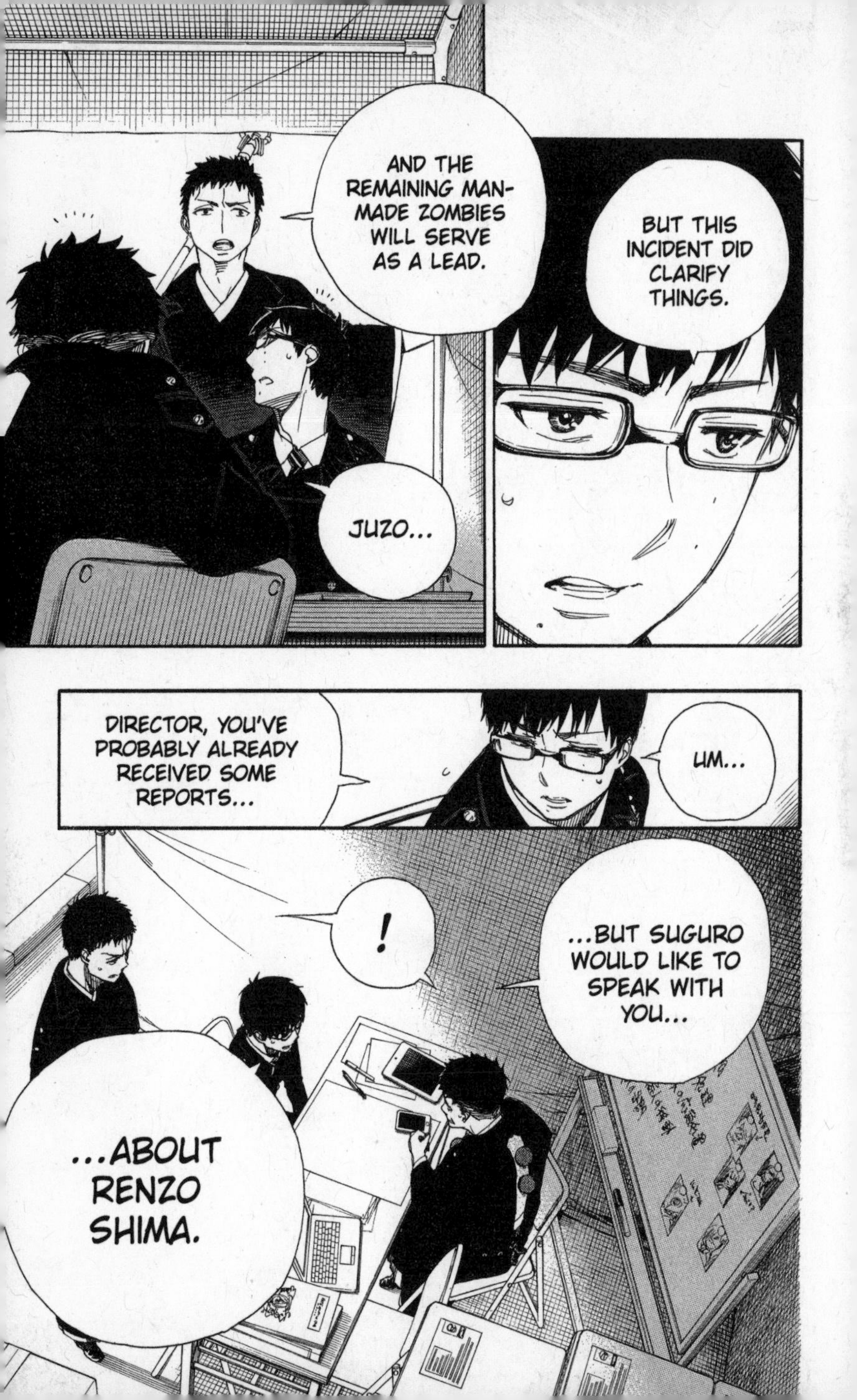

BUT THIS INCIDENT DID CLARIFY THINGS.
AND THE REMAINING MAN-MADE ZOMBIES WILL SERVE AS A LEAD.
JUZO...
UM...
DIRECTOR, YOU'VE PROBABLY ALREADY RECEIVED SOME REPORTS...
...BUT SUGURO WOULD LIKE TO SPEAK WITH YOU...
!
...ABOUT RENZO SHIMA.

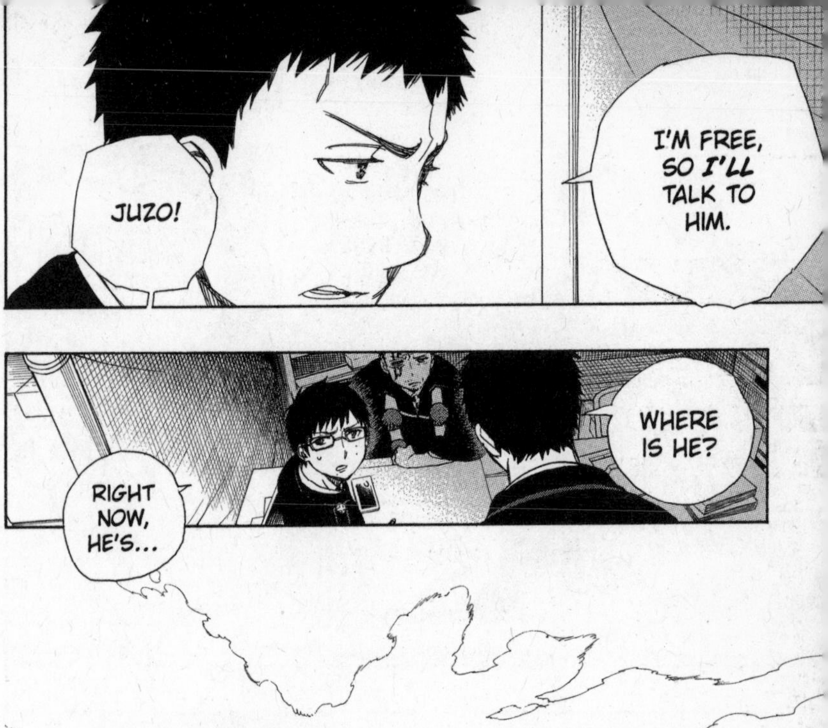
I'M FREE, SO *I'LL* TALK TO HIM.
JUZO!
WHERE IS HE?
RIGHT NOW, HE'S...

Chapter 64: I'll Come Again

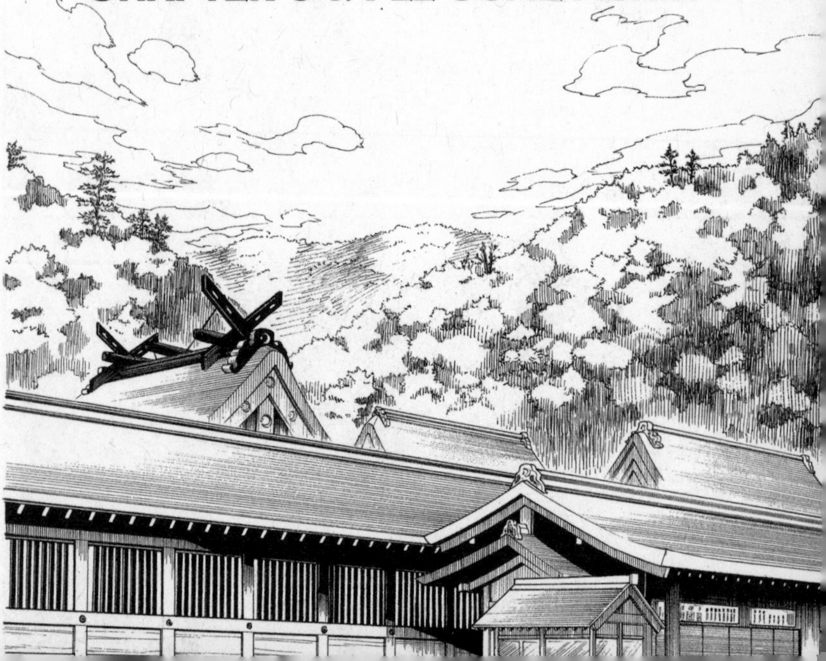

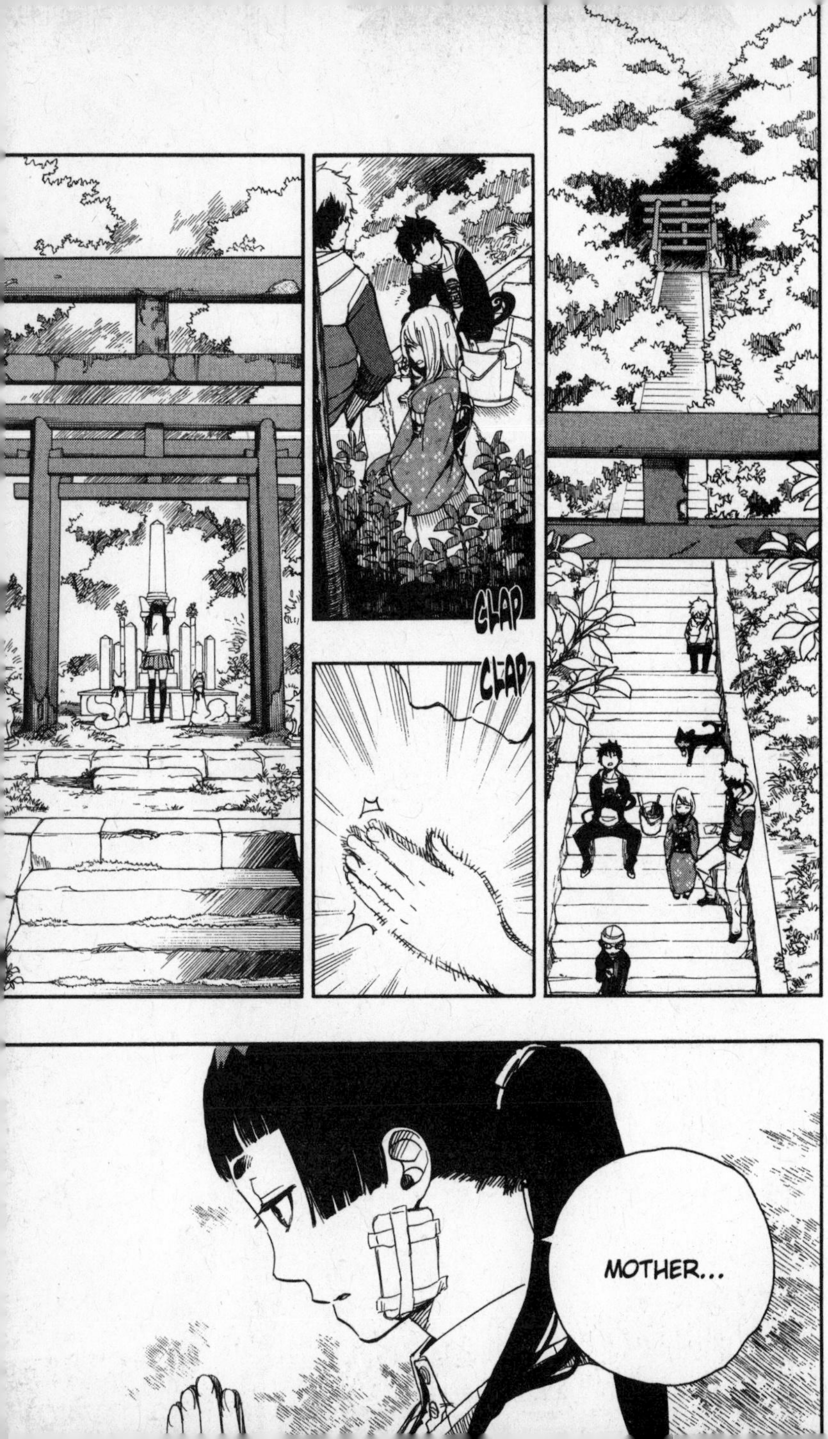
CLAP
CLAP
MOTHER...

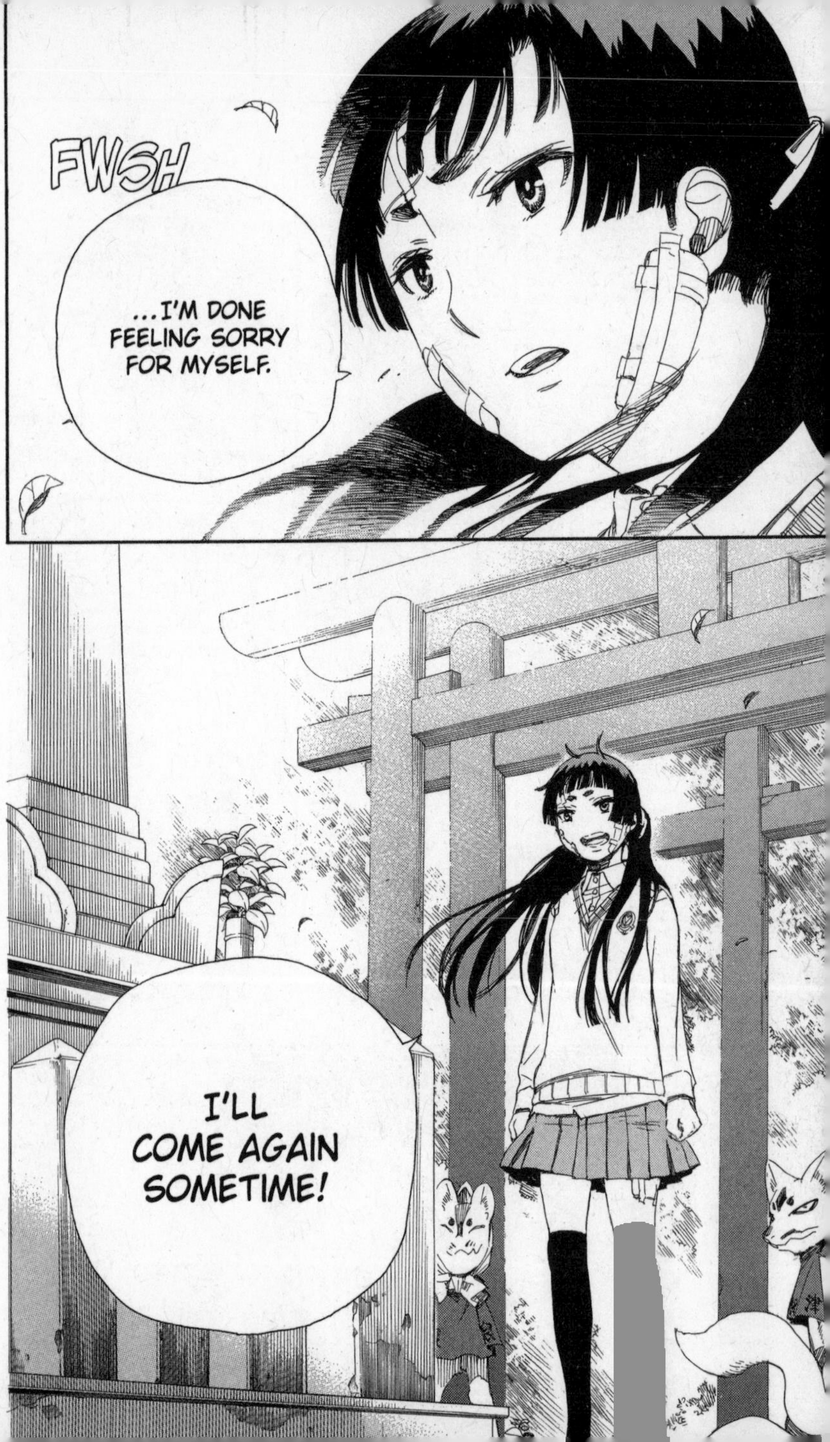
FWSH
...I'M DONE FEELING SORRY FOR MYSELF.
I'LL COME AGAIN SOMETIME!

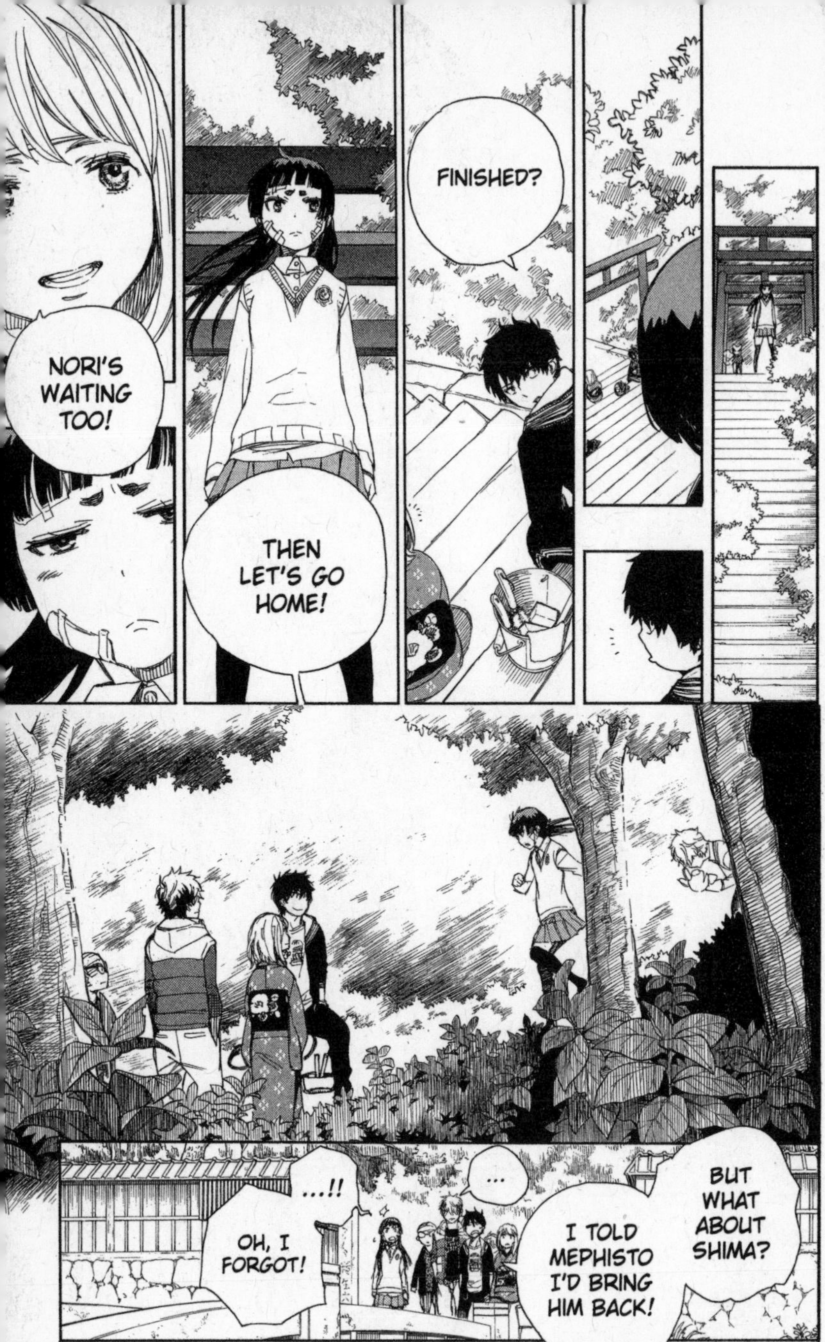

FINISHED?
THEN LET'S GO HOME!
NORI'S WAITING TOO!
BUT WHAT ABOUT SHIMA?
...
I TOLD MEPHISTO I'D BRING HIM BACK!
...!!
OH, I FORGOT!

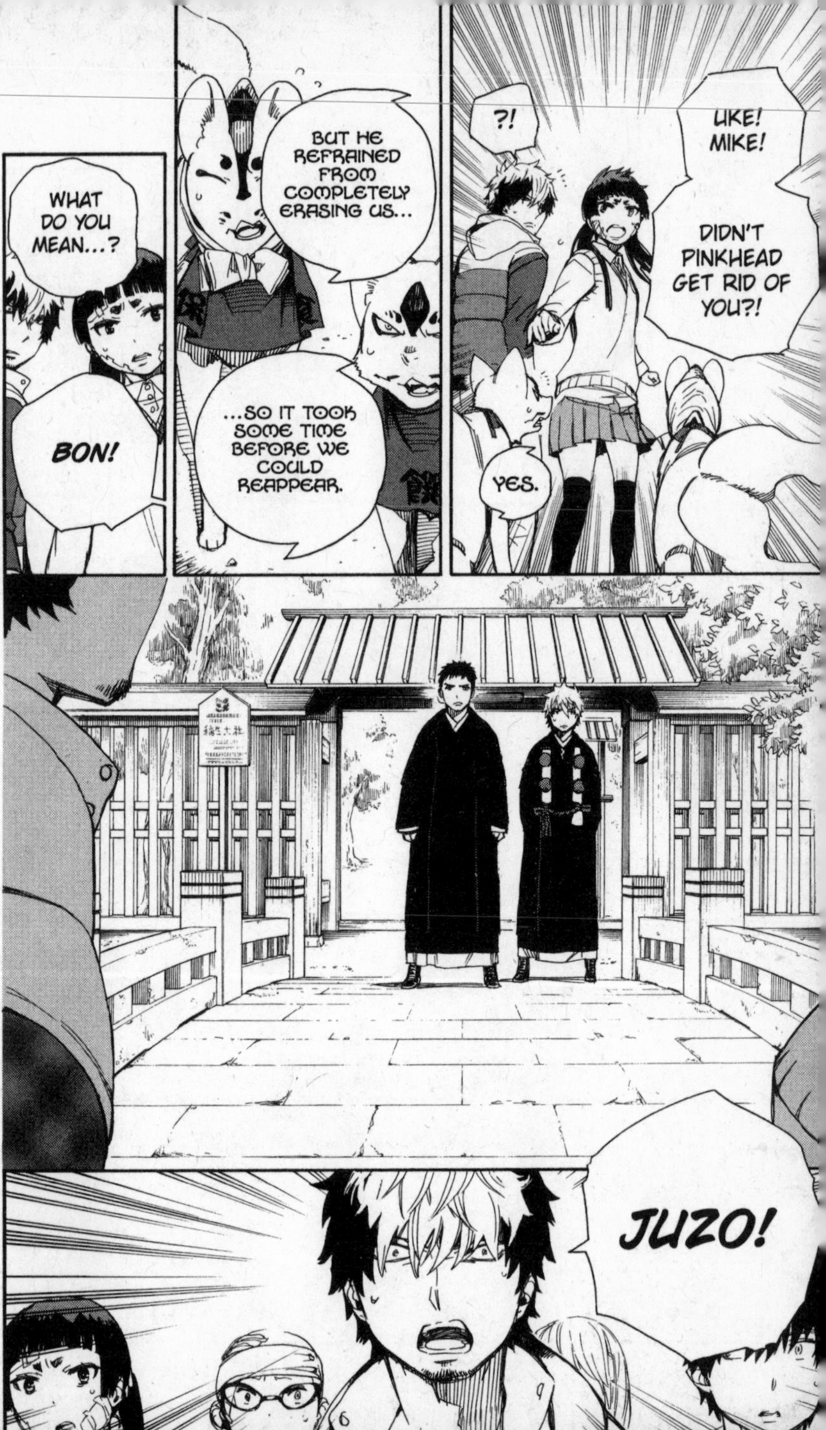
UKE! MIKE!
DIDN'T PINKHEAD GET RID OF YOU?!
?!
YES.
BUT HE REFRAINED FROM COMPLETELY ERASING US...
...SO IT TOOK SOME TIME BEFORE WE COULD REAPPEAR.
WHAT DO YOU MEAN...?
BON!
JUZO!

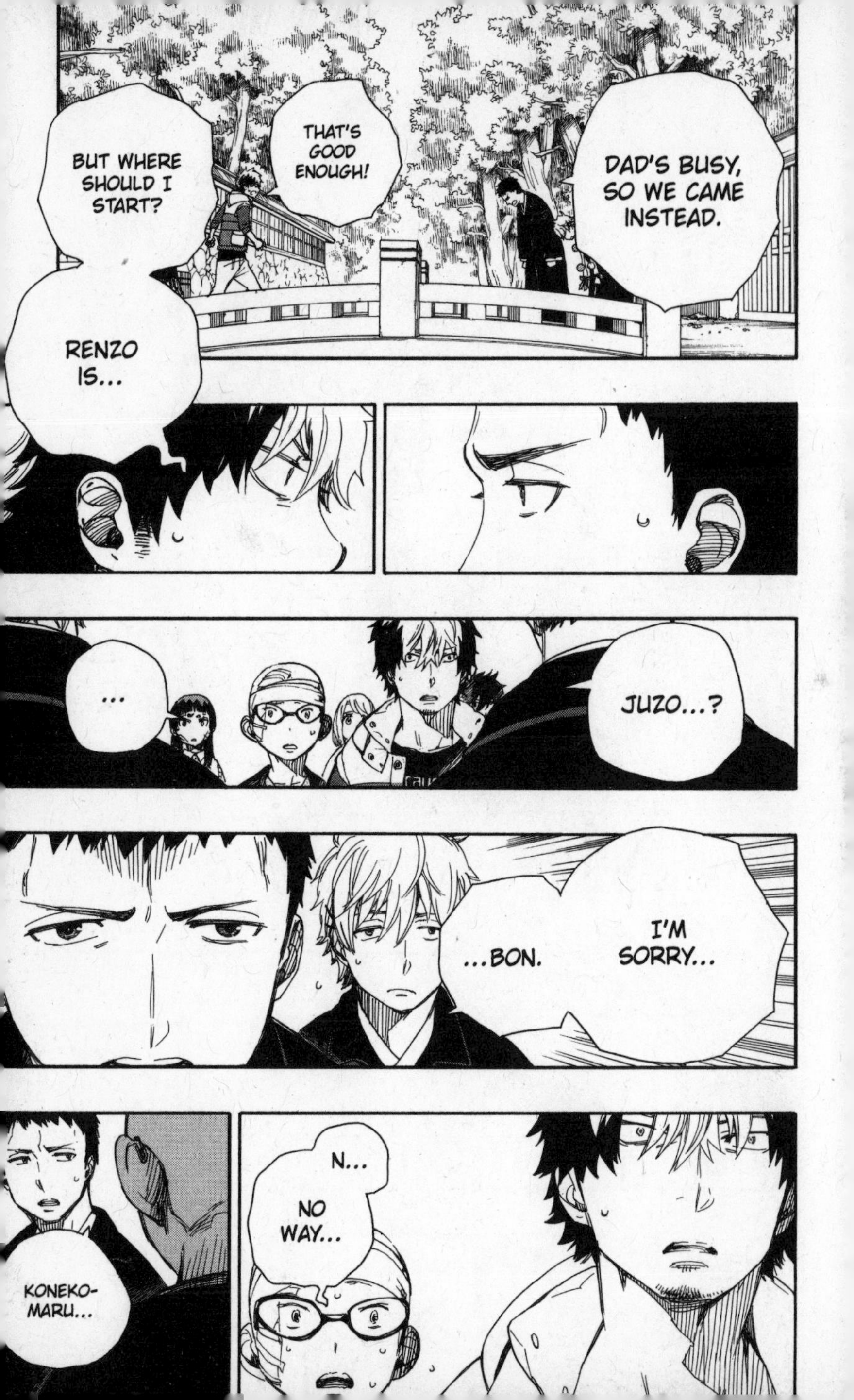
DAD'S BUSY, SO WE CAME INSTEAD.
THAT'S GOOD ENOUGH!
BUT WHERE SHOULD I START?
RENZO IS...
JUZO...?
...
I'M SORRY...
...BON.
N... NO WAY...
KONEKO-MARU...

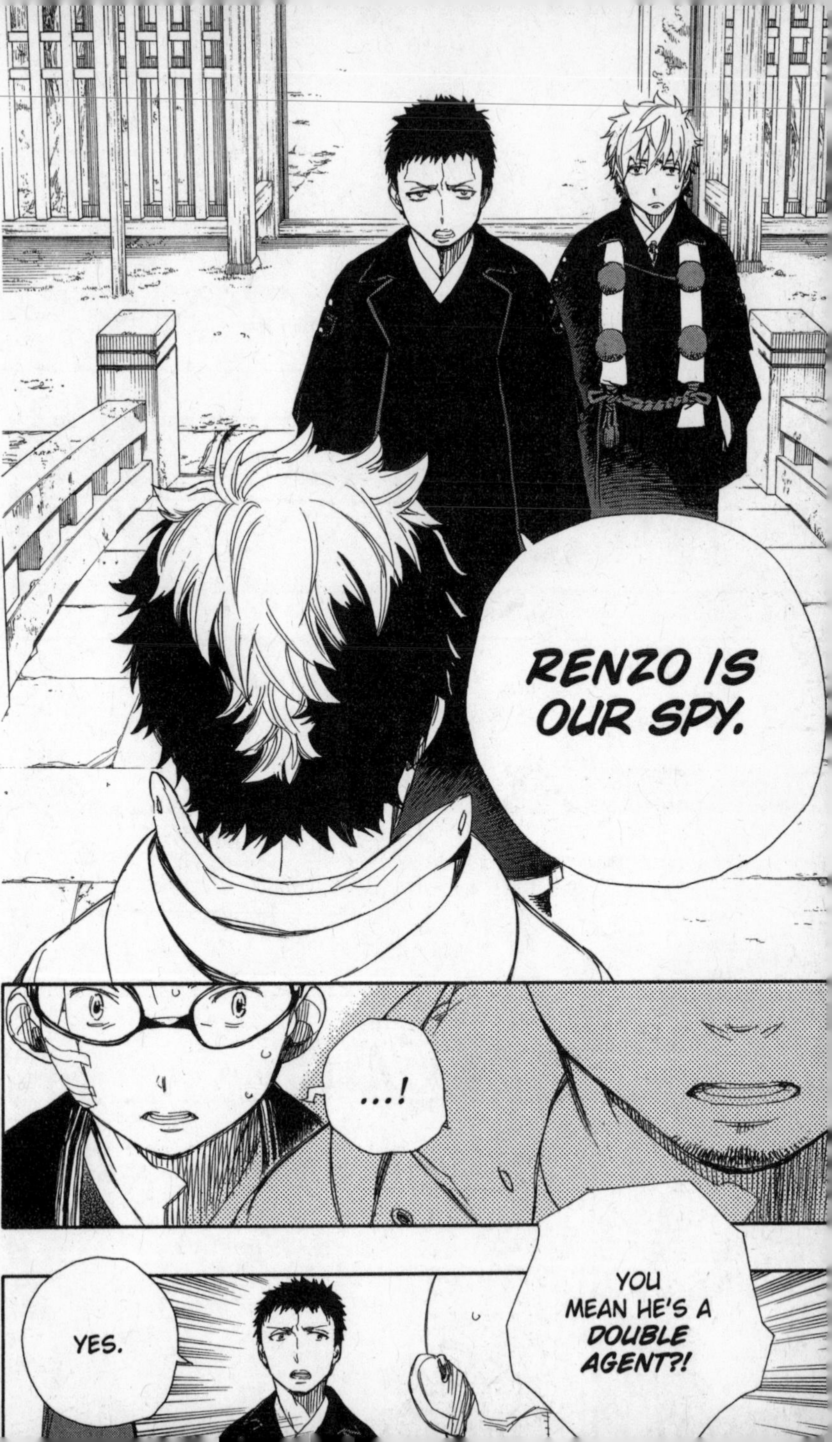
RENZO IS OUR SPY.
...!
YOU MEAN HE'S A DOUBLE AGENT?!
YES.

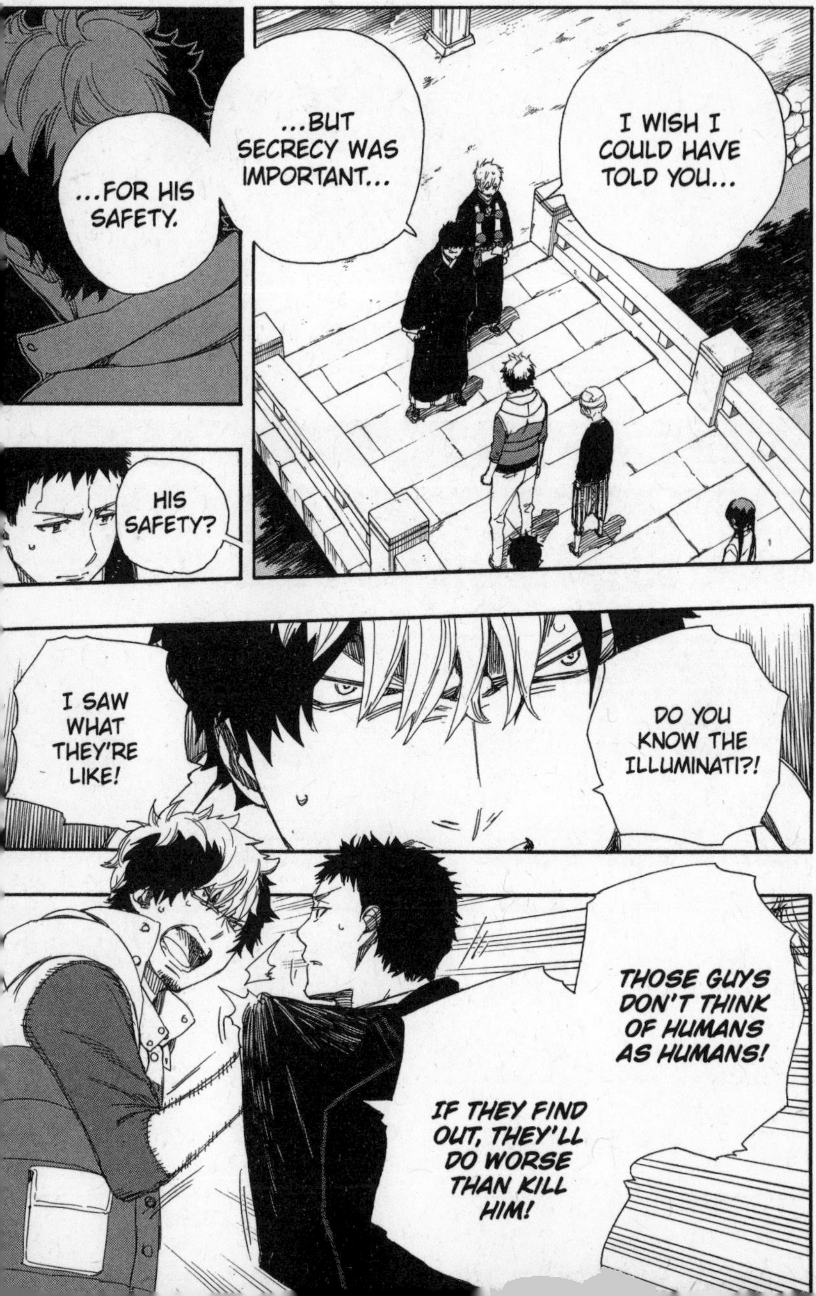
I WISH I COULD HAVE TOLD YOU...
...BUT SECRECY WAS IMPORTANT...
...FOR HIS SAFETY.
HIS SAFETY?
DO YOU KNOW THE ILLUMINATI?!
I SAW WHAT THEY'RE LIKE!
THOSE GUYS DON'T THINK OF HUMANS AS HUMANS!
IF THEY FIND OUT, THEY'LL DO WORSE THAN KILL HIM!

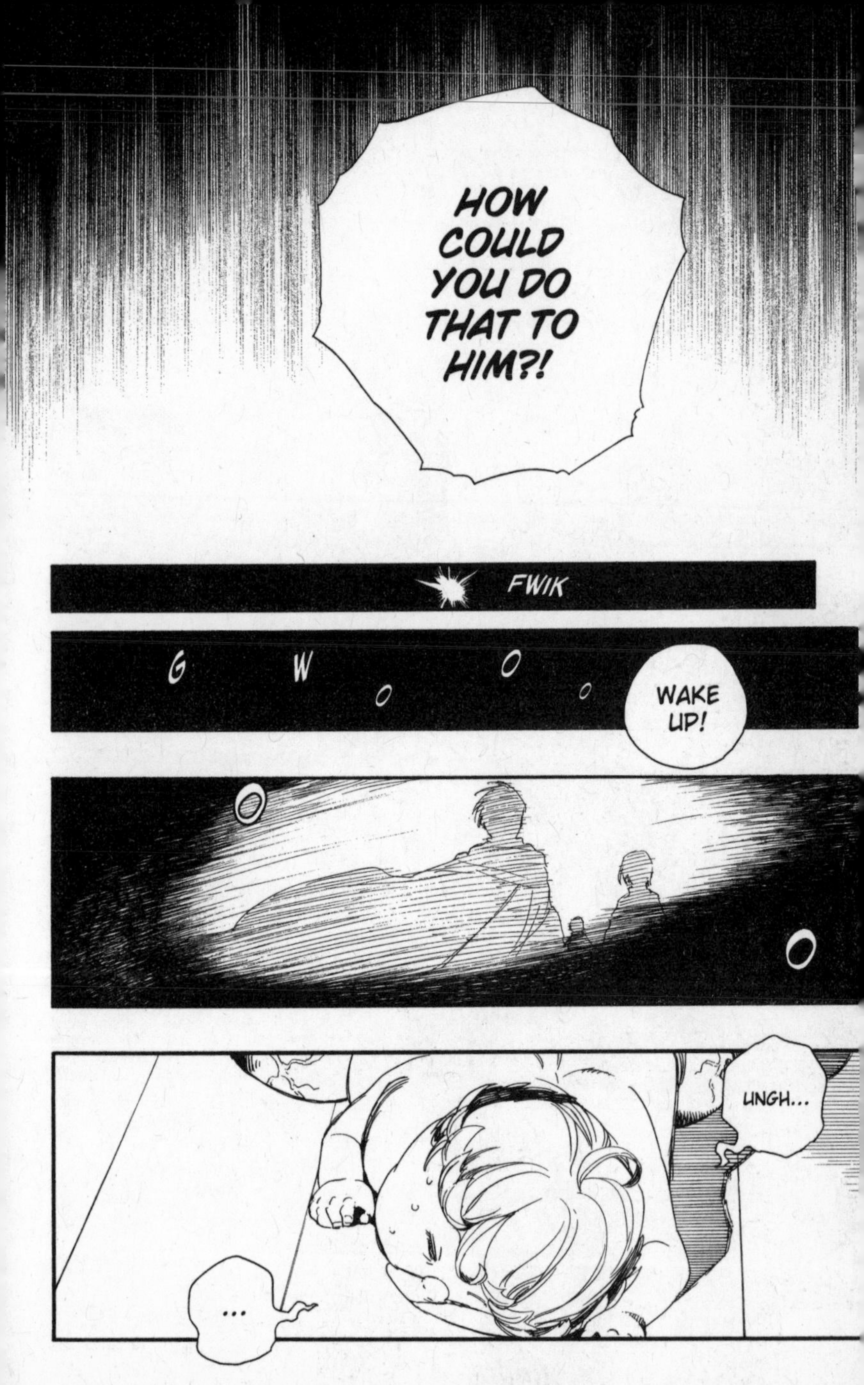
HOW COULD YOU DO THAT TO HIM?!
FWIK
WAKE UP!
G W O O O O
O O
UNGH...
...

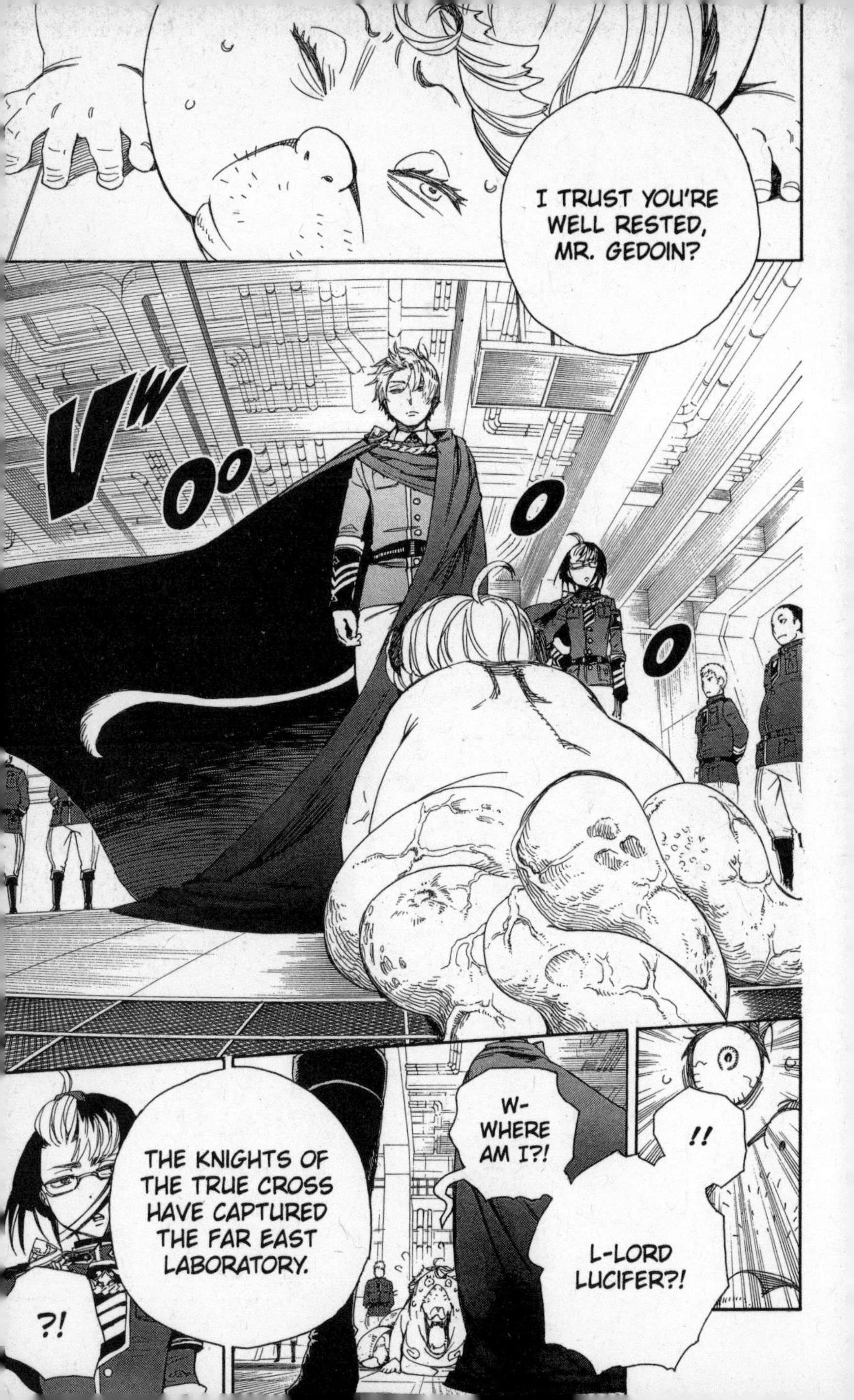
I TRUST YOU'RE WELL RESTED, MR. GEDOIN?
VWOOOO
W-WHERE AM I?!
!!
L-LORD LUCIFER?!
THE KNIGHTS OF THE TRUE CROSS HAVE CAPTURED THE FAR EAST LABORATORY.
?!

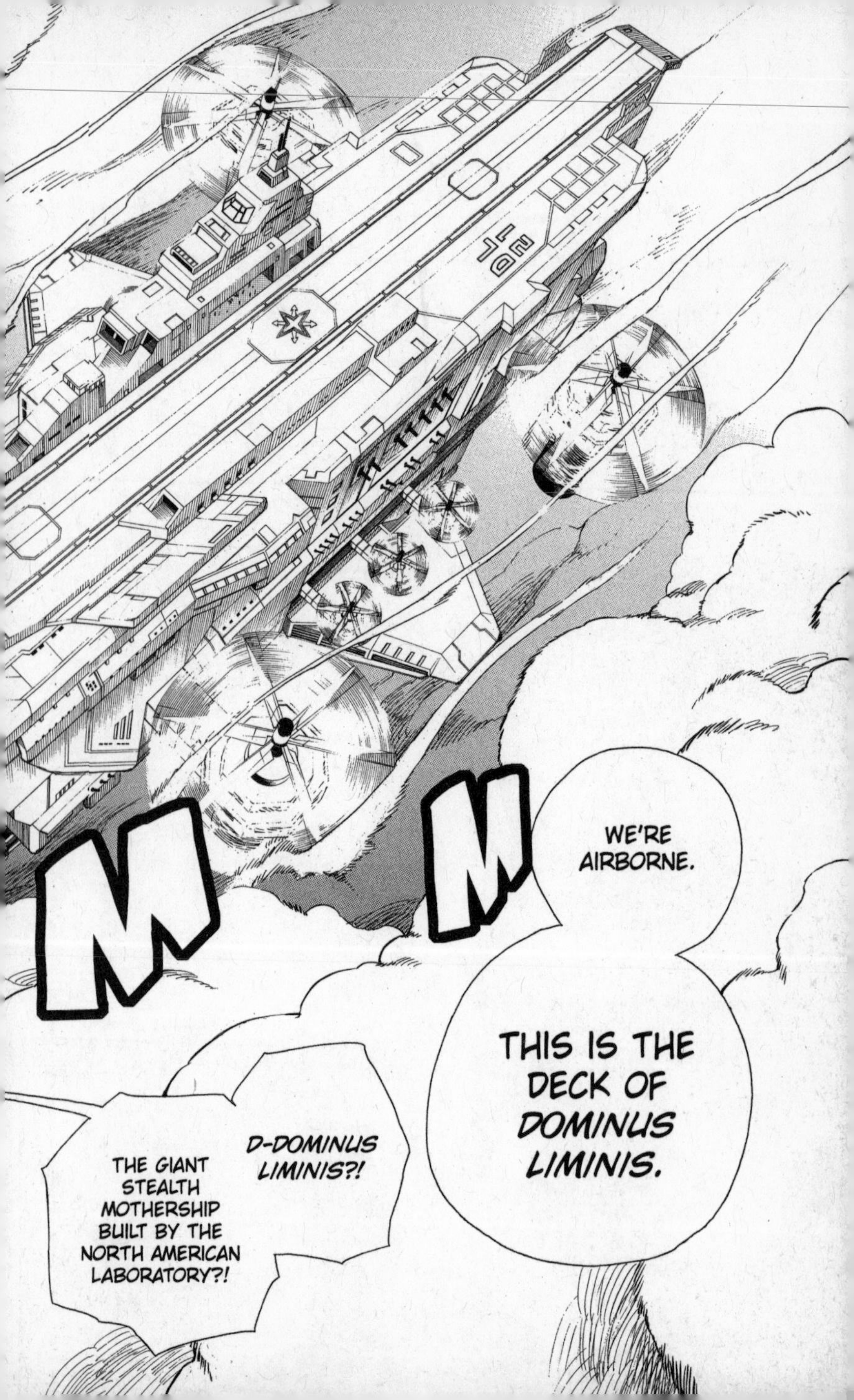
M
M
WE'RE AIRBORNE.
THIS IS THE DECK OF DOMINUS LIMINIS.
D-DOMINUS LIMINIS?!
THE GIANT STEALTH MOTHERSHIP BUILT BY THE NORTH AMERICAN LABORATORY?!

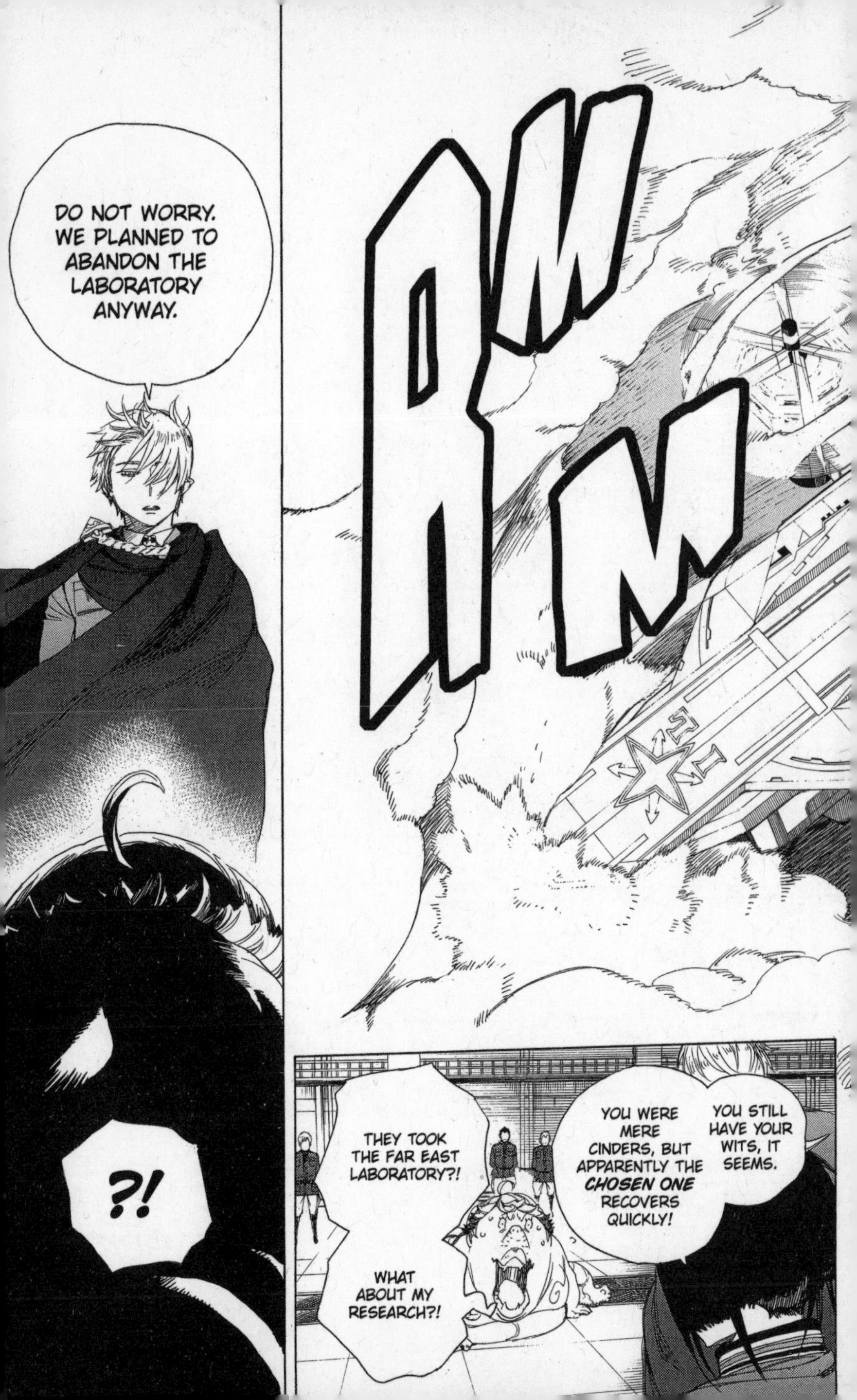
YOU STILL HAVE YOUR WITS, IT SEEMS.
YOU WERE MERE CINDERS, BUT APPARENTLY THE *CHOSEN ONE* RECOVERS QUICKLY!
THEY TOOK THE FAR EAST LABORATORY?!
WHAT ABOUT MY RESEARCH?!
DO NOT WORRY. WE PLANNED TO ABANDON THE LABORATORY ANYWAY.
?!

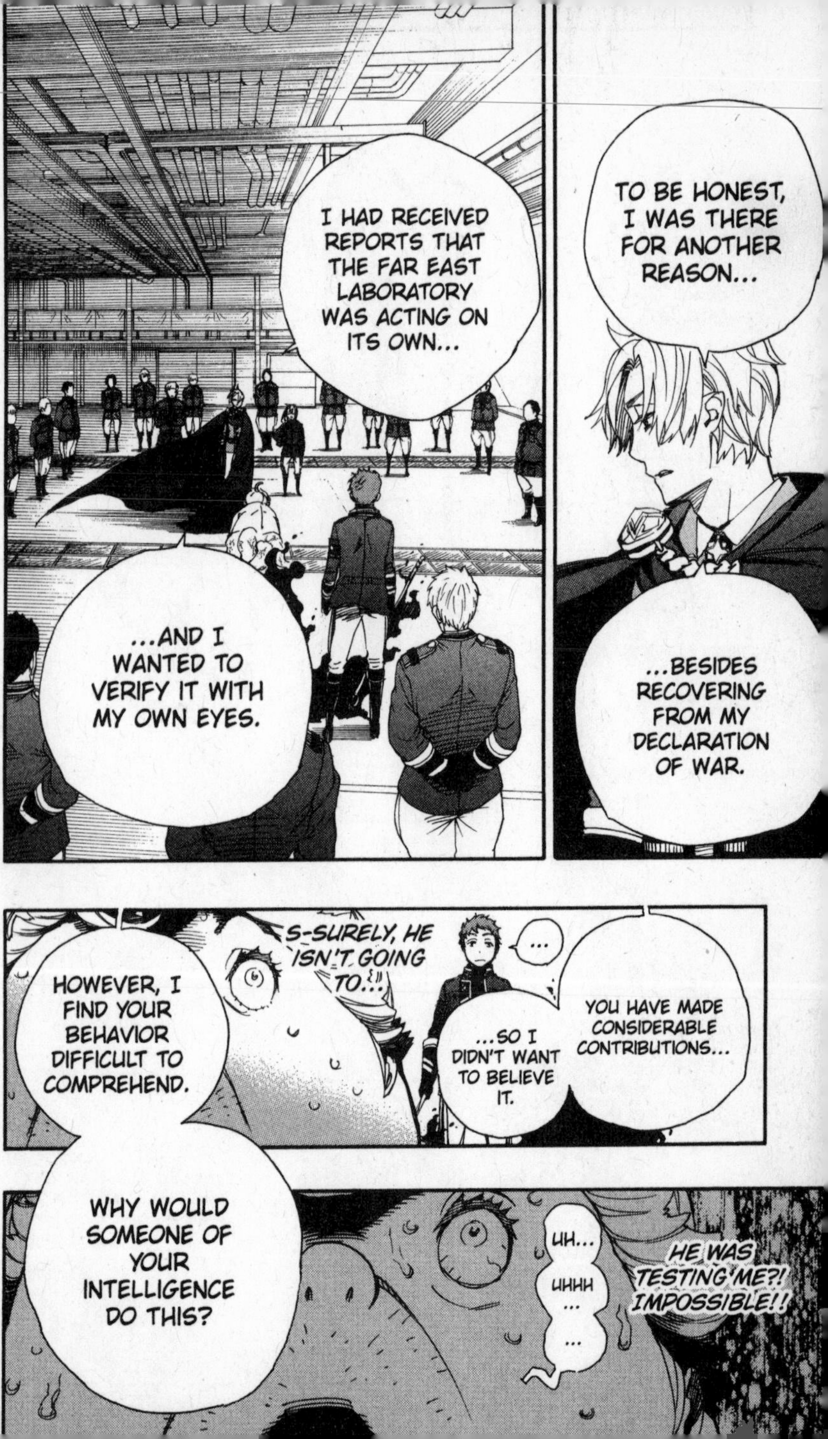
TO BE HONEST, I WAS THERE FOR ANOTHER REASON...
...BESIDES RECOVERING FROM MY DECLARATION OF WAR.
I HAD RECEIVED REPORTS THAT THE FAR EAST LABORATORY WAS ACTING ON ITS OWN...
...AND I WANTED TO VERIFY IT WITH MY OWN EYES.
YOU HAVE MADE CONSIDERABLE CONTRIBUTIONS...
...
...SO I DIDN'T WANT TO BELIEVE IT.
S-SURELY, HE ISN'T GOING TO...
HOWEVER, I FIND YOUR BEHAVIOR DIFFICULT TO COMPREHEND.
HE WAS TESTING ME?! IMPOSSIBLE!!
UH... UHHH ... ...
WHY WOULD SOMEONE OF YOUR INTELLIGENCE DO THIS?

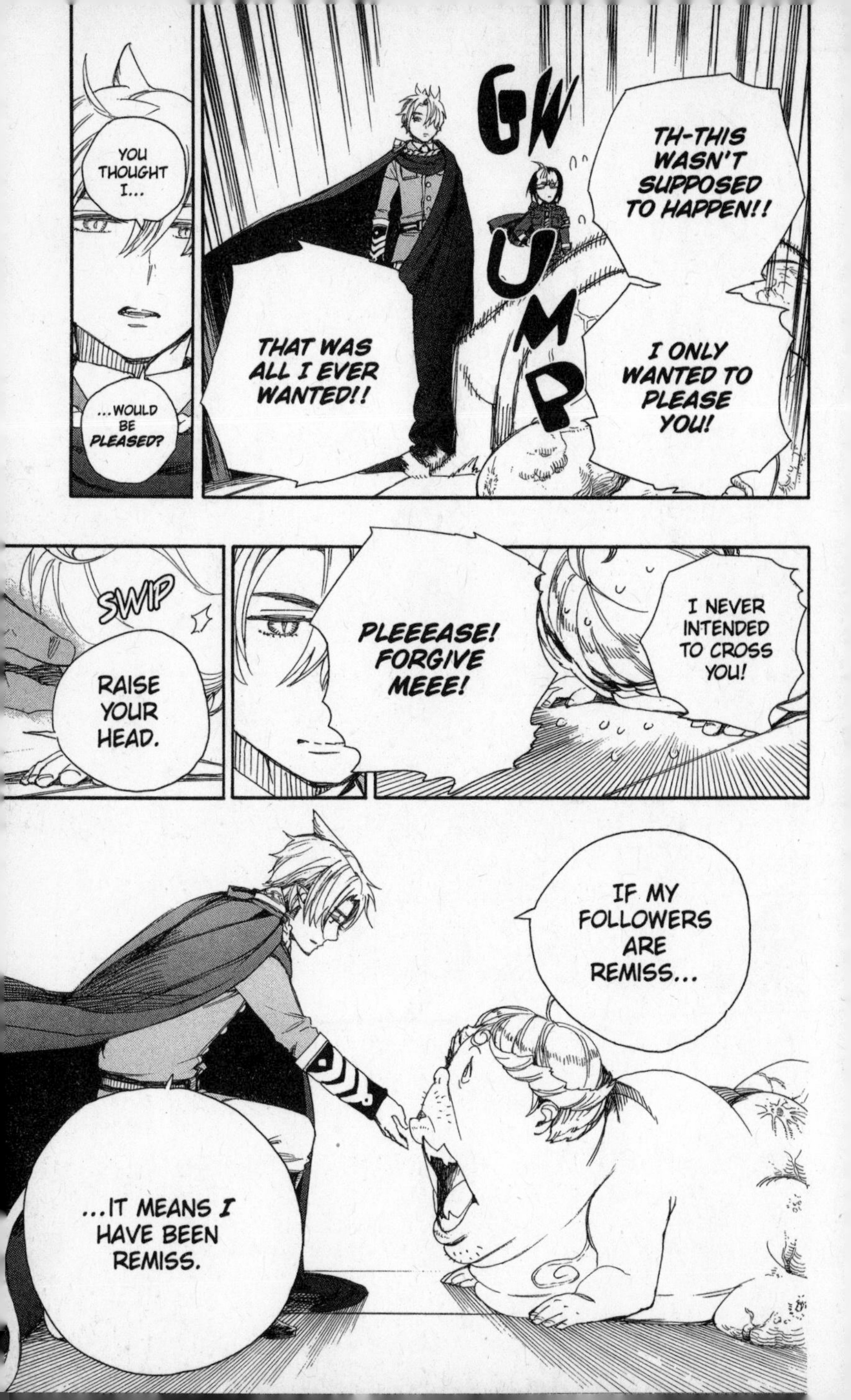
TH-THIS WASN'T SUPPOSED TO HAPPEN!!
GWUMP
I ONLY WANTED TO PLEASE YOU!
THAT WAS ALL I EVER WANTED!!
YOU THOUGHT I...
...WOULD BE *PLEASED?*
I NEVER INTENDED TO CROSS YOU!
PLEEEASE! FORGIVE MEEE!
SWIP
RAISE YOUR HEAD.
IF MY FOLLOWERS ARE REMISS...
...IT MEANS *I* HAVE BEEN REMISS.

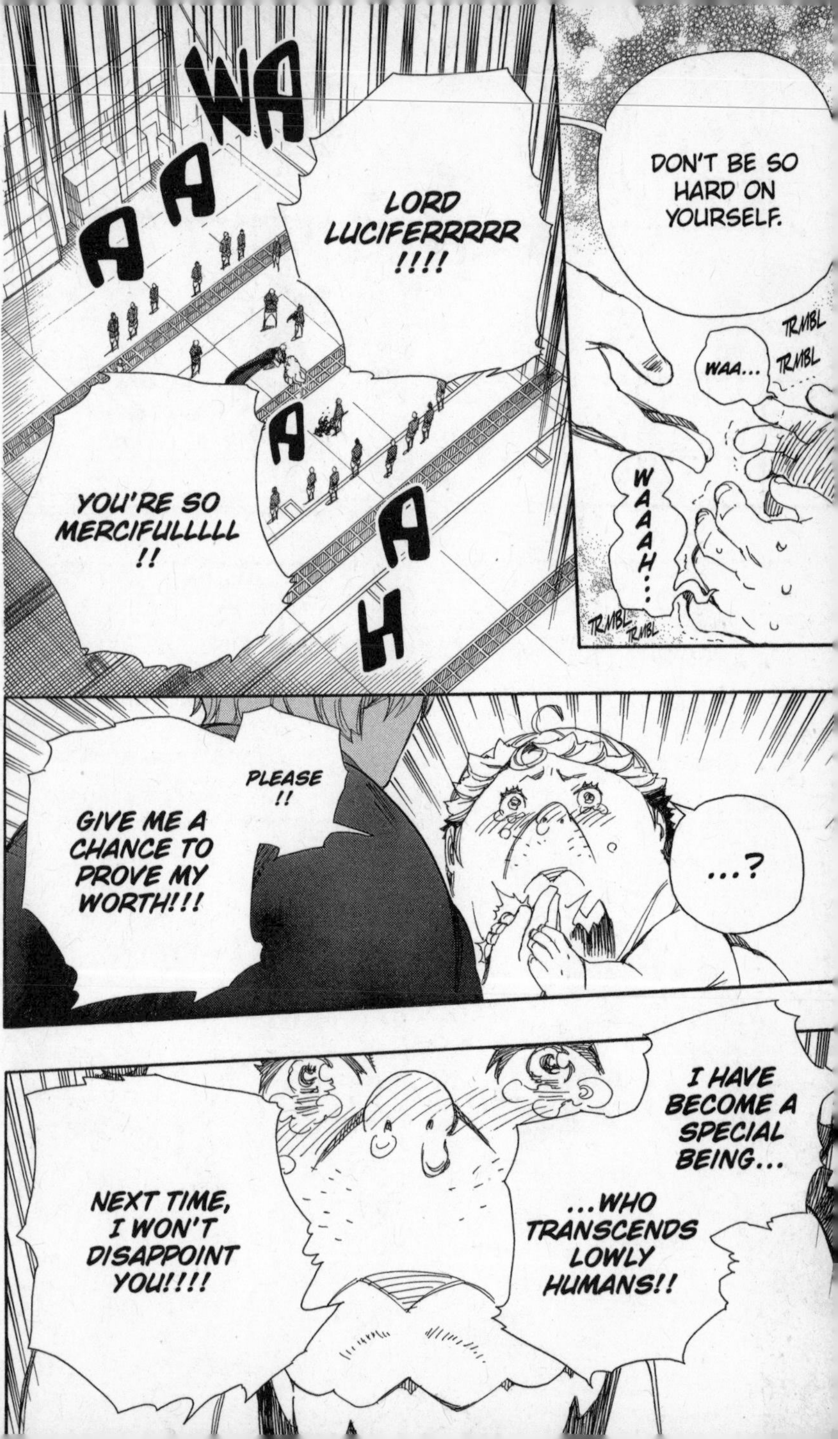
DON'T BE SO HARD ON YOURSELF.
TRMBL
TRMBL
WAA...
WAAAAH...
TRMBL TRMBL
WAAAAAH
LORD LUCIFERRRRR!!!!
YOU'RE SO MERCIFULLLLL!!
...?
PLEASE!!
GIVE ME A CHANCE TO PROVE MY WORTH!!!
I HAVE BECOME A SPECIAL BEING...
...WHO TRANSCENDS LOWLY HUMANS!!
NEXT TIME, I WON'T DISAPPOINT YOU!!!!

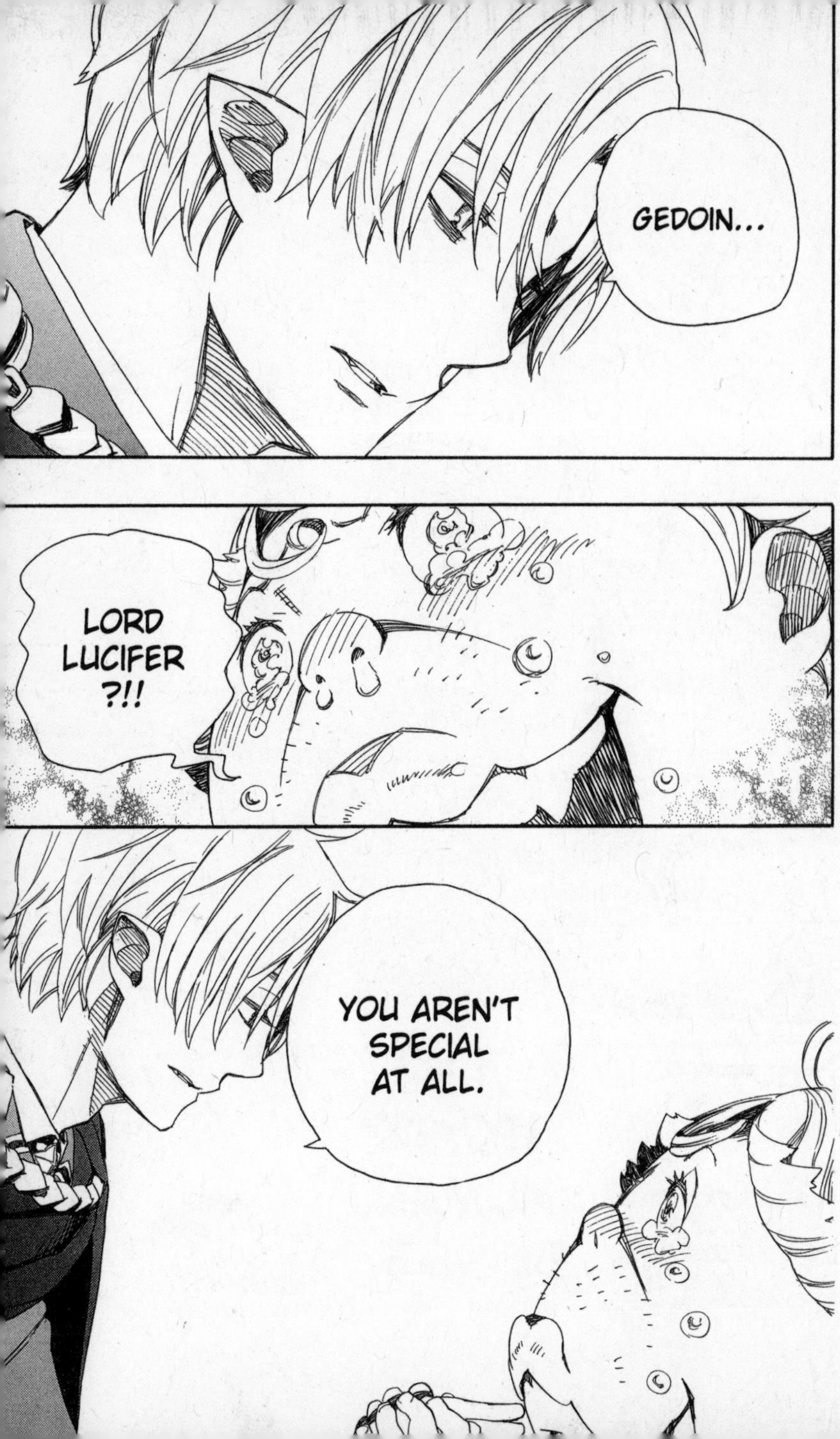
GEDOIN...
LORD LUCIFER ?!!
YOU AREN'T SPECIAL AT ALL.

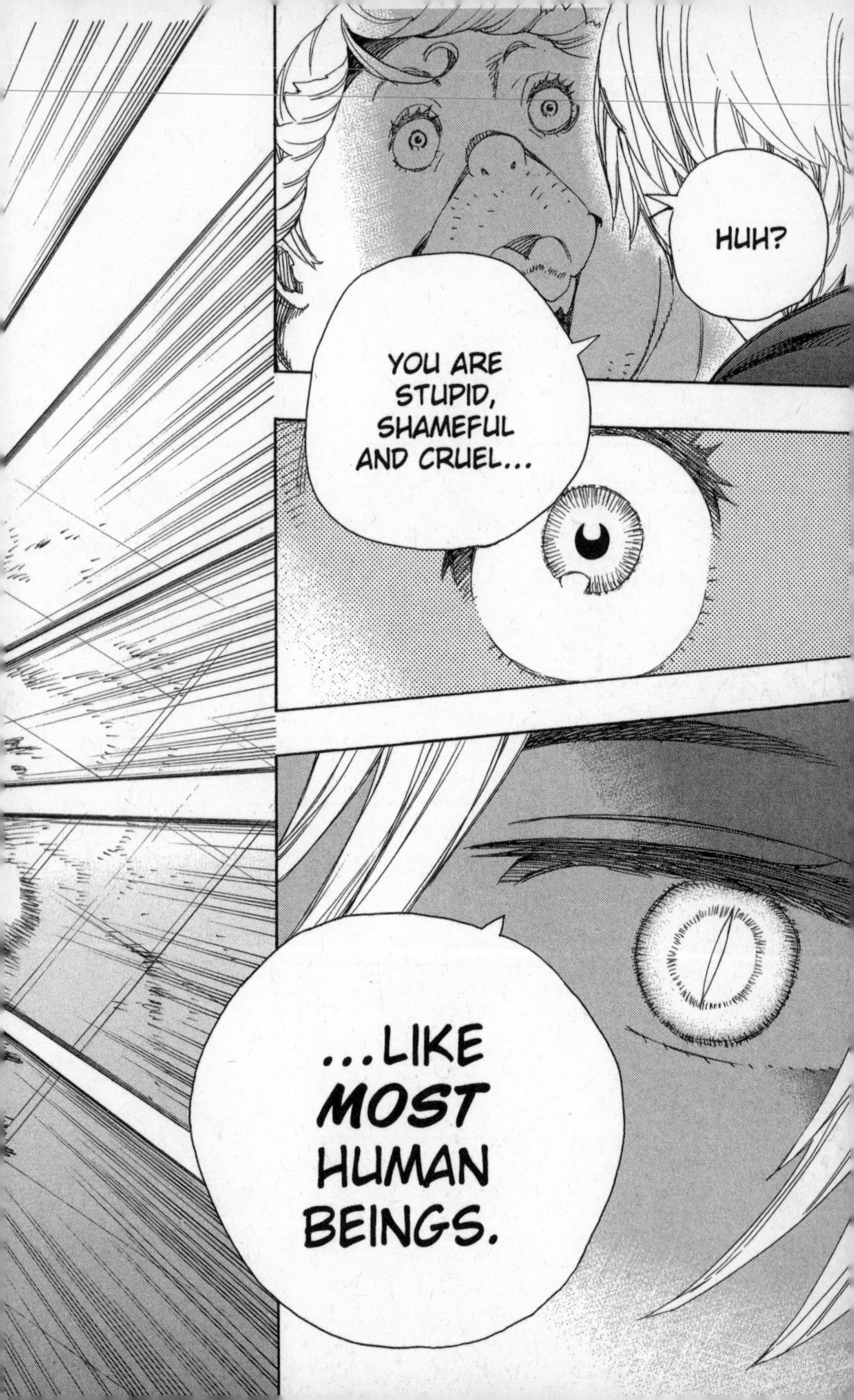
HUH?
YOU ARE STUPID, SHAMEFUL AND CRUEL...
...LIKE *MOST* HUMAN BEINGS.

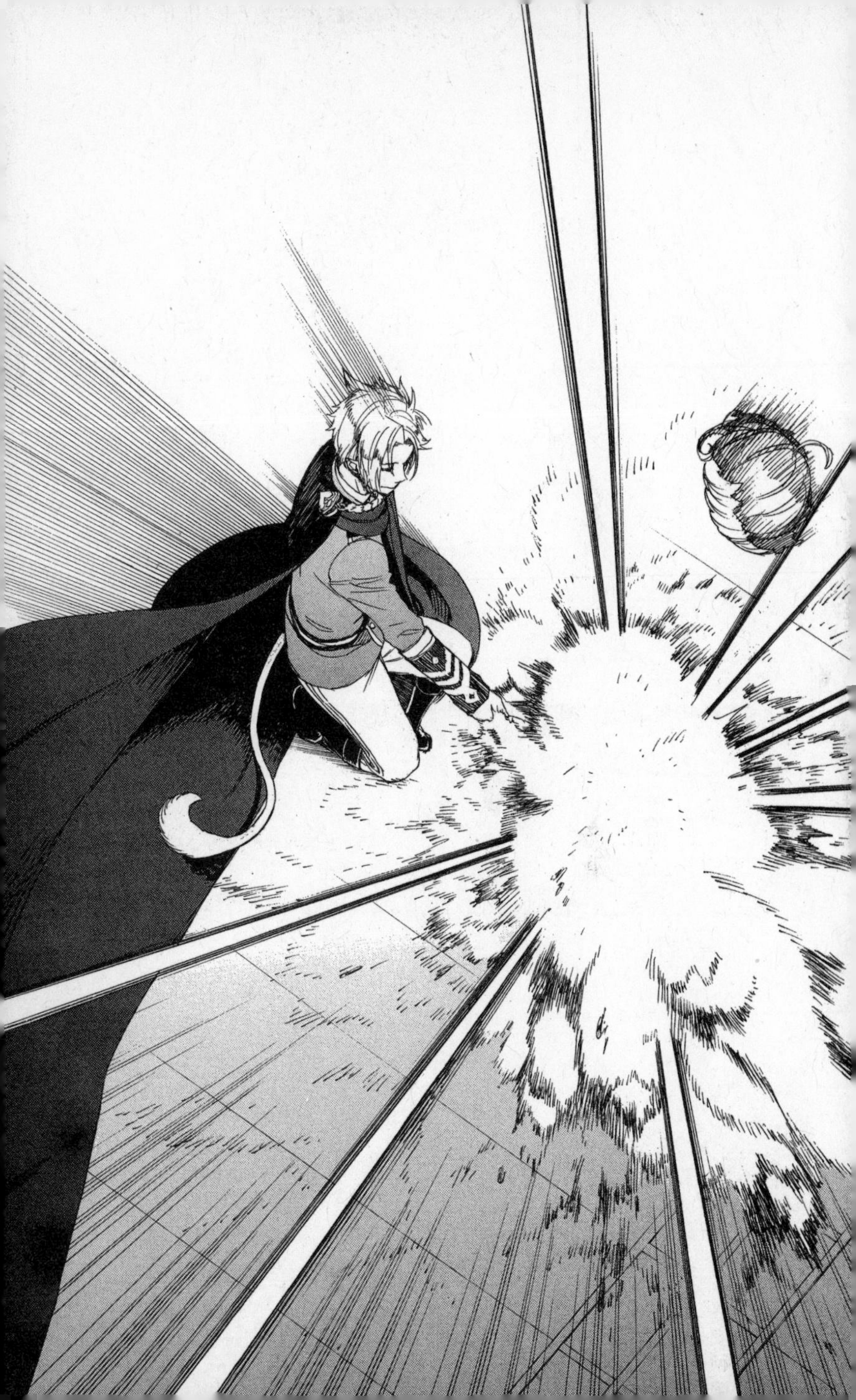

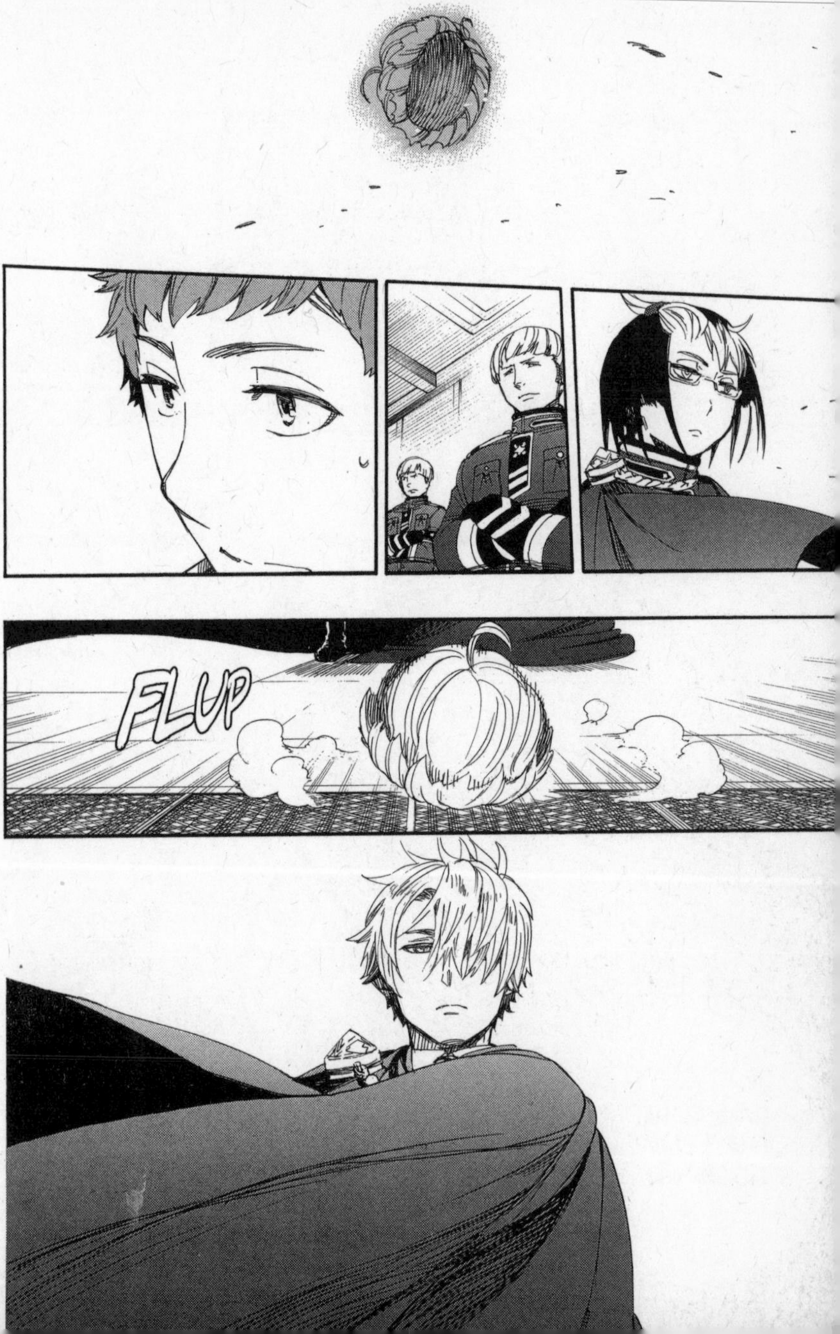
FLUP

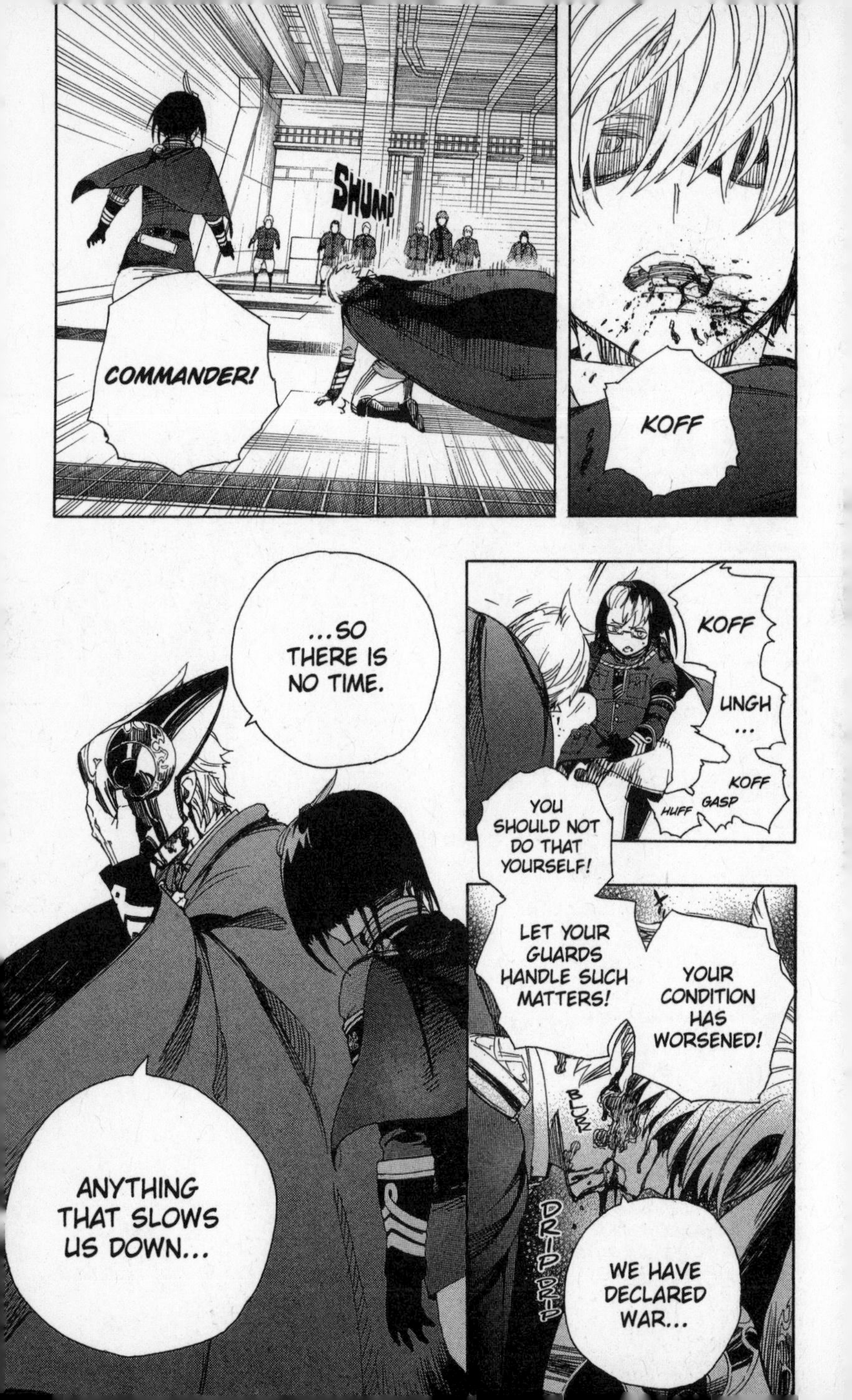
KOFF
SHUMP
COMMANDER!
KOFF
UNGH ...
KOFF
GASP
HUFF
YOU SHOULD NOT DO THAT YOURSELF!
LET YOUR GUARDS HANDLE SUCH MATTERS!
YOUR CONDITION HAS WORSENED!
DRIP DRIP
WE HAVE DECLARED WAR...
...SO THERE IS NO TIME.
ANYTHING THAT SLOWS US DOWN...

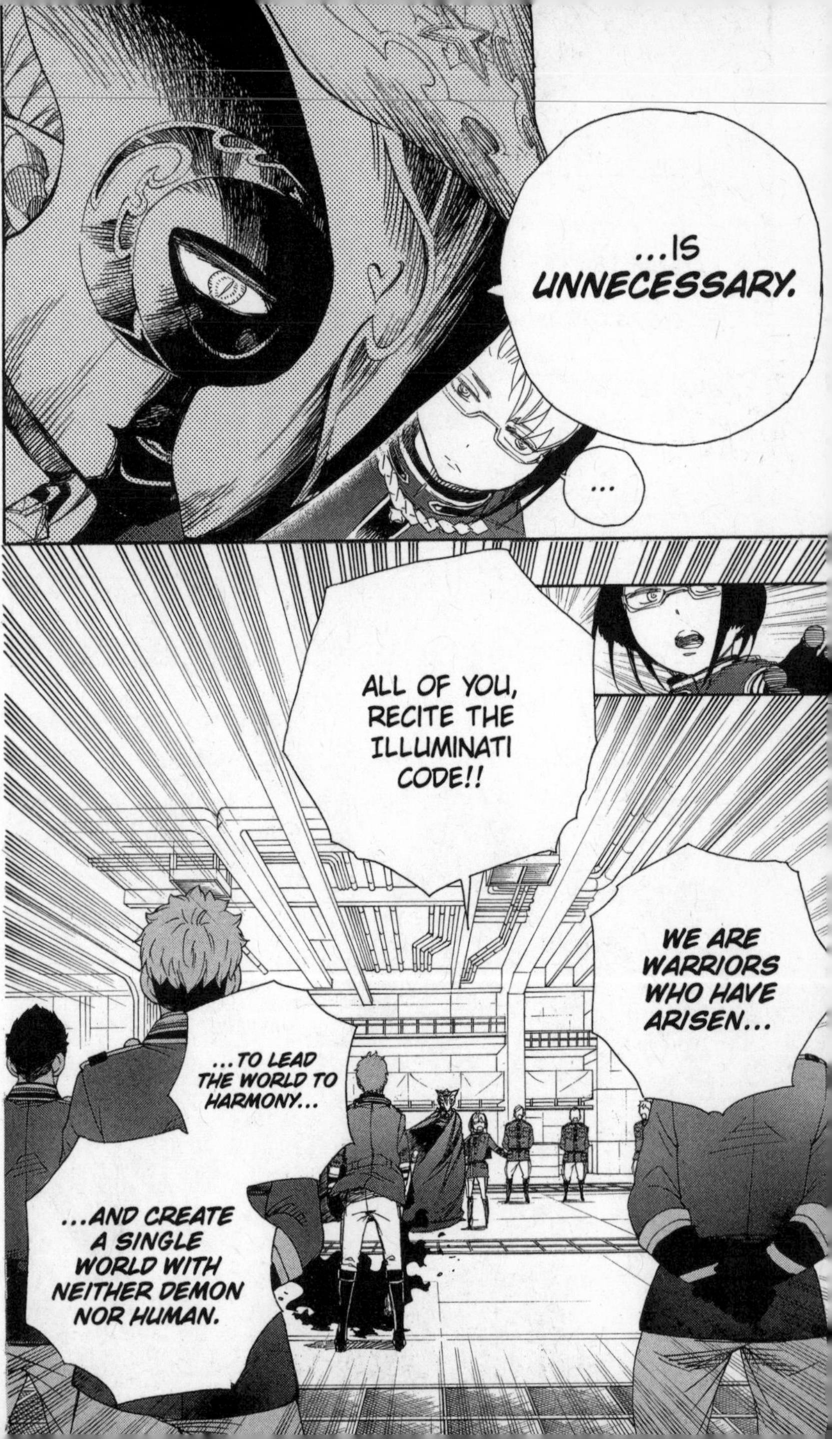
...IS UNNECESSARY.
...
ALL OF YOU, RECITE THE ILLUMINATI CODE!!
WE ARE WARRIORS WHO HAVE ARISEN...
...TO LEAD THE WORLD TO HARMONY...
...AND CREATE A SINGLE WORLD WITH NEITHER DEMON NOR HUMAN.

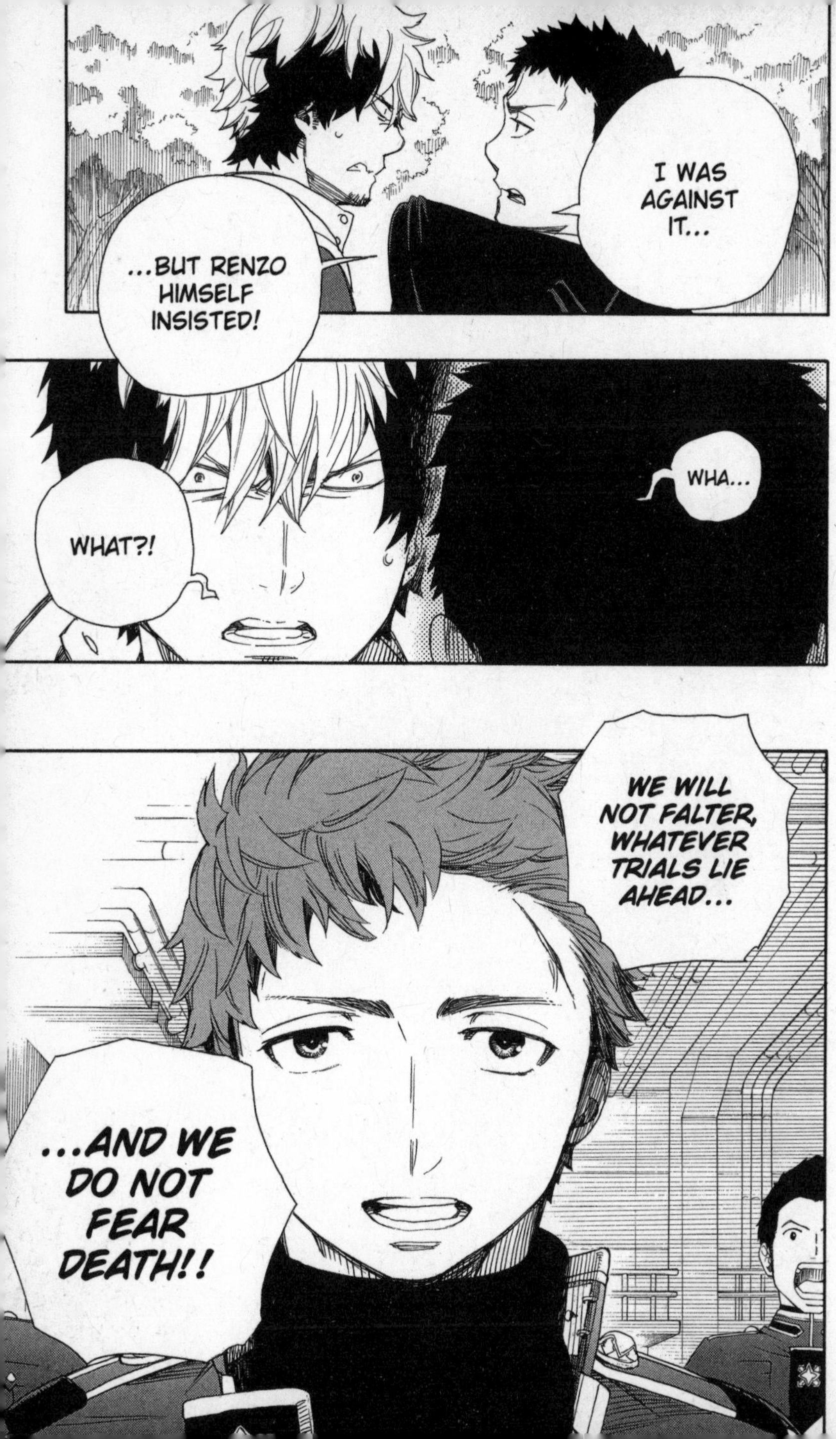
I WAS AGAINST IT...
...BUT RENZO HIMSELF INSISTED!
WHA...
WHAT?!
WE WILL NOT FALTER, WHATEVER TRIALS LIE AHEAD...
...AND WE DO NOT FEAR DEATH!!

Blue Exorcist Chapter 64: I'll Come Again

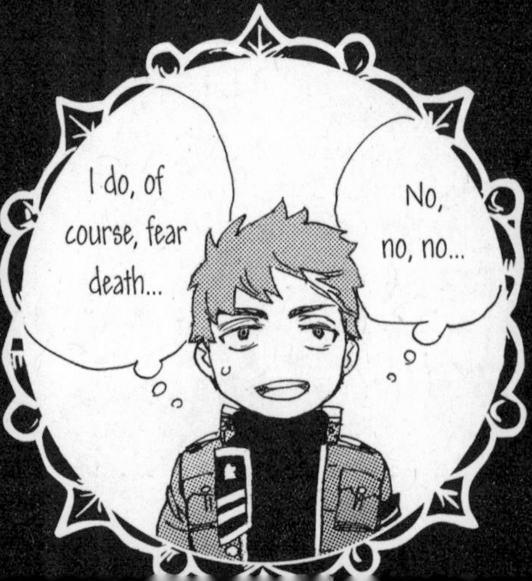
No, no, no...
I do, of course, fear death...

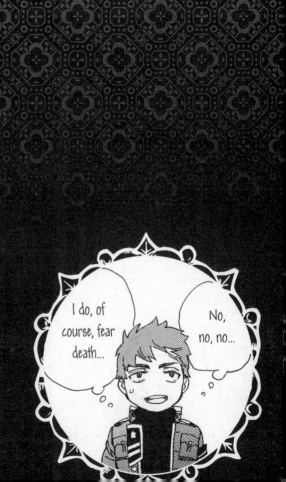

Chapter 64.5: Welcome Home

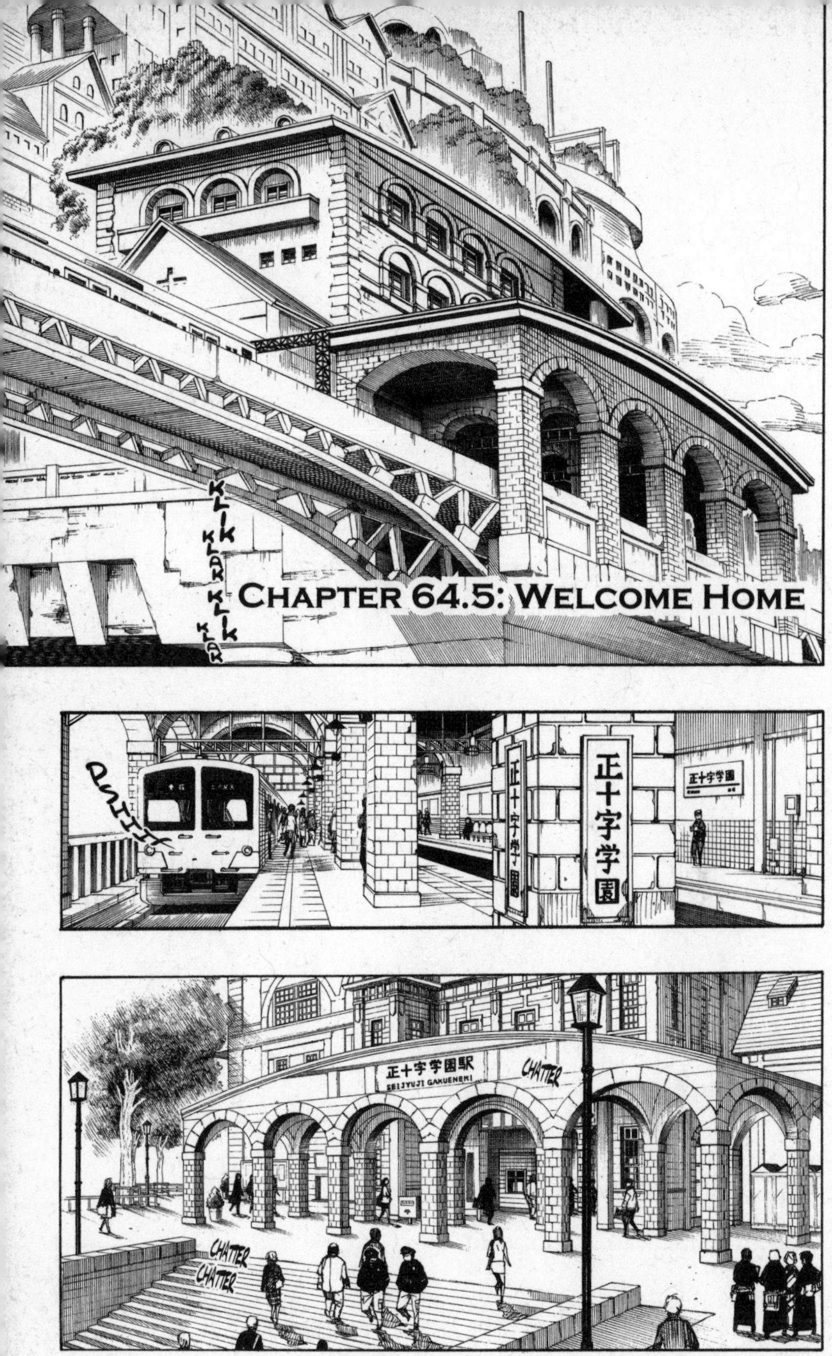
KLIK KLAK KLIK KLAK
PSHHH
正十字学園
正十字学園
正十字学園
正十字学園駅
SEIJYUJI GAKUENEKI
CHATTER
CHATTER CHATTER

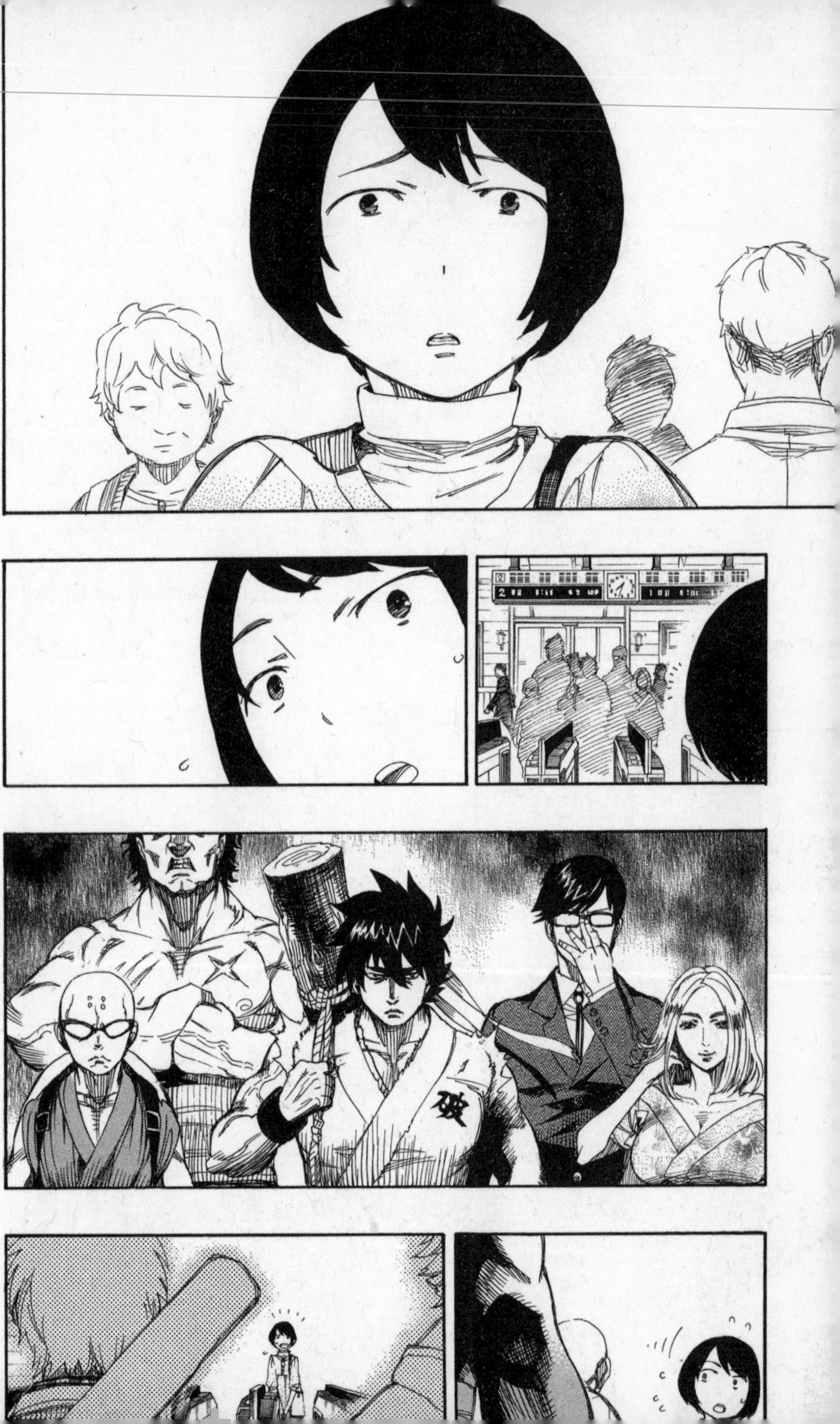

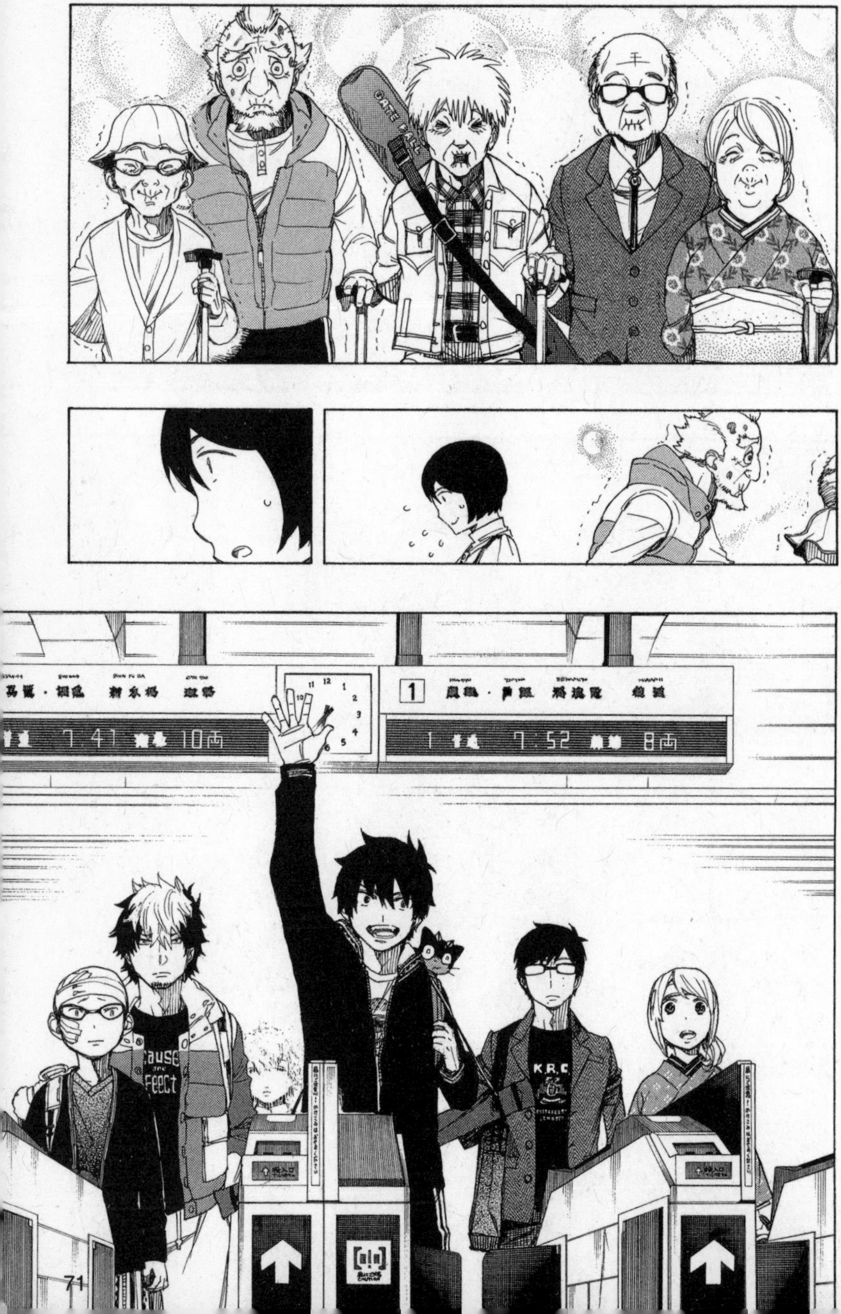
GAME BALL
7:41
7:52
K.R.C

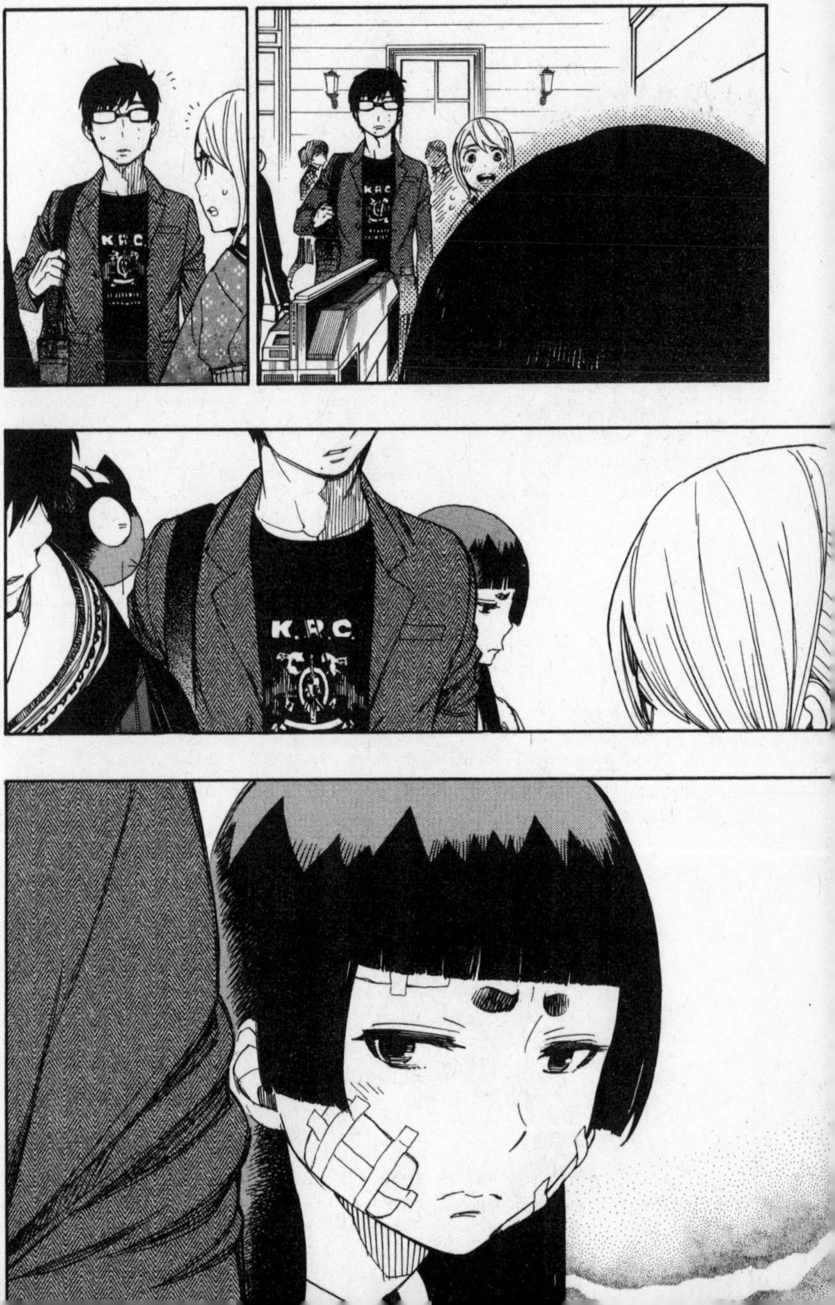
K.R.C.
K.R.C.

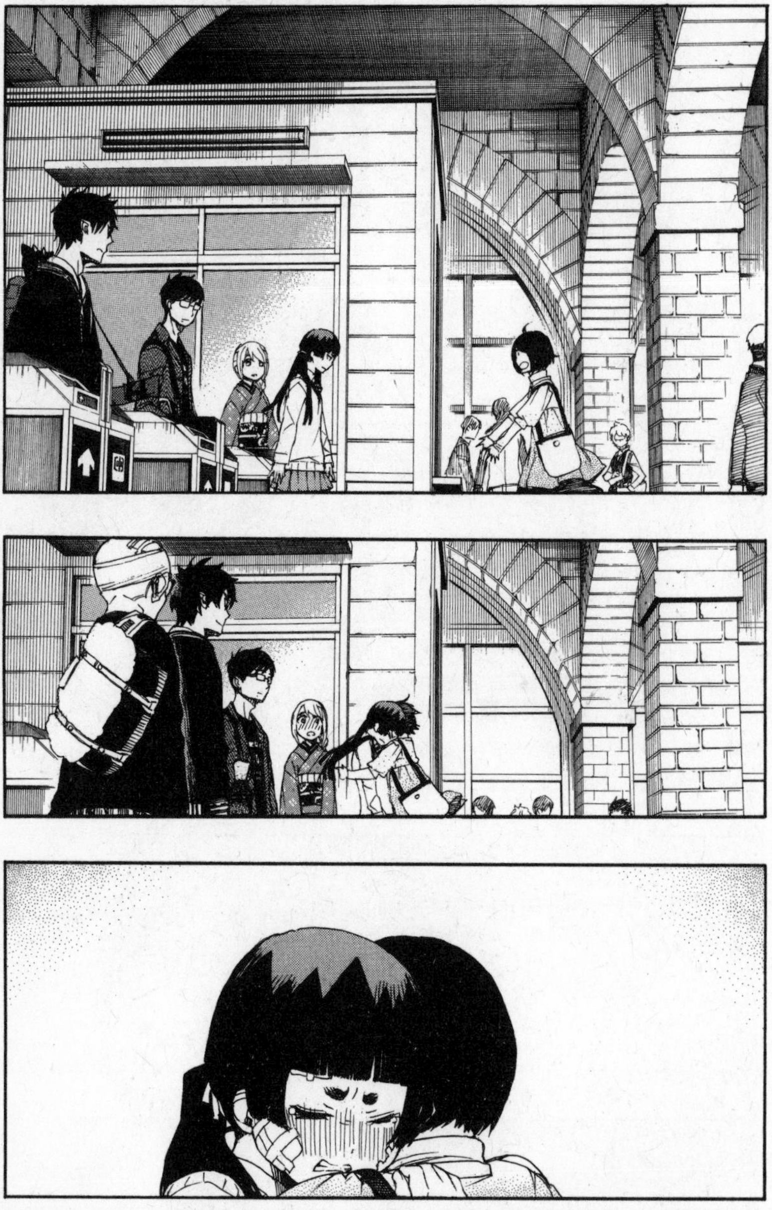

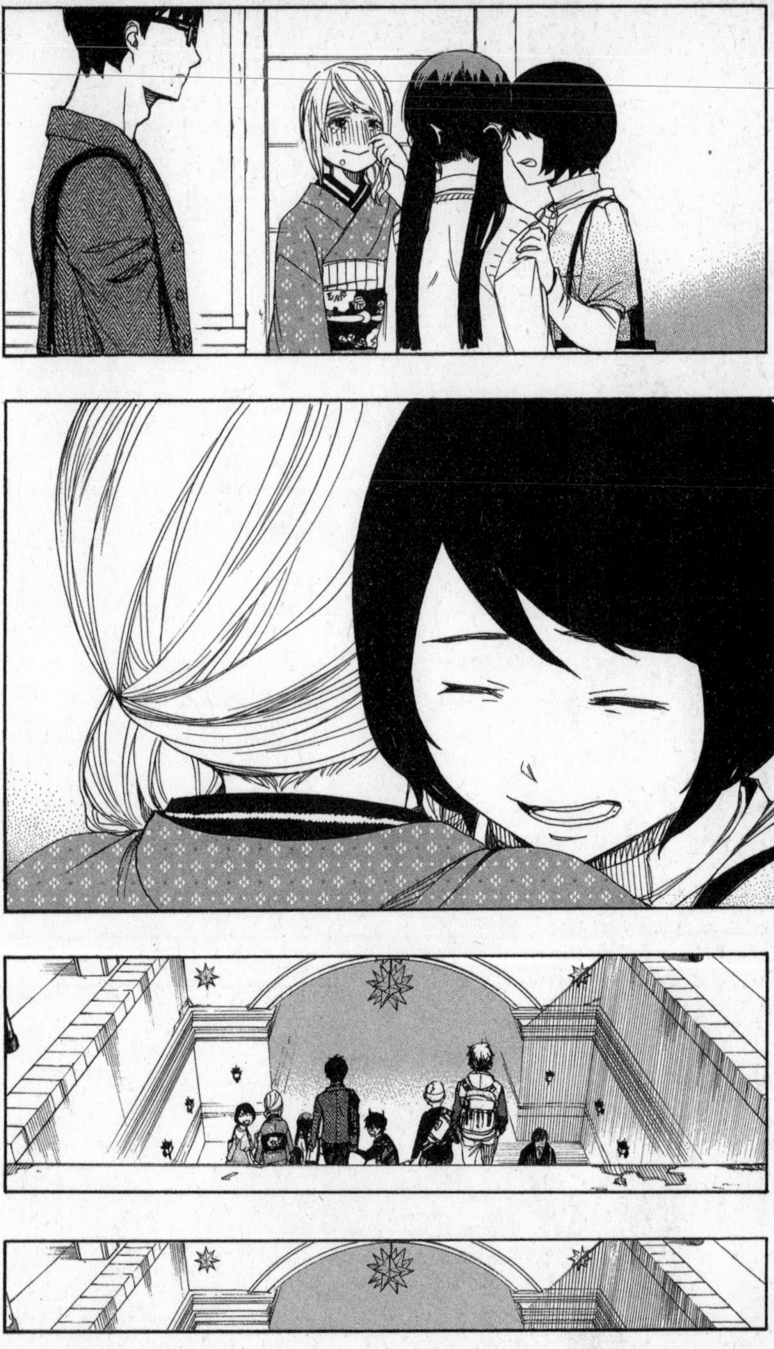

Blue Exorcist Chapter 64.5: Welcome Home

Chapter 65: Pink Spider: Part 1

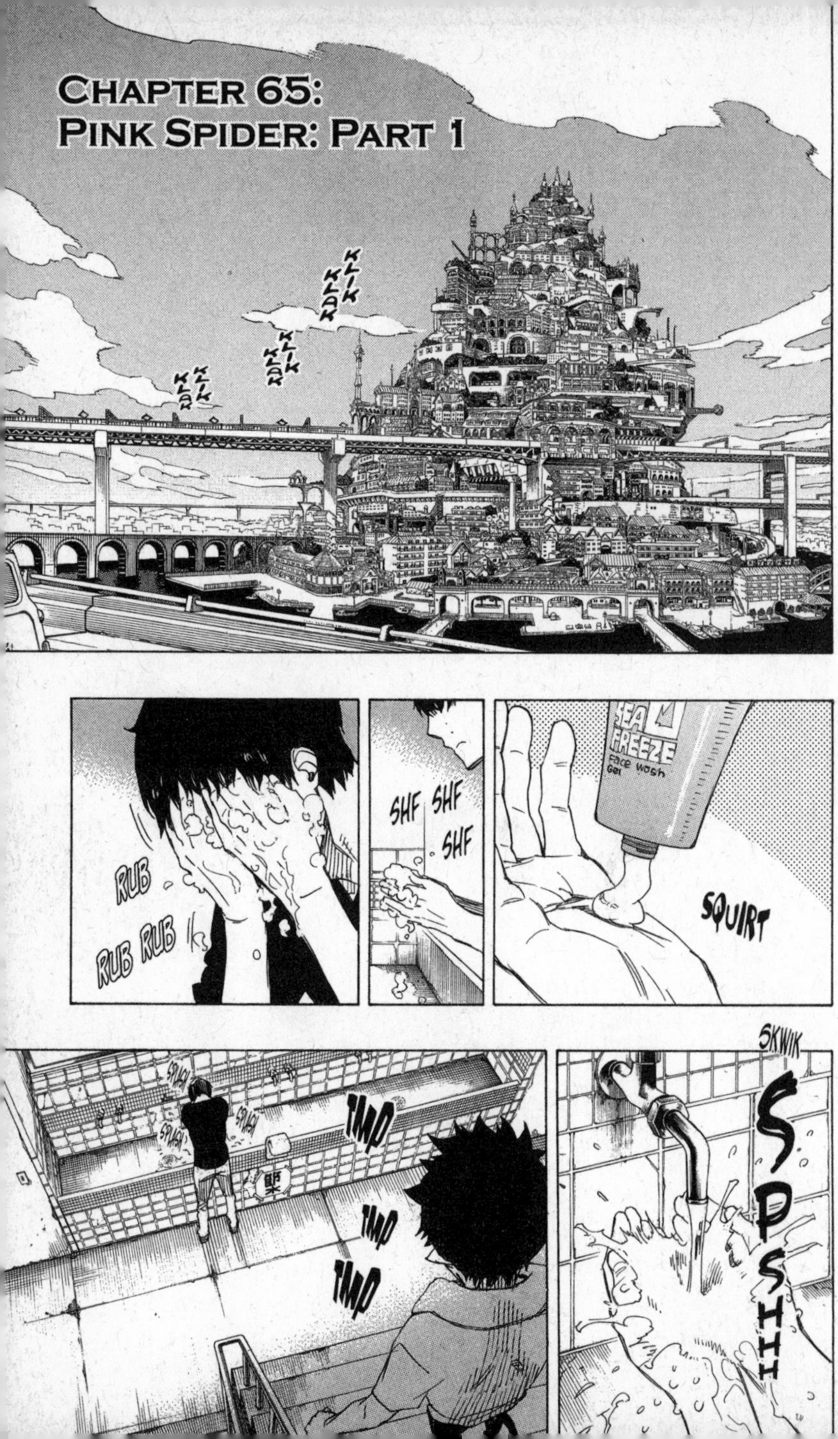
KLIK KLAK
KLIK KLAK
KLIK KLAK
SEA FREEZE face wash gel
SQUIRT
SHF SHF SHF
RUB RUB RUB
SKWIK
SPSHHH
TMP TMP TMP
SPLASH SPLASH SPLASH

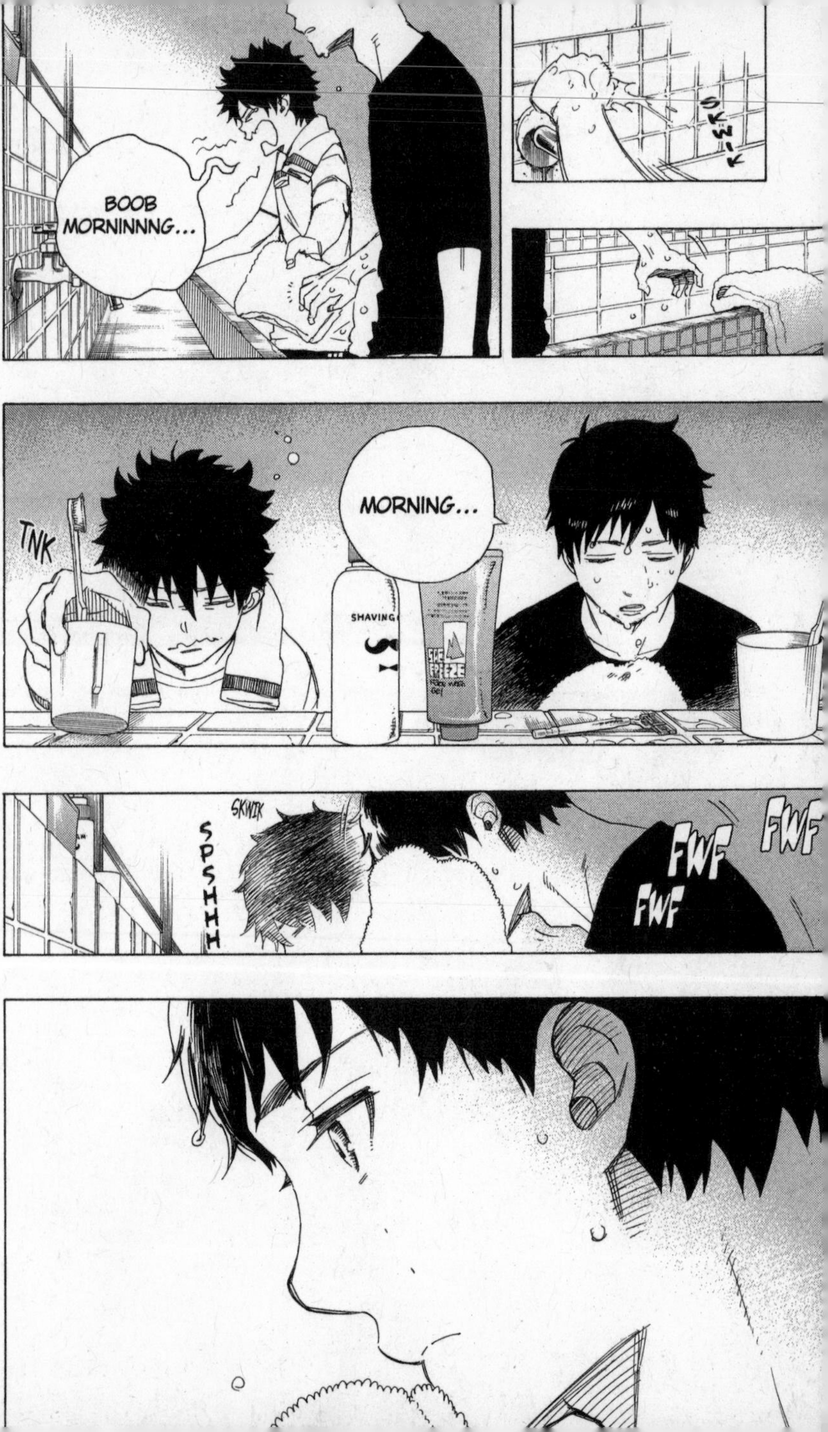
SKWIK
BOOB MORNINNNG...
MORNING...
SHAVING
TNK
FWF
FWF
FWF
SKWIK
SPSHHH

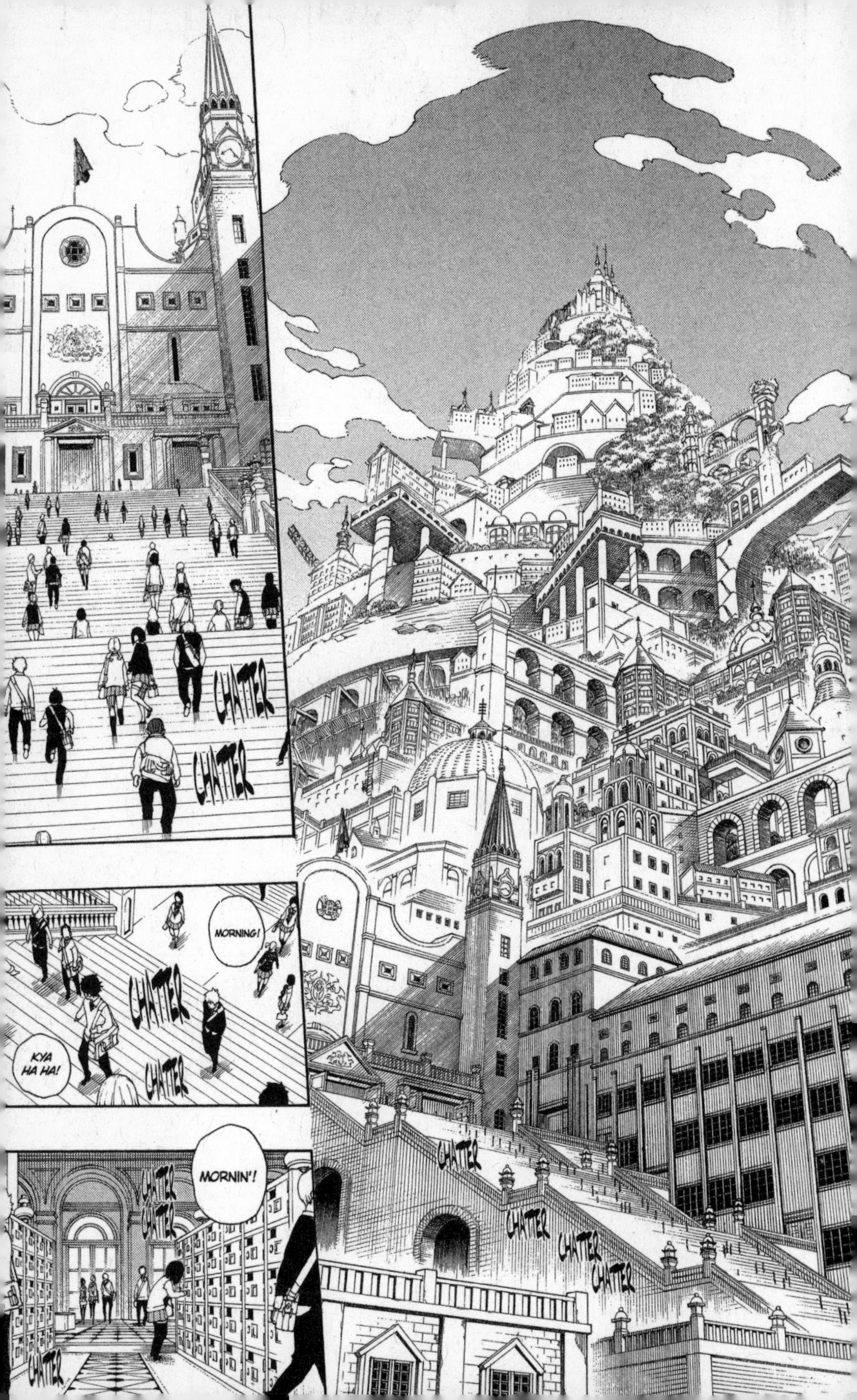
CHATTER
CHATTER
CHATTER
CHATTER
CHATTER
CHATTER
MORNING!
CHATTER
KYA HA HA!
CHATTER
MORNIN'!
CHATTER
CHATTER
CHATTER

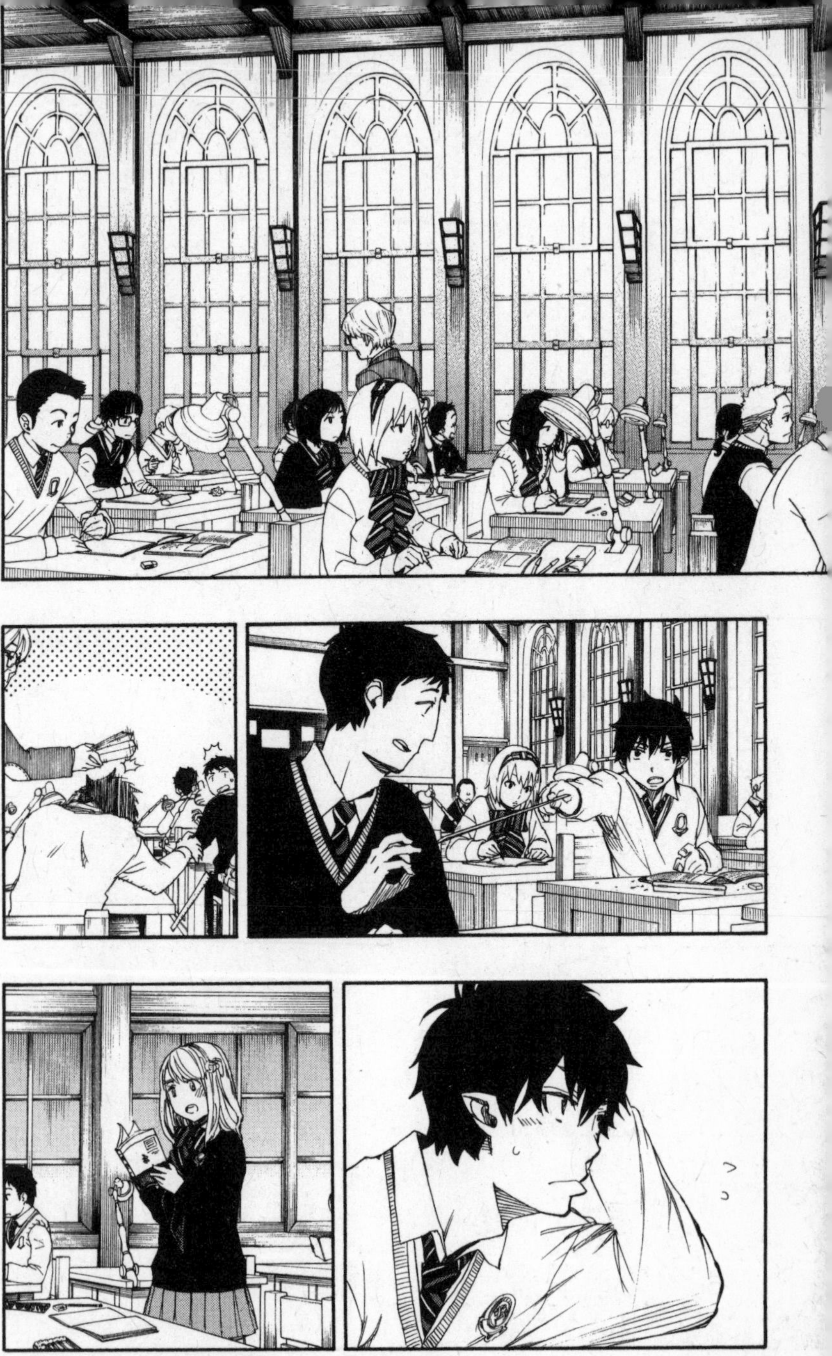

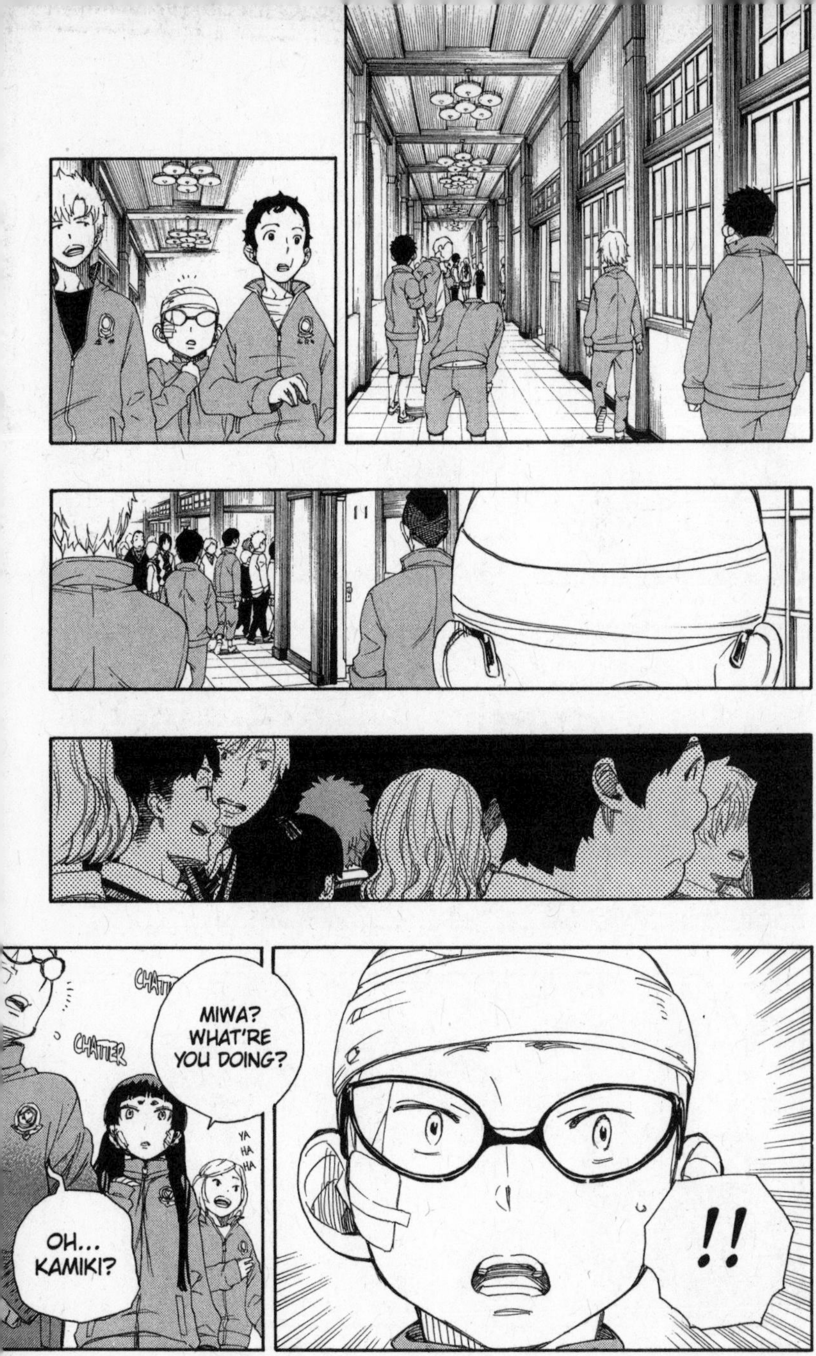
!!
MIWA? WHAT'RE YOU DOING?
YA HA HA
CHATTER
OH... KAMIKI?

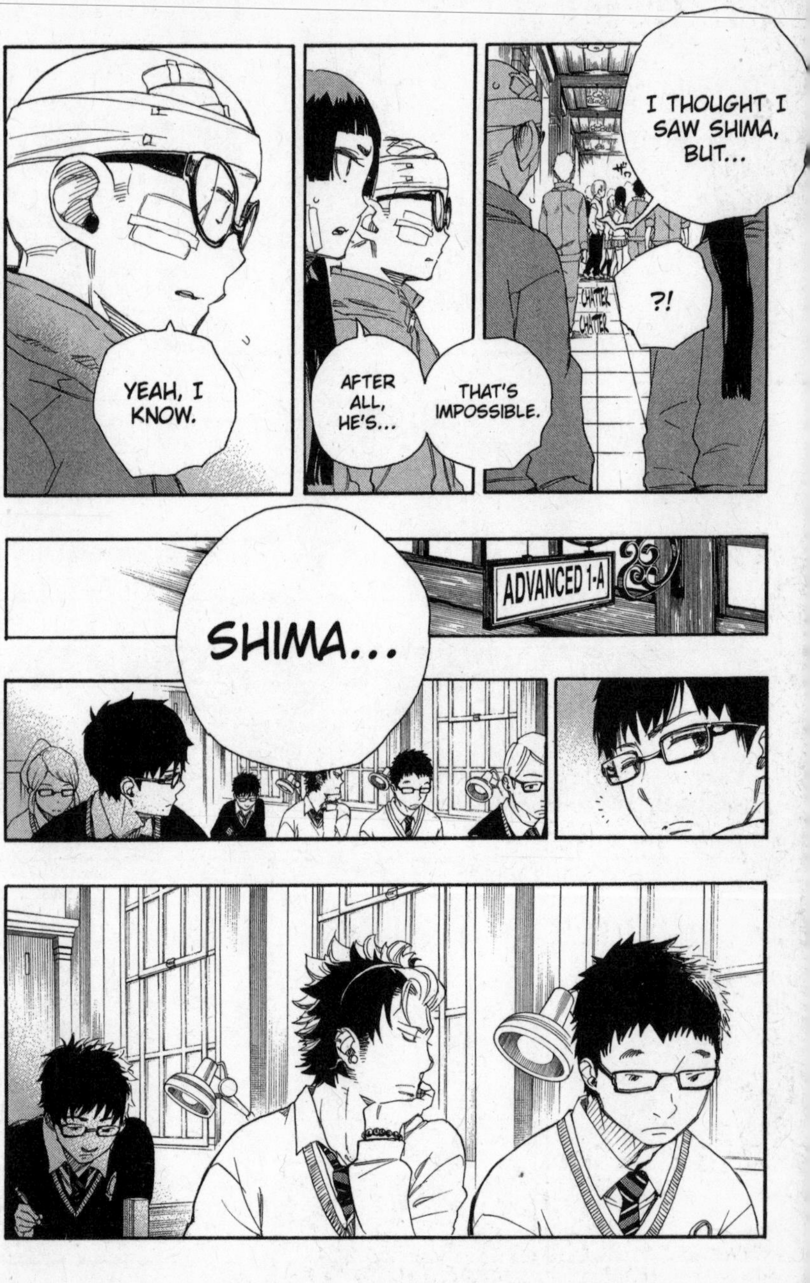
I THOUGHT I SAW SHIMA, BUT...
?!
CHATTER CHATTER
THAT'S IMPOSSIBLE.
AFTER ALL, HE'S...
YEAH, I KNOW.
ADVANCED 1-A
SHIMA...

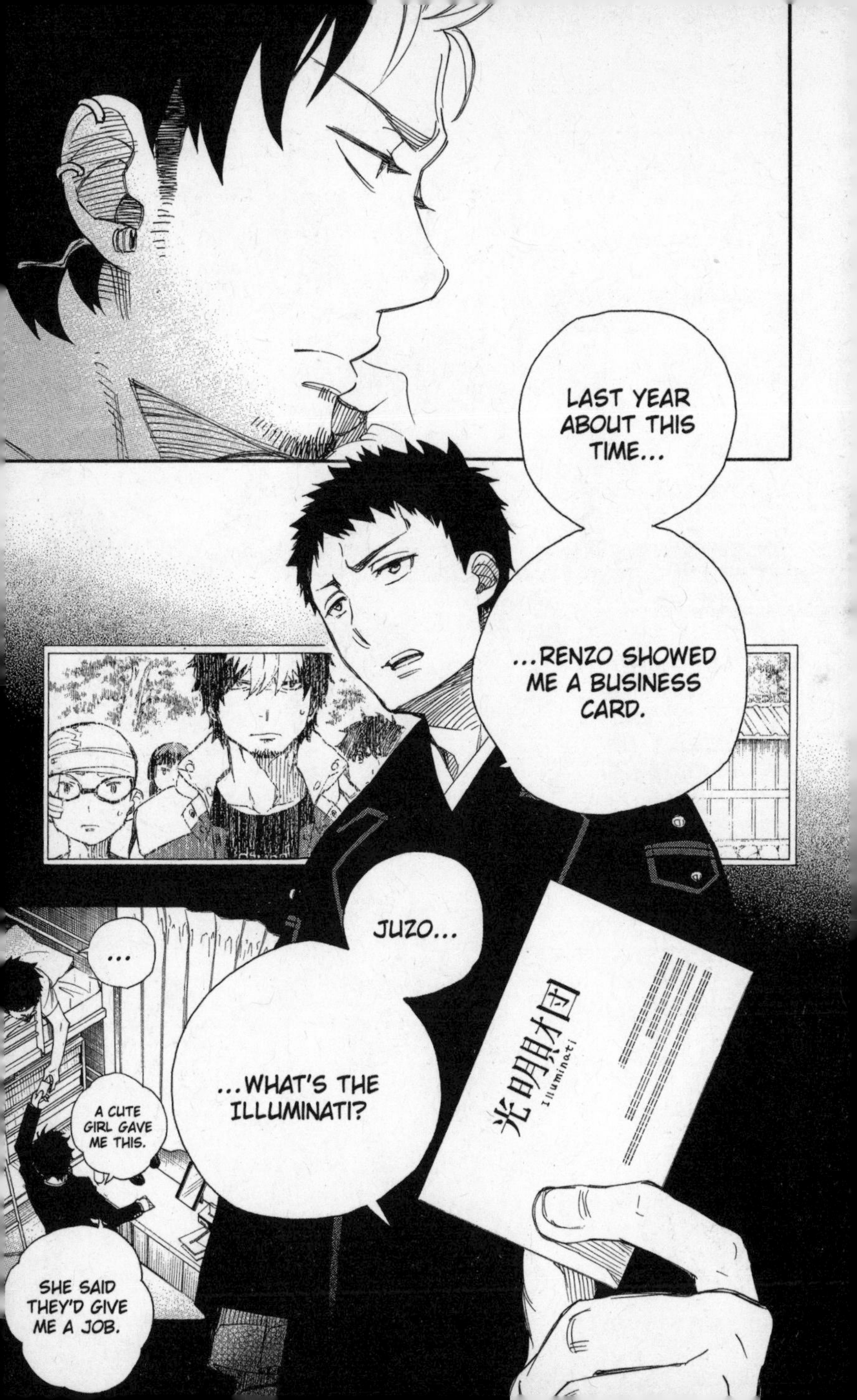
LAST YEAR ABOUT THIS TIME...
...RENZO SHOWED ME A BUSINESS CARD.
JUZO...
...WHAT'S THE ILLUMINATI?
光明財団
Illuminati
...
A CUTE GIRL GAVE ME THIS.
SHE SAID THEY'D GIVE ME A JOB.

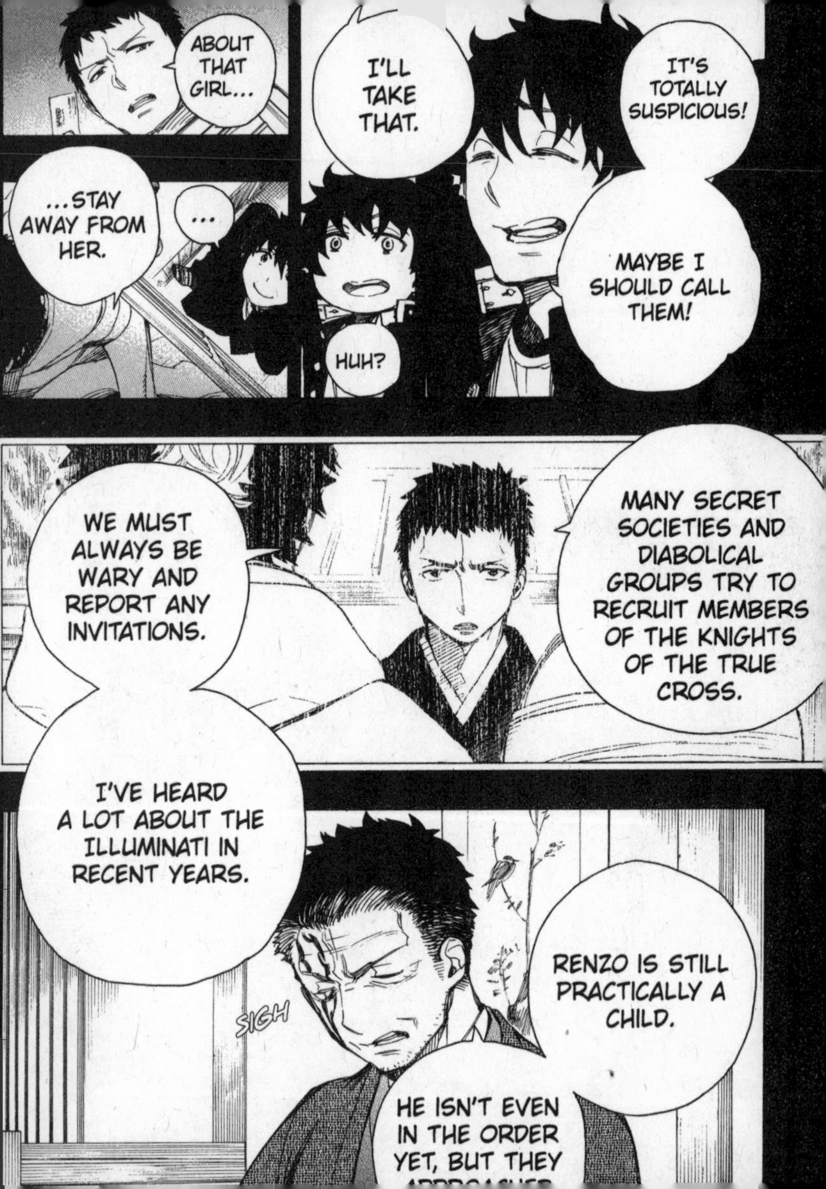
IT'S TOTALLY SUSPICIOUS!
I'LL TAKE THAT.
MAYBE I SHOULD CALL THEM!
HUH?
ABOUT THAT GIRL...
...STAY AWAY FROM HER.
...
MANY SECRET SOCIETIES AND DIABOLICAL GROUPS TRY TO RECRUIT MEMBERS OF THE KNIGHTS OF THE TRUE CROSS.
WE MUST ALWAYS BE WARY AND REPORT ANY INVITATIONS.
I'VE HEARD A LOT ABOUT THE ILLUMINATI IN RECENT YEARS.
RENZO IS STILL PRACTICALLY A CHILD.
SIGH
HE ISN'T EVEN IN THE ORDER YET, BUT THEY

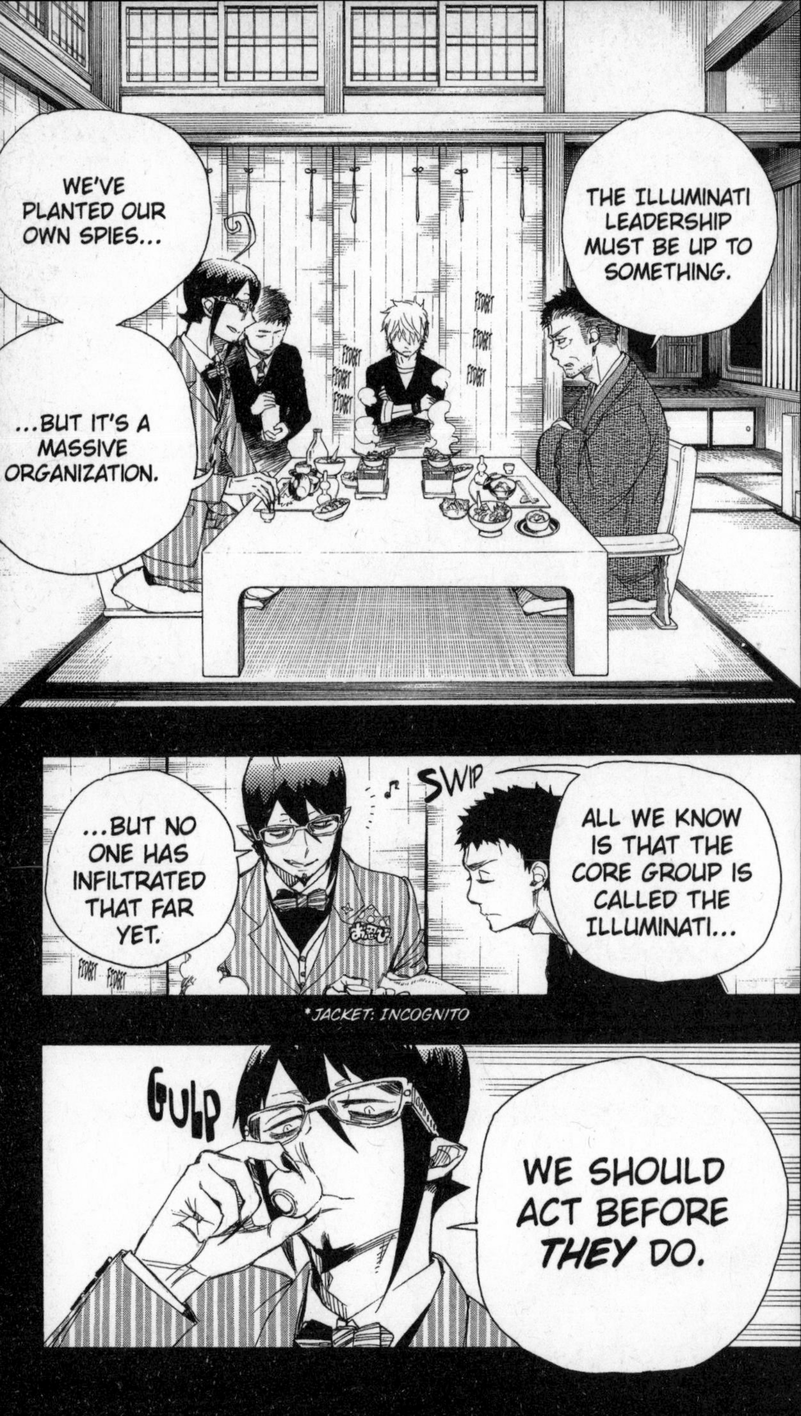
THE ILLUMINATI LEADERSHIP MUST BE UP TO SOMETHING.
FIDGET FIDGET FIDGET
FIDGET FIDGET FIDGET
WE'VE PLANTED OUR OWN SPIES...
...BUT IT'S A MASSIVE ORGANIZATION.
SWIP
ALL WE KNOW IS THAT THE CORE GROUP IS CALLED THE ILLUMINATI...
...BUT NO ONE HAS INFILTRATED THAT FAR YET.
FIDGET FIDGET
GULP
WE SHOULD ACT BEFORE *THEY* DO.

*JACKET: INCOGNITO

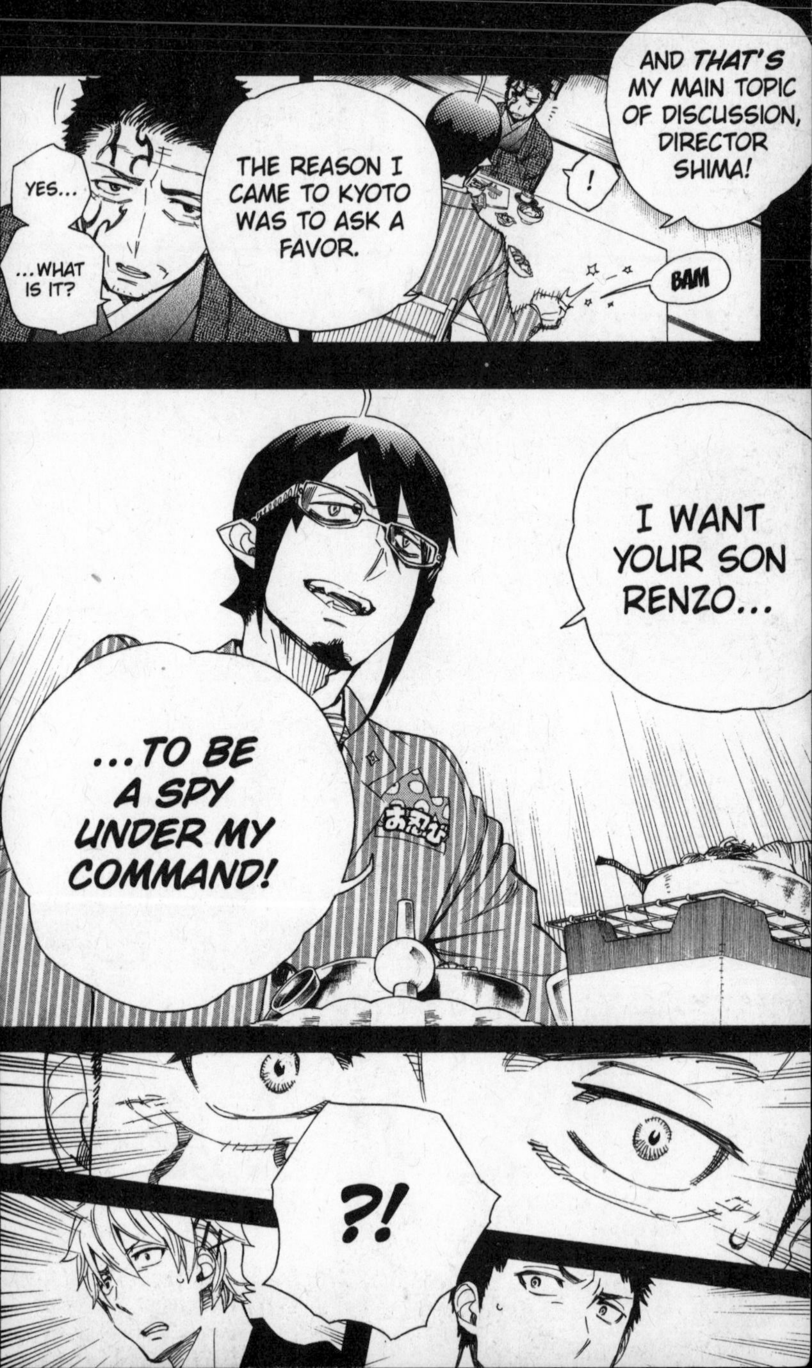
AND THAT'S MY MAIN TOPIC OF DISCUSSION, DIRECTOR SHIMA!
!
BAM
THE REASON I CAME TO KYOTO WAS TO ASK A FAVOR.
YES...
...WHAT IS IT?
I WANT YOUR SON RENZO...
お忍び
...TO BE A SPY UNDER MY COMMAND!
?!

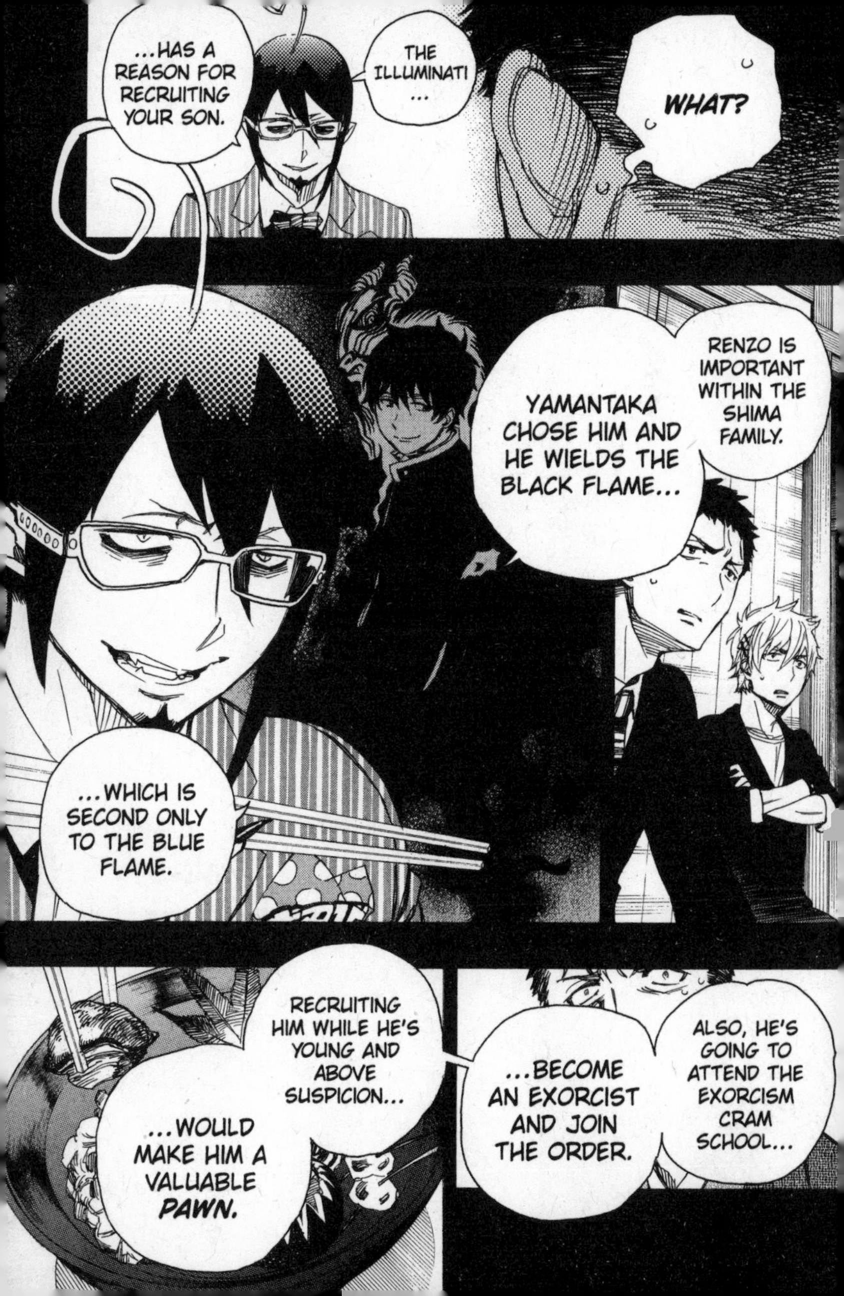
WHAT?
THE ILLUMINATI ...
...HAS A REASON FOR RECRUITING YOUR SON.
RENZO IS IMPORTANT WITHIN THE SHIMA FAMILY.
YAMANTAKA CHOSE HIM AND HE WIELDS THE BLACK FLAME...
...WHICH IS SECOND ONLY TO THE BLUE FLAME.
ALSO, HE'S GOING TO ATTEND THE EXORCISM CRAM SCHOOL...
...BECOME AN EXORCIST AND JOIN THE ORDER.
RECRUITING HIM WHILE HE'S YOUNG AND ABOVE SUSPICION...
...WOULD MAKE HIM A VALUABLE PAWN.

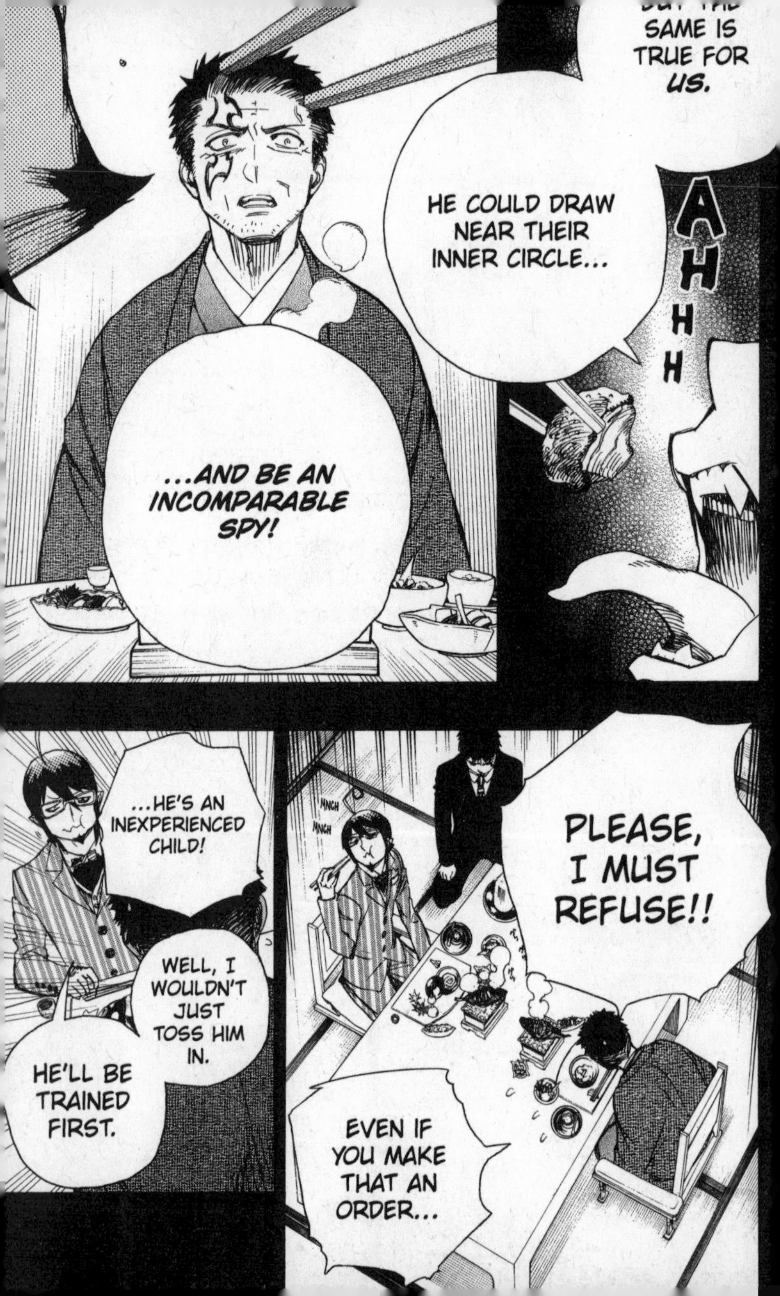
SAME IS TRUE FOR US.
AHHH
HE COULD DRAW NEAR THEIR INNER CIRCLE...
...AND BE AN INCOMPARABLE SPY!
PLEASE, I MUST REFUSE!!
MNCH
MNCH
EVEN IF YOU MAKE THAT AN ORDER...
...HE'S AN INEXPERIENCED CHILD!
WELL, I WOULDN'T JUST TOSS HIM IN.
HE'LL BE TRAINED FIRST.

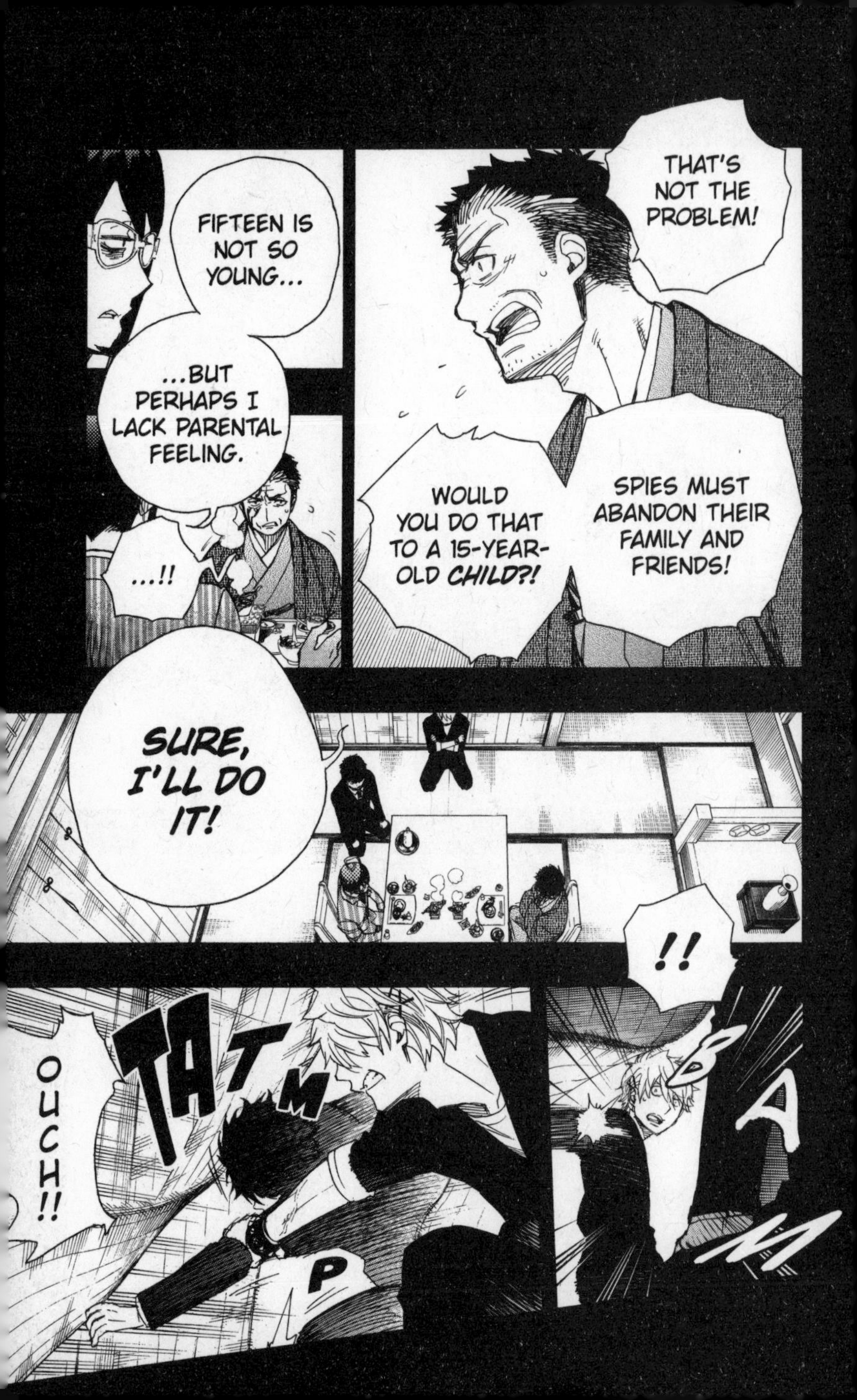
THAT'S NOT THE PROBLEM!
SPIES MUST ABANDON THEIR FAMILY AND FRIENDS!
WOULD YOU DO THAT TO A 15-YEAR-OLD CHILD?!
FIFTEEN IS NOT SO YOUNG...
...BUT PERHAPS I LACK PARENTAL FEELING.
...!!
SURE, I'LL DO IT!
!!
BAM
TATMP
OUCH!!

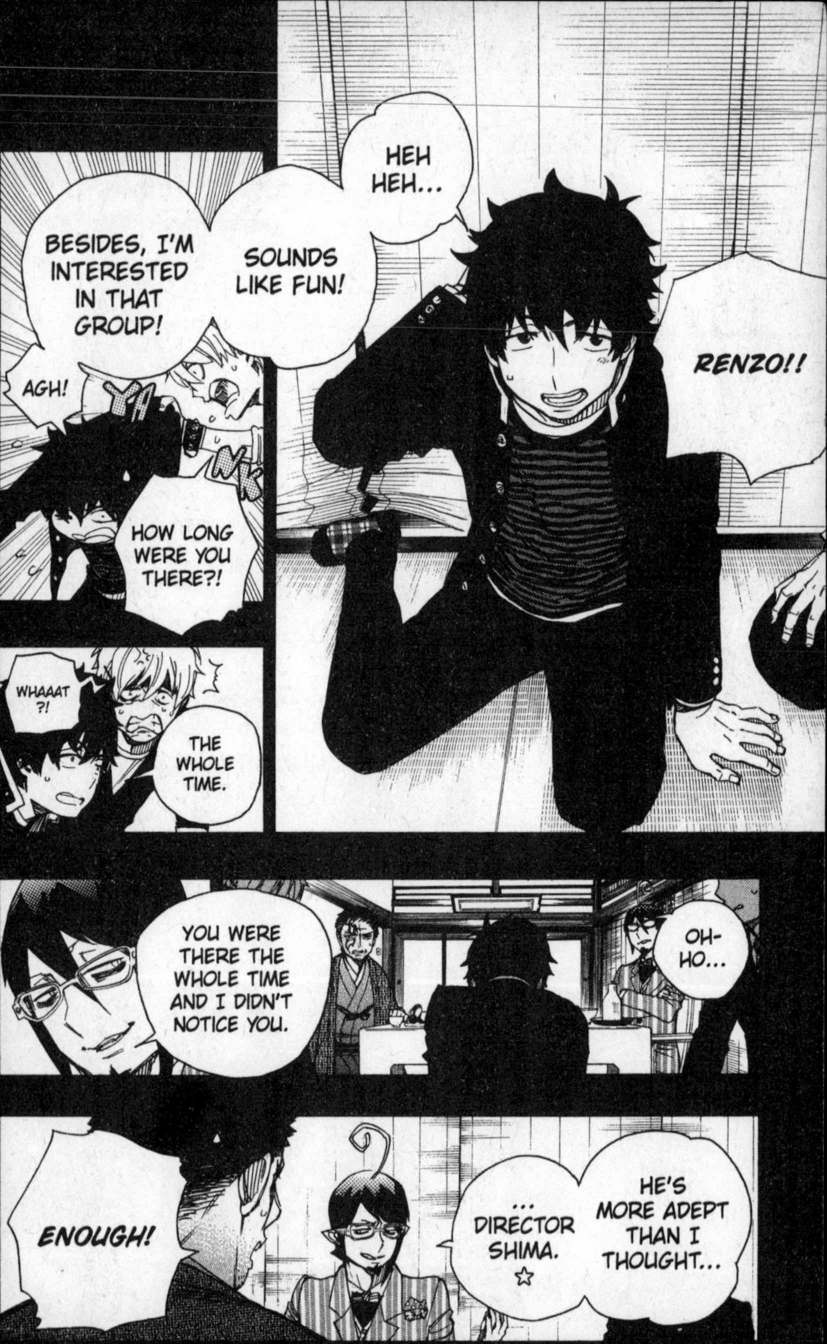
HEH HEH...
SOUNDS LIKE FUN!
BESIDES, I'M INTERESTED IN THAT GROUP!
RENZO!!
AGH!
YANK
HOW LONG WERE YOU THERE?!
WHAAAT?!
THE WHOLE TIME.
OH-HO...
YOU WERE THERE THE WHOLE TIME AND I DIDN'T NOTICE YOU.
HE'S MORE ADEPT THAN I THOUGHT...
... DIRECTOR SHIMA. ☆
ENOUGH!

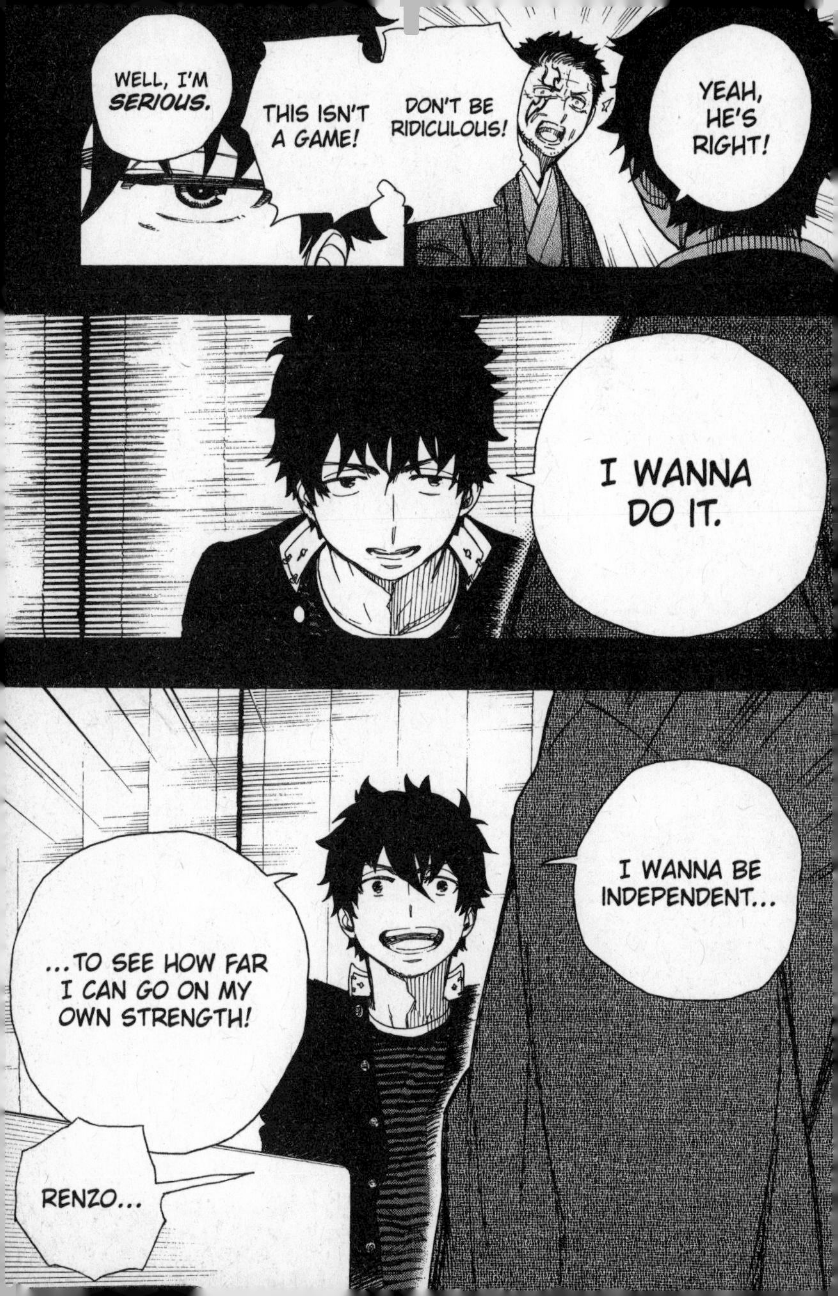
YEAH, HE'S RIGHT!
DON'T BE RIDICULOUS!
THIS ISN'T A GAME!
WELL, I'M *SERIOUS.*
I WANNA DO IT.
I WANNA BE INDEPENDENT...
...TO SEE HOW FAR I CAN GO ON MY OWN STRENGTH!
RENZO...

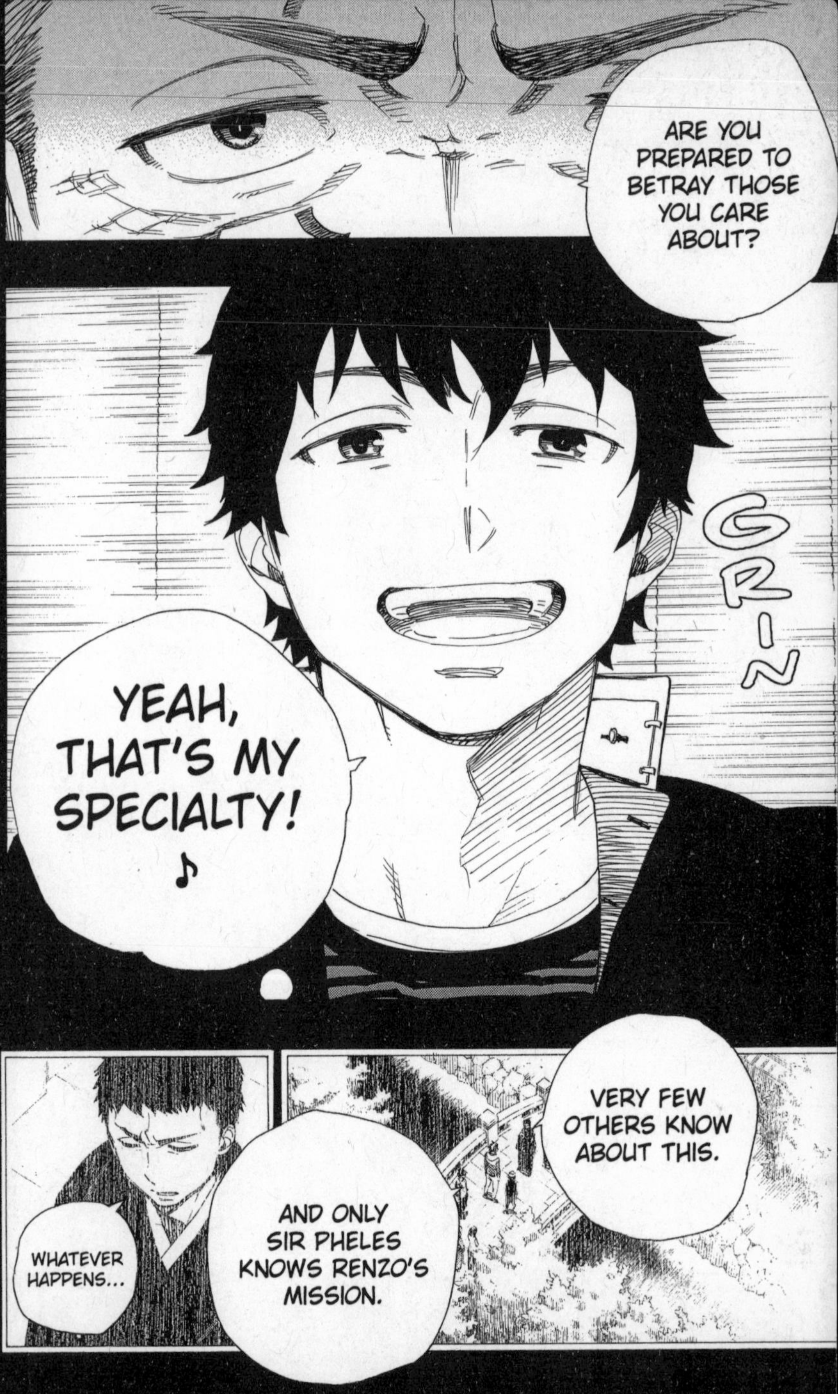
ARE YOU PREPARED TO BETRAY THOSE YOU CARE ABOUT?
GRIN
YEAH, THAT'S MY SPECIALTY! ♪
VERY FEW OTHERS KNOW ABOUT THIS.
AND ONLY SIR PHELES KNOWS RENZO'S MISSION.
WHATEVER HAPPENS...

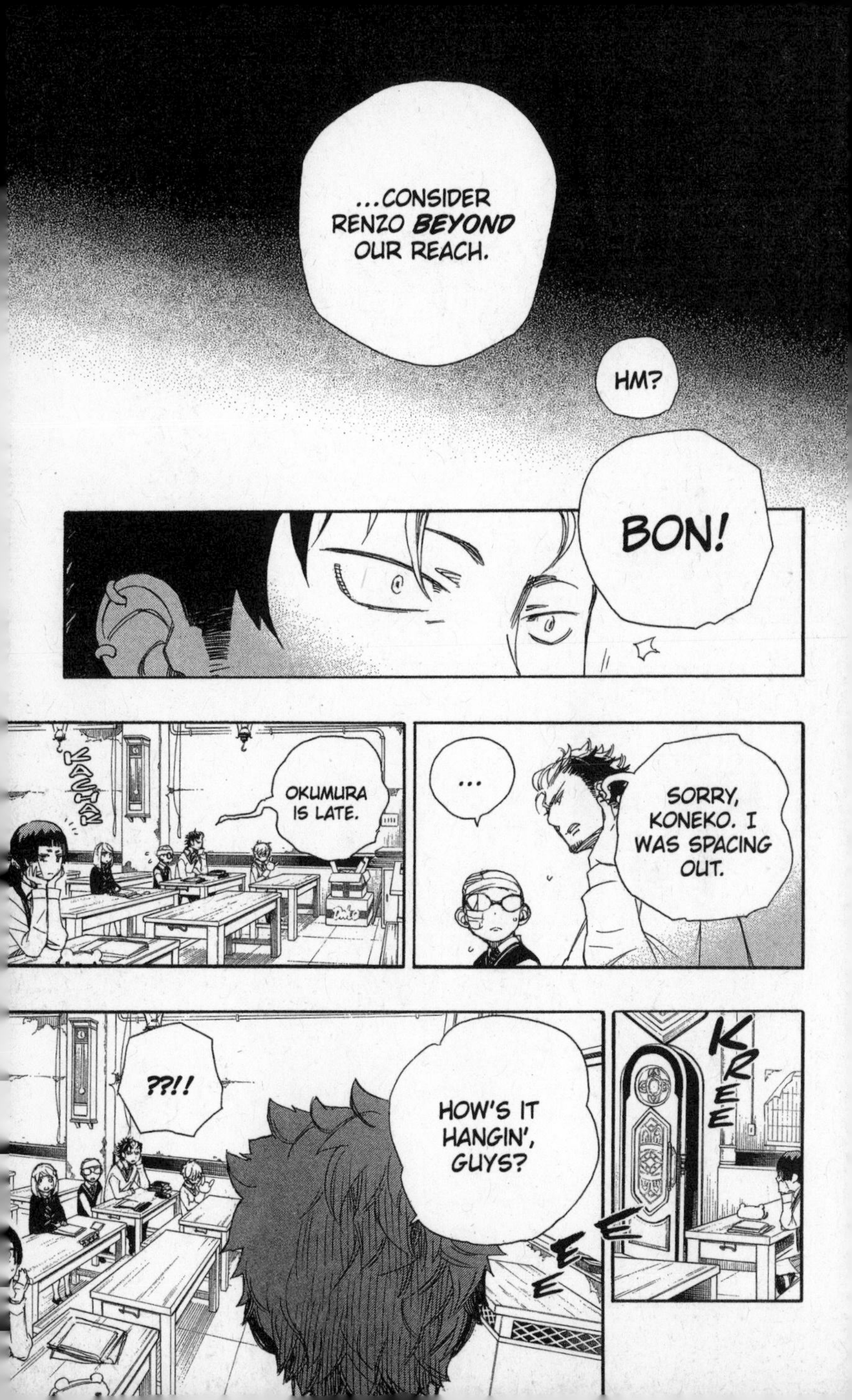
...CONSIDER RENZO BEYOND OUR REACH.
HM?
BON!
...
SORRY, KONEKO. I WAS SPACING OUT.
OKUMURA IS LATE.
KACHA!
KREEEEEE
HOW'S IT HANGIN', GUYS?
??!!

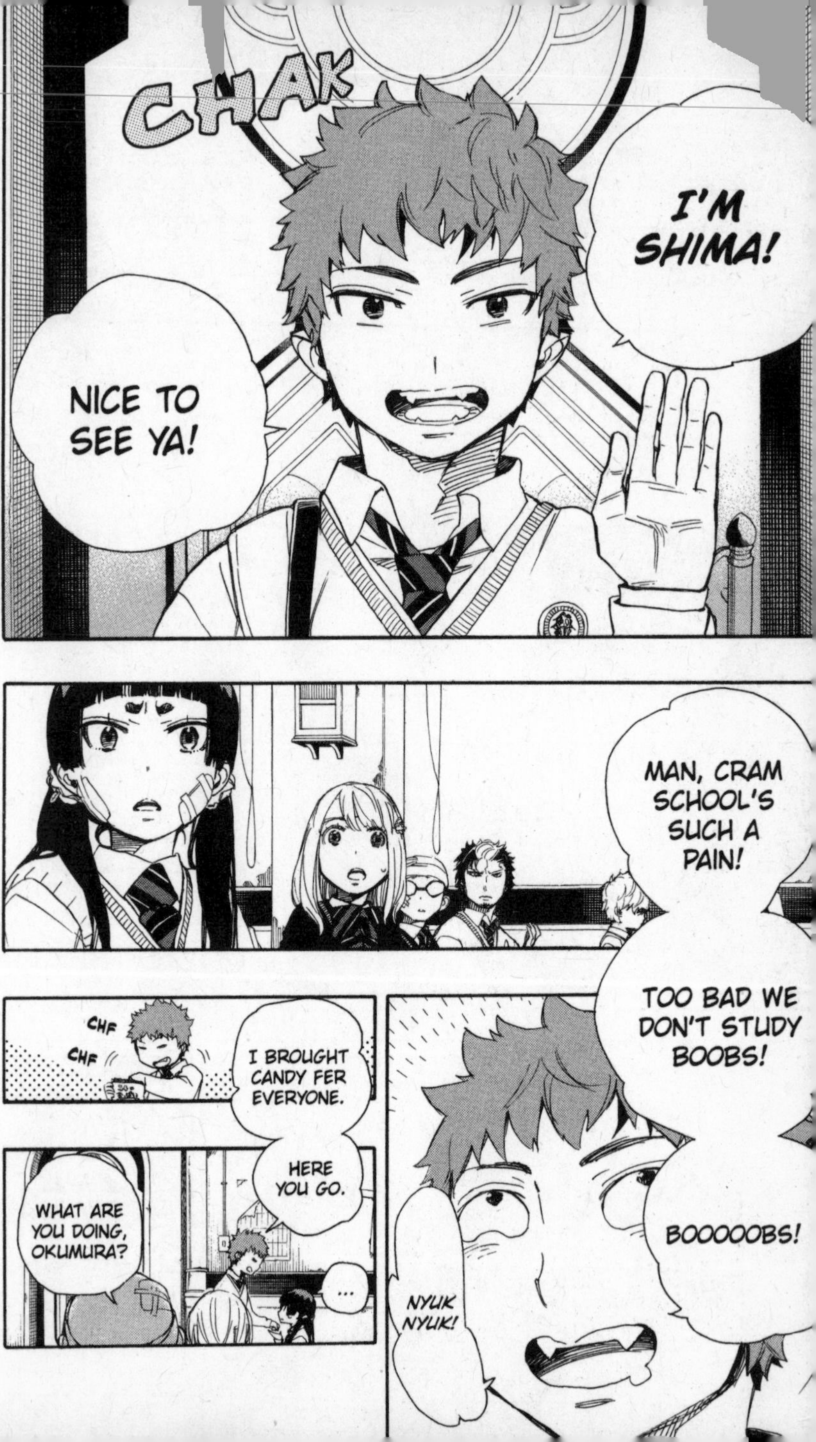
CHAK
I'M SHIMA!
NICE TO SEE YA!
MAN, CRAM SCHOOL'S SUCH A PAIN!
TOO BAD WE DON'T STUDY BOOBS!
BOOOOOBS!
NYUK NYUK!
CHF CHF
I BROUGHT CANDY FER EVERYONE.
HERE YOU GO.
...
WHAT ARE YOU DOING, OKUMURA?

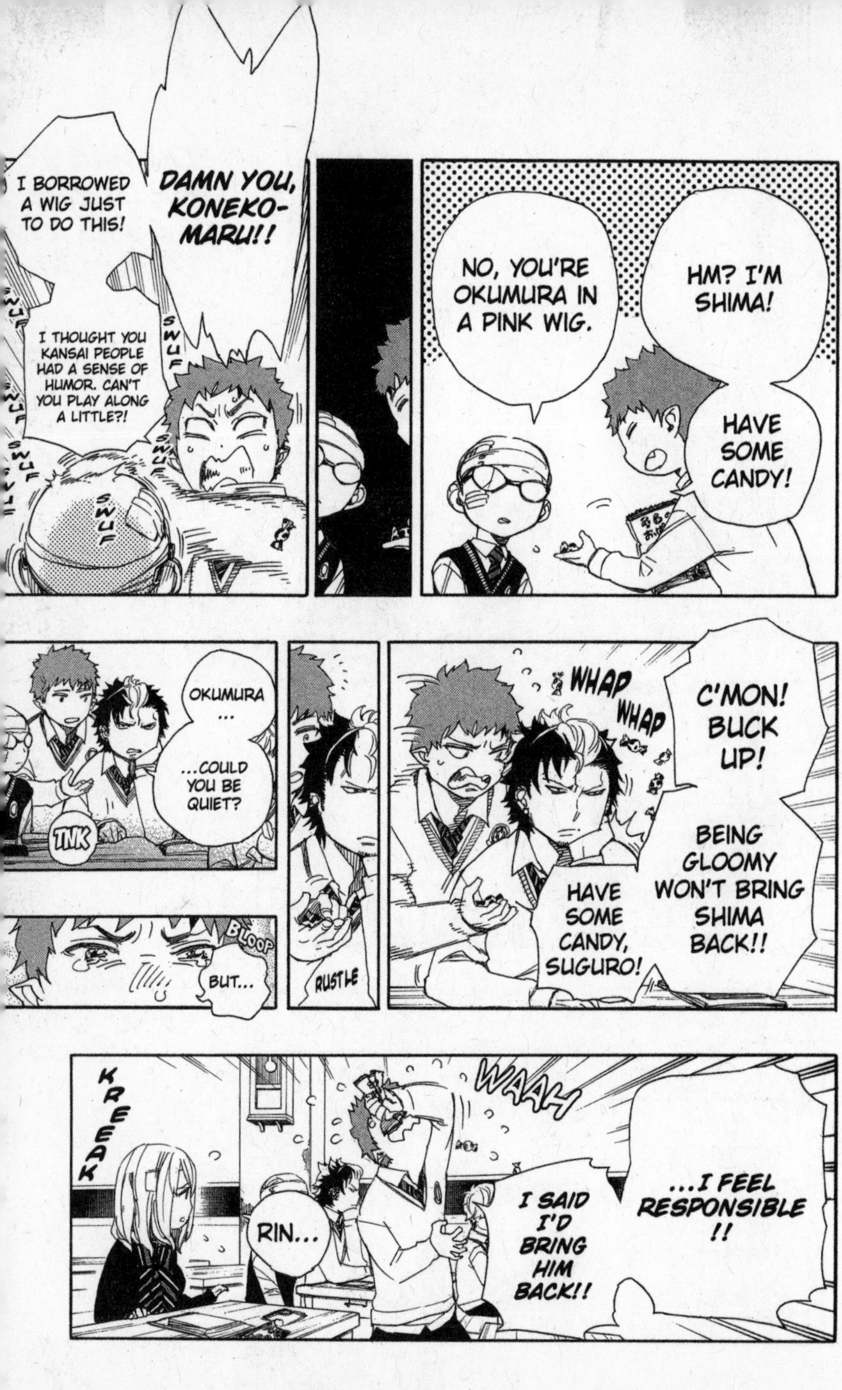
HM? I'M SHIMA!
NO, YOU'RE OKUMURA IN A PINK WIG.
HAVE SOME CANDY!
DAMN YOU, KONEKO-MARU!!
I BORROWED A WIG JUST TO DO THIS!
SWUF
I THOUGHT YOU KANSAI PEOPLE HAD A SENSE OF HUMOR. CAN'T YOU PLAY ALONG A LITTLE?!
SWUF
SWUF
SWUF
C'MON! BUCK UP!
WHAP
WHAP
BEING GLOOMY WON'T BRING SHIMA BACK!!
HAVE SOME CANDY, SUGURO!
RUSTLE
OKUMURA ...
...COULD YOU BE QUIET?
TNK
BLOOP
BUT...
WAAH
...I FEEL RESPONSIBLE!!
I SAID I'D BRING HIM BACK!!
RIN...
KREEAK

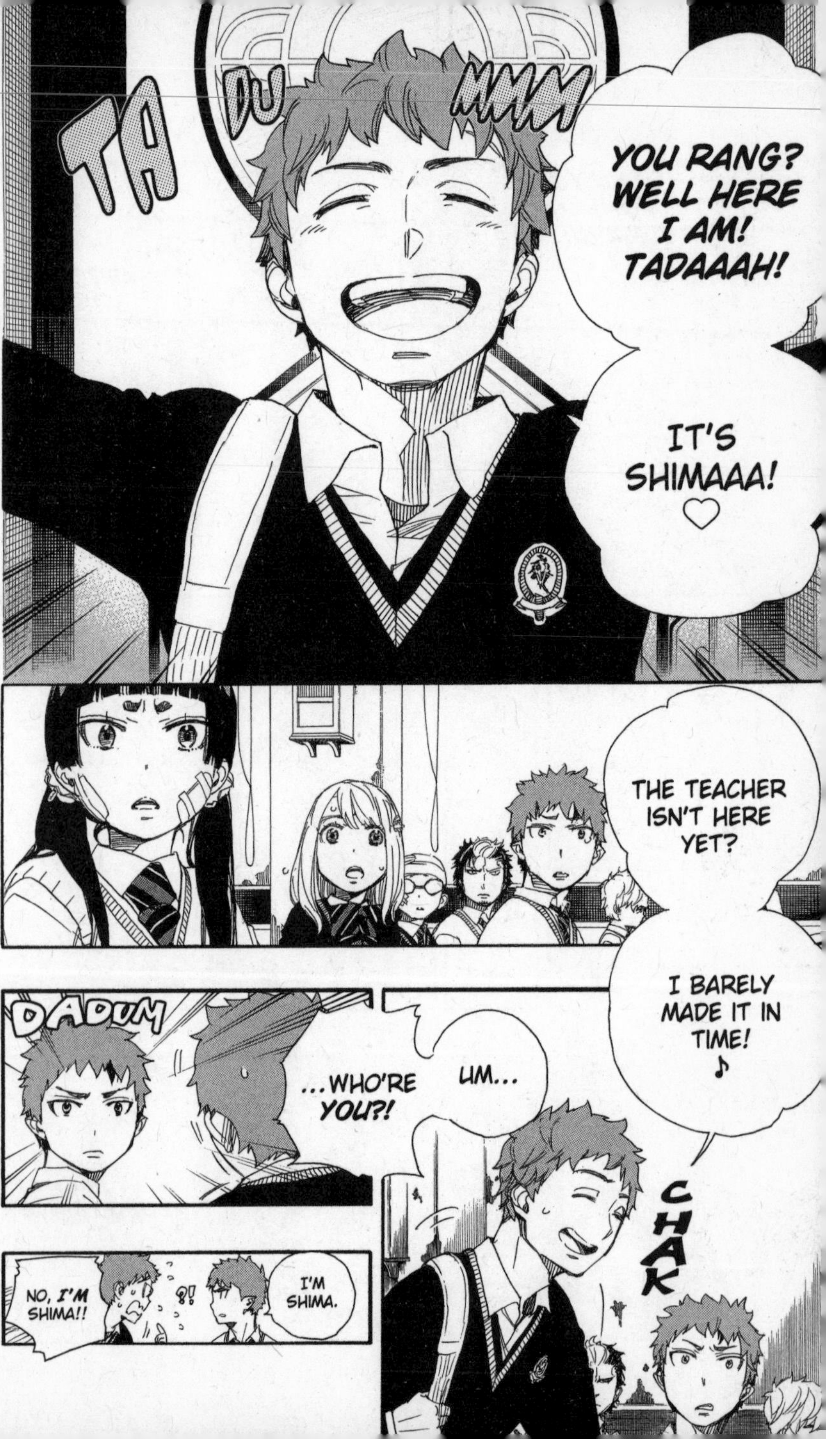
TA DU MMM
YOU RANG? WELL HERE I AM! TADAAAH!
IT'S SHIMAAA! ♡
THE TEACHER ISN'T HERE YET?
I BARELY MADE IT IN TIME! ♪
CHAK
UM...
DADUM
...WHO'RE *YOU*?!
I'M SHIMA.
?!
NO, *I'M* SHIMA!!

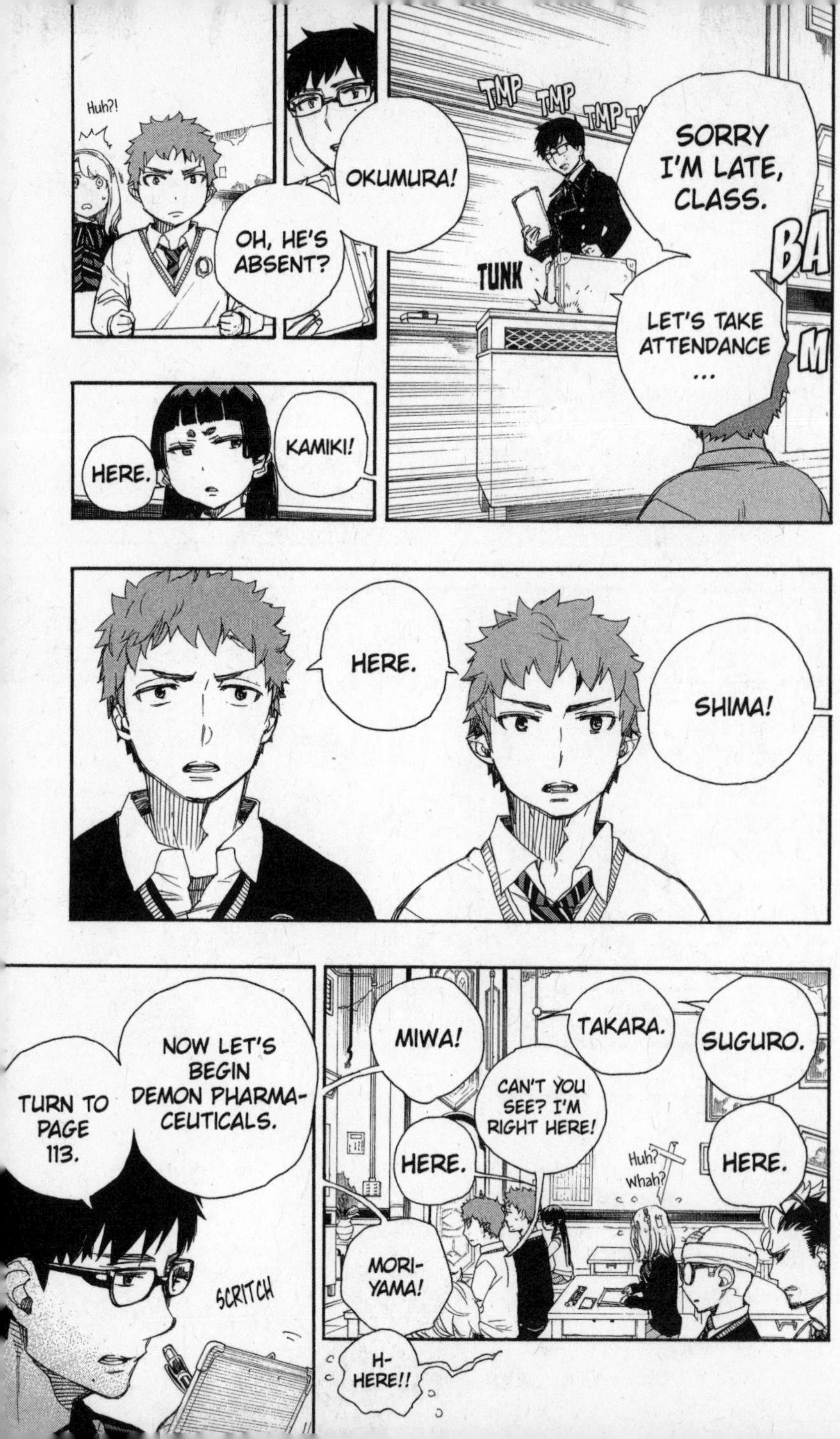
TMP TMP TMP
SORRY I'M LATE, CLASS.
BAM
TUNK
LET'S TAKE ATTENDANCE ...
OKUMURA!
Huh?!
OH, HE'S ABSENT?
KAMIKI!
HERE.
SHIMA!
HERE.
SUGURO.
HERE.
TAKARA.
CAN'T YOU SEE? I'M RIGHT HERE!
Huh? Whah?
MIWA!
HERE.
MORI-YAMA!
H-HERE!!
NOW LET'S BEGIN DEMON PHARMA-CEUTICALS.
TURN TO PAGE 113.
SCRITCH

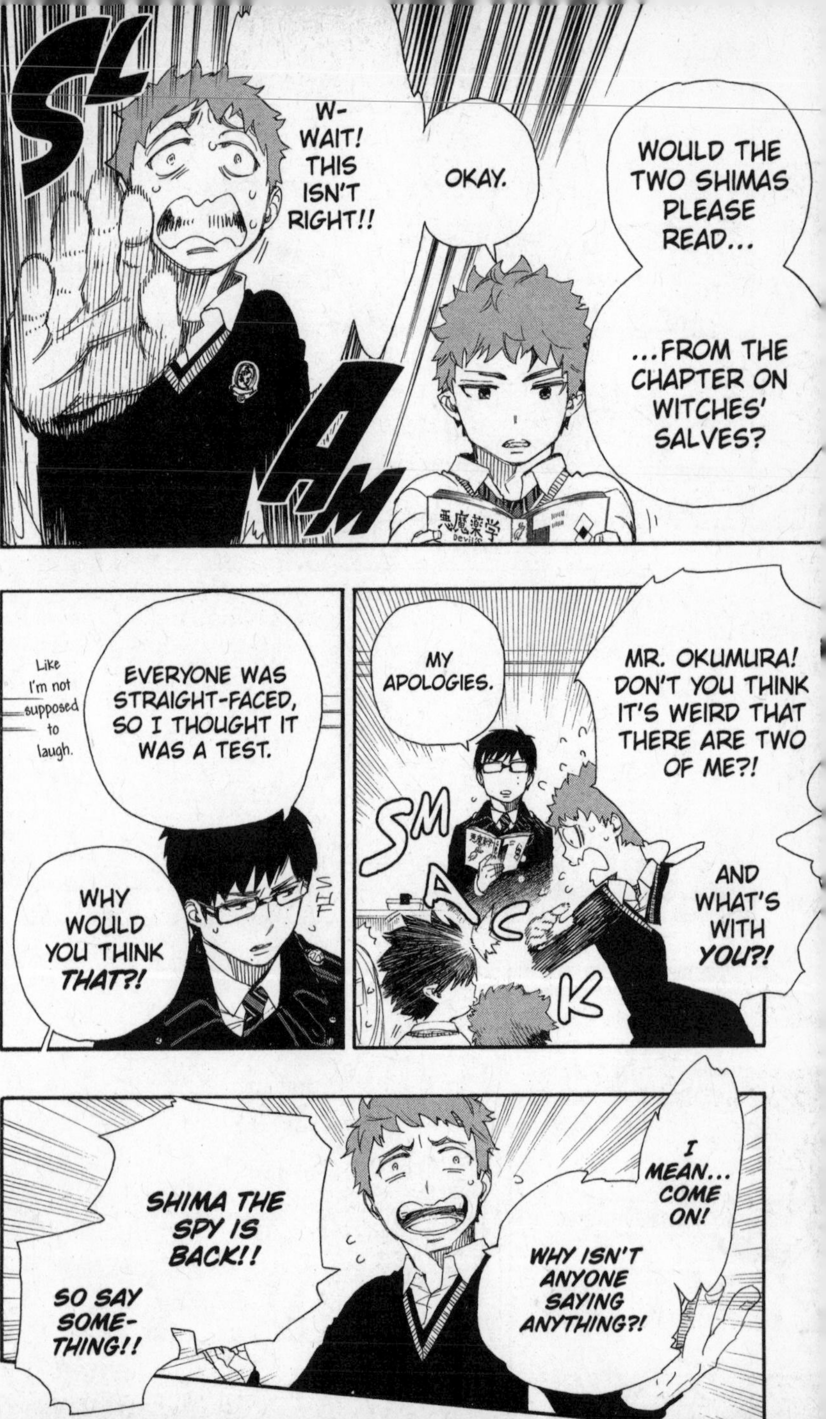
WOULD THE TWO SHIMAS PLEASE READ...
...FROM THE CHAPTER ON WITCHES' SALVES?
OKAY.
W- WAIT! THIS ISN'T RIGHT!!
SL
AM
MR. OKUMURA! DON'T YOU THINK IT'S WEIRD THAT THERE ARE TWO OF ME?!
AND WHAT'S WITH *YOU?!*
MY APOLOGIES.
SMACK
EVERYONE WAS STRAIGHT-FACED, SO I THOUGHT IT WAS A TEST.
Like I'm not supposed to laugh.
WHY WOULD YOU THINK *THAT?!*
I MEAN... COME ON!
WHY ISN'T ANYONE SAYING ANYTHING?!
SHIMA THE SPY IS BACK!!
SO SAY SOME-THING!!

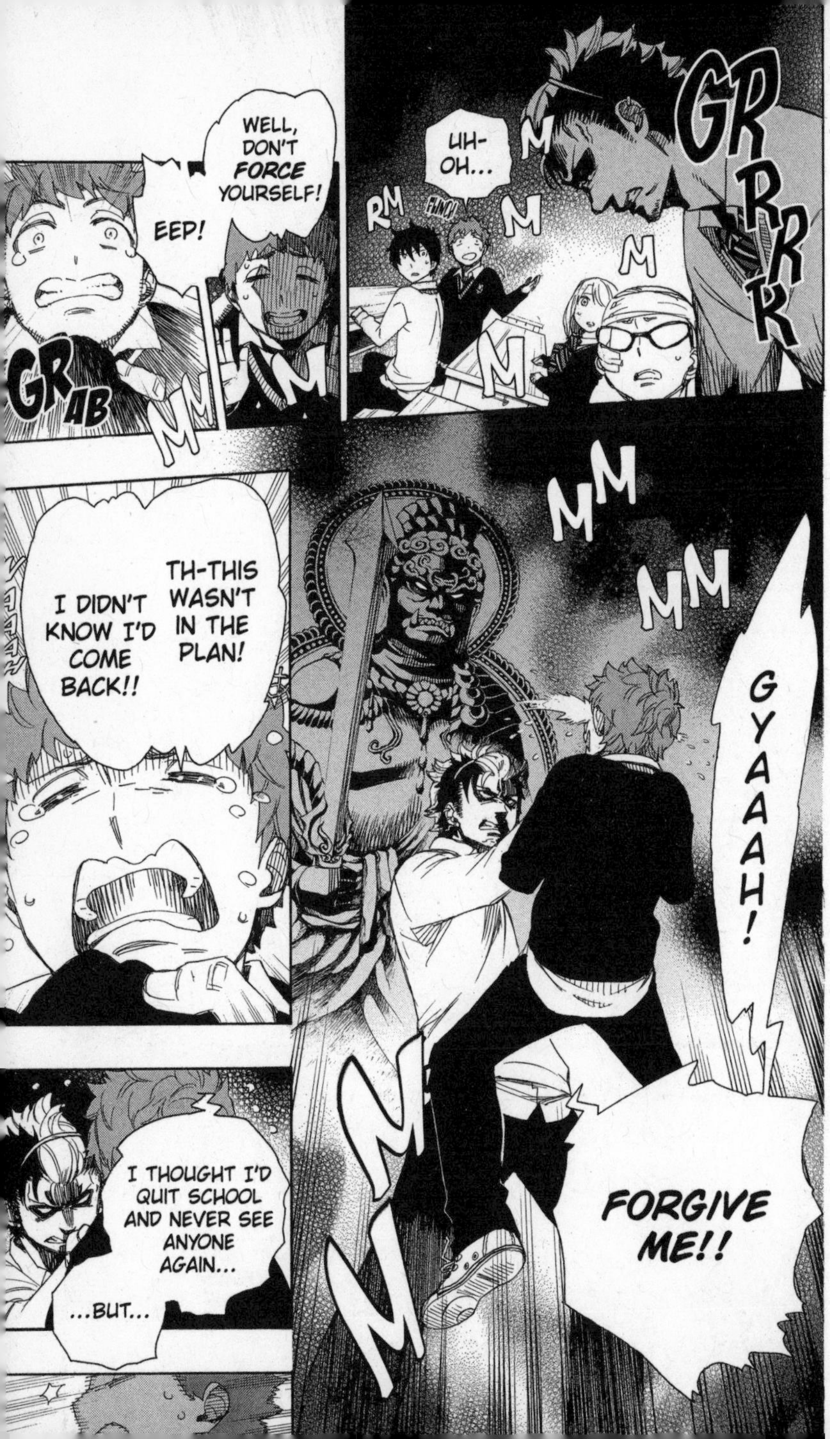
GRRRRR
M
UH-OH...
FLINCH
RM
M
M
M
M
WELL, DON'T FORCE YOURSELF!
EEP!
GRAB
MMM
MM
MM
GYAAAH!
FORGIVE ME!!
MMM
TH-THIS WASN'T IN THE PLAN!
I DIDN'T KNOW I'D COME BACK!!
I THOUGHT I'D QUIT SCHOOL AND NEVER SEE ANYONE AGAIN...
...BUT...

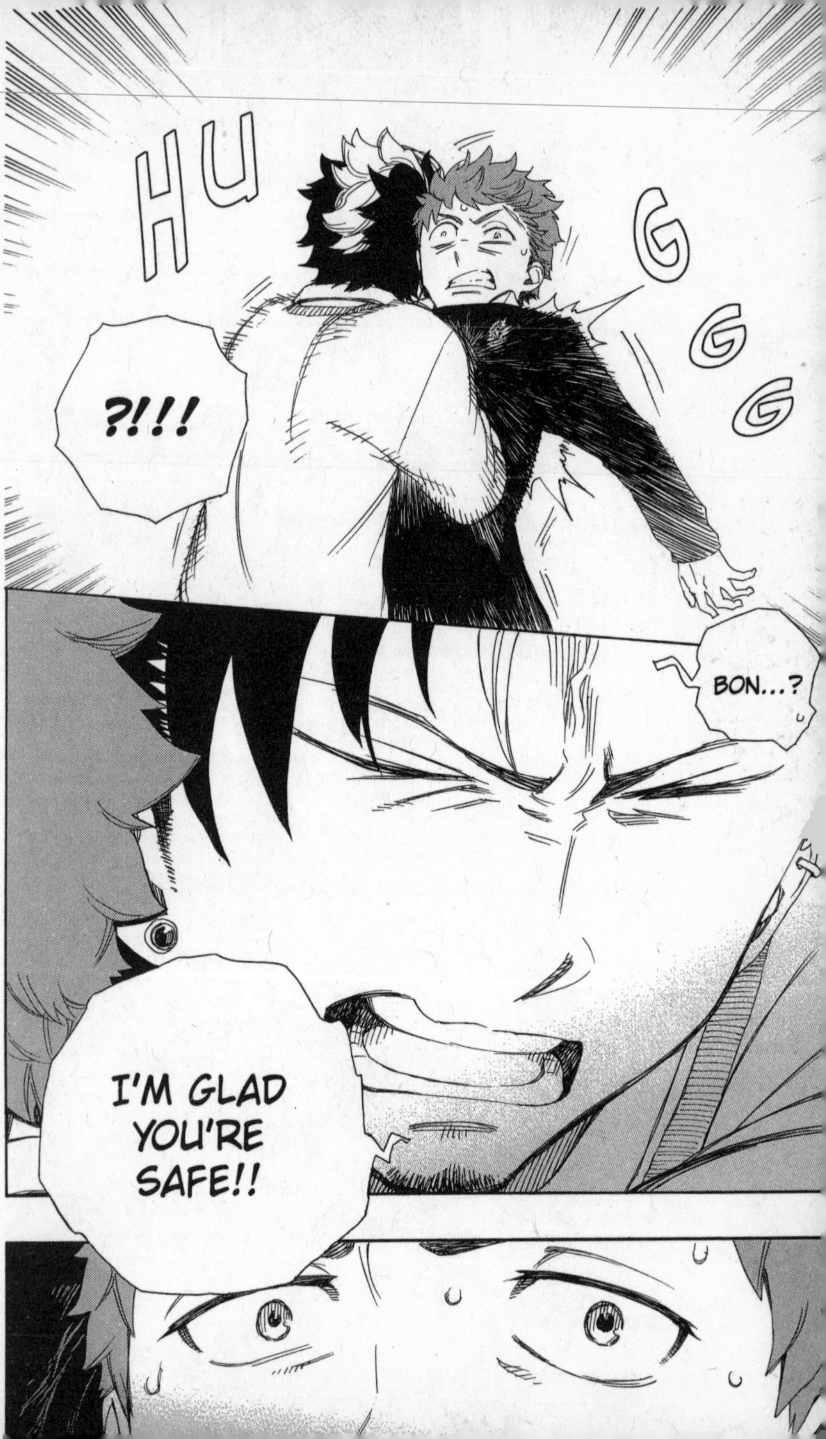
HUGGG
?!!!
BON...?
I'M GLAD YOU'RE SAFE!!

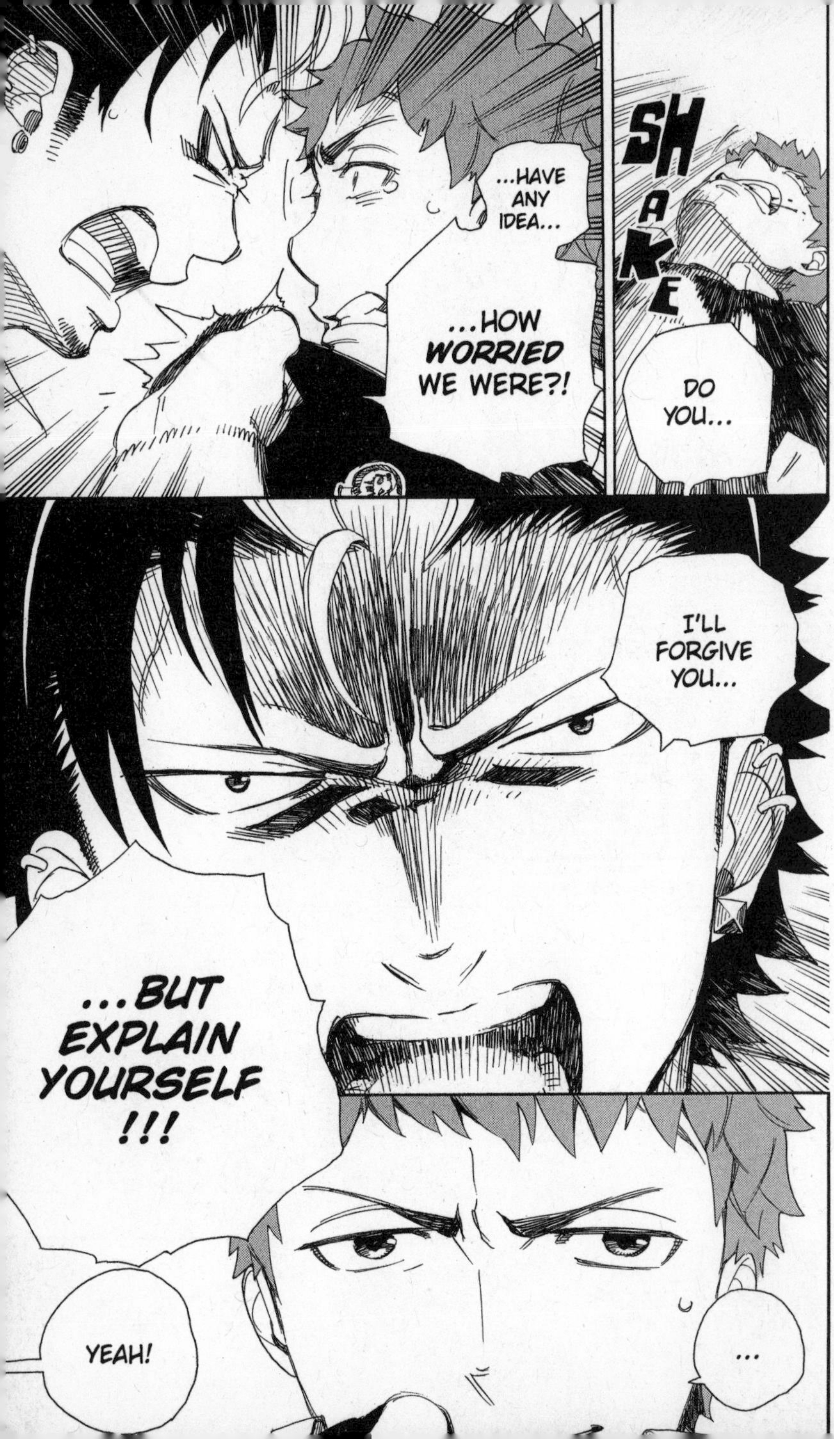
SHAKE
DO YOU...
...HAVE ANY IDEA...
...HOW WORRIED WE WERE?!
I'LL FORGIVE YOU...
...BUT EXPLAIN YOURSELF!!!
...
YEAH!

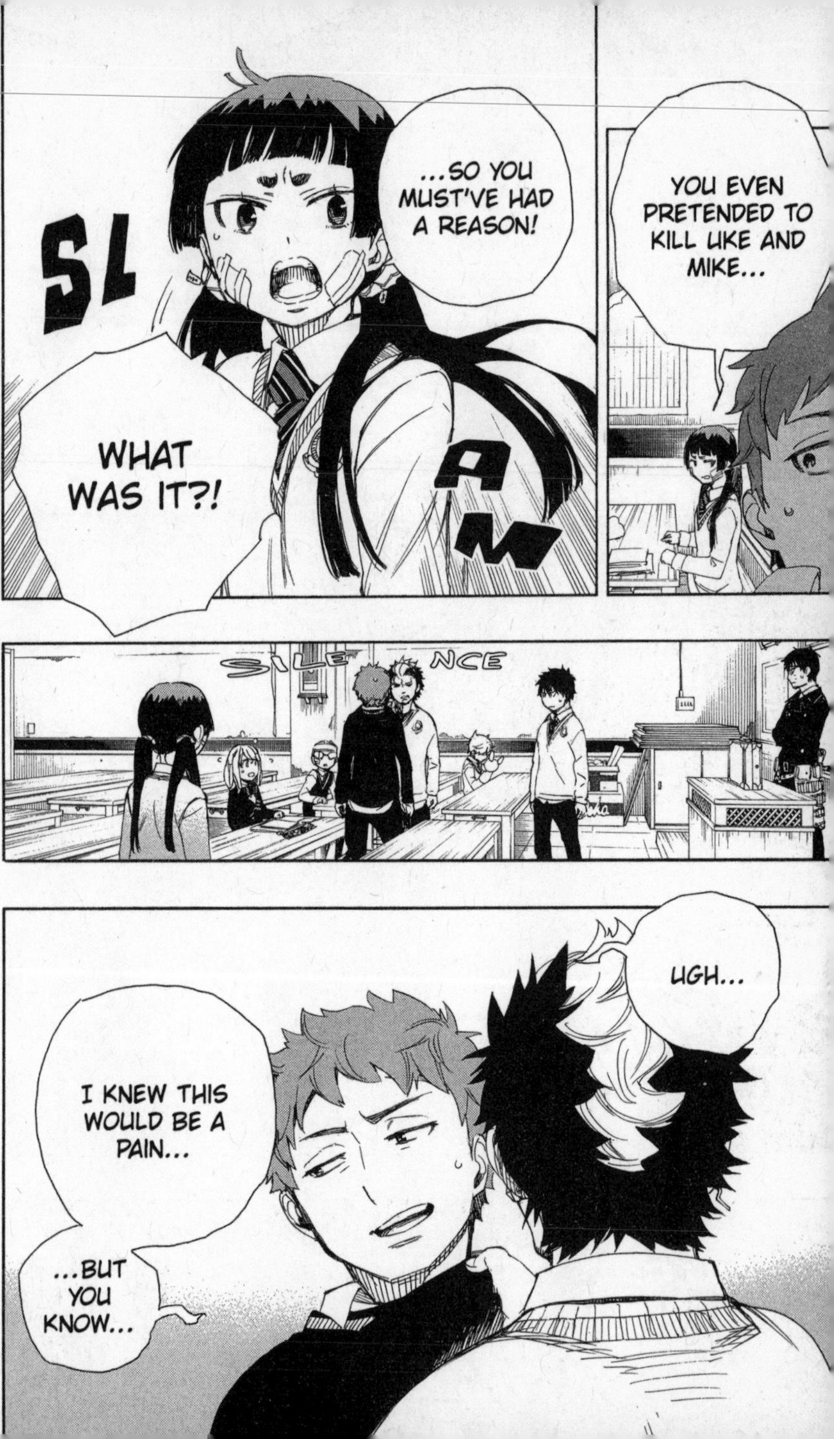
YOU EVEN PRETENDED TO KILL UKE AND MIKE...
...SO YOU MUST'VE HAD A REASON!
SLAM
WHAT WAS IT?!
SILENCE
UGH...
I KNEW THIS WOULD BE A PAIN...
...BUT YOU KNOW...

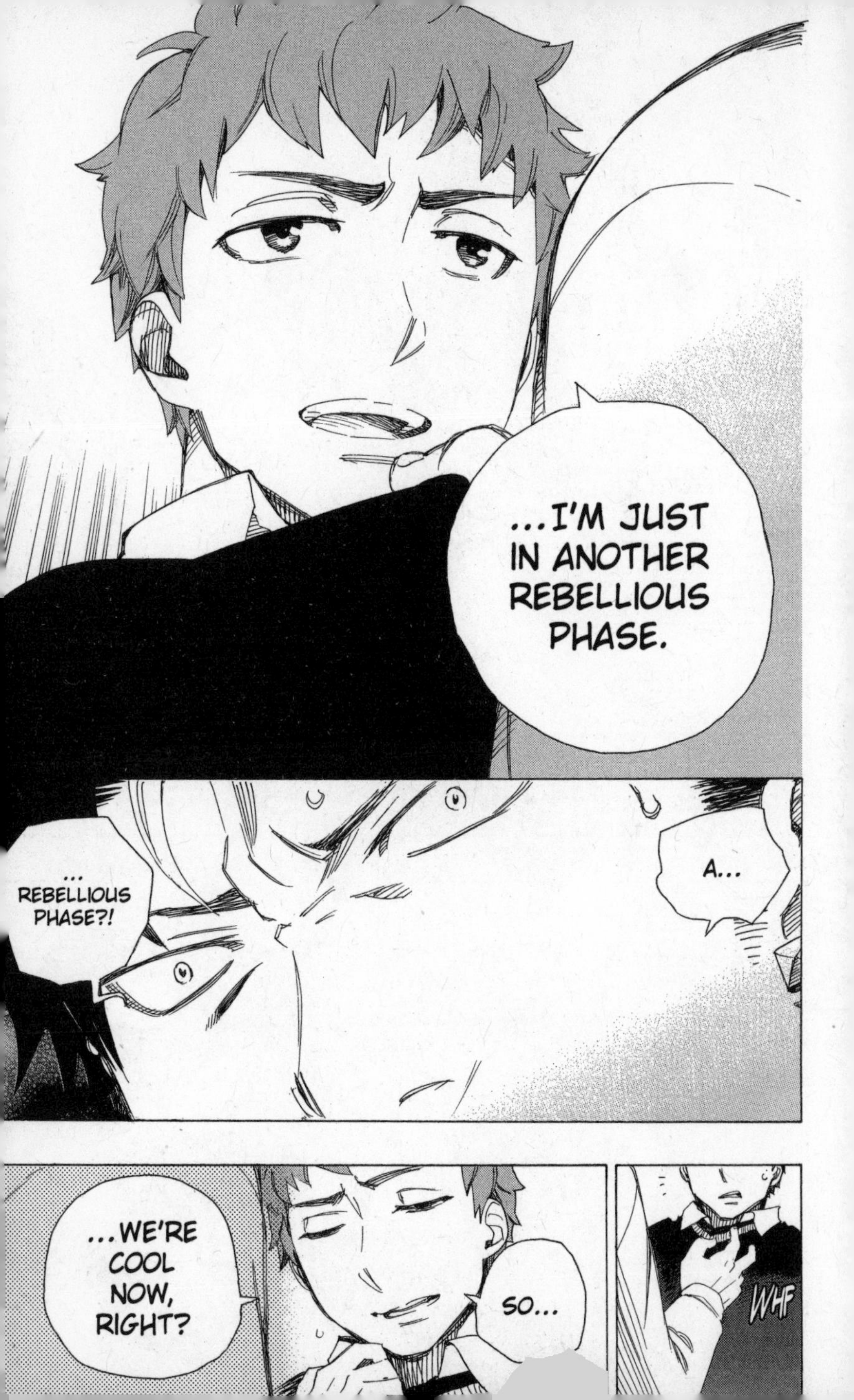
...I'M JUST IN ANOTHER REBELLIOUS PHASE.
A...
... REBELLIOUS PHASE?!
WHF
SO...
...WE'RE COOL NOW, RIGHT?

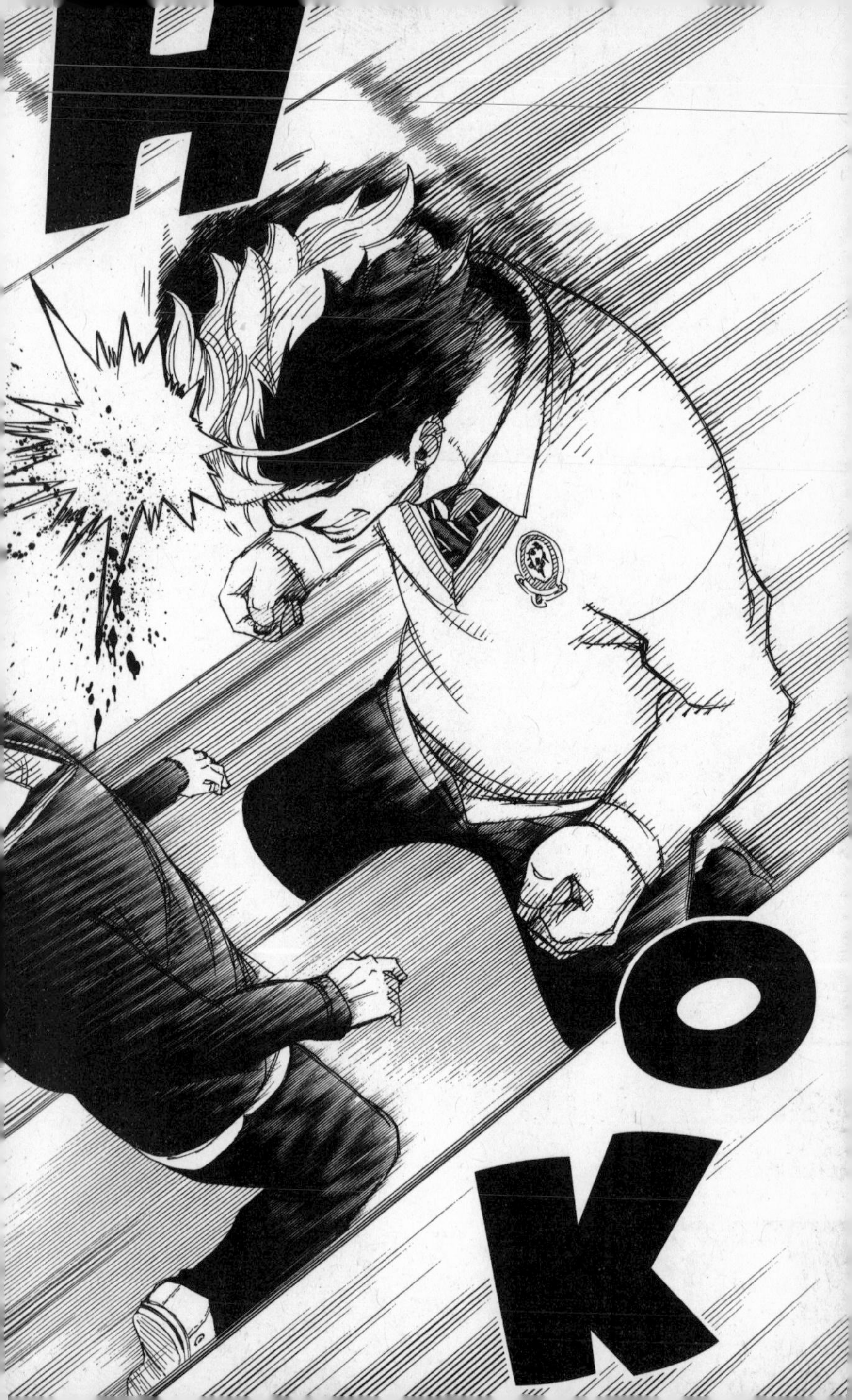
HOK

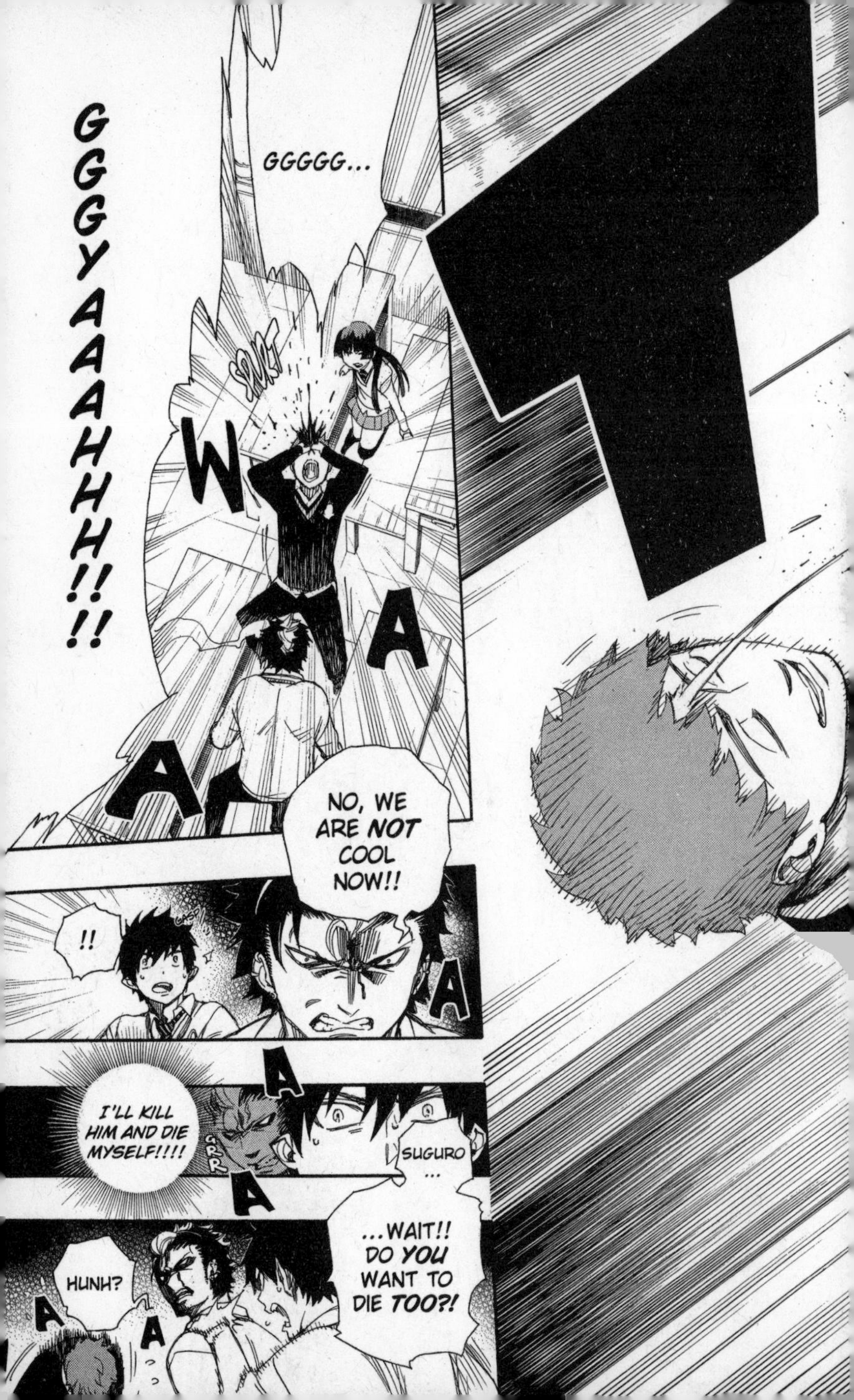
GGGGG...
GGGYAAAAHHHH!!!!
WAAAAAAA
NO, WE ARE NOT COOL NOW!!
!!
I'LL KILL HIM AND DIE MYSELF!!!!
GRR
SUGURO ...
...WAIT!! DO YOU WANT TO DIE TOO?!
HUNH?

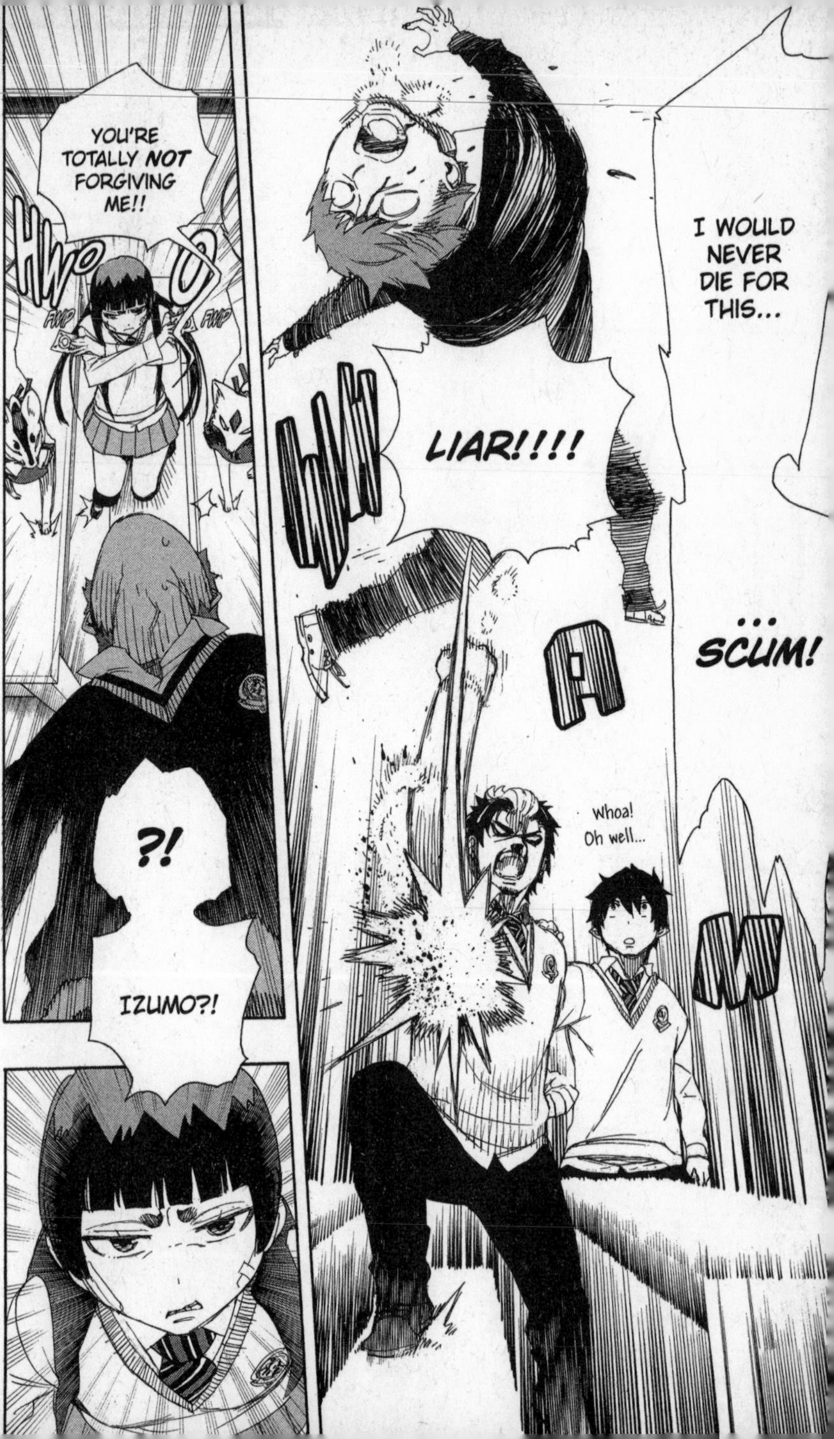
I WOULD NEVER DIE FOR THIS...
LIAR!!!!
...SCÜM!
Whoa! Oh well...
YOU'RE TOTALLY NOT FORGIVING ME!!
?!
IZUMO?!

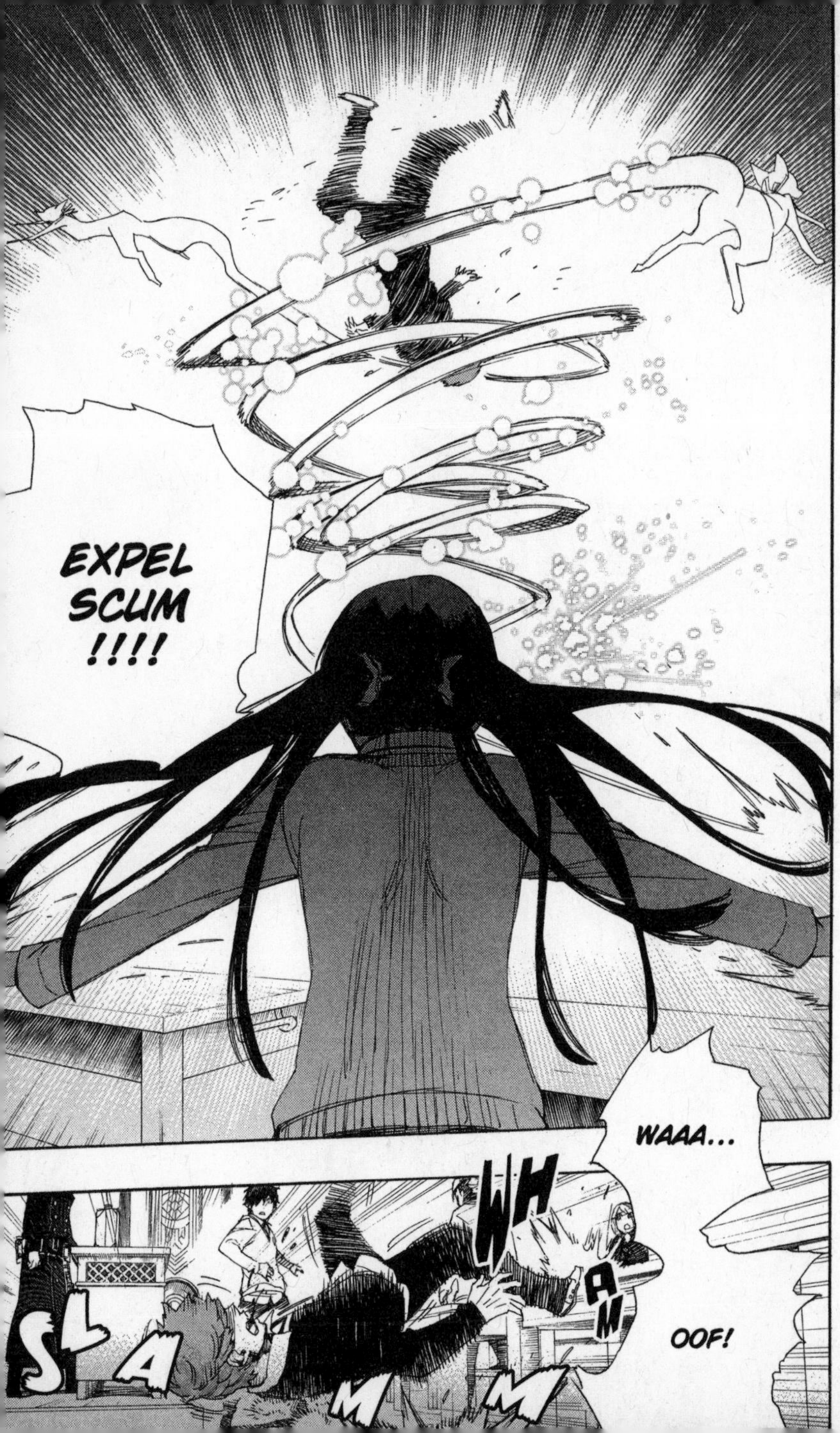
EXPEL SCUM !!!!
WAAA...
WHAM
OOF!
SLAMM

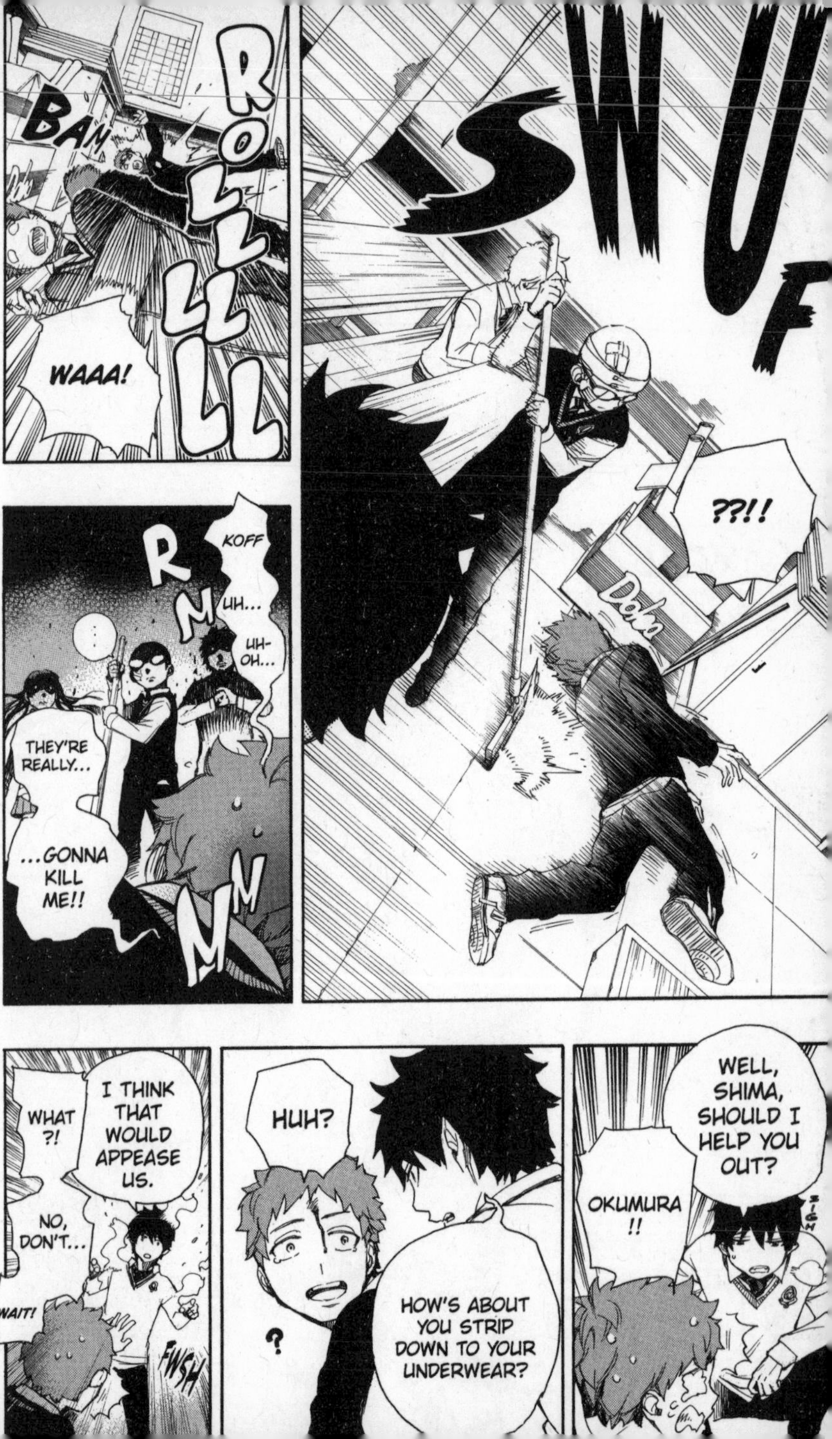
SWUF
??!!
Doko
BAM
ROLLLLL
WAAA!
KOFF
RMMM
UH...
UH-OH...
...
THEY'RE REALLY...
...GONNA KILL ME!!
WELL, SHIMA, SHOULD I HELP YOU OUT?
SIGH
OKUMURA!!
HUH?
HOW'S ABOUT YOU STRIP DOWN TO YOUR UNDERWEAR?
?
I THINK THAT WOULD APPEASE US.
WHAT?!
NO, DON'T...
WAIT!
FWSH

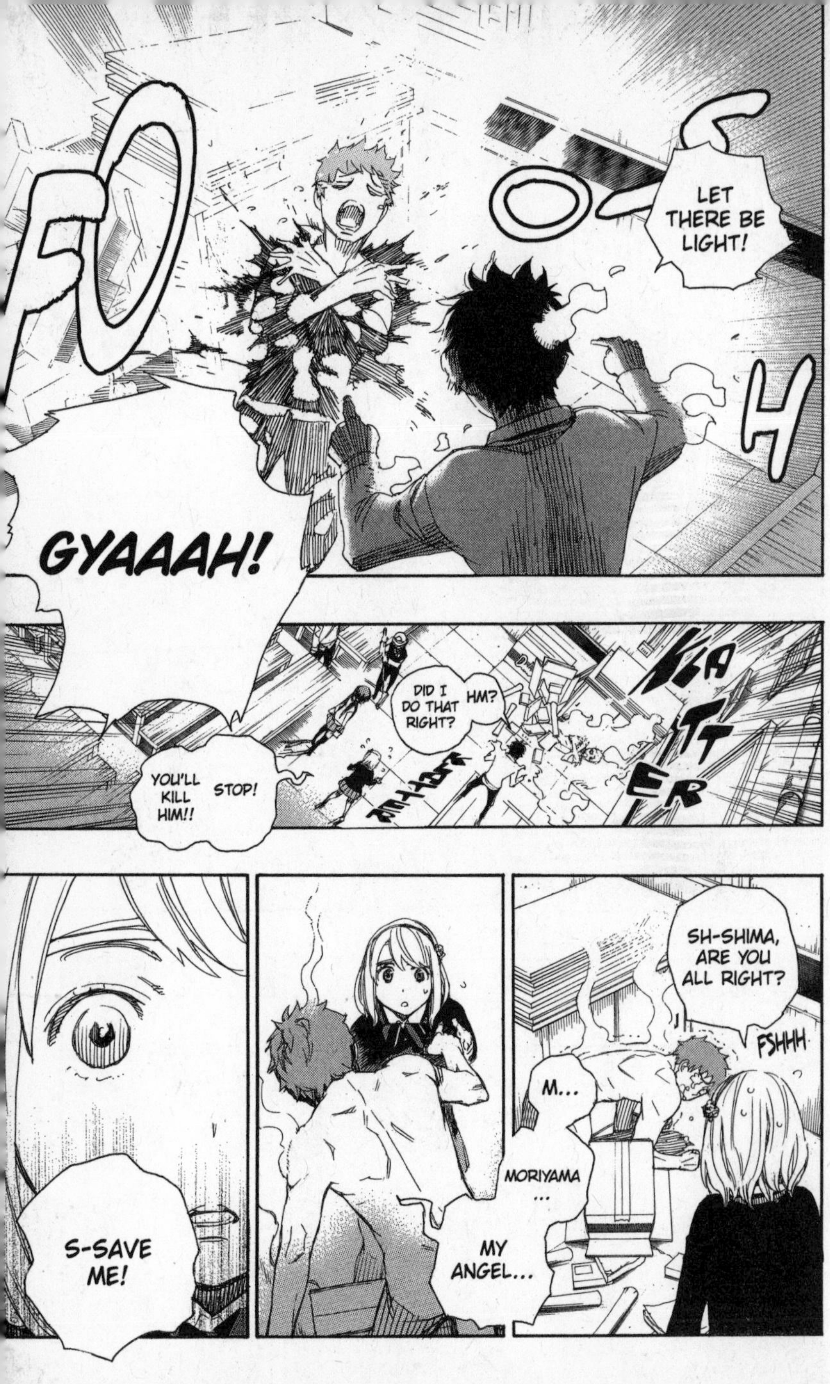
LET THERE BE LIGHT!
GYAAAH!
HM?
DID I DO THAT RIGHT?
STOP!
YOU'LL KILL HIM!!
SH-SHIMA, ARE YOU ALL RIGHT?
FSHHH
M...
MORIYAMA ...
MY ANGEL...
S-SAVE ME!

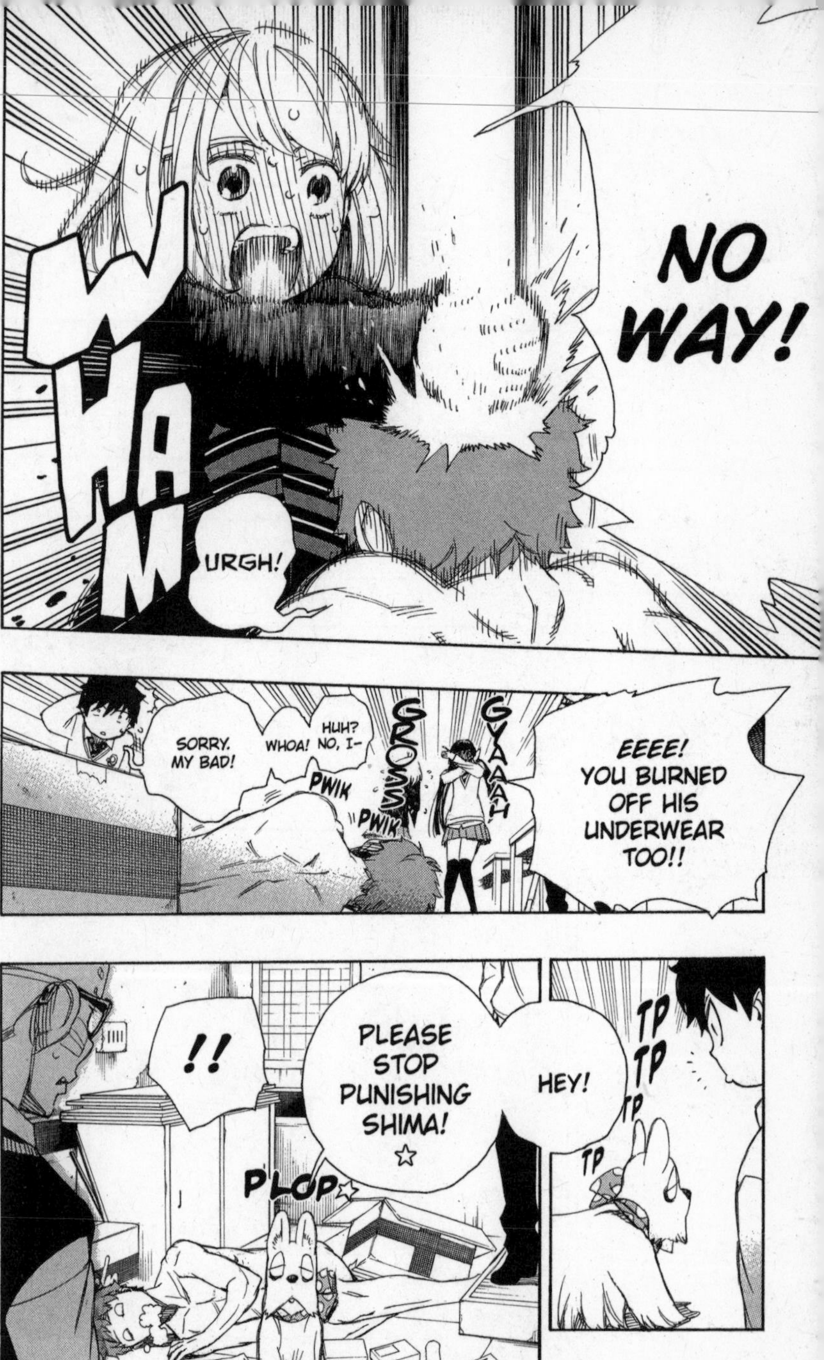
NO WAY!
WHAM
URGH!
EEEE! YOU BURNED OFF HIS UNDERWEAR TOO!!
GYAAAAH
GROSS
PWIK
PWIK
HUH? NO, I–
WHOA!
SORRY. MY BAD!
TP
TP
TP
TP
HEY!
PLEASE STOP PUNISHING SHIMA! ☆
!!
PLOP☆

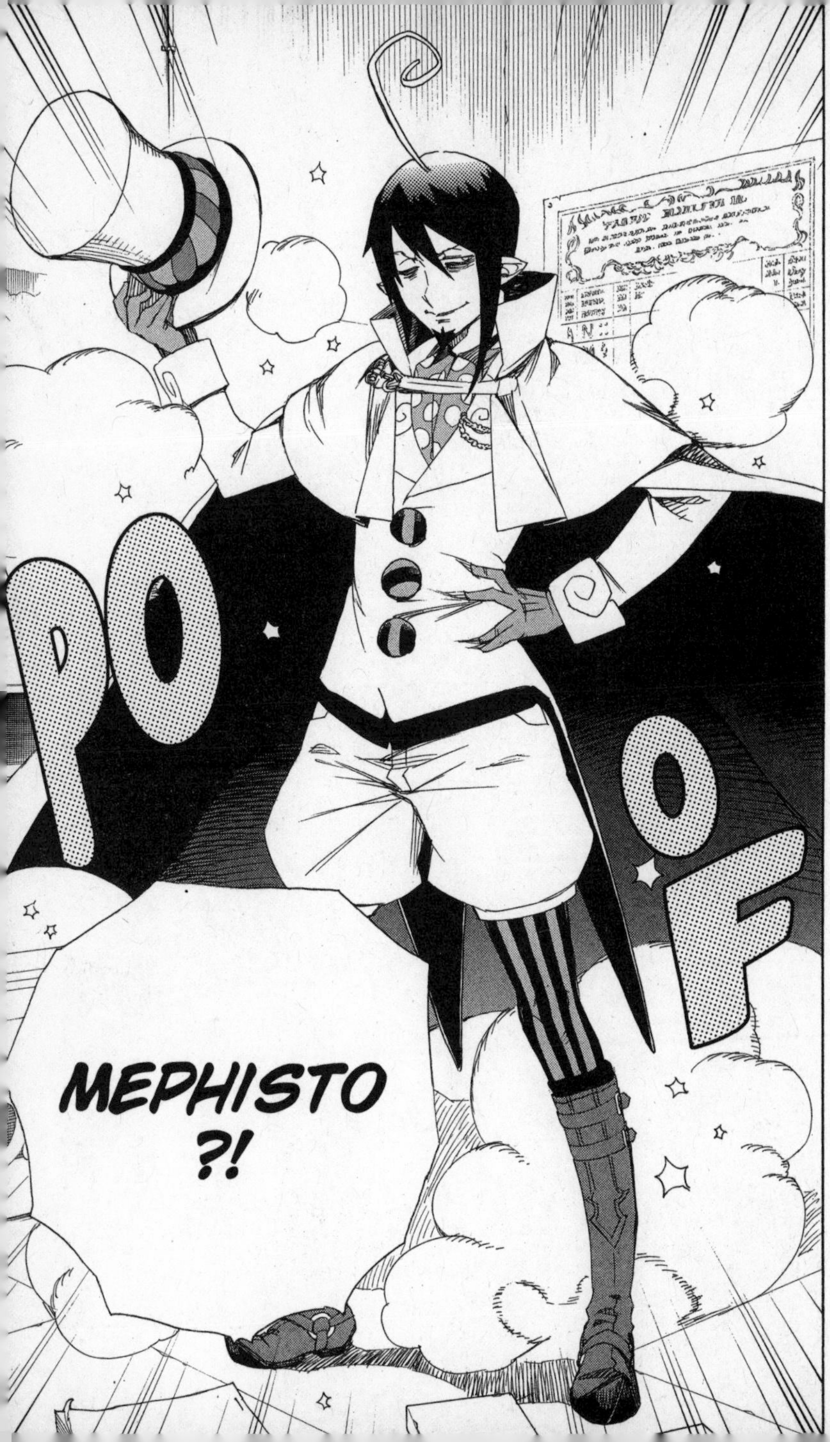
POOF
MEPHISTO ?!

Blue Exorcist Chapter 65: Pink Spider: Part 1

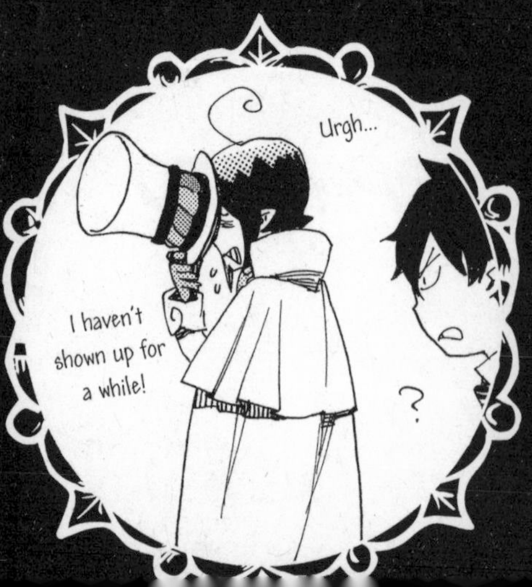
Urgh...
I haven't shown up for a while!
?

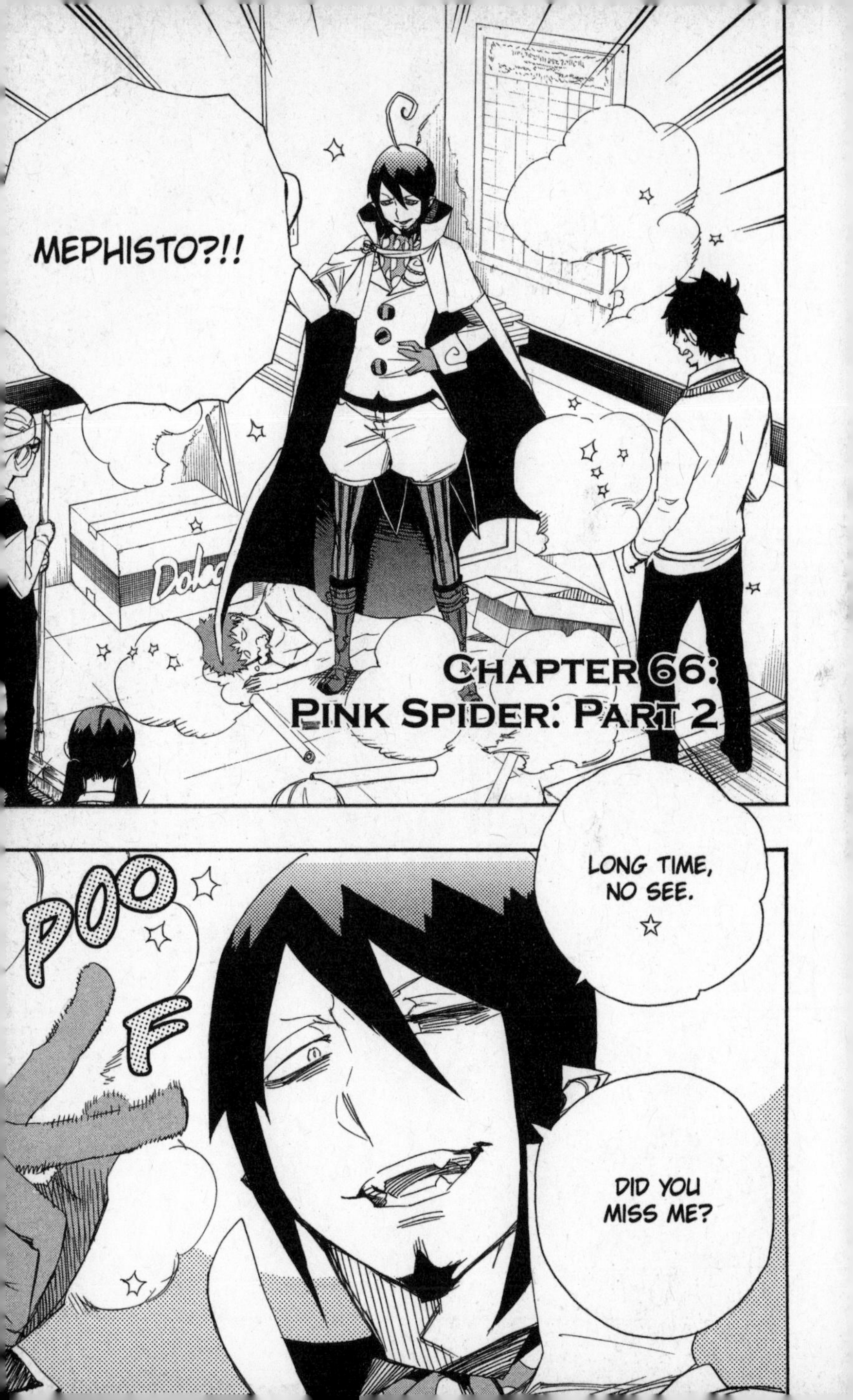
MEPHISTO?!!
Chapter 66:
Pink Spider: Part 2
LONG TIME, NO SEE. ☆
POOF
DID YOU MISS ME?

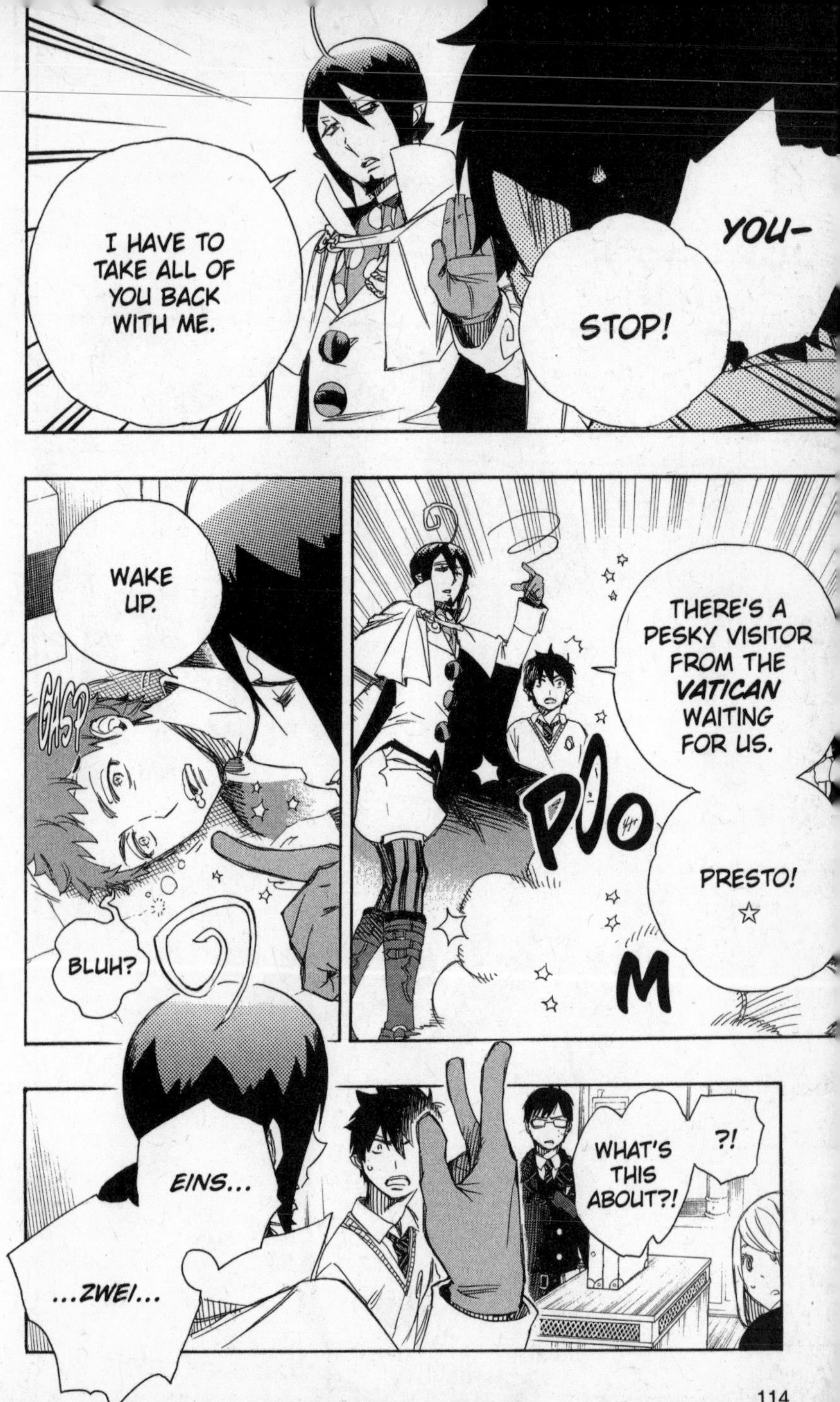
YOU-
STOP!
I HAVE TO TAKE ALL OF YOU BACK WITH ME.
THERE'S A PESKY VISITOR FROM THE VATICAN WAITING FOR US.
POOM
PRESTO! ☆
WAKE UP.
GASP
BLUH?
?!
WHAT'S THIS ABOUT?!
EINS...
...ZWEI...

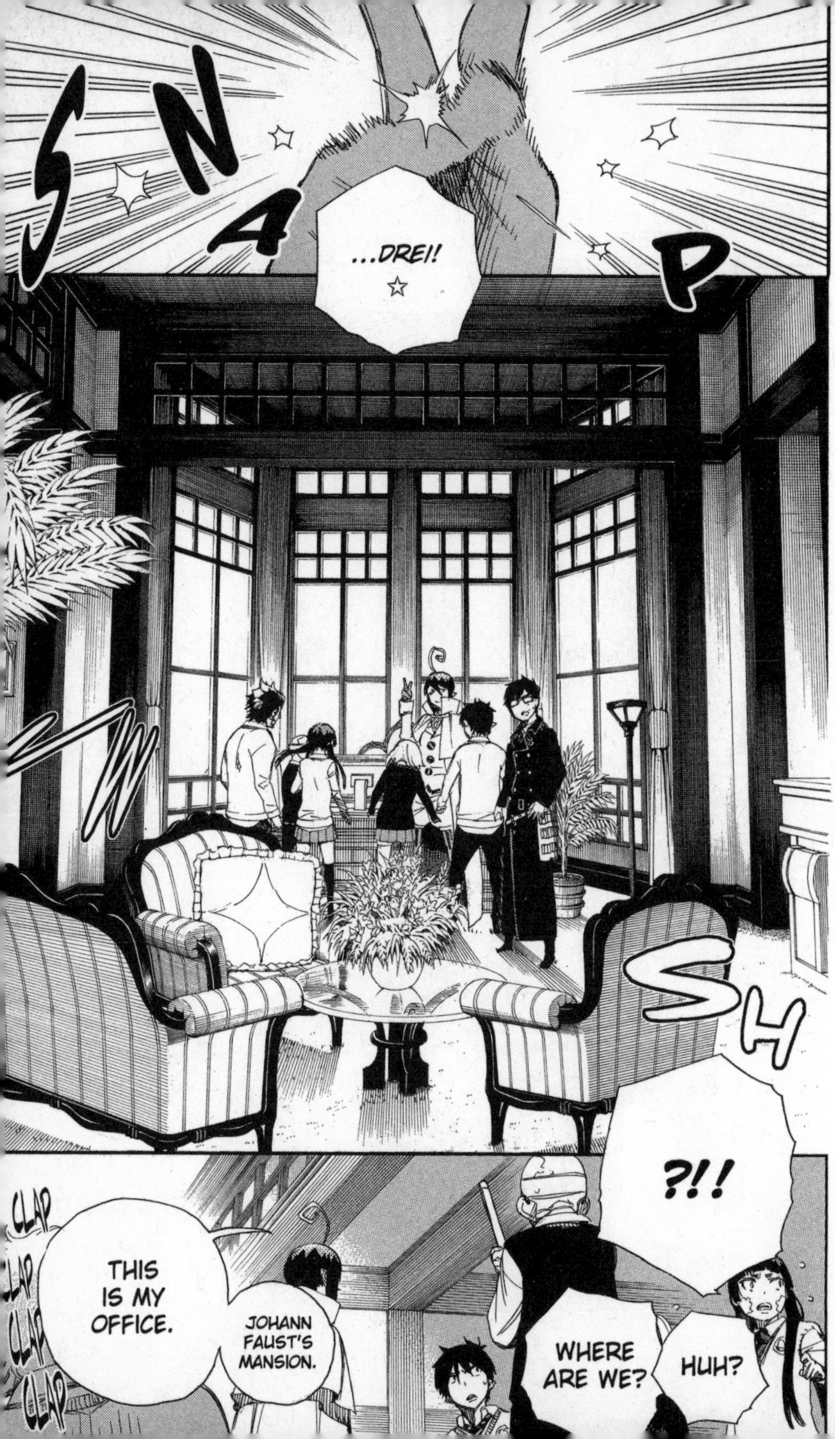
SNAP
...DREI! ☆
SH
?!!
HUH?
WHERE ARE WE?
JOHANN FAUST'S MANSION.
THIS IS MY OFFICE.
CLAP CLAP CLAP CLAP

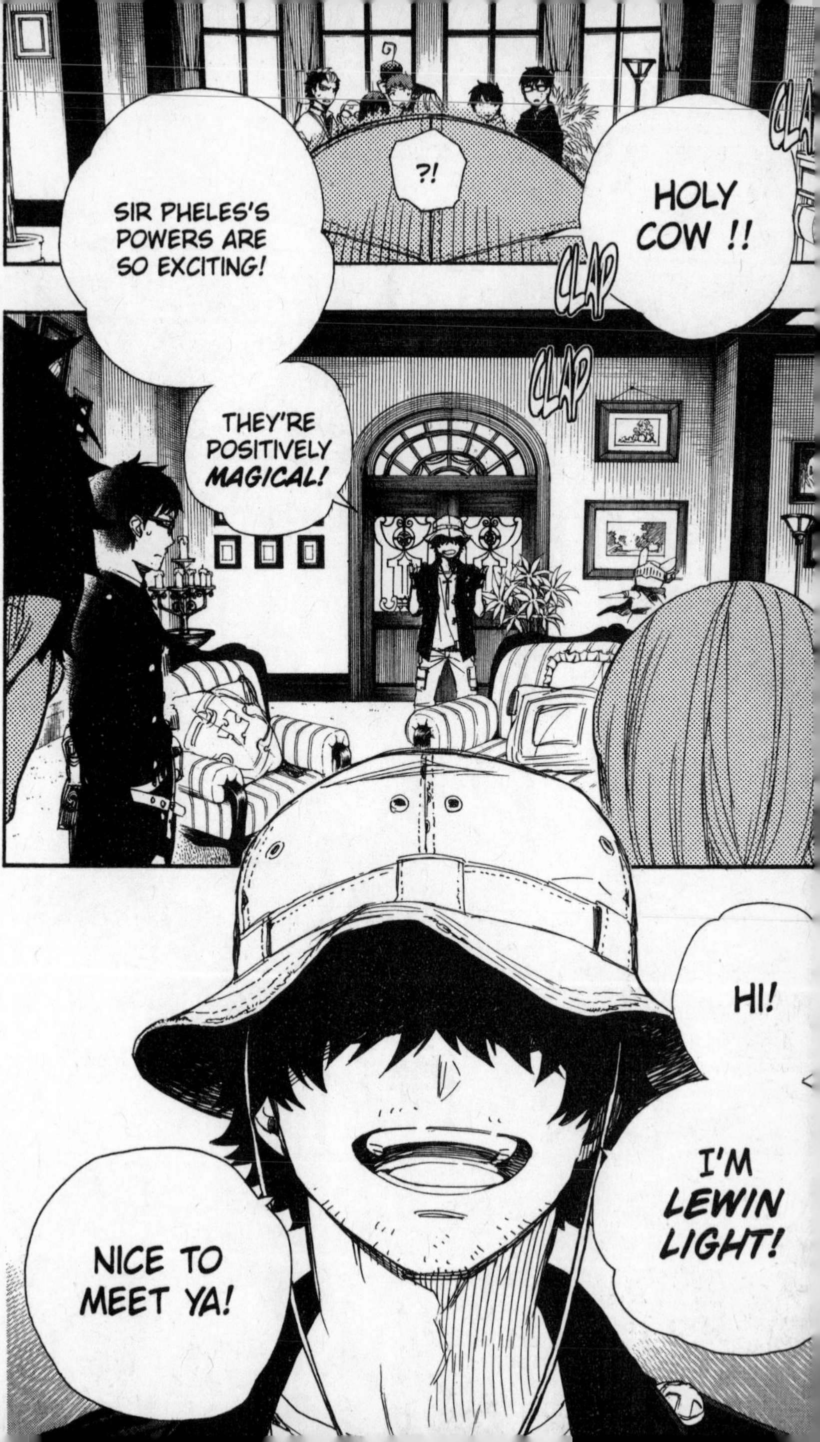
HOLY COW !!
CLAP
?!
SIR PHELES'S POWERS ARE SO EXCITING!
CLAP
THEY'RE POSITIVELY *MAGICAL!*
HI!
I'M *LEWIN LIGHT!*
NICE TO MEET YA!

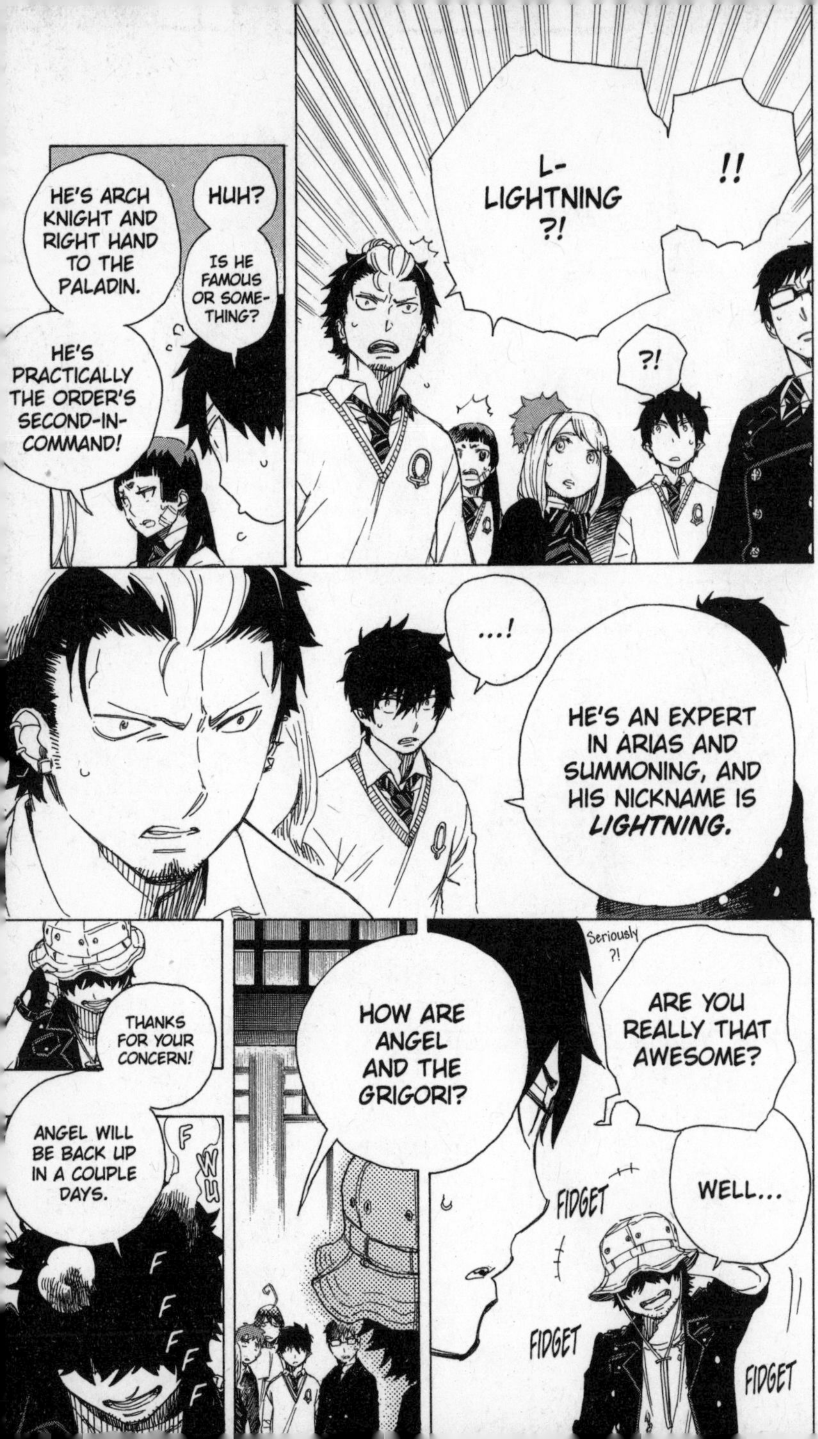
L-LIGHTNING ?!
!!
?!
HUH?
IS HE FAMOUS OR SOMETHING?
HE'S ARCH KNIGHT AND RIGHT HAND TO THE PALADIN.
HE'S PRACTICALLY THE ORDER'S SECOND-IN-COMMAND!
HE'S AN EXPERT IN ARIAS AND SUMMONING, AND HIS NICKNAME IS *LIGHTNING.*
...!
Seriously ?!
ARE YOU REALLY THAT AWESOME?
WELL...
FIDGET
FIDGET
FIDGET
HOW ARE ANGEL AND THE GRIGORI?
THANKS FOR YOUR CONCERN!
ANGEL WILL BE BACK UP IN A COUPLE DAYS.
FWU
FFFFF

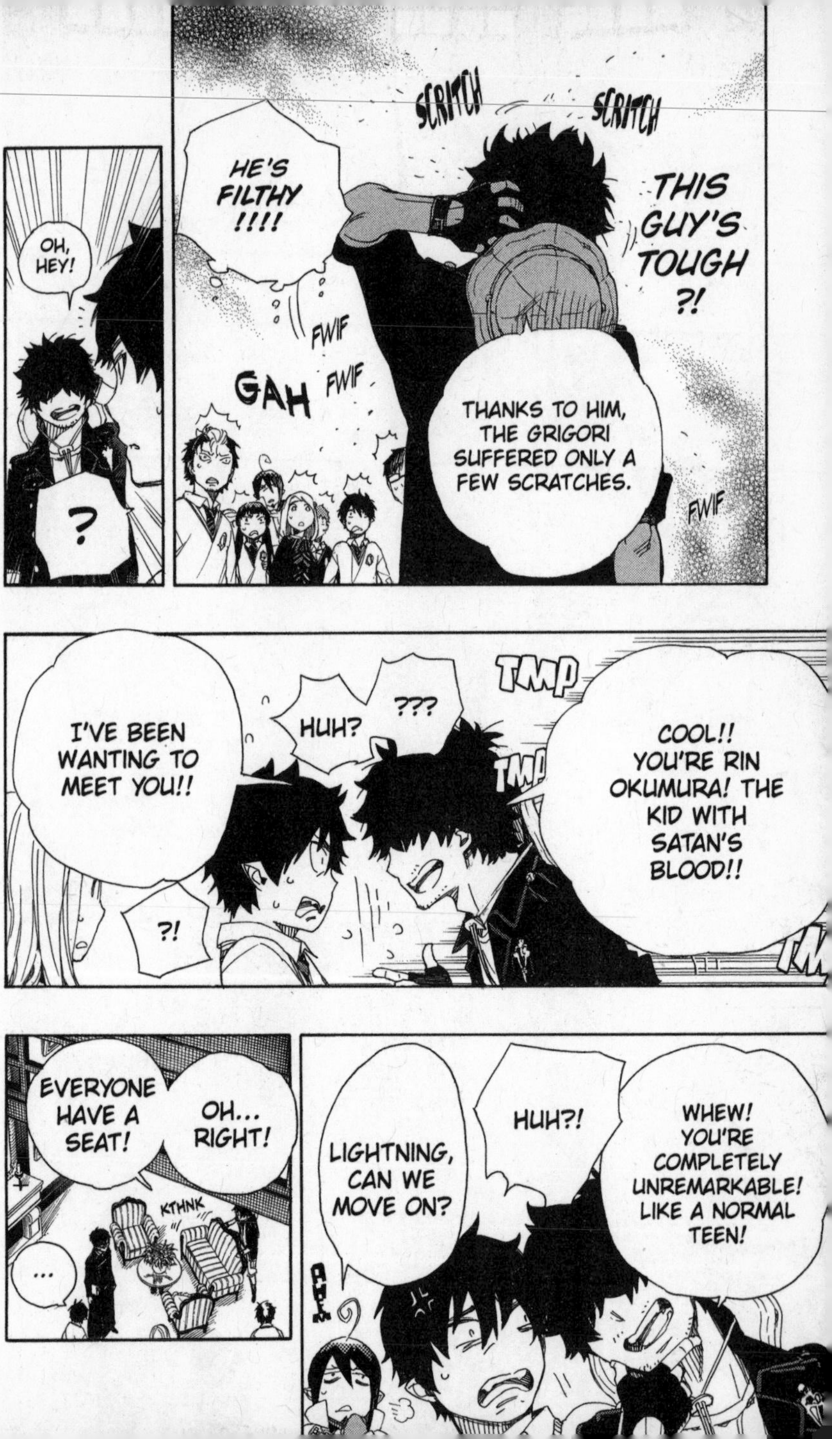
SCRITCH
SCRITCH
THIS GUY'S TOUGH ?!
HE'S FILTHY !!!!
THANKS TO HIM, THE GRIGORI SUFFERED ONLY A FEW SCRATCHES.
FWIF
GAH
FWIF
FWIF
OH, HEY!
?
TMP
COOL!! YOU'RE RIN OKUMURA! THE KID WITH SATAN'S BLOOD!!
TMP
???
HUH?
I'VE BEEN WANTING TO MEET YOU!!
?!
WHEW! YOU'RE COMPLETELY UNREMARKABLE! LIKE A NORMAL TEEN!
HUH?!
LIGHTNING, CAN WE MOVE ON?
OH... RIGHT!
EVERYONE HAVE A SEAT!
KTHNK
...

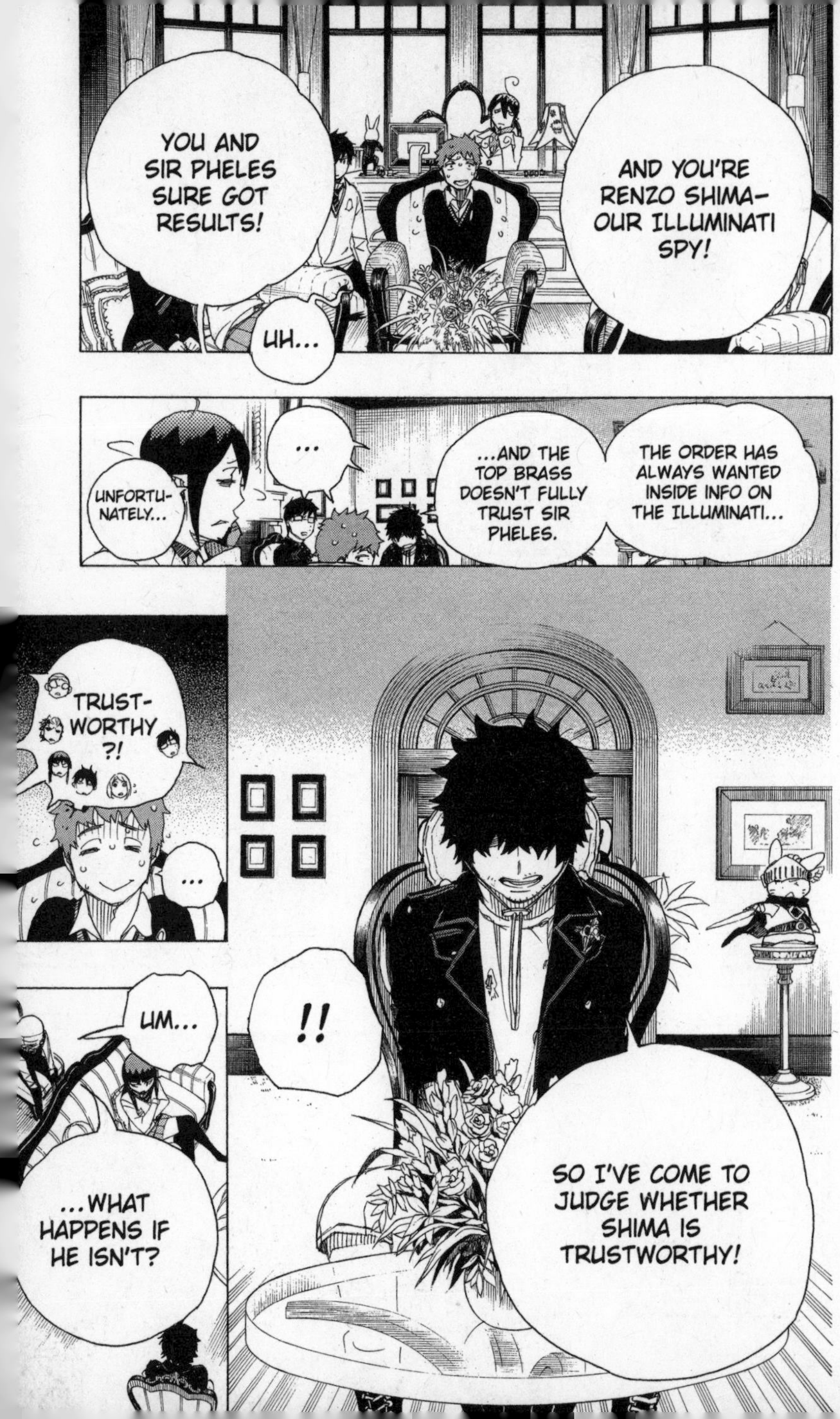
AND YOU'RE RENZO SHIMA—OUR ILLUMINATI SPY!
YOU AND SIR PHELES SURE GOT RESULTS!
UH...
THE ORDER HAS ALWAYS WANTED INSIDE INFO ON THE ILLUMINATI...
...AND THE TOP BRASS DOESN'T FULLY TRUST SIR PHELES.
...
UNFORTU-NATELY...
SO I'VE COME TO JUDGE WHETHER SHIMA IS TRUSTWORTHY!
!!
TRUST-WORTHY ?!
...
UM...
...WHAT HAPPENS IF HE ISN'T?

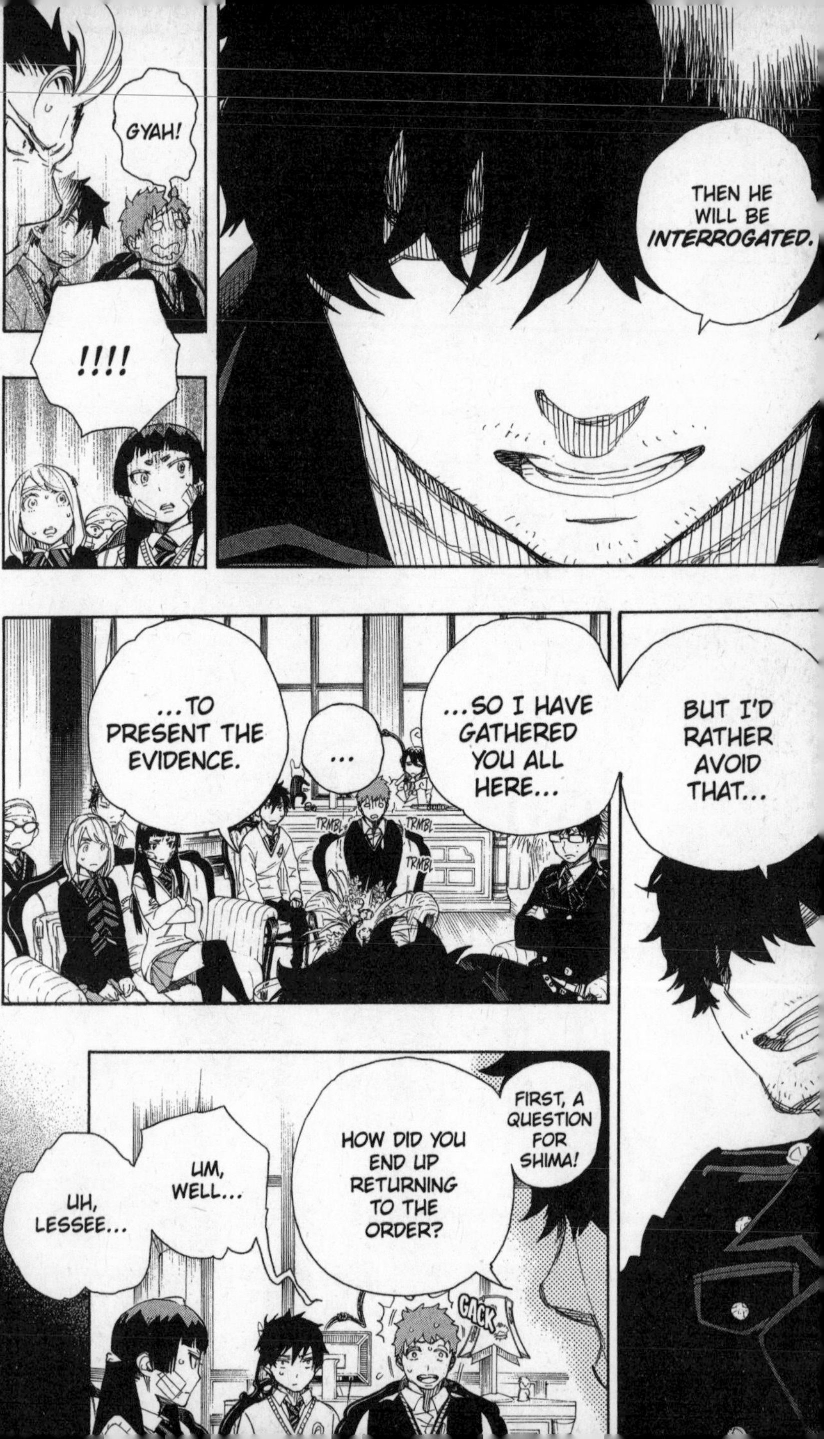
THEN HE WILL BE INTERROGATED.
GYAH!
!!!!
BUT I'D RATHER AVOID THAT...
...SO I HAVE GATHERED YOU ALL HERE...
TRMBL
TRMBL
TRMBL
...
...TO PRESENT THE EVIDENCE.
FIRST, A QUESTION FOR SHIMA!
HOW DID YOU END UP RETURNING TO THE ORDER?
GACK
UM, WELL...
UH, LESSEE...

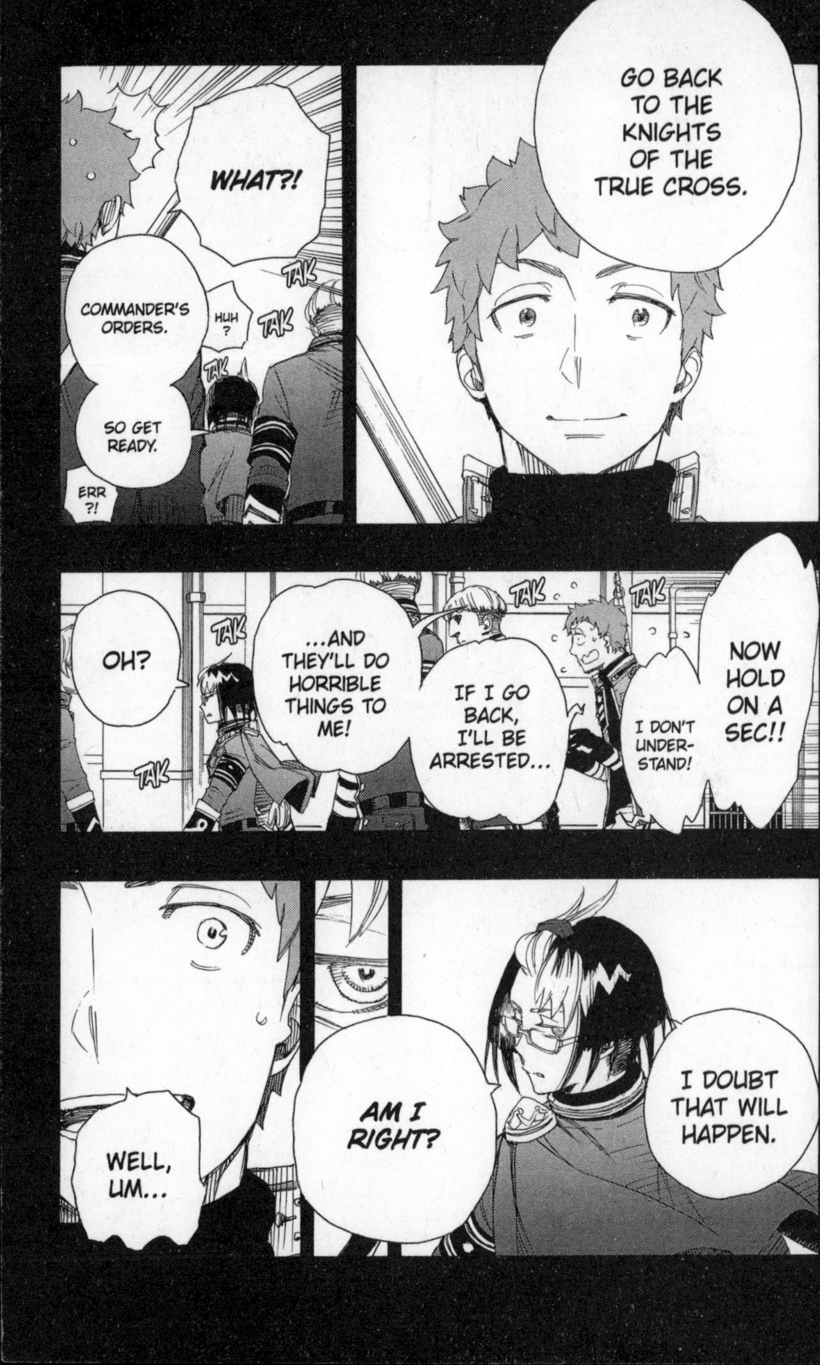
GO BACK TO THE KNIGHTS OF THE TRUE CROSS.
WHAT?!
TAK
COMMANDER'S ORDERS.
HUH ?
TAK
TAK
SO GET READY.
ERR ?!
NOW HOLD ON A SEC!!
I DON'T UNDER-STAND!
TAK
TAK
IF I GO BACK, I'LL BE ARRESTED...
...AND THEY'LL DO HORRIBLE THINGS TO ME!
TAK
OH?
TAK
I DOUBT THAT WILL HAPPEN.
AM I RIGHT?
WELL, UM...

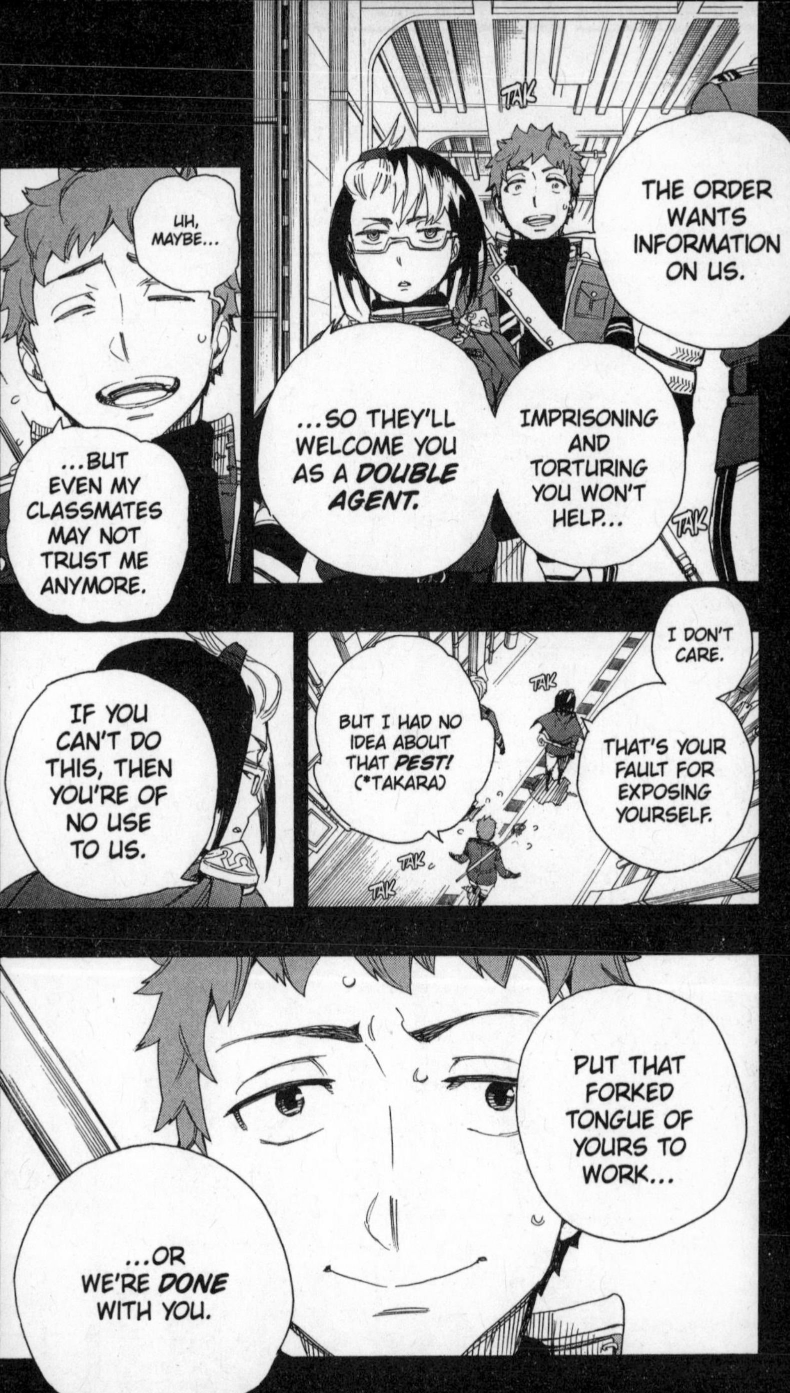
TAK
THE ORDER WANTS INFORMATION ON US.
IMPRISONING AND TORTURING YOU WON'T HELP...
...SO THEY'LL WELCOME YOU AS A *DOUBLE AGENT.*
TAK
UH, MAYBE...
...BUT EVEN MY CLASSMATES MAY NOT TRUST ME ANYMORE.
I DON'T CARE.
TAK
THAT'S YOUR FAULT FOR EXPOSING YOURSELF.
BUT I HAD NO IDEA ABOUT THAT *PEST!* (*TAKARA)
TAK
TAK
IF YOU CAN'T DO THIS, THEN YOU'RE OF NO USE TO US.
PUT THAT FORKED TONGUE OF YOURS TO WORK...
...OR WE'RE *DONE* WITH YOU.

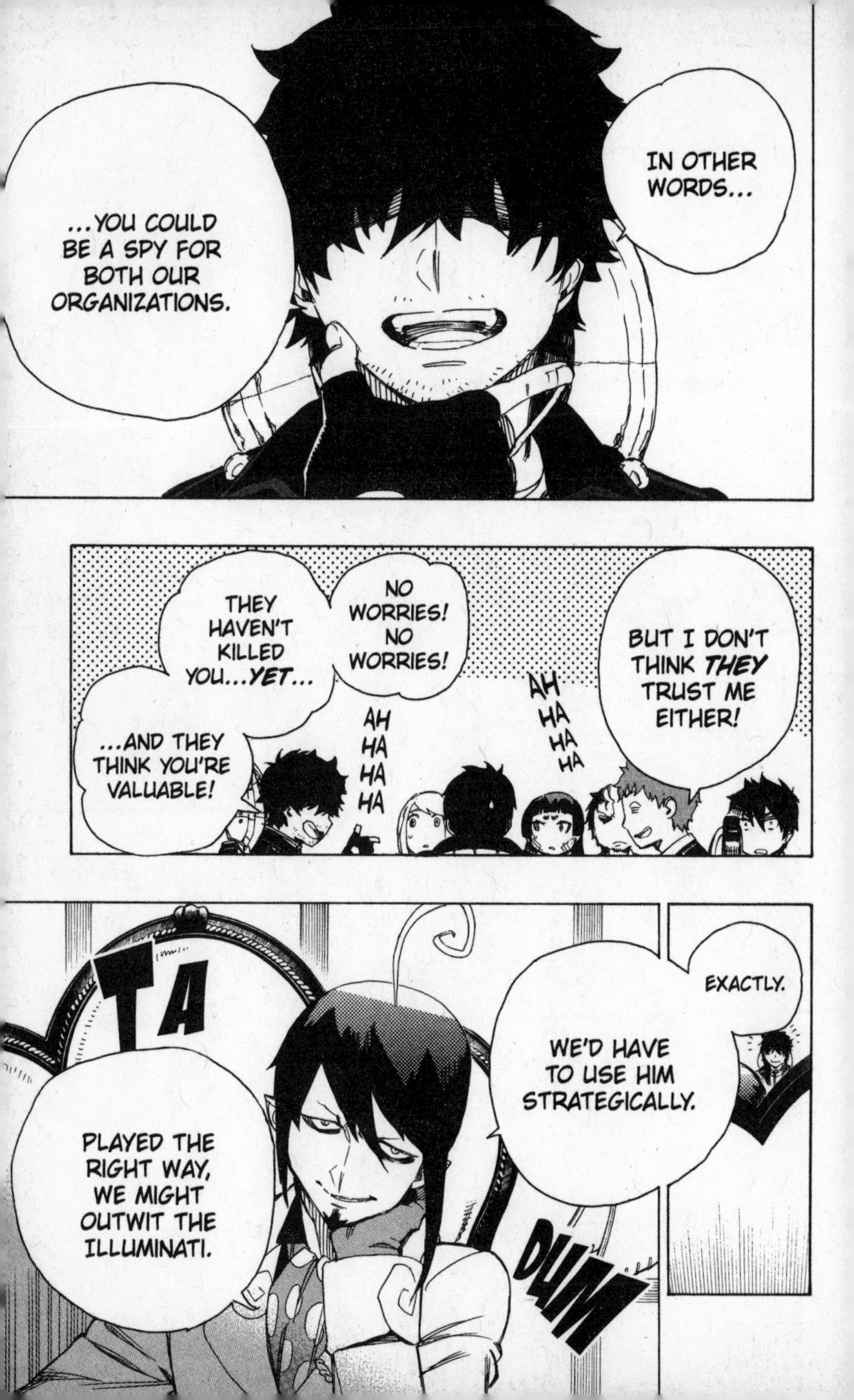
IN OTHER WORDS...
...YOU COULD BE A SPY FOR BOTH OUR ORGANIZATIONS.
BUT I DON'T THINK *THEY* TRUST ME EITHER!
AH HA HA HA
NO WORRIES! NO WORRIES!
AH HA HA HA
THEY HAVEN'T KILLED YOU...*YET*...
...AND THEY THINK YOU'RE VALUABLE!
EXACTLY.
WE'D HAVE TO USE HIM STRATEGICALLY.
TA
PLAYED THE RIGHT WAY, WE MIGHT OUTWIT THE ILLUMINATI.
DUM

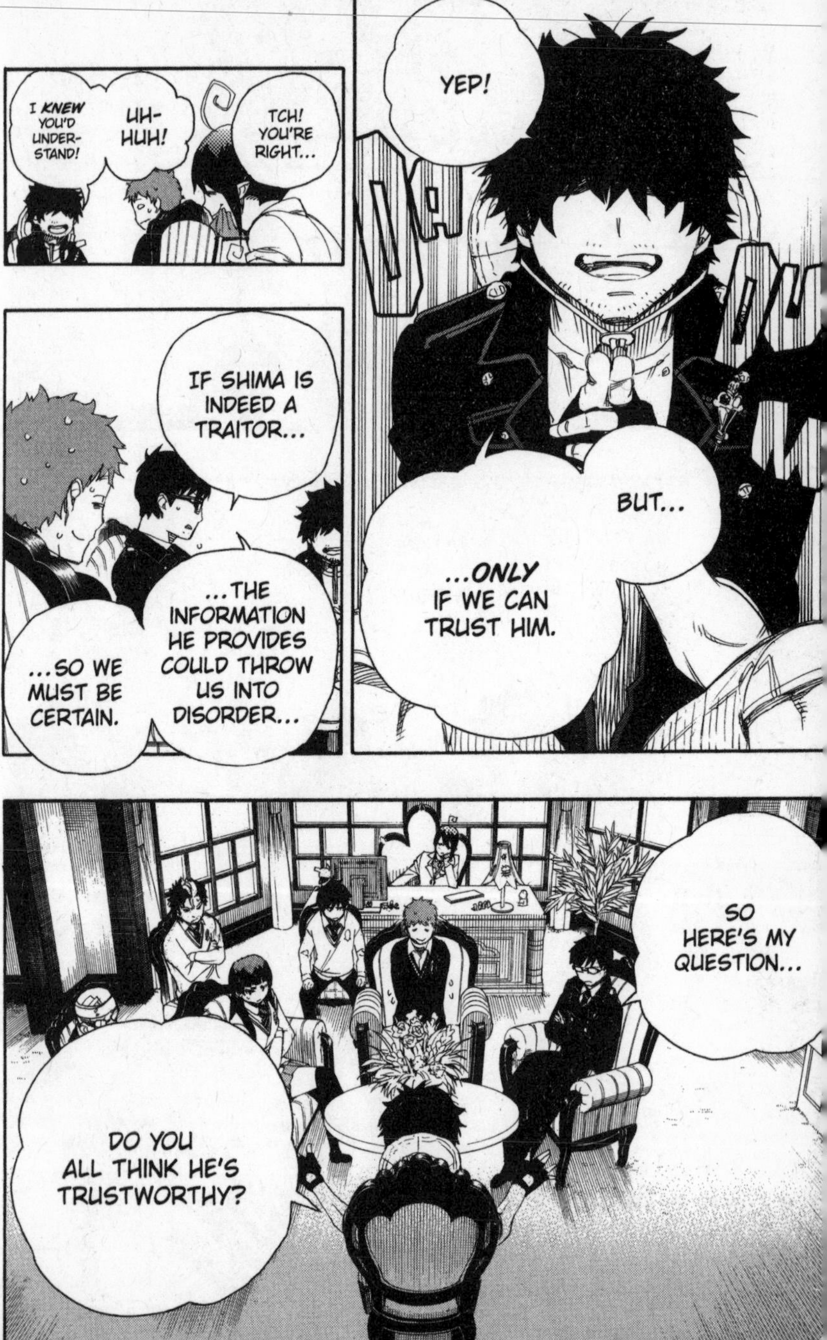
YEP!
BUT...
...*ONLY* IF WE CAN TRUST HIM.
TCH! YOU'RE RIGHT...
UH-HUH!
I *KNEW* YOU'D UNDER-STAND!
IF SHIMA IS INDEED A TRAITOR...
...THE INFORMATION HE PROVIDES COULD THROW US INTO DISORDER...
...SO WE MUST BE CERTAIN.
SO HERE'S MY QUESTION...
DO YOU ALL THINK HE'S TRUSTWORTHY?

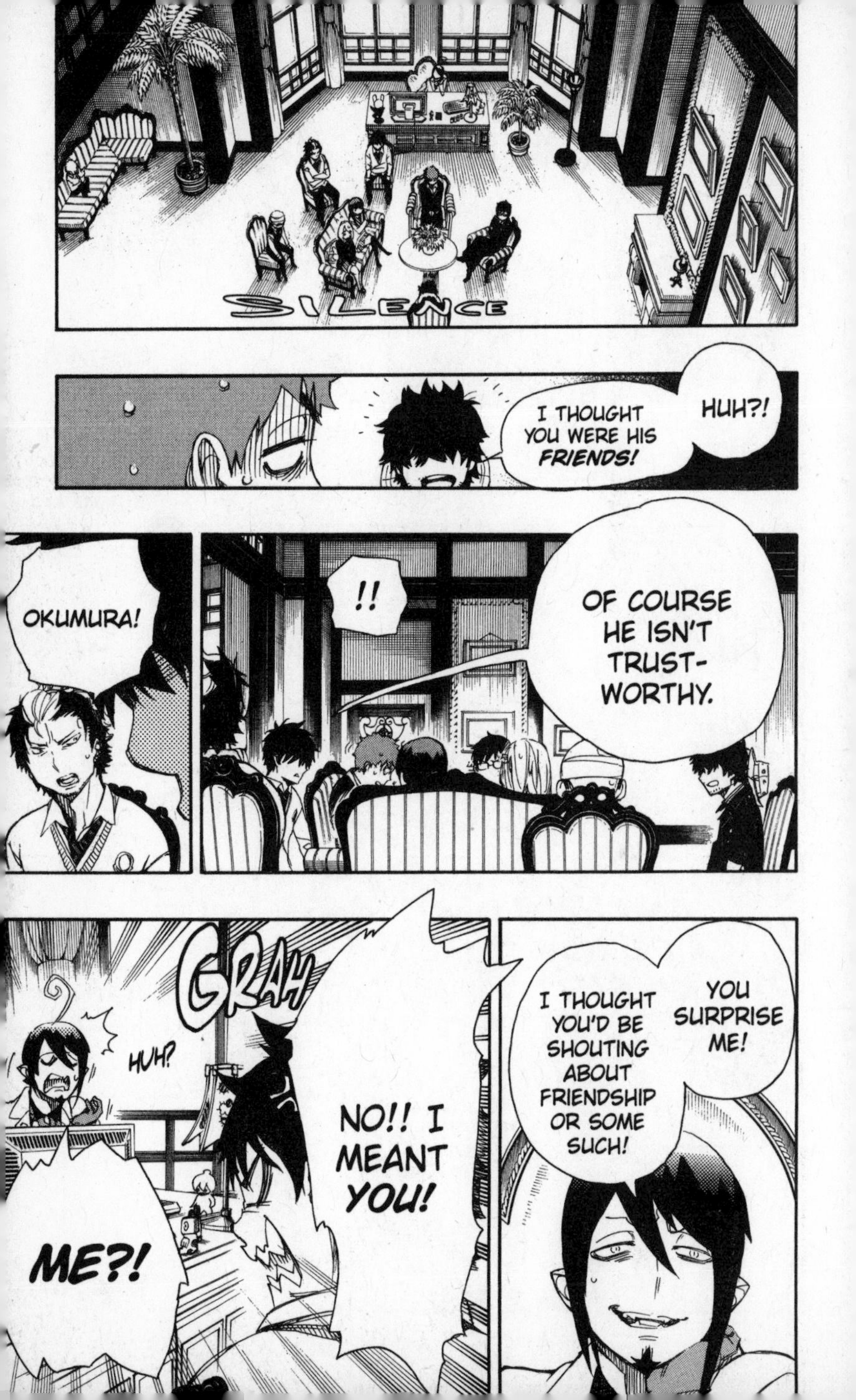
SILENCE
HUH?!
I THOUGHT YOU WERE HIS FRIENDS!
OF COURSE HE ISN'T TRUST-WORTHY.
!!
OKUMURA!
YOU SURPRISE ME!
I THOUGHT YOU'D BE SHOUTING ABOUT FRIENDSHIP OR SOME SUCH!
GRAH
NO!! I MEANT YOU!
HUH?
ME?!

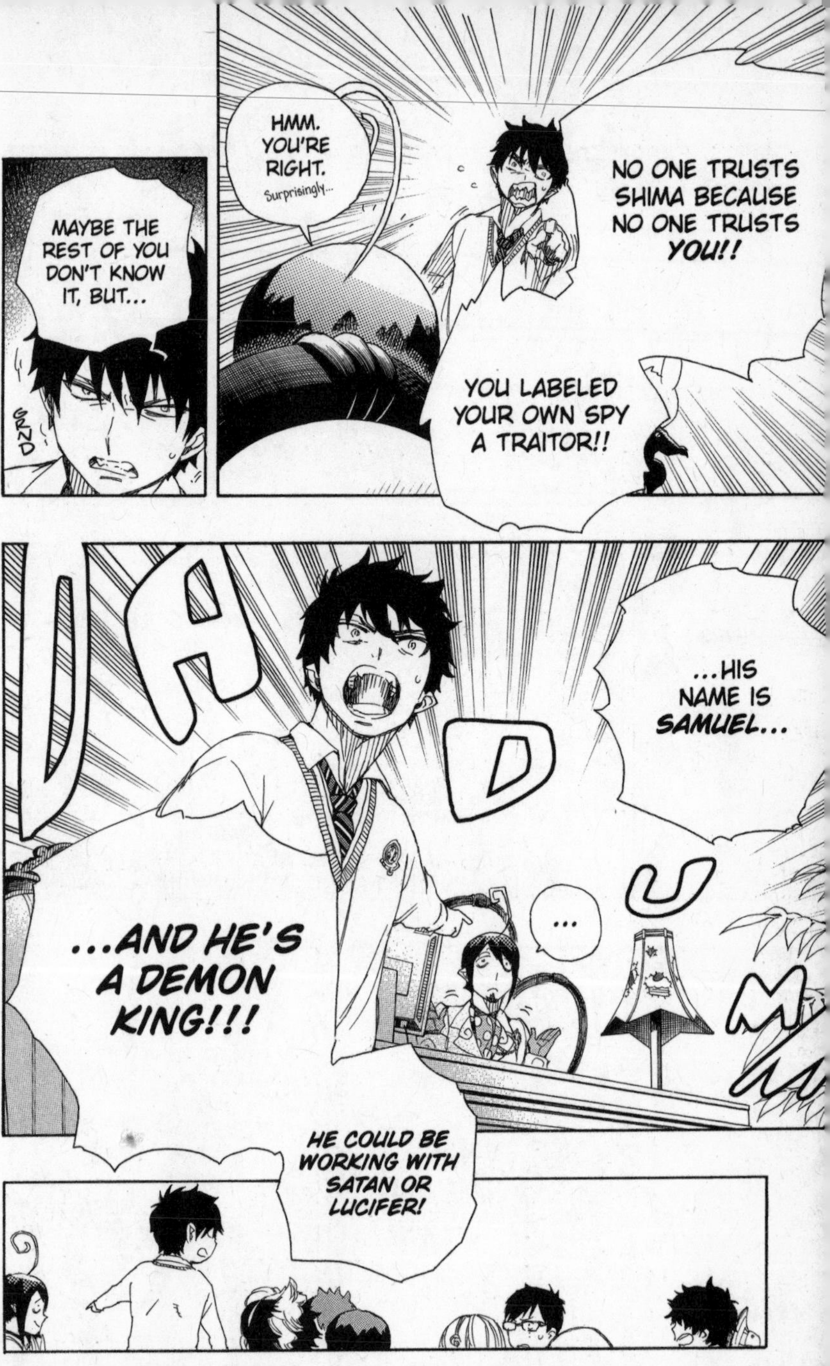

NO ONE TRUSTS SHIMA BECAUSE NO ONE TRUSTS YOU!!
YOU LABELED YOUR OWN SPY A TRAITOR!!
HMM. YOU'RE RIGHT.
Surprisingly...
MAYBE THE REST OF YOU DON'T KNOW IT, BUT...
GRND
...HIS NAME IS SAMUEL...
...
...AND HE'S A DEMON KING!!!
HE COULD BE WORKING WITH SATAN OR LUCIFER!

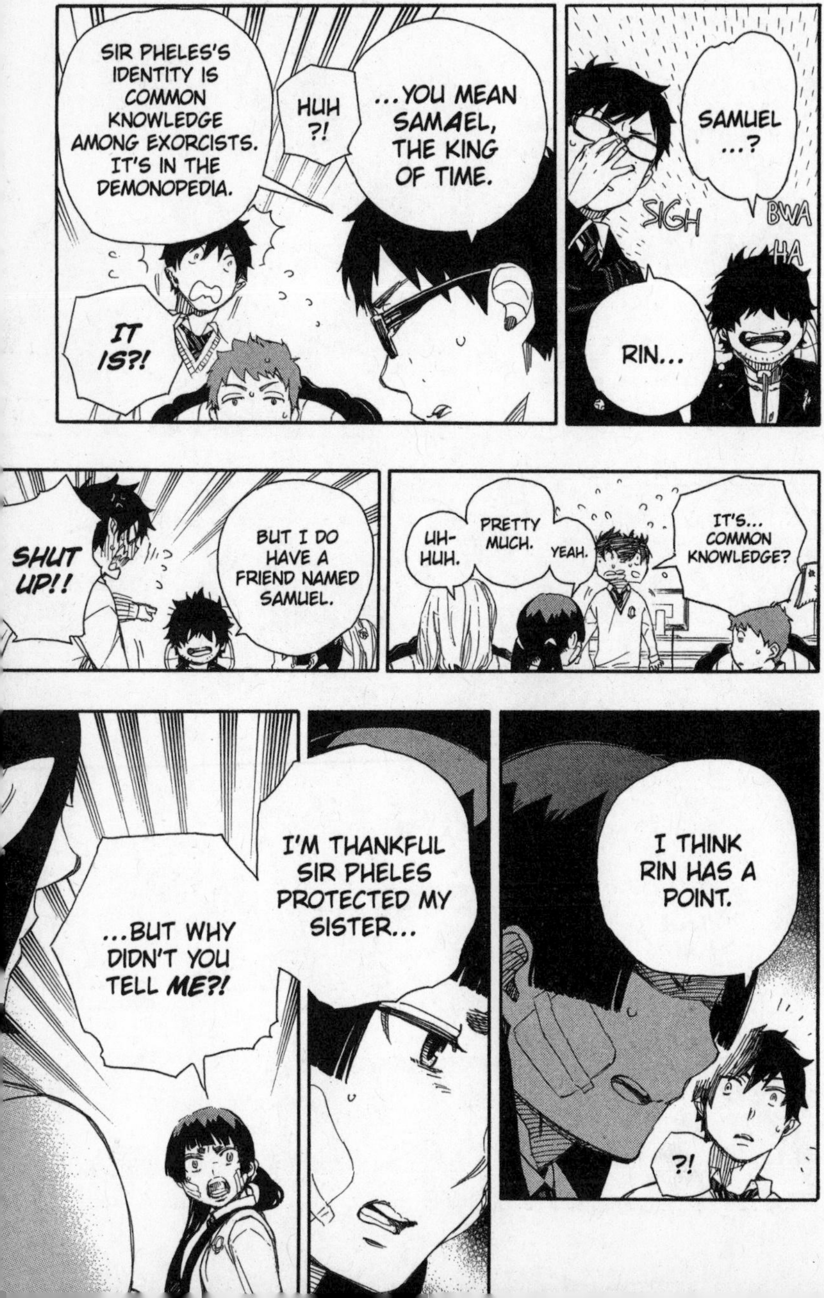
SAMUEL ...?
SIGH
BWA HA
RIN...
...YOU MEAN SAMAEL, THE KING OF TIME.
HUH ?!
SIR PHELES'S IDENTITY IS COMMON KNOWLEDGE AMONG EXORCISTS. IT'S IN THE DEMONOPEDIA.
IT IS?!
IT'S... COMMON KNOWLEDGE?
YEAH.
PRETTY MUCH.
UH-HUH.
BUT I DO HAVE A FRIEND NAMED SAMUEL.
SHUT UP!!
I THINK RIN HAS A POINT.
?!
I'M THANKFUL SIR PHELES PROTECTED MY SISTER...
...BUT WHY DIDN'T YOU TELL ME?!

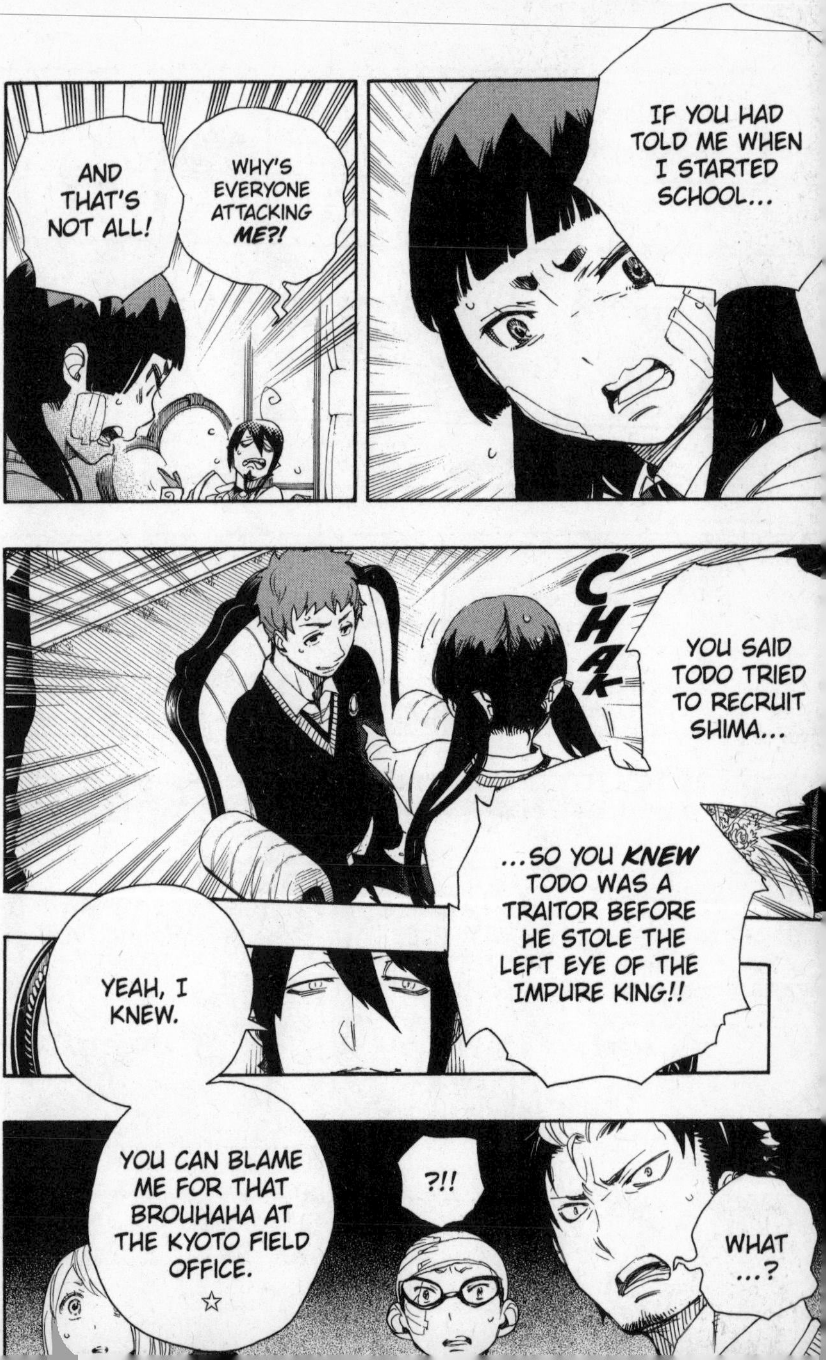
IF YOU HAD TOLD ME WHEN I STARTED SCHOOL...
WHY'S EVERYONE ATTACKING *ME?!*
AND THAT'S NOT ALL!
CHAK
YOU SAID TODO TRIED TO RECRUIT SHIMA...
...SO YOU *KNEW* TODO WAS A TRAITOR BEFORE HE STOLE THE LEFT EYE OF THE IMPURE KING!!
YEAH, I KNEW.
WHAT ...?
?!!
YOU CAN BLAME ME FOR THAT BROUHAHA AT THE KYOTO FIELD OFFICE. ☆

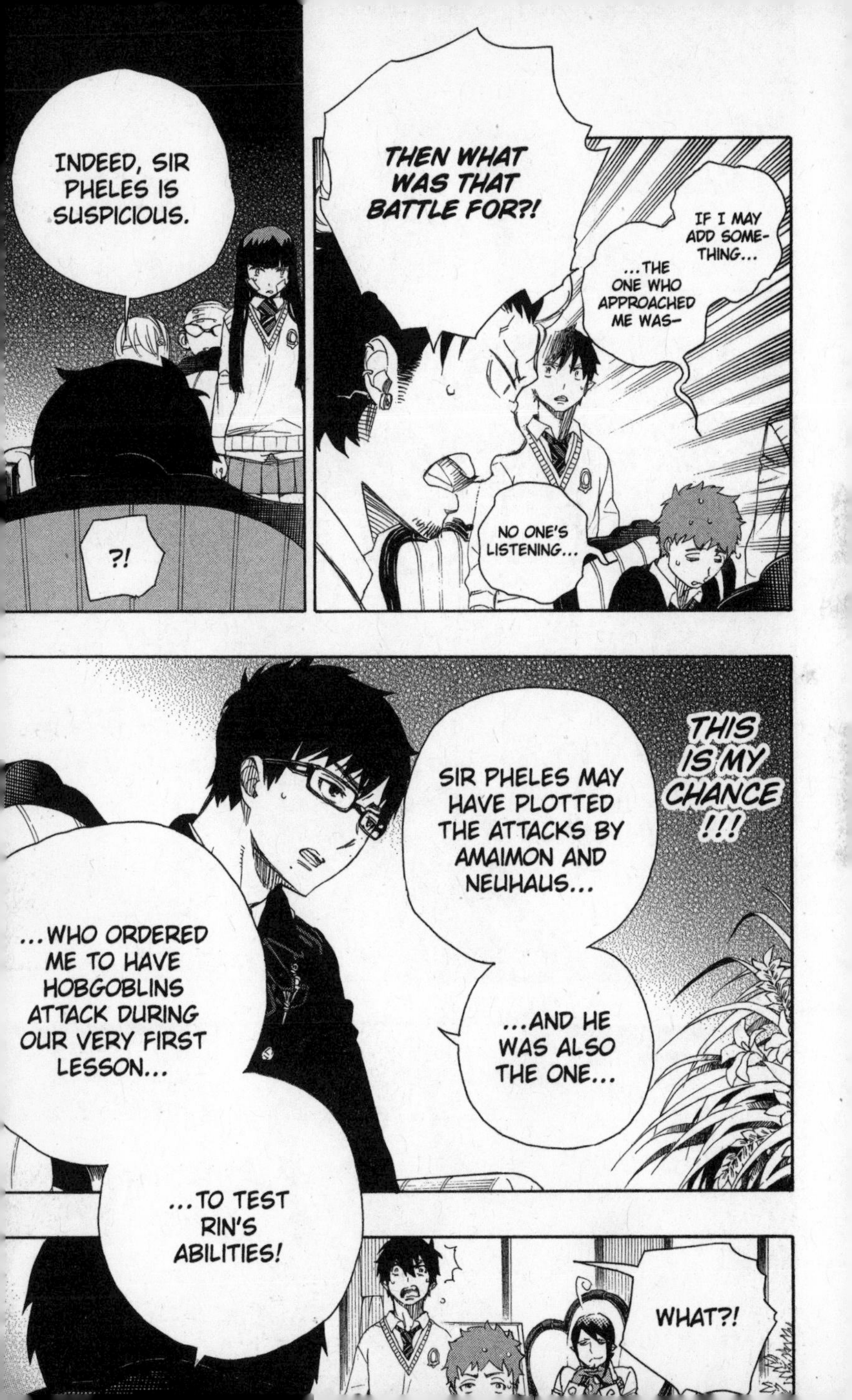
THEN WHAT WAS THAT BATTLE FOR?!
IF I MAY ADD SOME-THING...
...THE ONE WHO APPROACHED ME WAS-
NO ONE'S LISTENING...
INDEED, SIR PHELES IS SUSPICIOUS.
?!
THIS IS MY CHANCE!!!
SIR PHELES MAY HAVE PLOTTED THE ATTACKS BY AMAIMON AND NEUHAUS...
...AND HE WAS ALSO THE ONE...
...WHO ORDERED ME TO HAVE HOBGOBLINS ATTACK DURING OUR VERY FIRST LESSON...
...TO TEST RIN'S ABILITIES!
WHAT?!

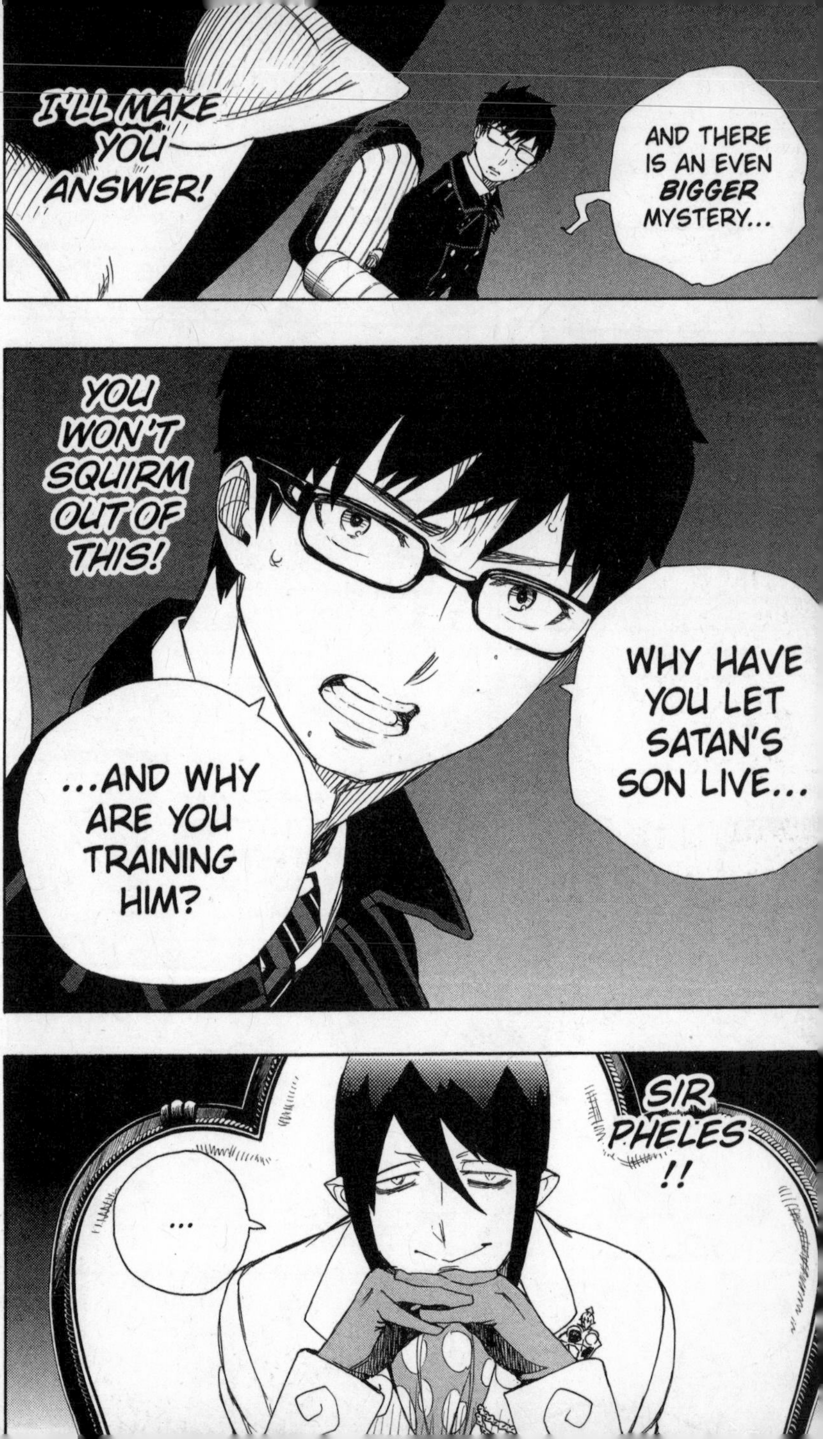
AND THERE IS AN EVEN BIGGER MYSTERY...
I'LL MAKE YOU ANSWER!
YOU WON'T SQUIRM OUT OF THIS!
WHY HAVE YOU LET SATAN'S SON LIVE...
...AND WHY ARE YOU TRAINING HIM?
SIR PHELES!!
...

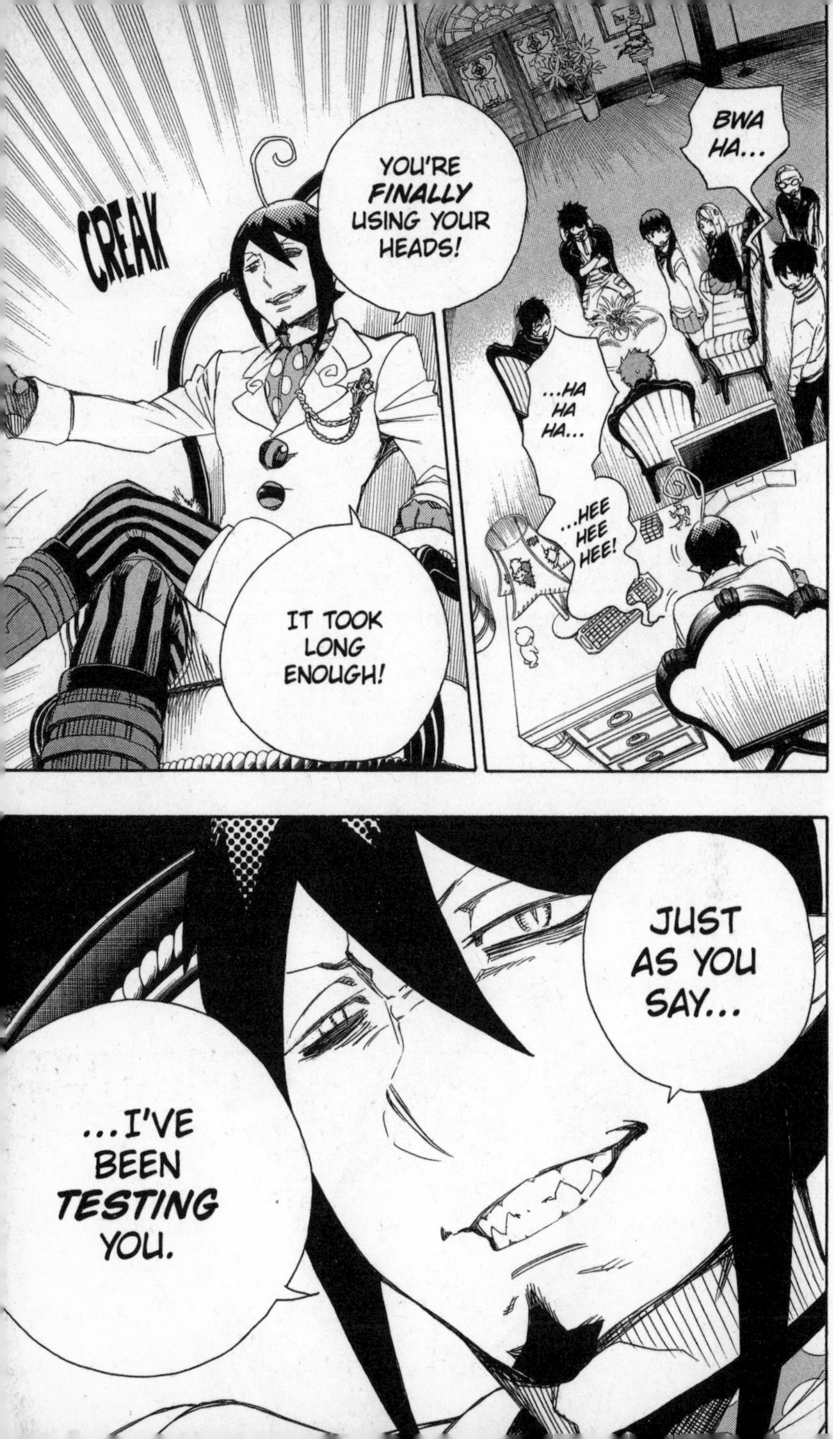
BWA HA...
...HA HA HA...
...HEE HEE HEE!
CREAK
YOU'RE *FINALLY* USING YOUR HEADS!
IT TOOK LONG ENOUGH!
JUST AS YOU SAY...
...I'VE BEEN *TESTING* YOU.

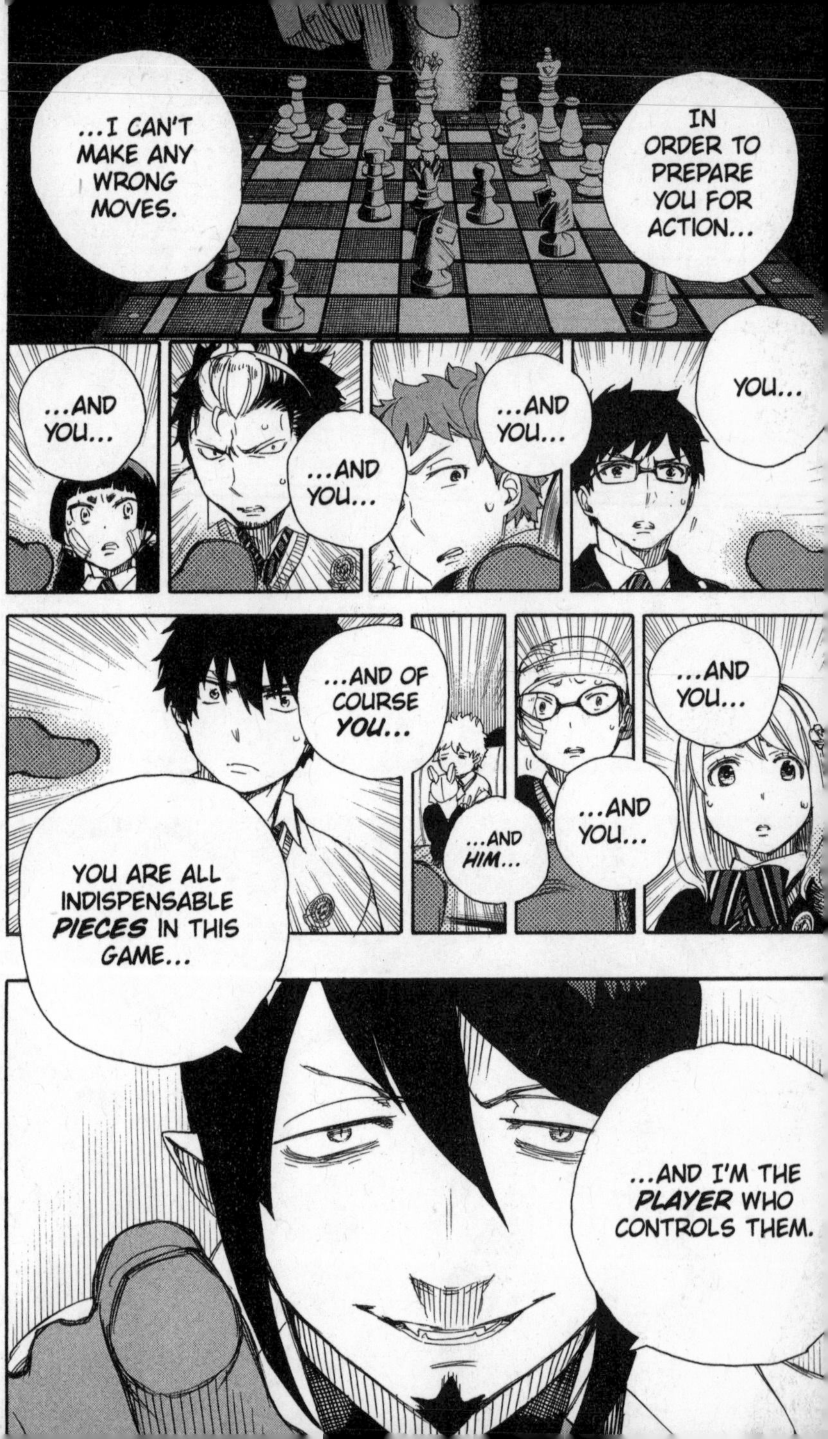
IN ORDER TO PREPARE YOU FOR ACTION...
...I CAN'T MAKE ANY WRONG MOVES.
YOU...
...AND YOU...
...AND YOU...
...AND YOU...
...AND YOU...
...AND YOU...
...AND HIM...
...AND OF COURSE YOU...
YOU ARE ALL INDISPENSABLE PIECES IN THIS GAME...
...AND I'M THE PLAYER WHO CONTROLS THEM.

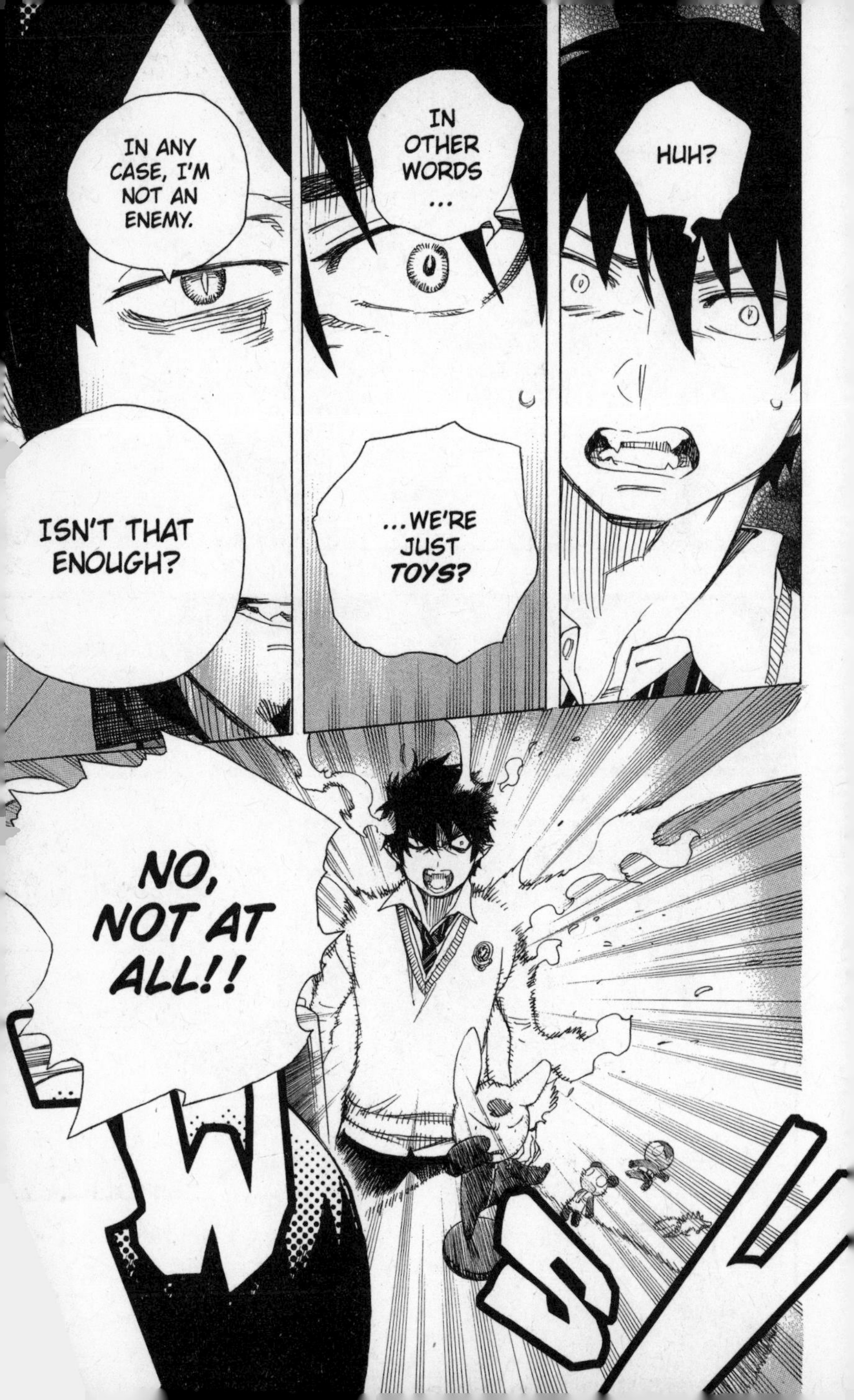
HUH?
IN OTHER WORDS ...
...WE'RE JUST TOYS?
IN ANY CASE, I'M NOT AN ENEMY.
ISN'T THAT ENOUGH?
NO, NOT AT ALL!!

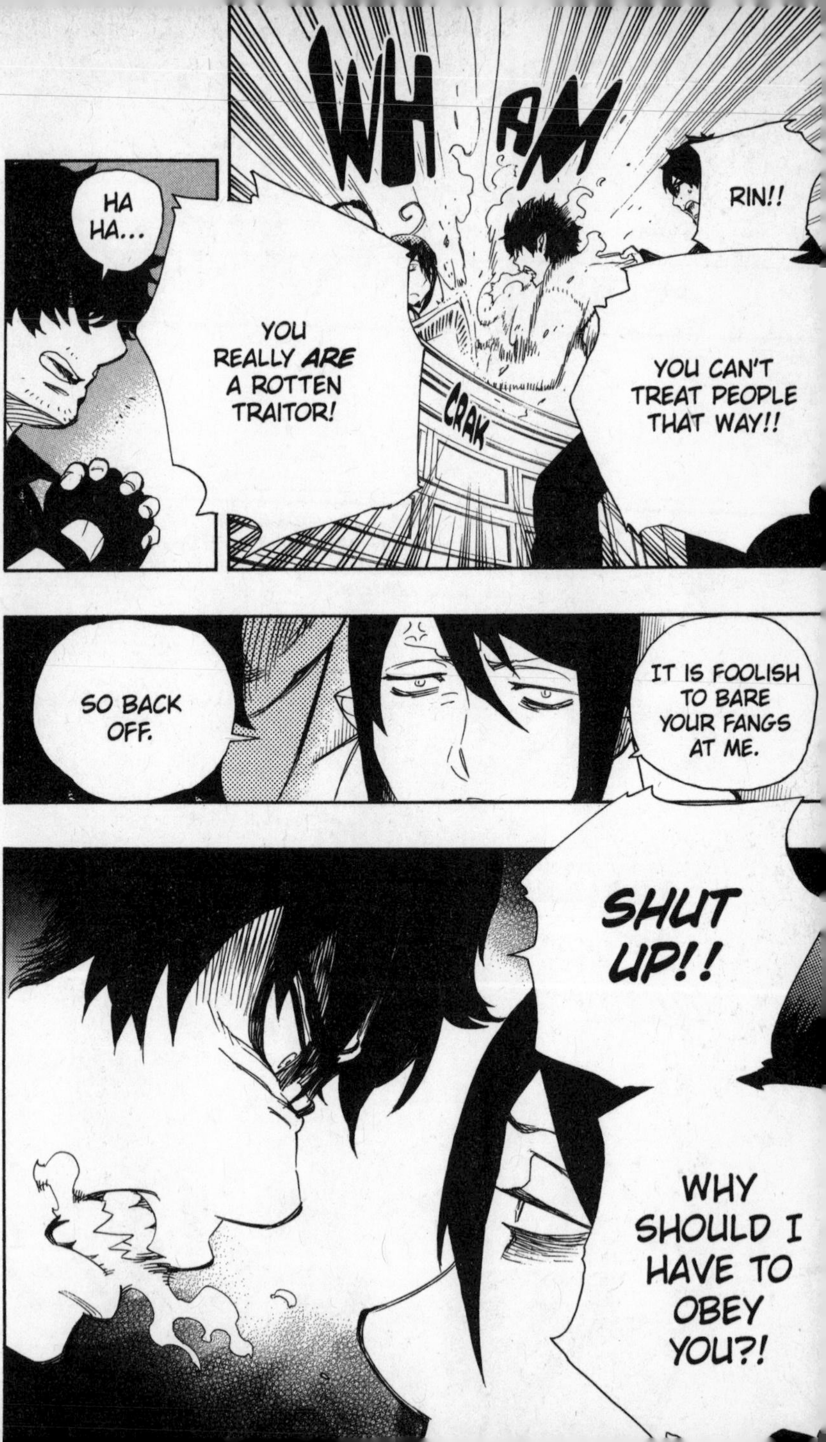
WHAM
RIN!!
YOU CAN'T TREAT PEOPLE THAT WAY!!
YOU REALLY ARE A ROTTEN TRAITOR!
CRAK
HA HA...
IT IS FOOLISH TO BARE YOUR FANGS AT ME.
SO BACK OFF.
SHUT UP!!
WHY SHOULD I HAVE TO OBEY YOU?!

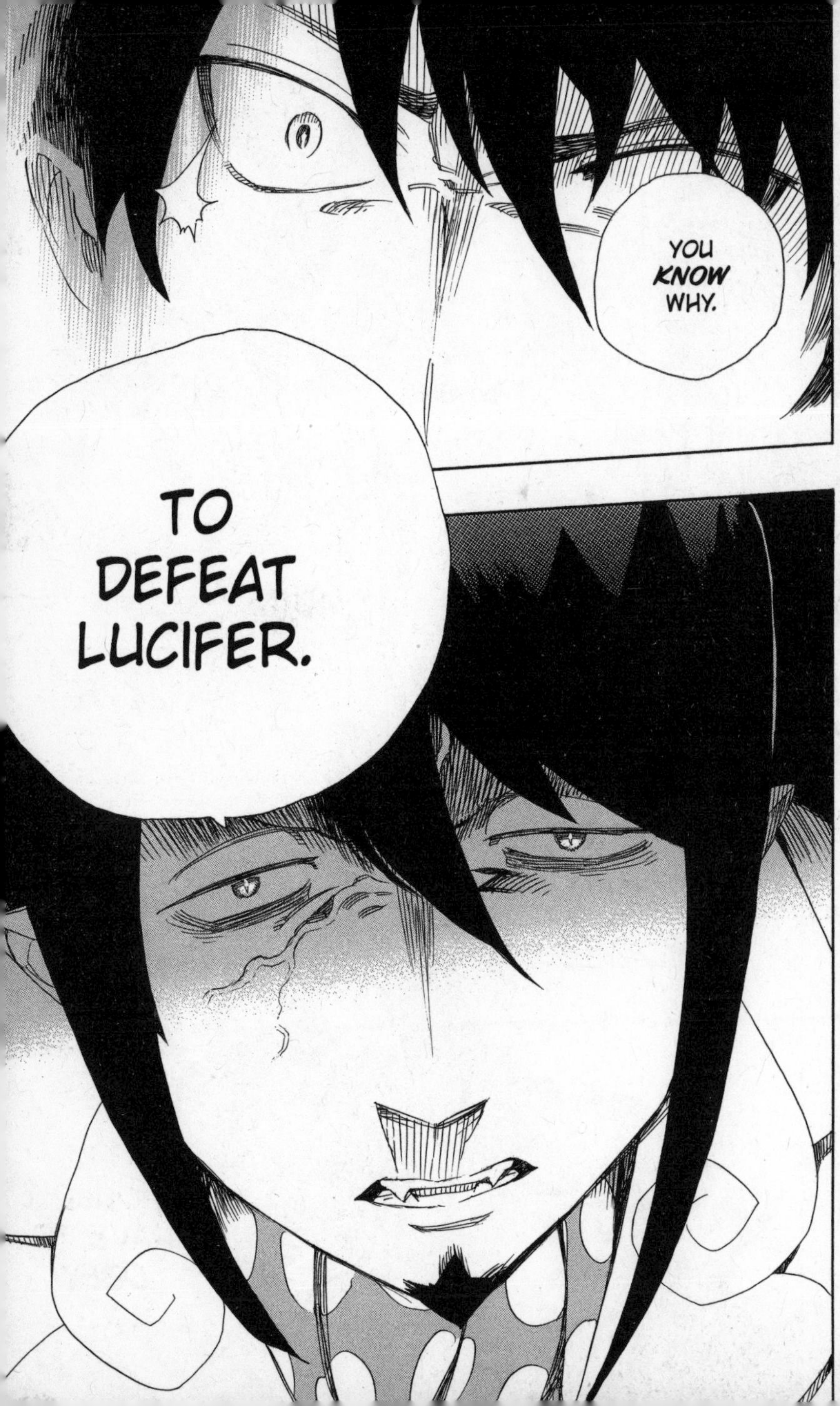
YOU KNOW WHY.
TO DEFEAT LUCIFER.

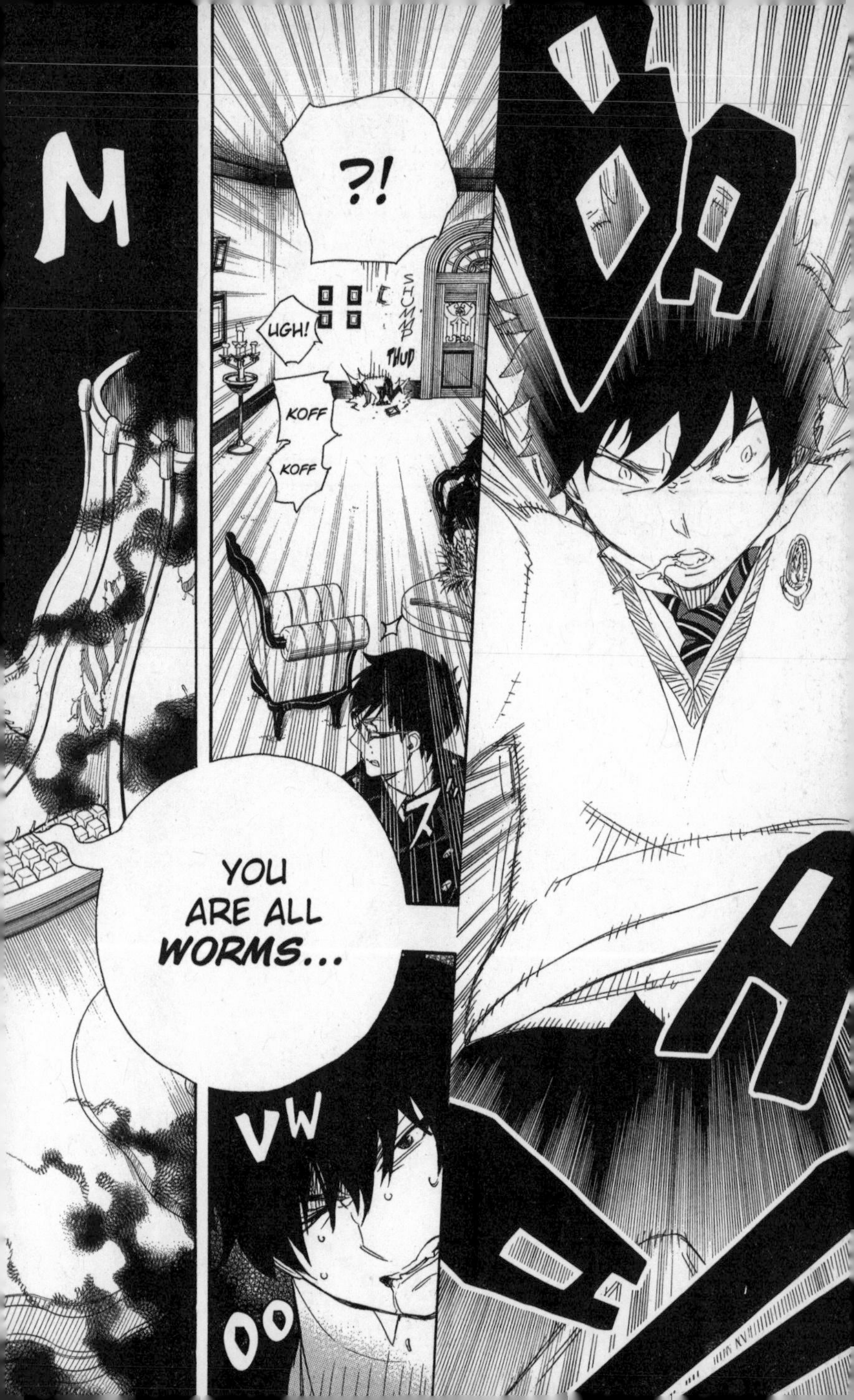
DA
?!
SHUMMP
THUD
UGH!
KOFF
KOFF
YOU ARE ALL WORMS...
VW
OO
M

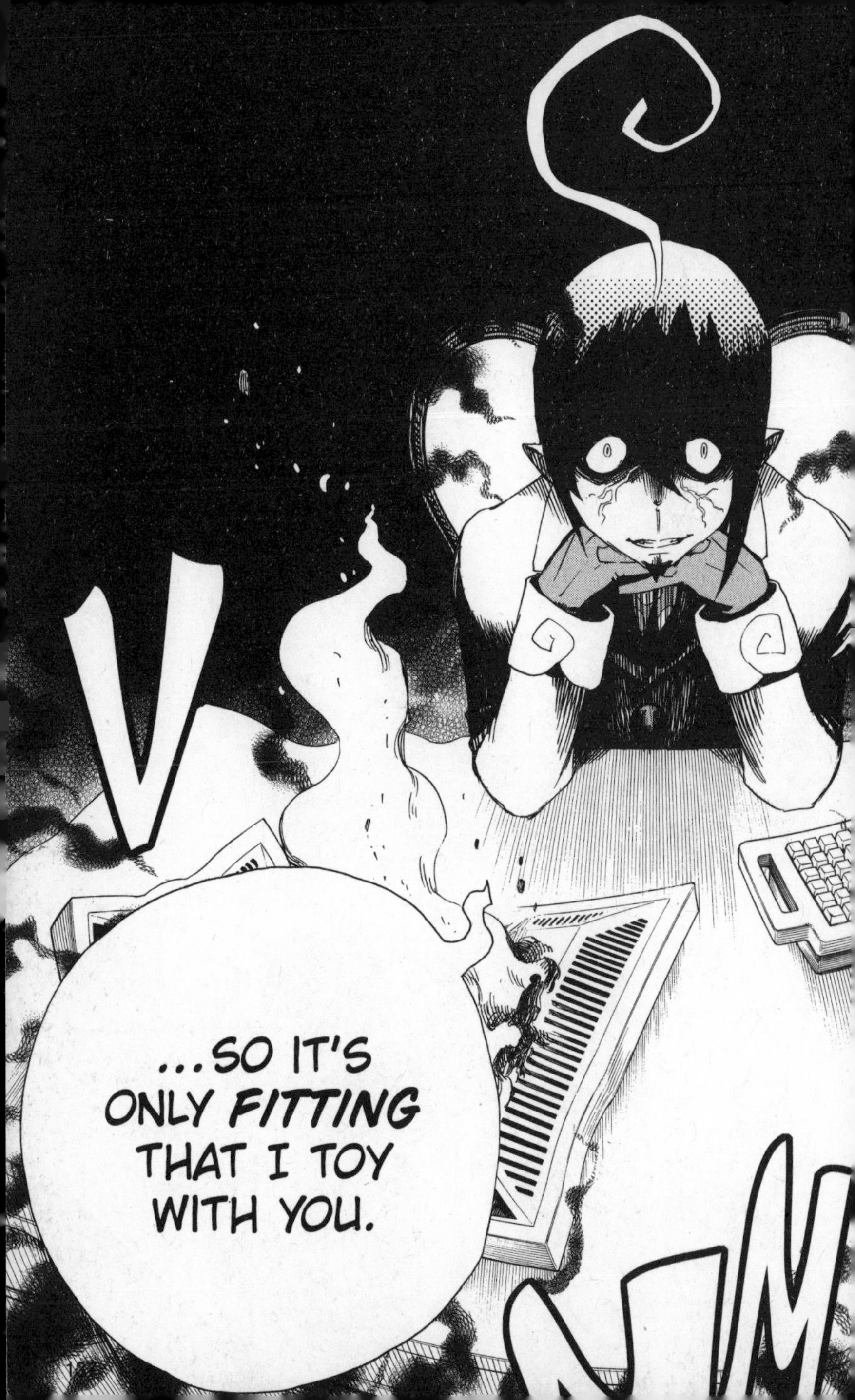
...SO IT'S ONLY *FITTING* THAT I TOY WITH YOU.

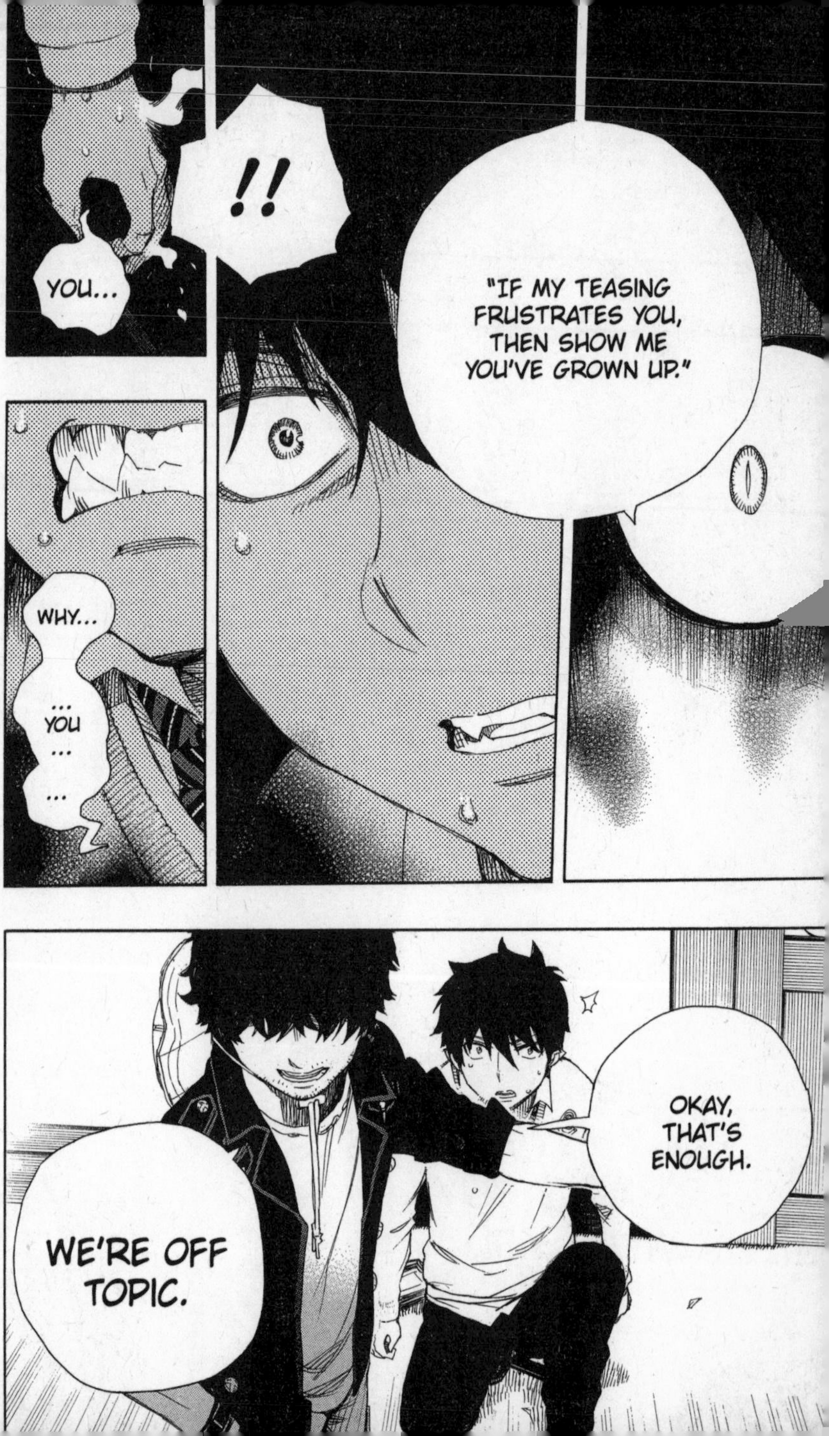
"IF MY TEASING FRUSTRATES YOU, THEN SHOW ME YOU'VE GROWN UP."
!!
YOU...
WHY...
... YOU ... ...
OKAY, THAT'S ENOUGH.
WE'RE OFF TOPIC.

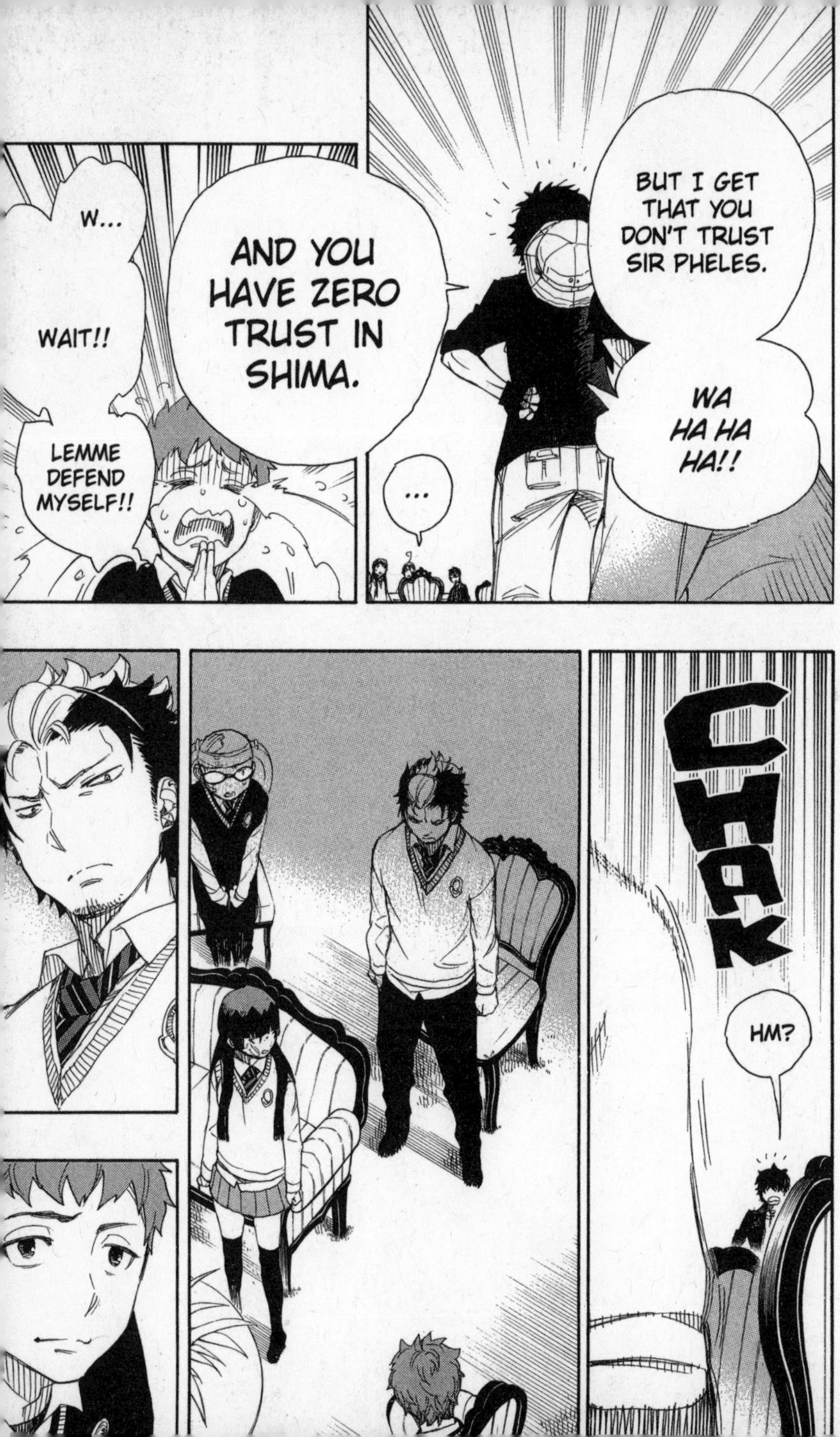
BUT I GET THAT YOU DON'T TRUST SIR PHELES.
WA HA HA HA!!
...
AND YOU HAVE ZERO TRUST IN SHIMA.
W...
WAIT!!
LEMME DEFEND MYSELF!!
CHAK
HM?

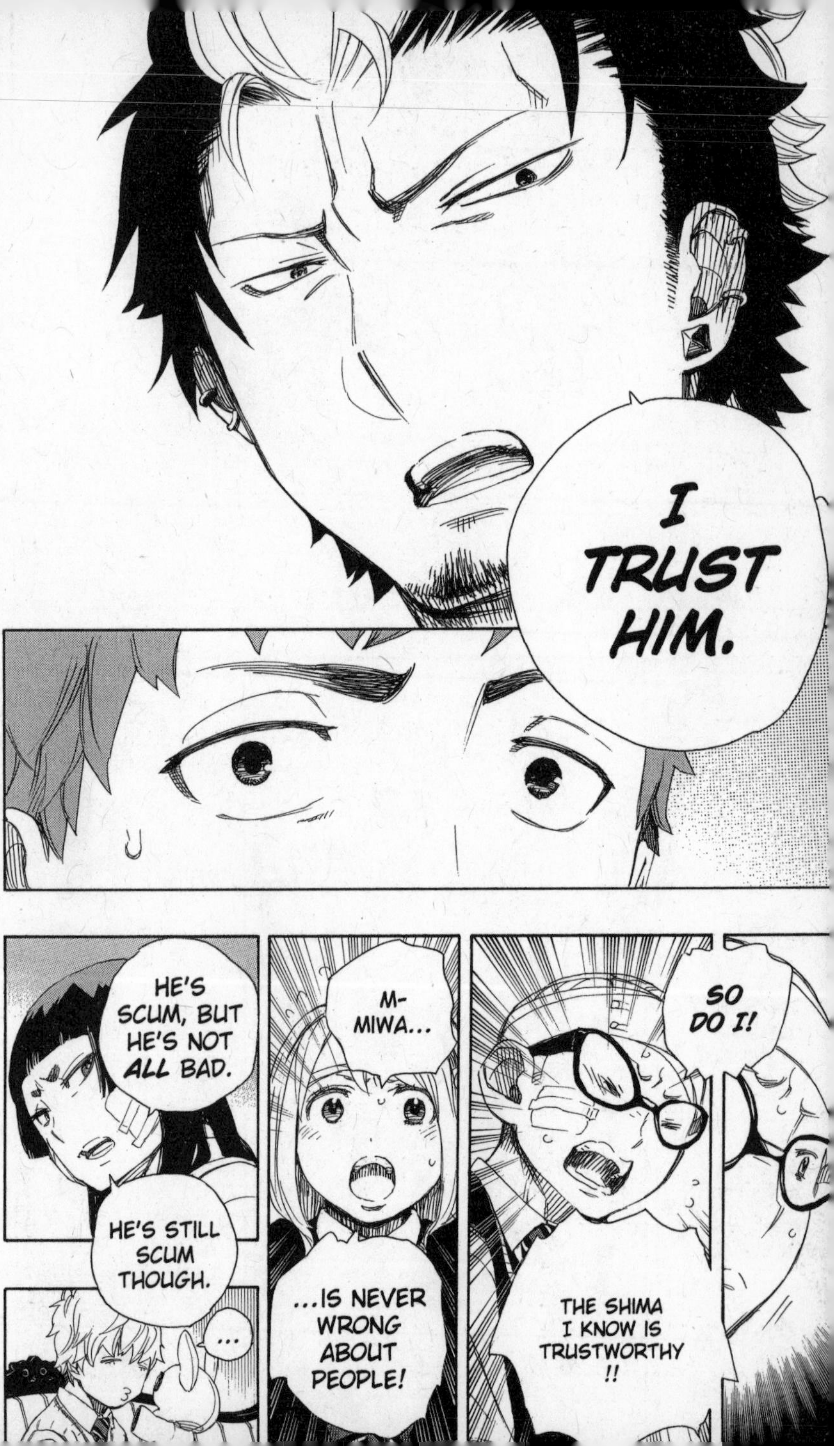
I TRUST HIM.
SO DO I!
THE SHIMA I KNOW IS TRUSTWORTHY !!
M-MIWA...
...IS NEVER WRONG ABOUT PEOPLE!
HE'S SCUM, BUT HE'S NOT ALL BAD.
HE'S STILL SCUM THOUGH.
...

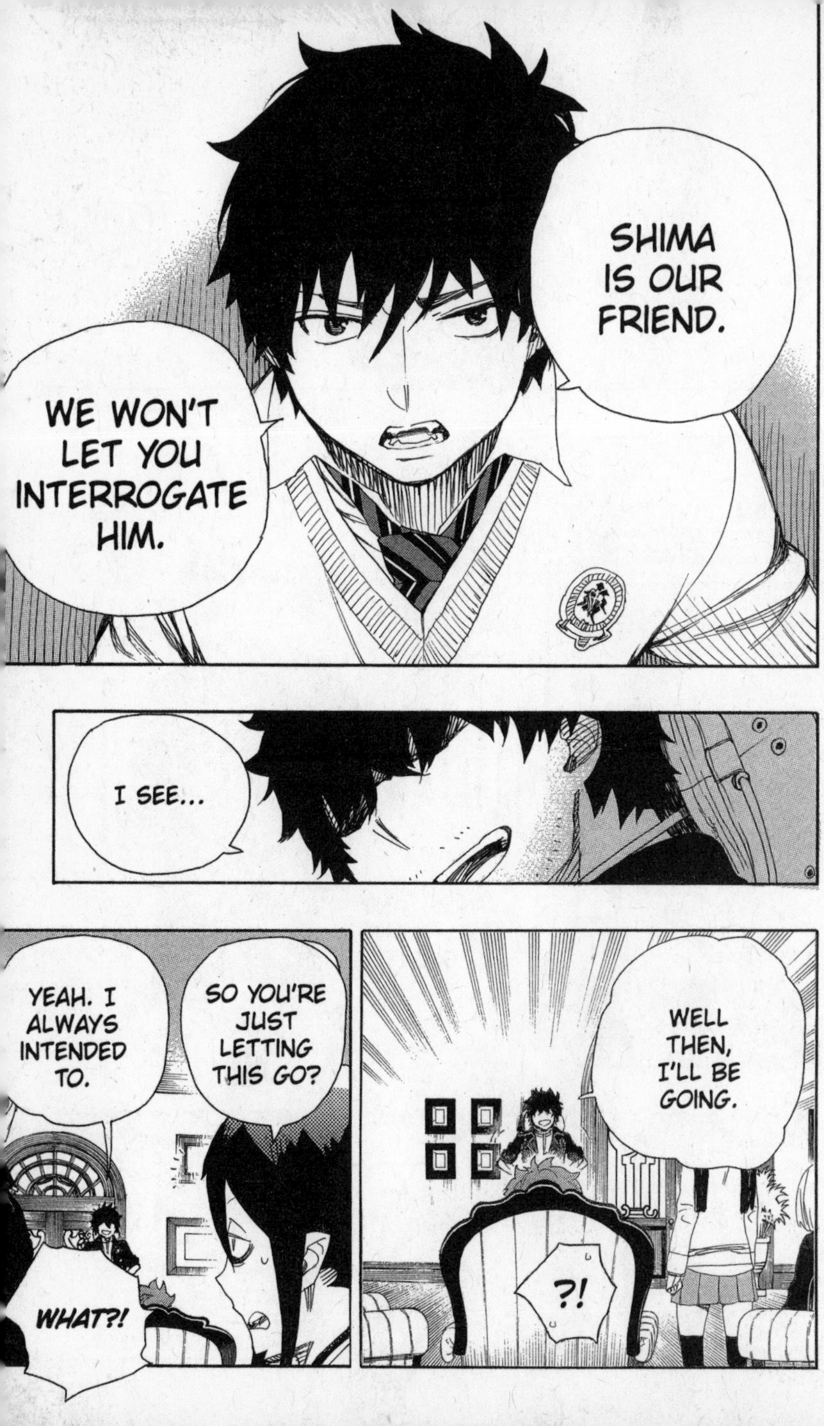
SHIMA IS OUR FRIEND.
WE WON'T LET YOU INTERROGATE HIM.
I SEE...
WELL THEN, I'LL BE GOING.
?!
SO YOU'RE JUST LETTING THIS GO?
YEAH. I ALWAYS INTENDED TO.
WHAT?!

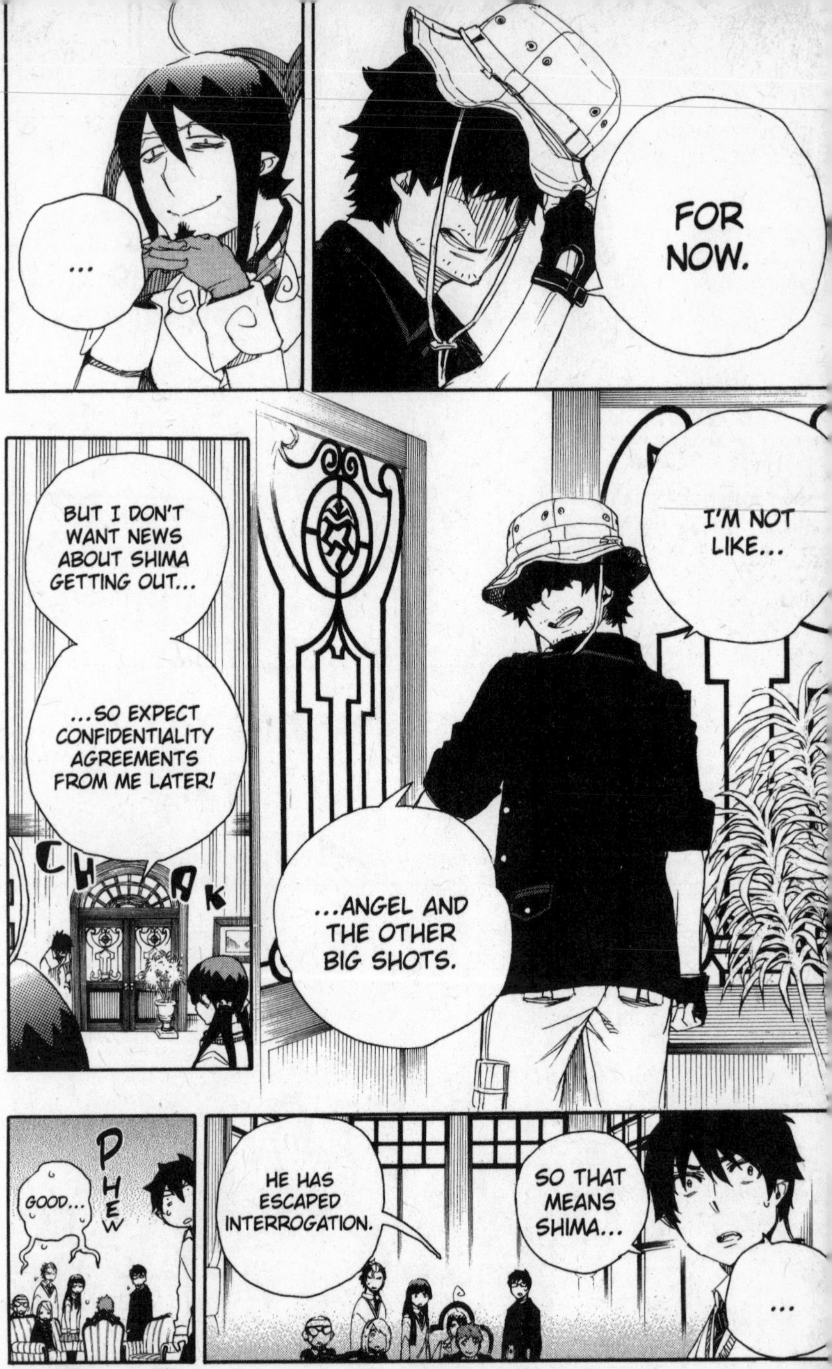
FOR NOW.
...
I'M NOT LIKE...
...ANGEL AND THE OTHER BIG SHOTS.
BUT I DON'T WANT NEWS ABOUT SHIMA GETTING OUT...
...SO EXPECT CONFIDENTIALITY AGREEMENTS FROM ME LATER!
CHAK
...
SO THAT MEANS SHIMA...
HE HAS ESCAPED INTERROGATION.
PHEW
GOOD...

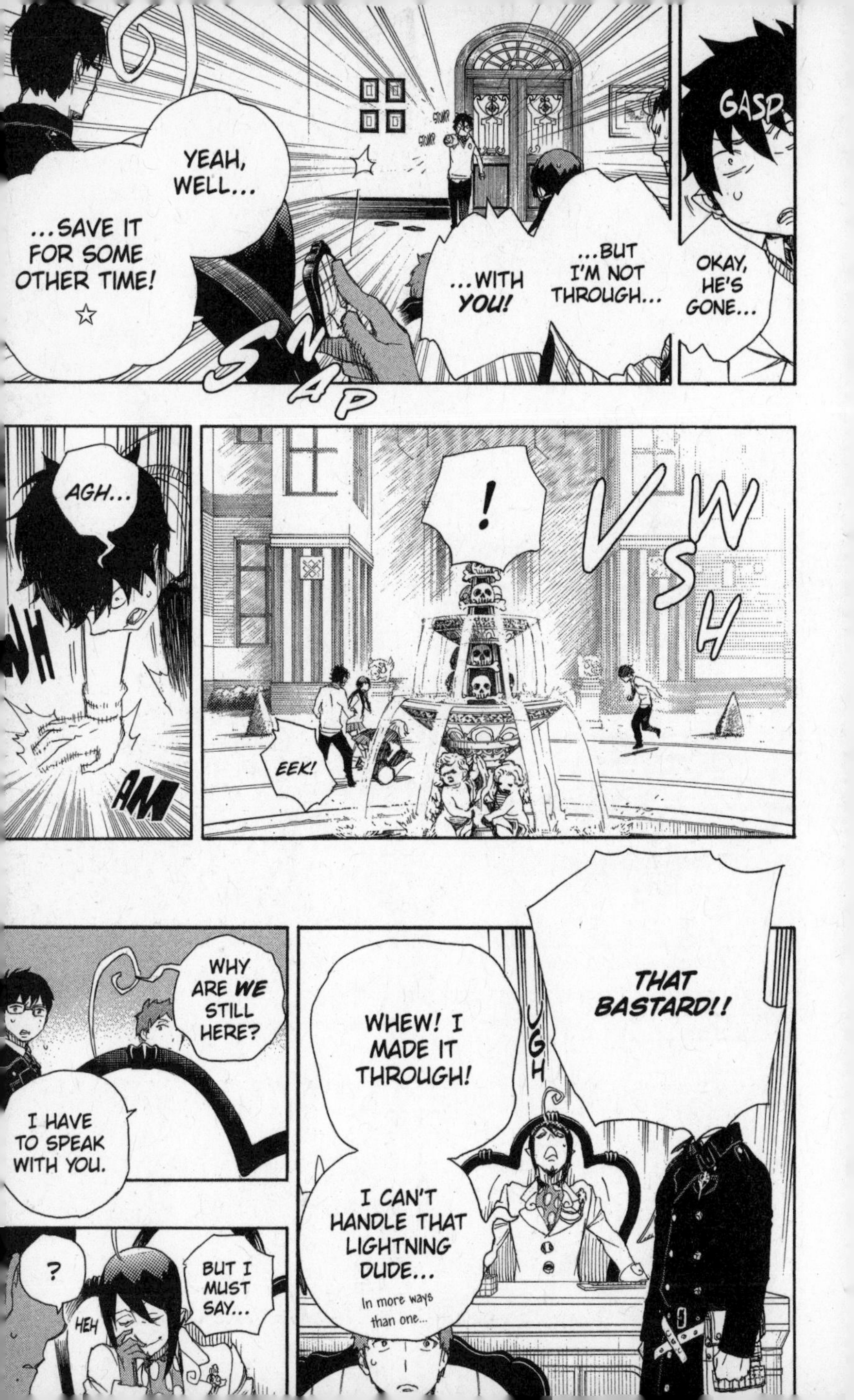
GASP
OKAY, HE'S GONE...
...BUT I'M NOT THROUGH...
...WITH YOU!
STOMP
STOMP
YEAH, WELL...
...SAVE IT FOR SOME OTHER TIME! ☆
SNAP
!
VWSH
EEK!
AGH...
NH
AM
THAT BASTARD!!
UGH
WHEW! I MADE IT THROUGH!
I CAN'T HANDLE THAT LIGHTNING DUDE...
In more ways than one...
WHY ARE WE STILL HERE?
I HAVE TO SPEAK WITH YOU.
BUT I MUST SAY...
?
HEH

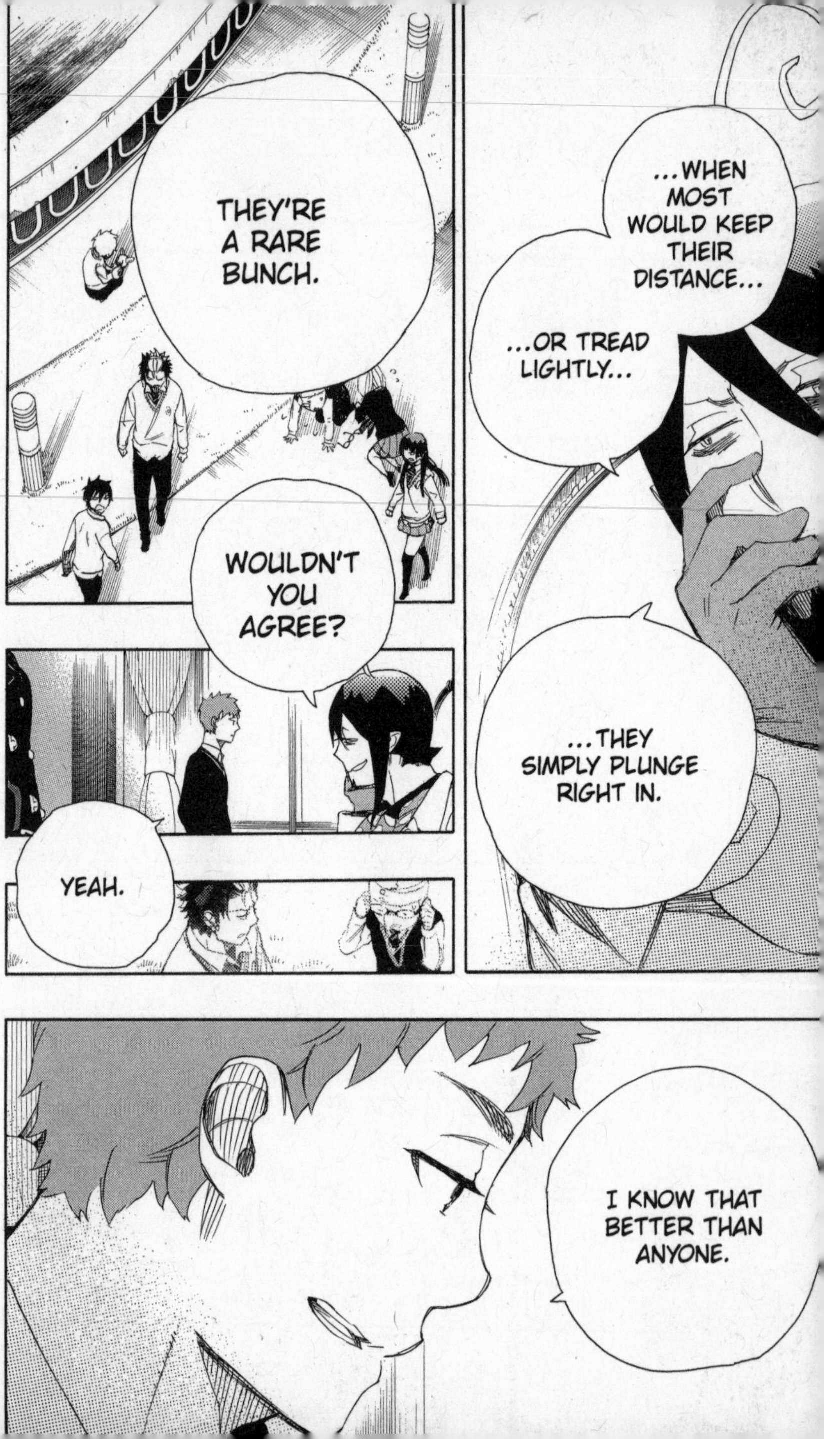
...WHEN MOST WOULD KEEP THEIR DISTANCE...
...OR TREAD LIGHTLY...
...THEY SIMPLY PLUNGE RIGHT IN.
THEY'RE A RARE BUNCH.
WOULDN'T YOU AGREE?
YEAH.
I KNOW THAT BETTER THAN ANYONE.

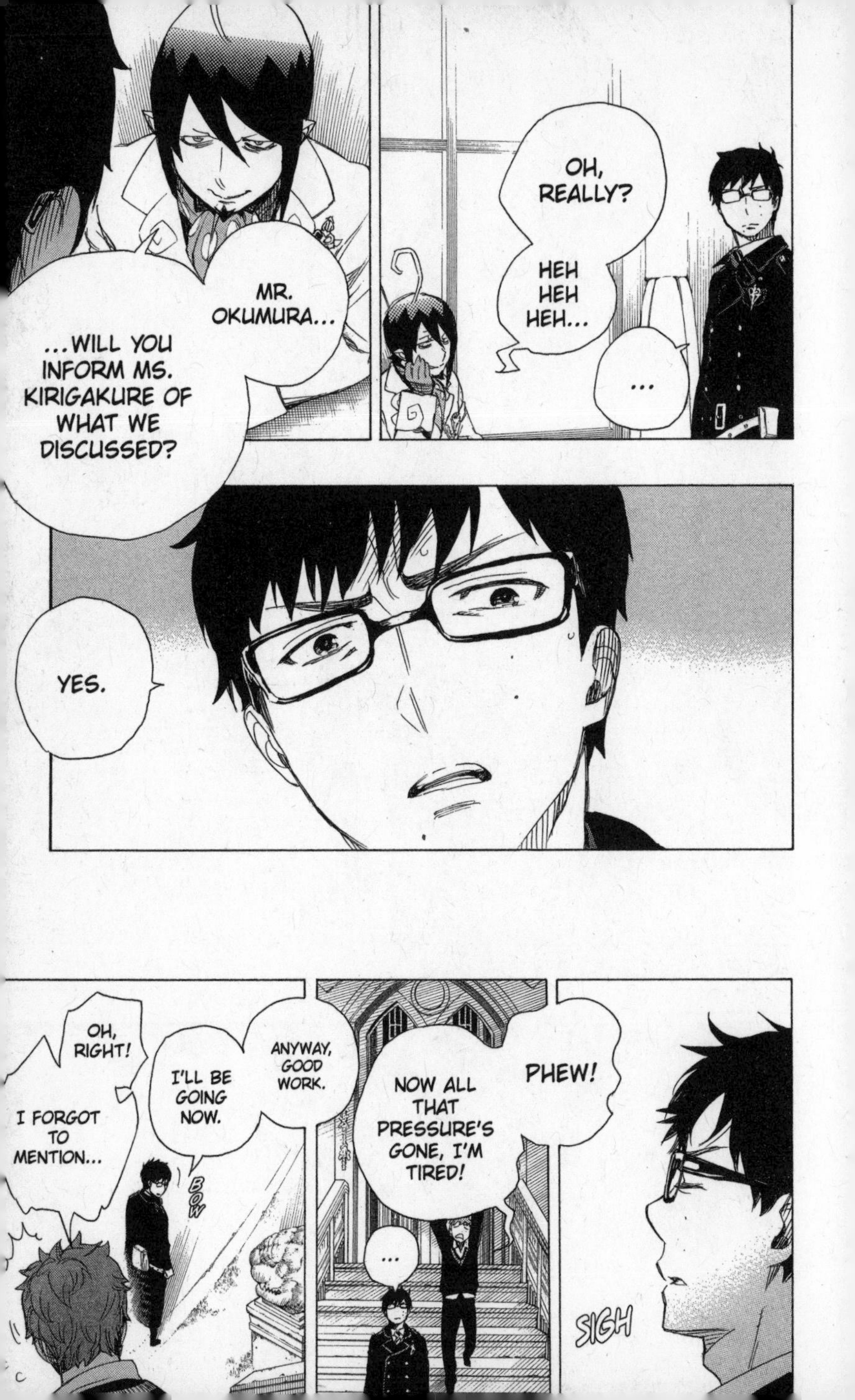
OH, REALLY?
HEH HEH HEH...
...
MR. OKUMURA...
...WILL YOU INFORM MS. KIRIGAKURE OF WHAT WE DISCUSSED?
YES.
PHEW!
SIGH
NOW ALL THAT PRESSURE'S GONE, I'M TIRED!
...
ANYWAY, GOOD WORK.
I'LL BE GOING NOW.
BOW
OH, RIGHT!
I FORGOT TO MENTION...

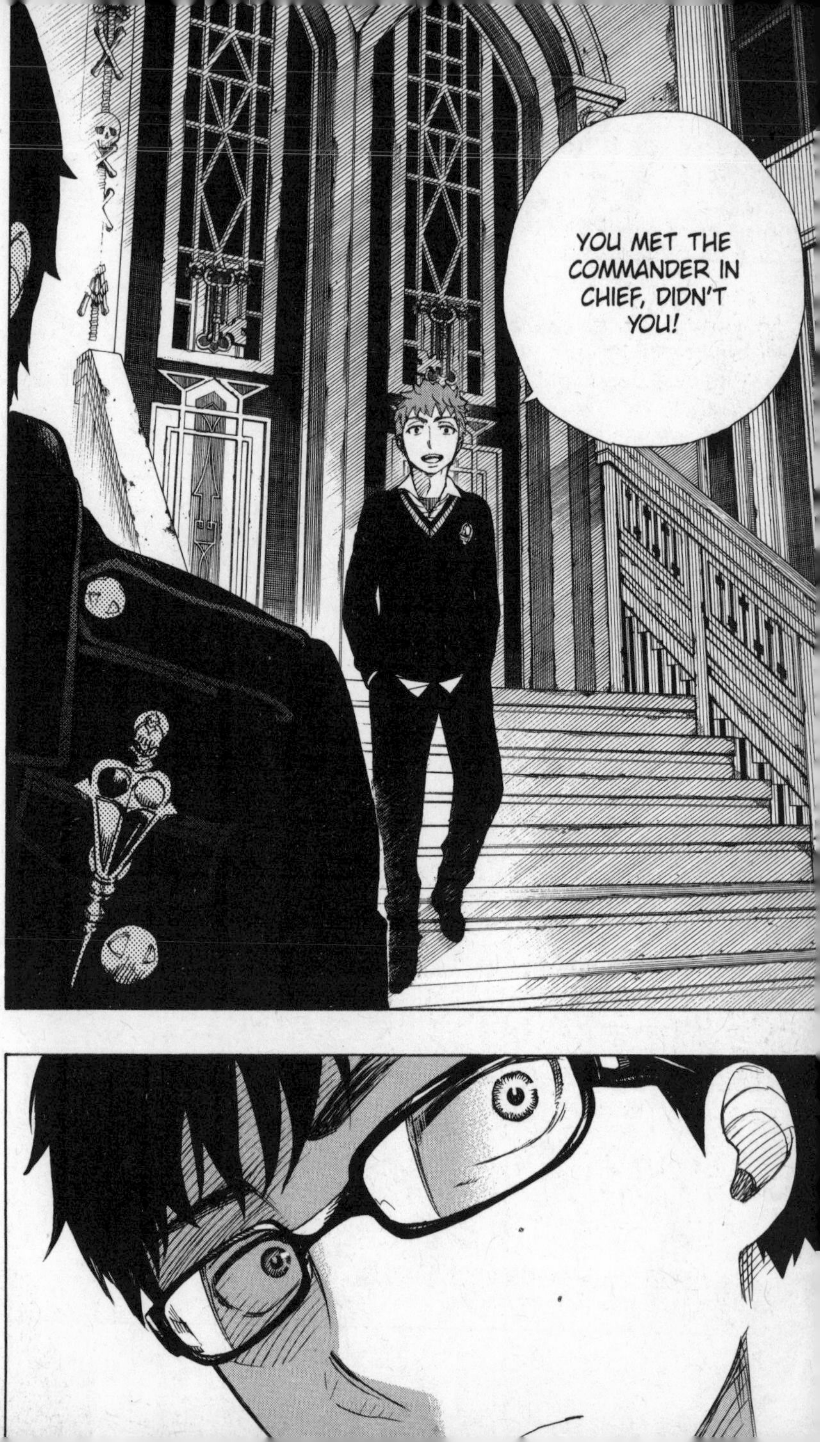
YOU MET THE COMMANDER IN CHIEF, DIDN'T YOU!

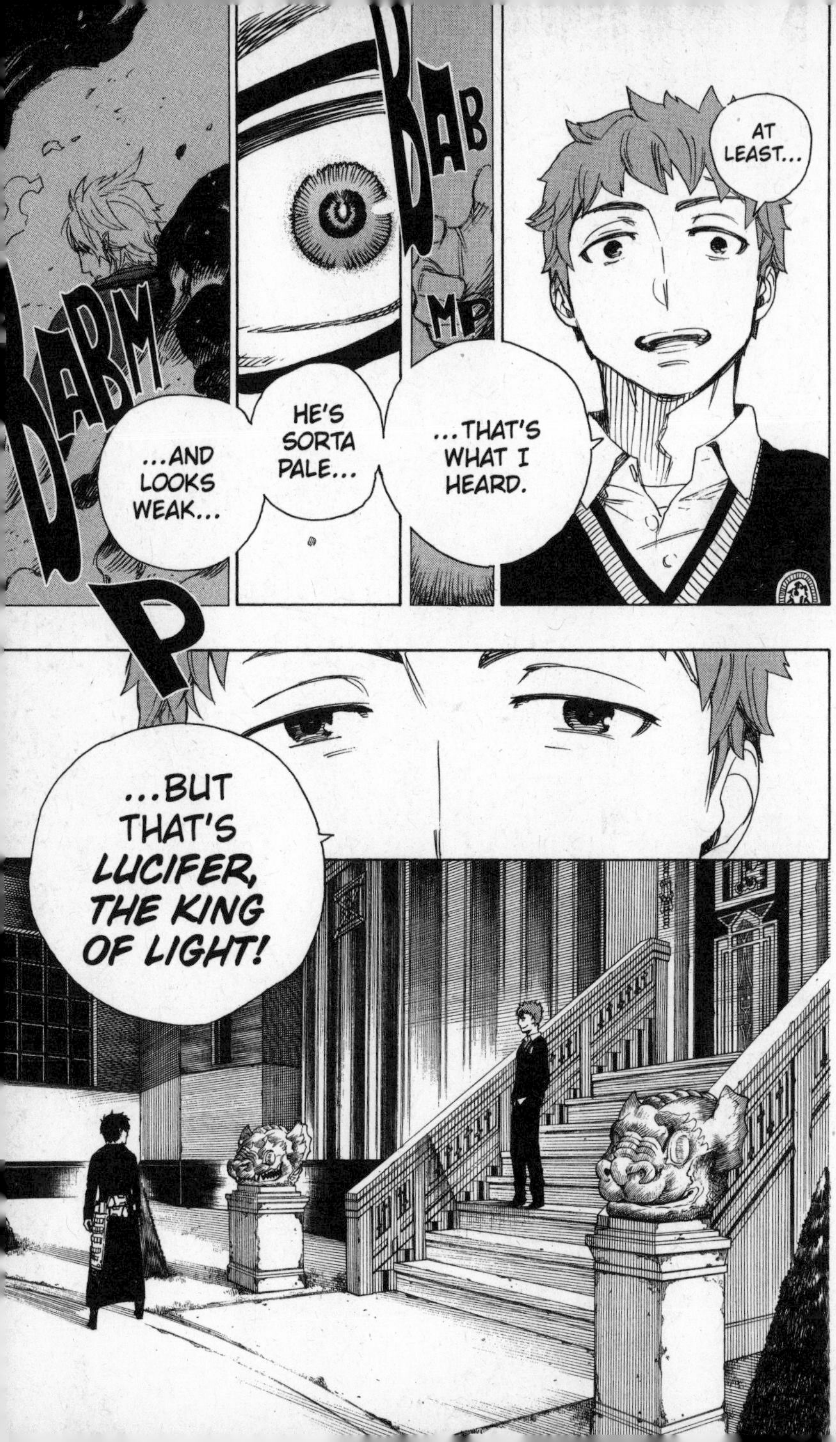
AT LEAST...
...THAT'S WHAT I HEARD.
DABMP
HE'S SORTA PALE...
...AND LOOKS WEAK...
DABMP
...BUT THAT'S *LUCIFER, THE KING OF LIGHT!*

Blue Exorcist Chapter 66: Pink Spider: Part 2

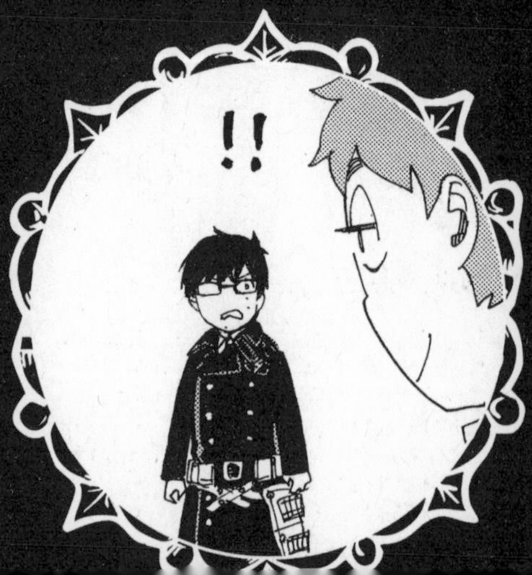
!!

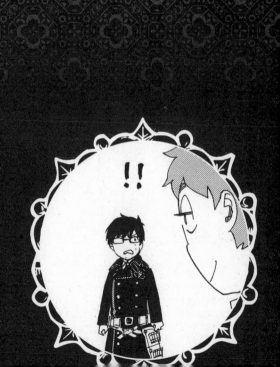

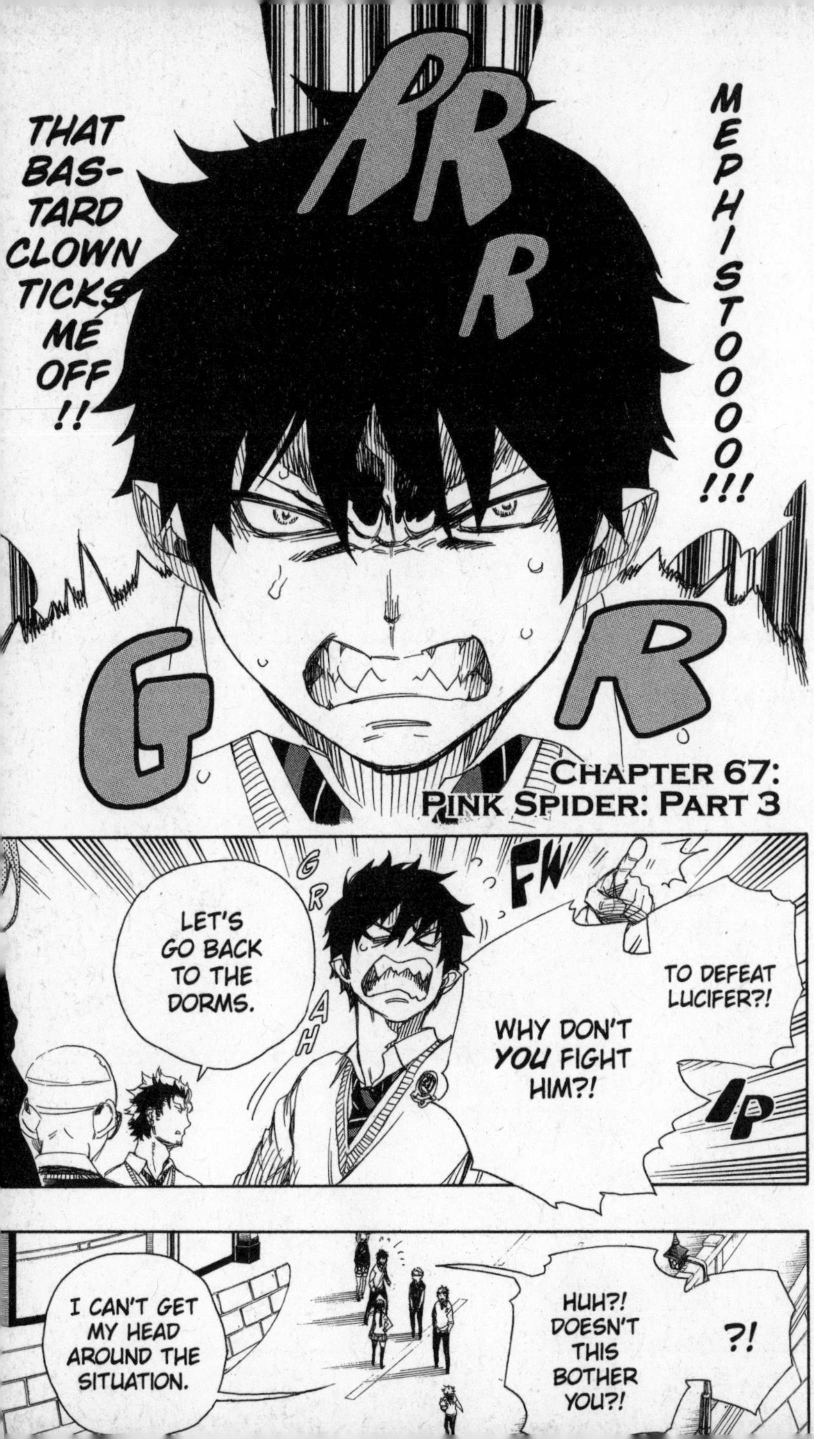
MEPHISTOOOOO!!!
RRR
THAT BASTARD CLOWN TICKS ME OFF!!
GR
CHAPTER 67: PINK SPIDER: PART 3
TO DEFEAT LUCIFER?!
WHY DON'T YOU FIGHT HIM?!
FWIP
GRAH
LET'S GO BACK TO THE DORMS.
?!
HUH?! DOESN'T THIS BOTHER YOU?!
I CAN'T GET MY HEAD AROUND THE SITUATION.

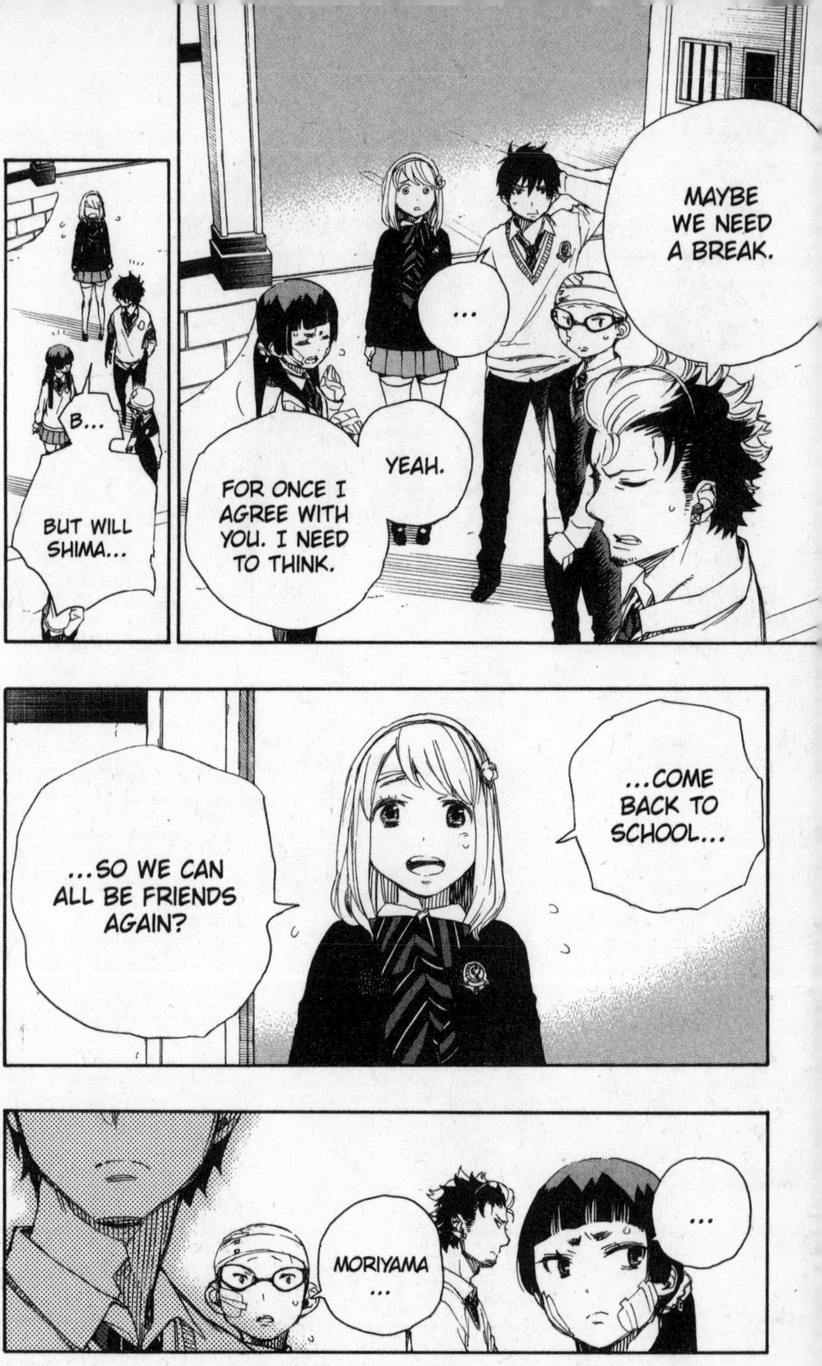
MAYBE WE NEED A BREAK.
...
YEAH.
FOR ONCE I AGREE WITH YOU. I NEED TO THINK.
B...
BUT WILL SHIMA...
...COME BACK TO SCHOOL...
...SO WE CAN ALL BE FRIENDS AGAIN?
...
MORIYAMA ...

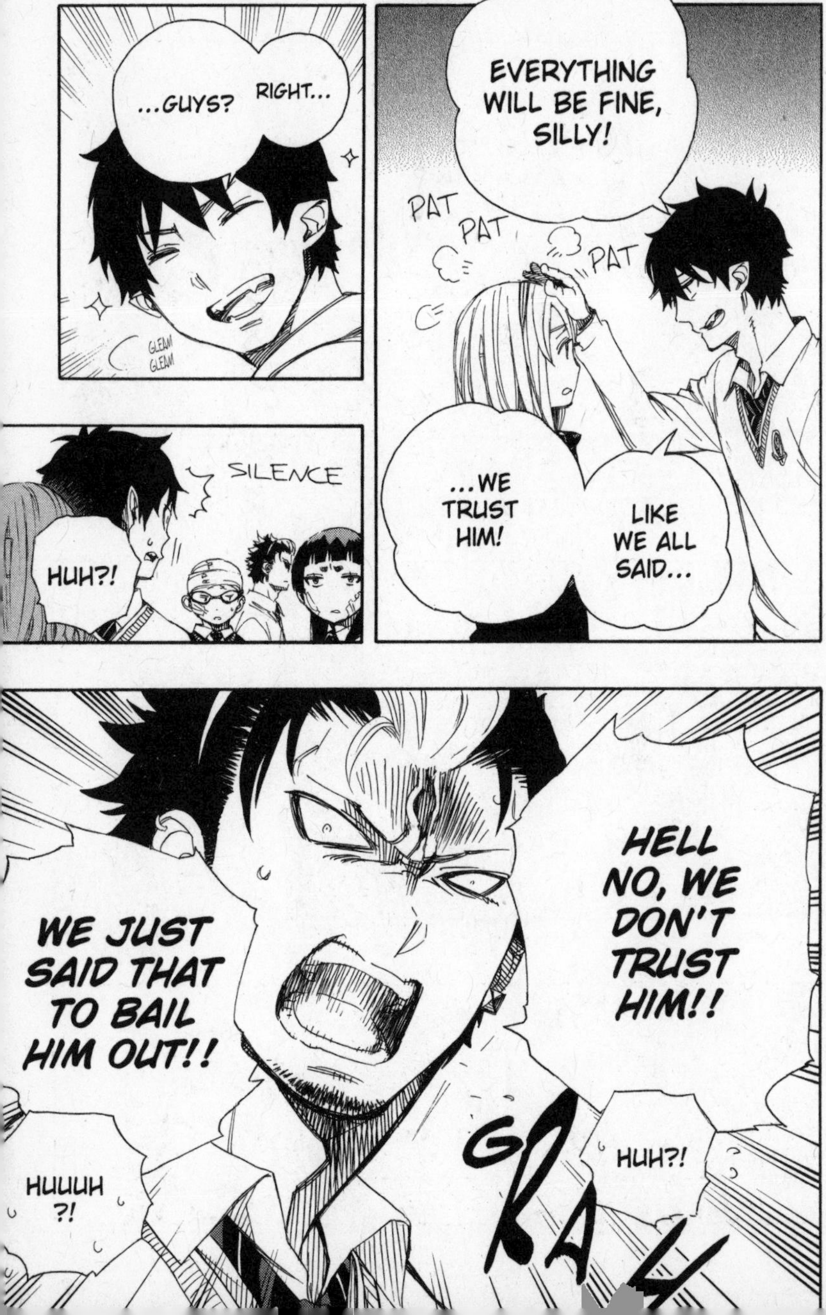
EVERYTHING WILL BE FINE, SILLY!
PAT
PAT
PAT
LIKE WE ALL SAID...
...WE TRUST HIM!
RIGHT...
...GUYS?
GLEAM GLEAM
SILENCE
HUH?!
HELL NO, WE DON'T TRUST HIM!!
WE JUST SAID THAT TO BAIL HIM OUT!!
HUH?!
GRAH
HUUUH ?!

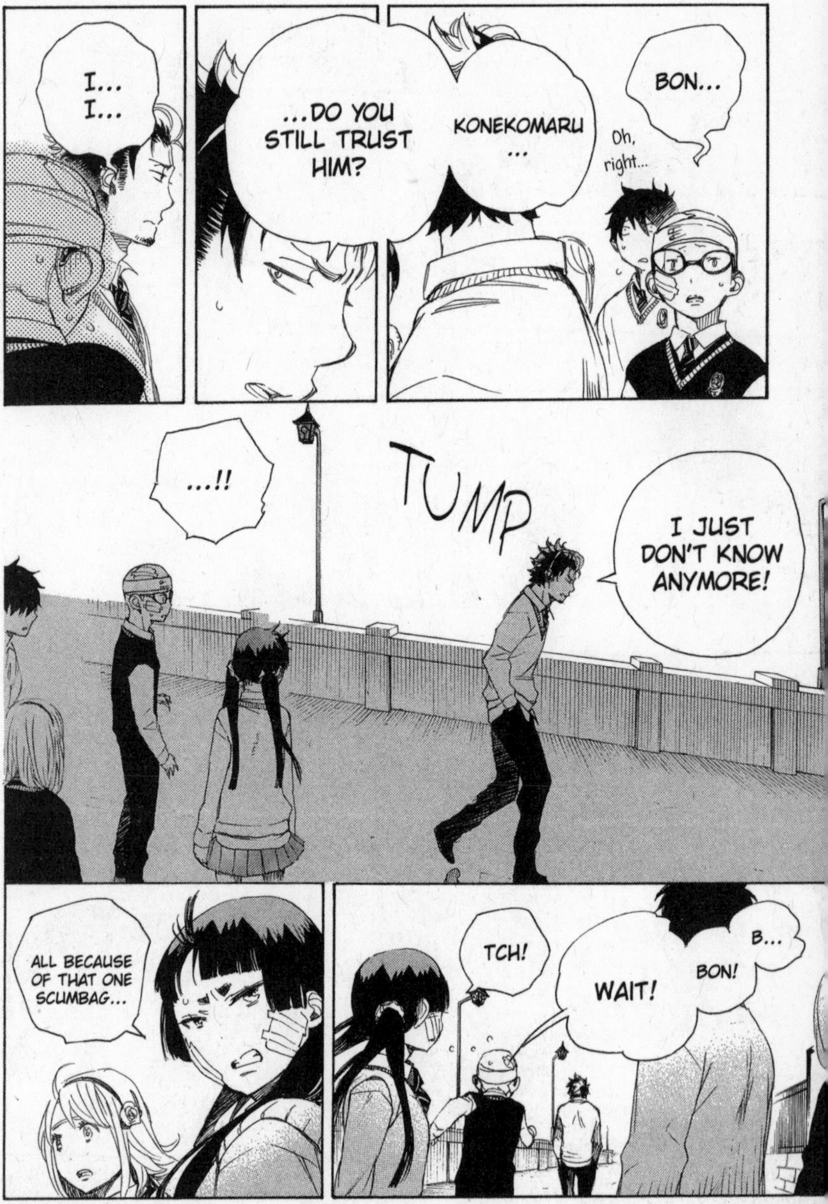
BON...
Oh, right...
KONEKOMARU ...
...DO YOU STILL TRUST HIM?
I... I...
I JUST DON'T KNOW ANYMORE!
TUMP
...!!
B... BON!
WAIT!
TCH!
ALL BECAUSE OF THAT ONE SCUMBAG...

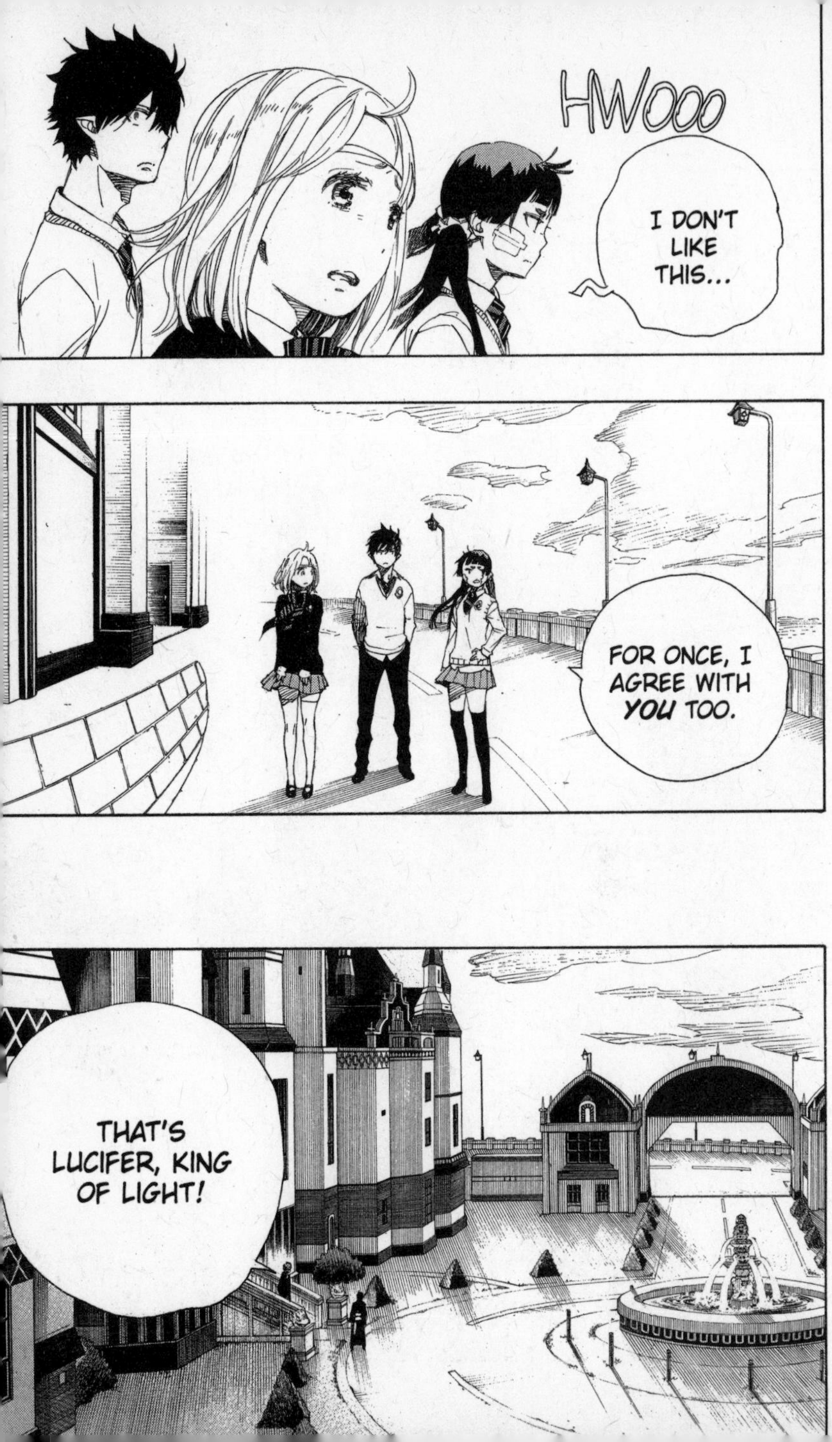
HWOOO
I DON'T LIKE THIS...
FOR ONCE, I AGREE WITH YOU TOO.
THAT'S LUCIFER, KING OF LIGHT!

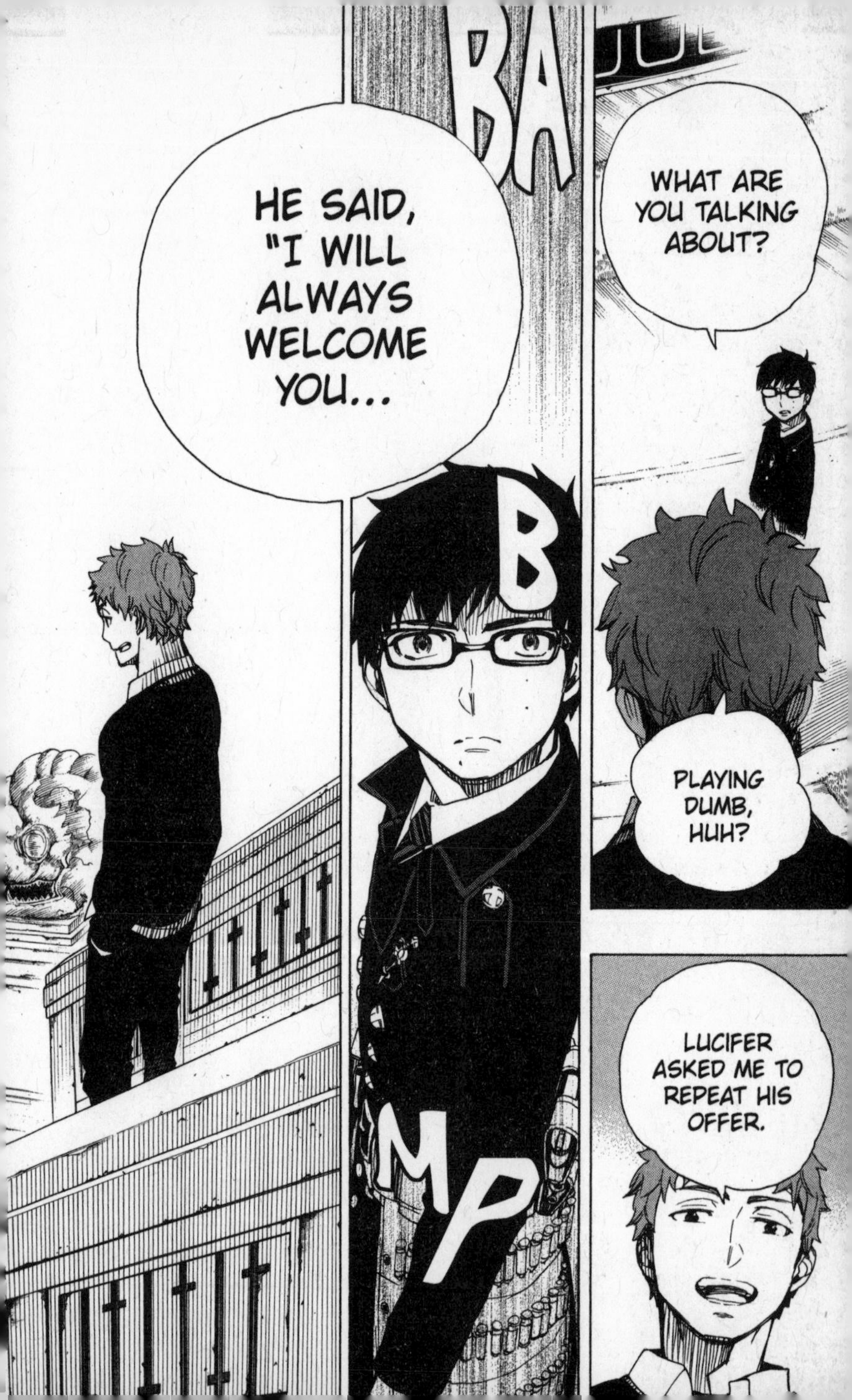
WHAT ARE YOU TALKING ABOUT?
PLAYING DUMB, HUH?
LUCIFER ASKED ME TO REPEAT HIS OFFER.
BA
B
MP
HE SAID, "I WILL ALWAYS WELCOME YOU...

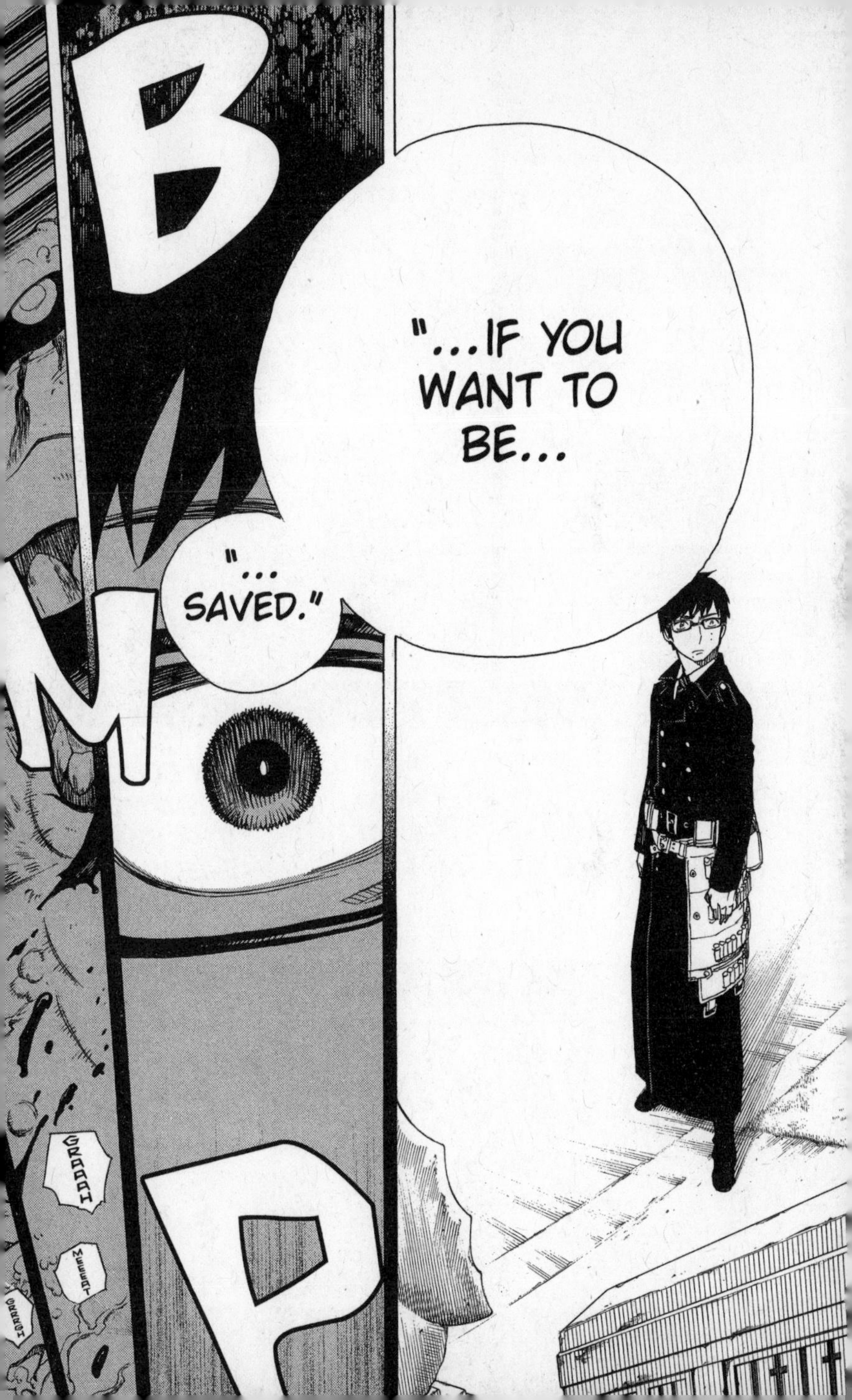
"...IF YOU WANT TO BE...
"... SAVED."
BOMP
GRAAAH
MEEEAT
GRRRGH

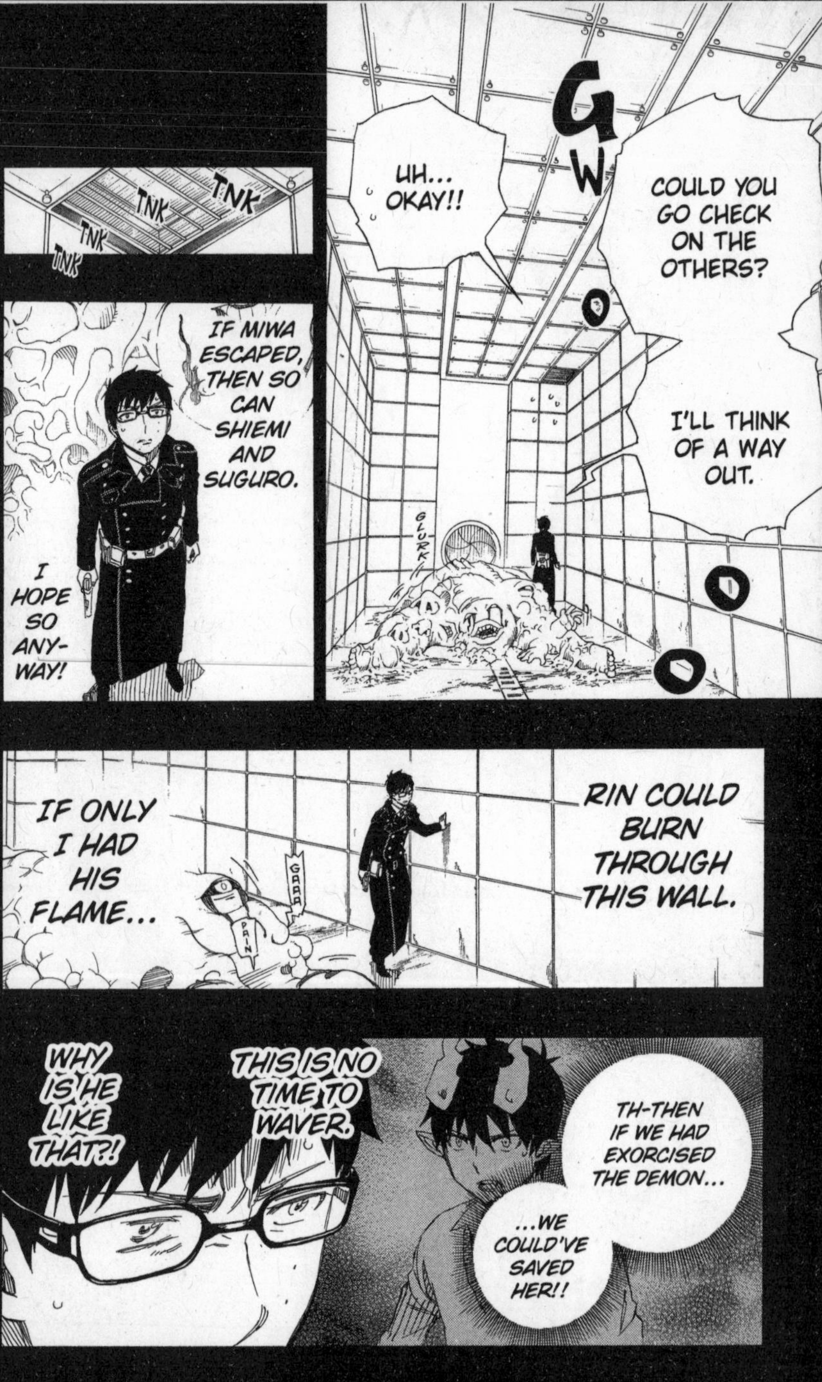
GW
COULD YOU GO CHECK ON THE OTHERS?
I'LL THINK OF A WAY OUT.
UH... OKAY!!
GLURK
TNK
TNK
TNK
TNK
IF MIWA ESCAPED, THEN SO CAN SHIEMI AND SUGURO.
I HOPE SO ANYWAY!
RIN COULD BURN THROUGH THIS WALL.
GAAA
PAIN
IF ONLY I HAD HIS FLAME...
TH-THEN IF WE HAD EXORCISED THE DEMON...
...WE COULD'VE SAVED HER!!
THIS IS NO TIME TO WAVER.
WHY IS HE LIKE THAT?!

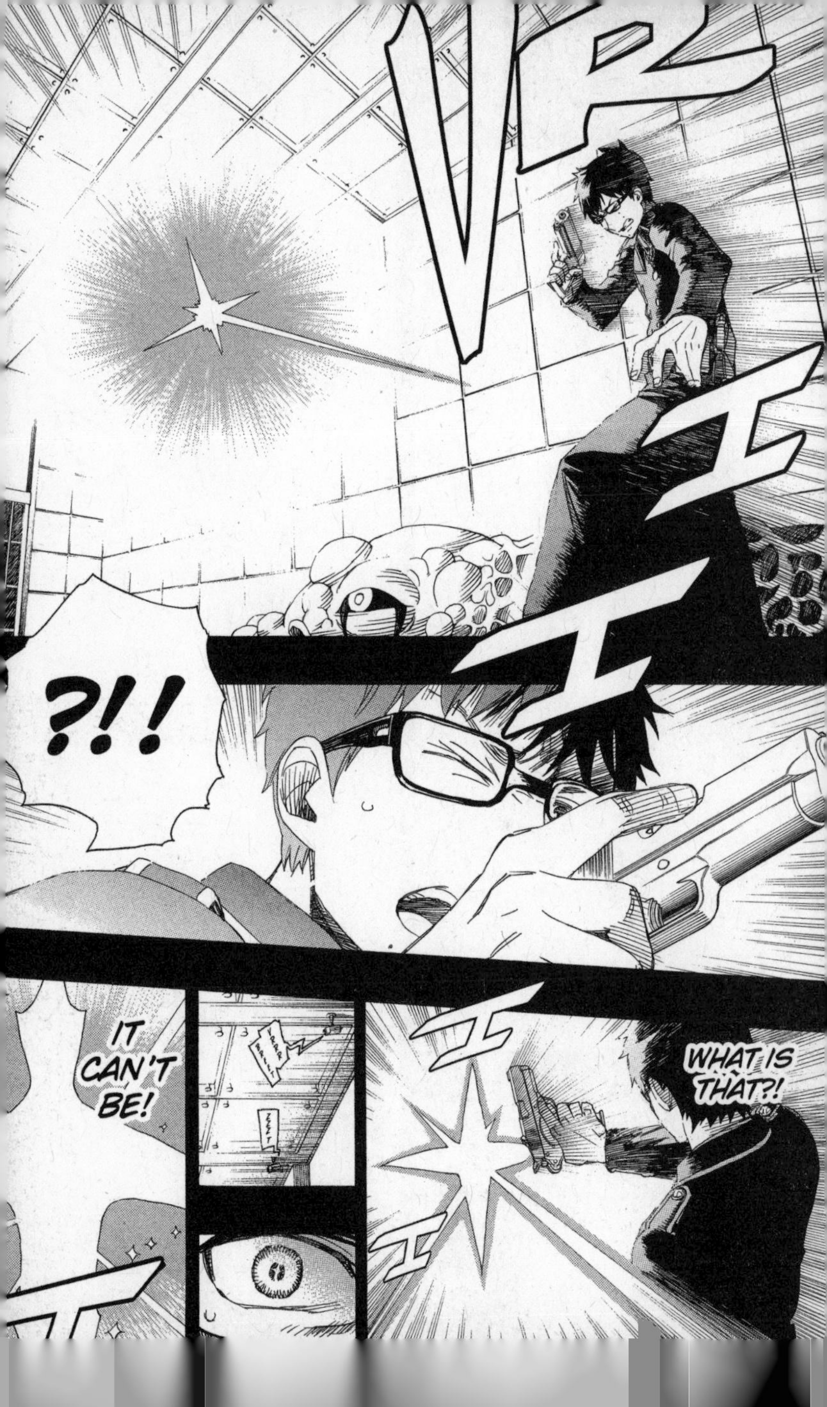
VRII
?!!
WHAT IS THAT?!
IT CAN'T BE!

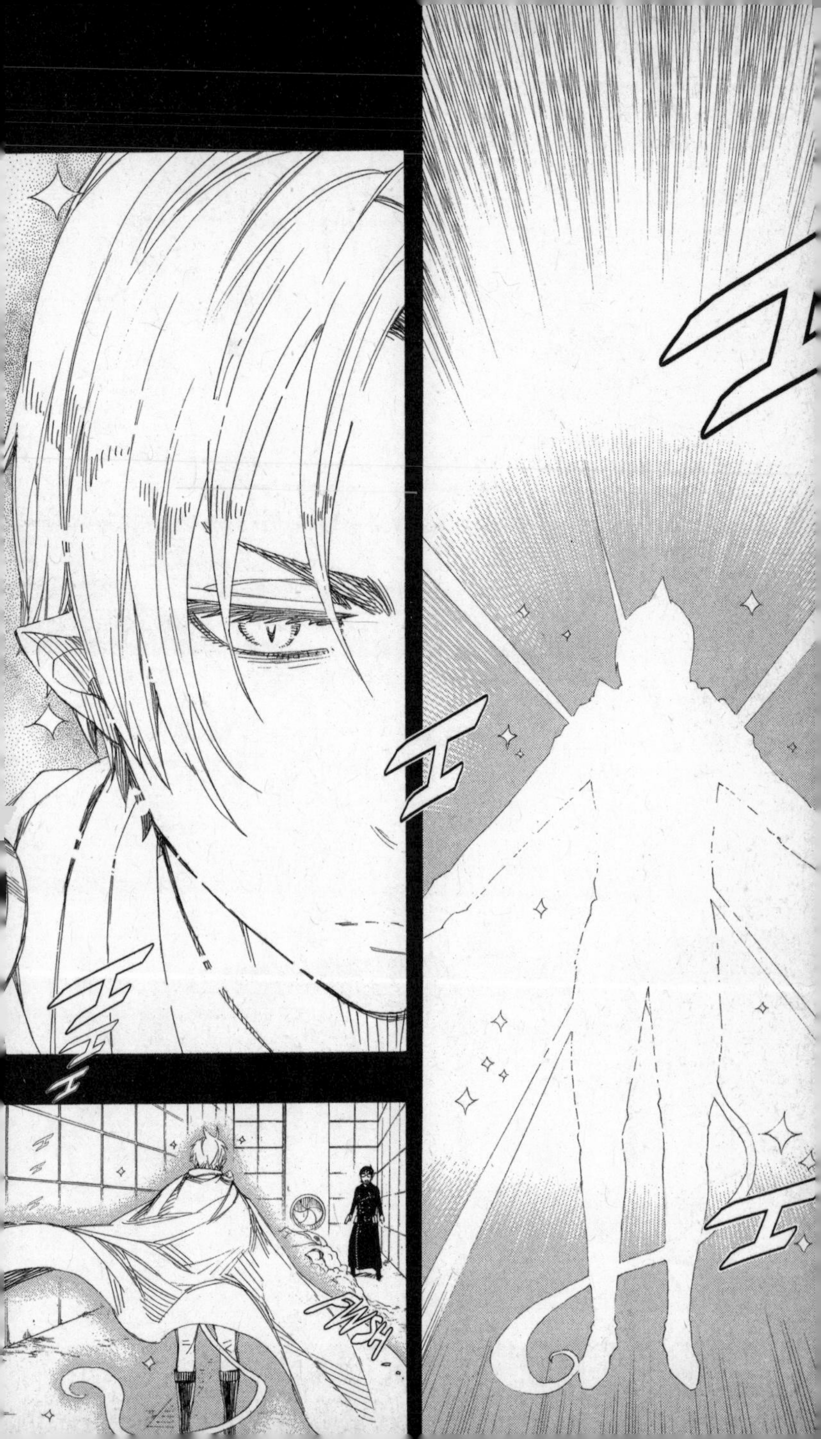
FWSH

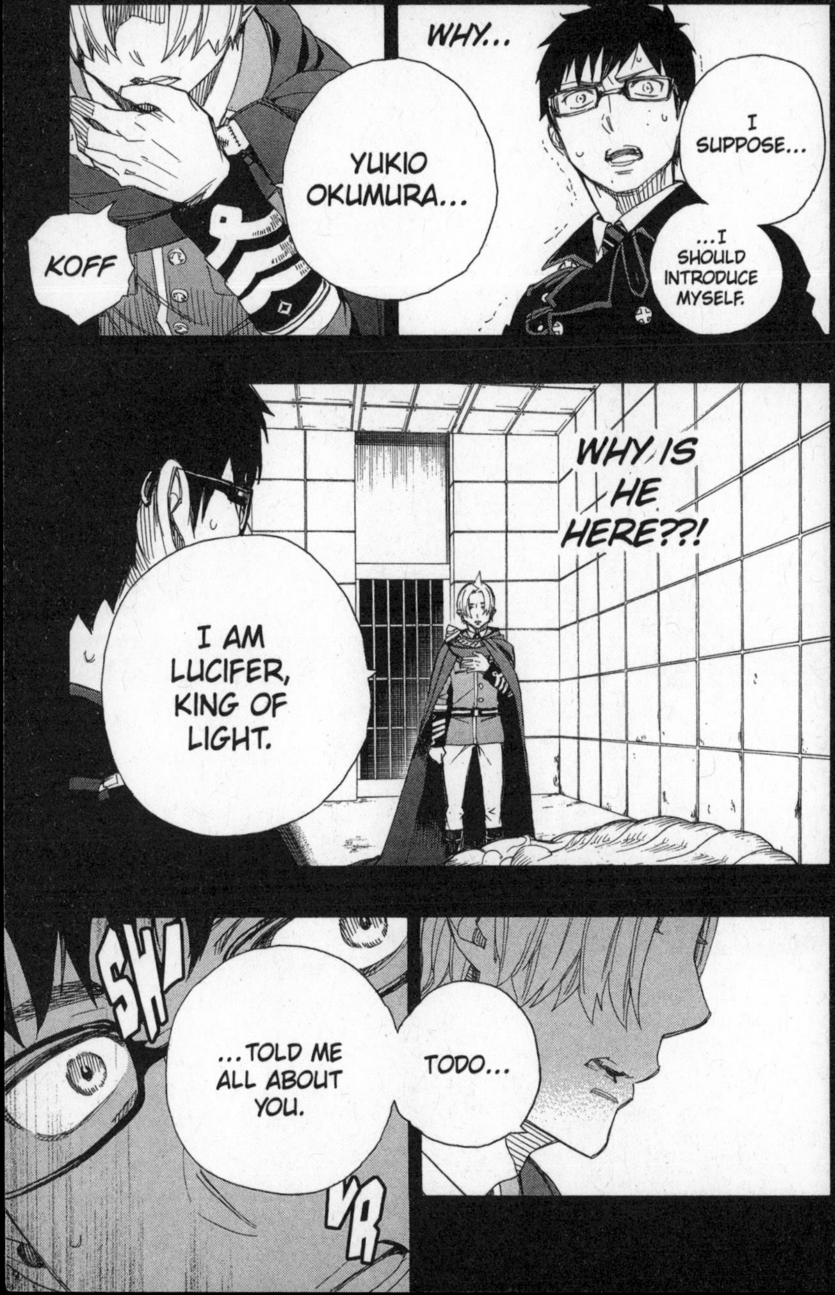
WHY...
I SUPPOSE...
...I SHOULD INTRODUCE MYSELF.
YUKIO OKUMURA...
KOFF
WHY IS HE HERE??!
I AM LUCIFER, KING OF LIGHT.
TODO...
...TOLD ME ALL ABOUT YOU.
SH
VR

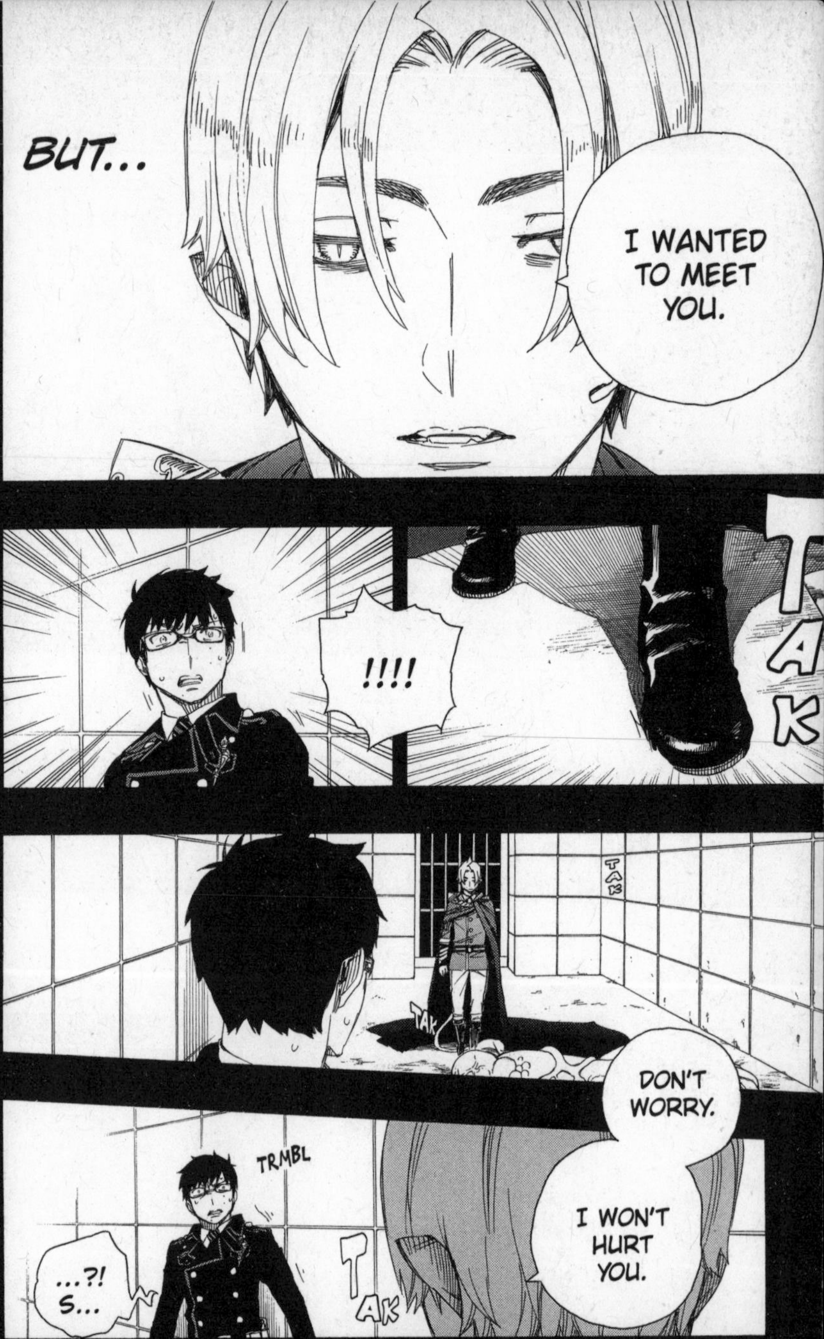
BUT...
I WANTED TO MEET YOU.
TAK
!!!!
TAK
TAK
DON'T WORRY.
I WON'T HURT YOU.
TRMBL
TAK
...?! S...

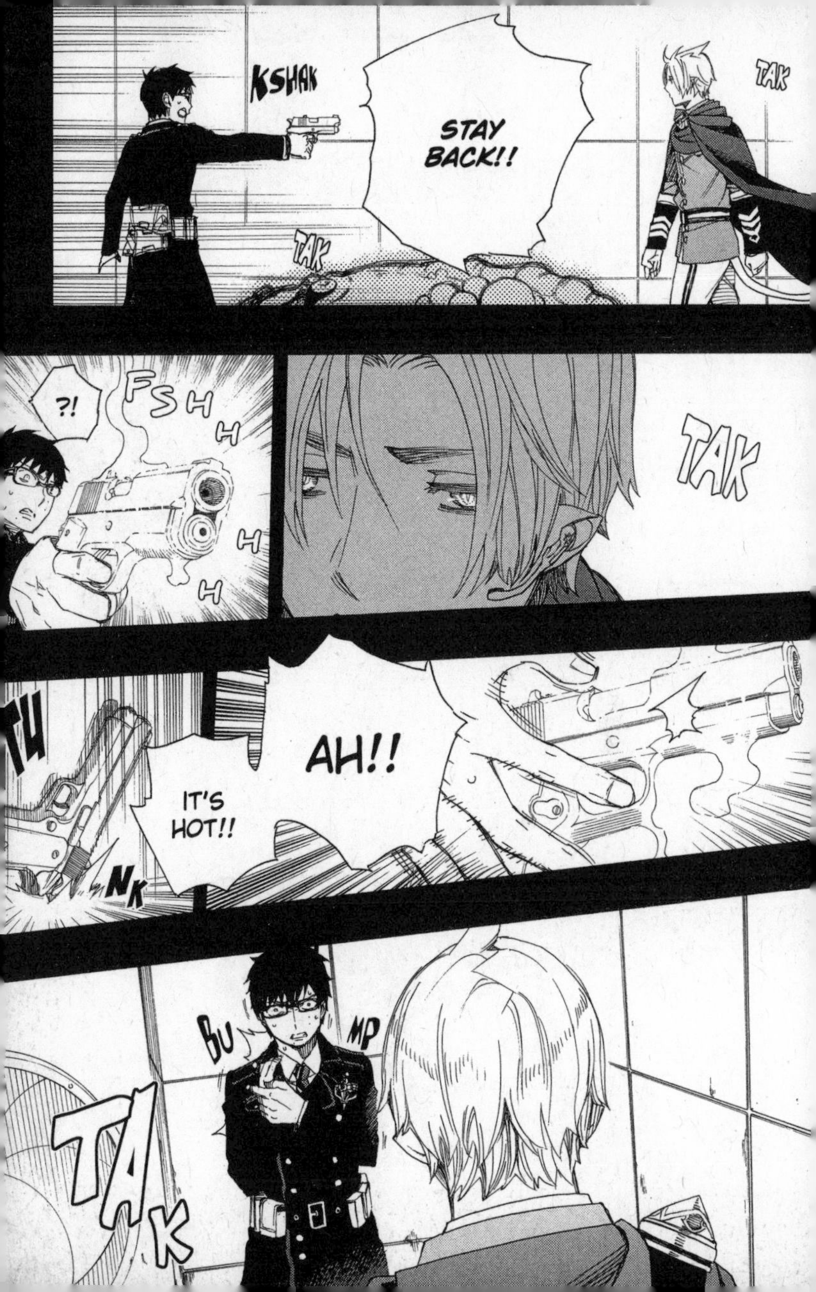
TAK
STAY BACK!!
KSHAK
TAK
TAK
?!
FSHHHHH
AH!!
IT'S HOT!!
TU
NK
BUMP
TAK

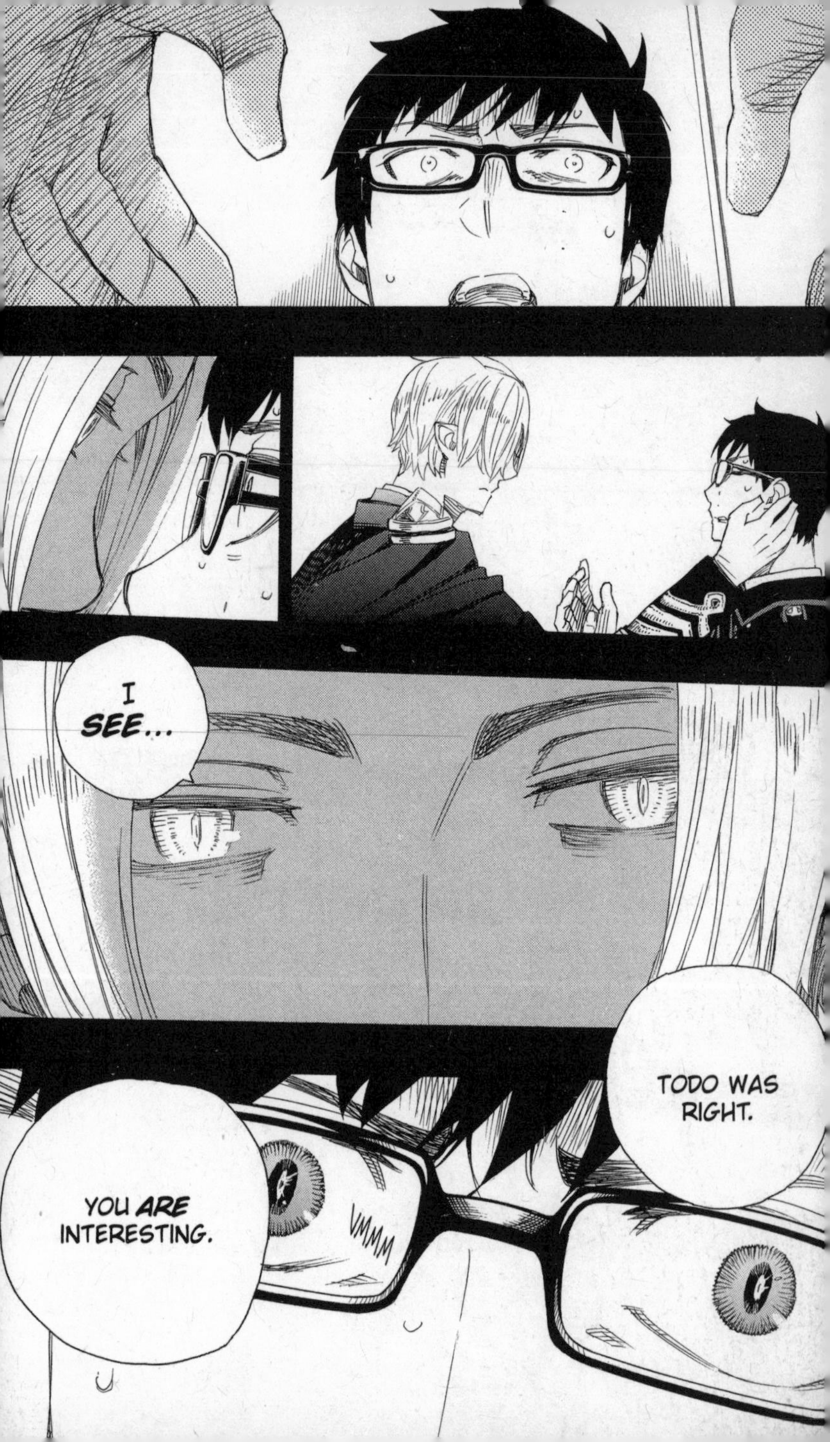
I SEE...
TODO WAS RIGHT.
VMMM
YOU ARE INTERESTING.

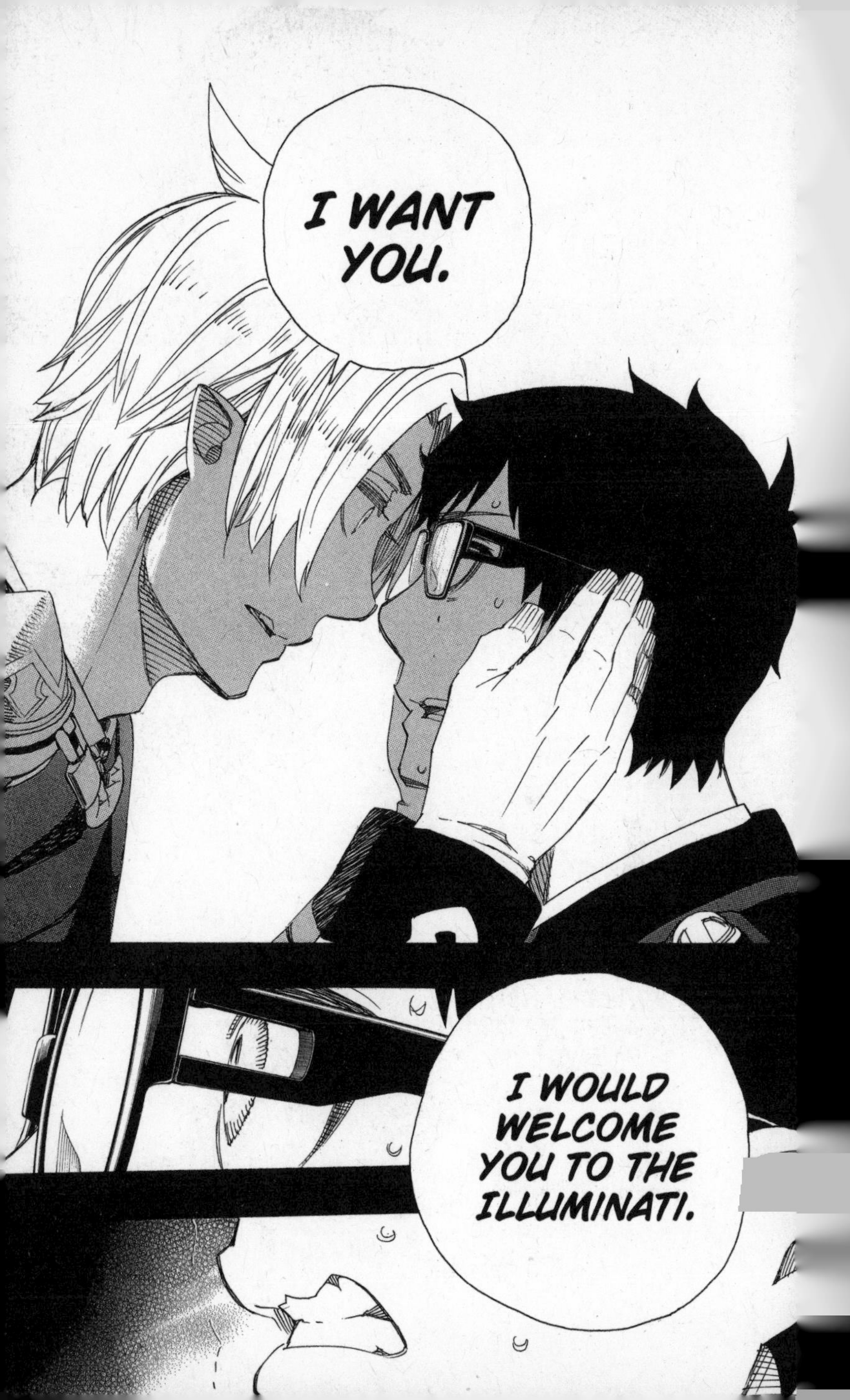
I WANT YOU.
I WOULD WELCOME YOU TO THE ILLUMINATI.

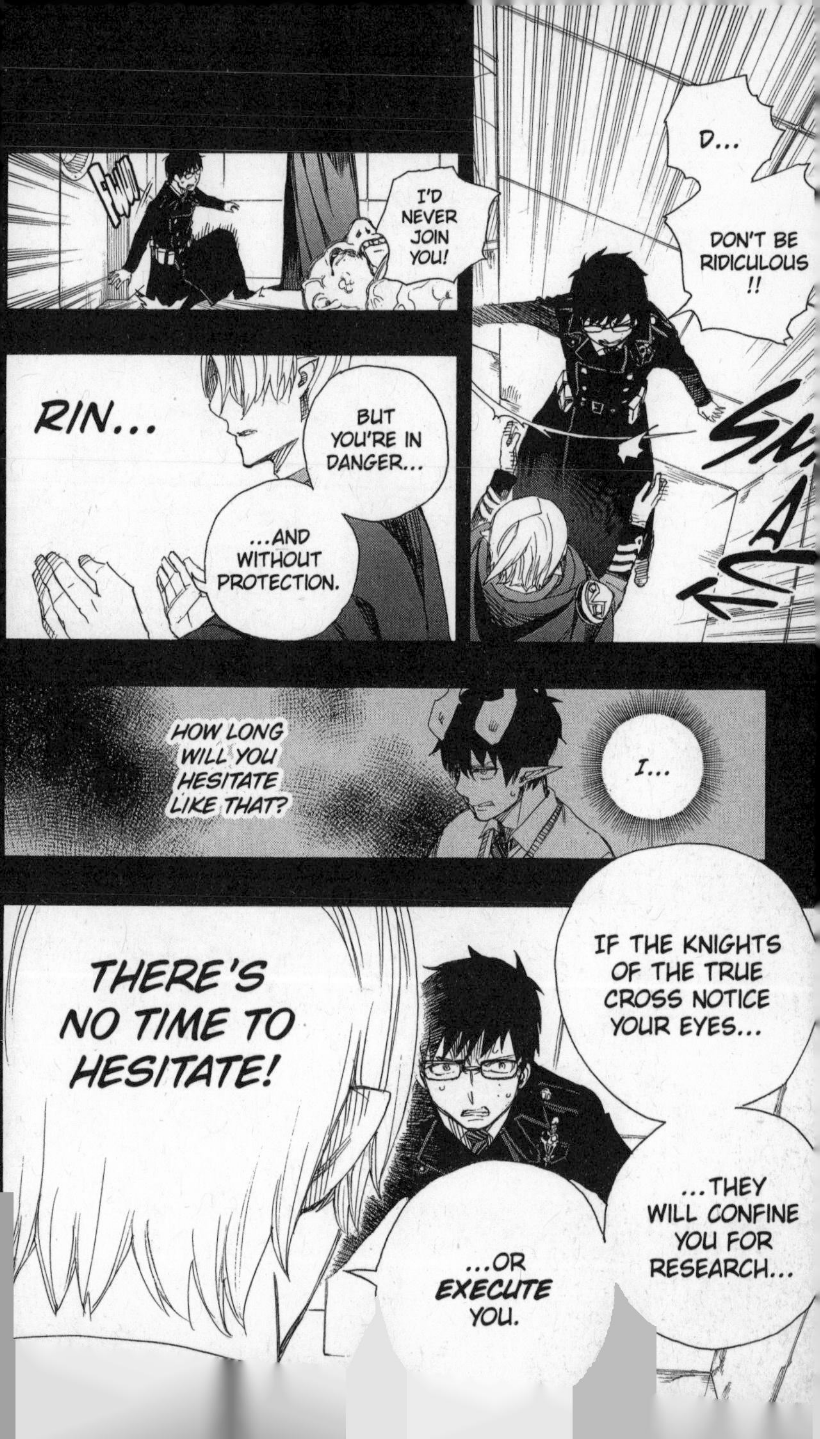
D...
DON'T BE RIDICULOUS !!
I'D NEVER JOIN YOU!
BUT YOU'RE IN DANGER...
RIN...
...AND WITHOUT PROTECTION.
I...
HOW LONG WILL YOU HESITATE LIKE THAT?
IF THE KNIGHTS OF THE TRUE CROSS NOTICE YOUR EYES...
...THEY WILL CONFINE YOU FOR RESEARCH...
...OR EXECUTE YOU.
THERE'S NO TIME TO HESITATE!

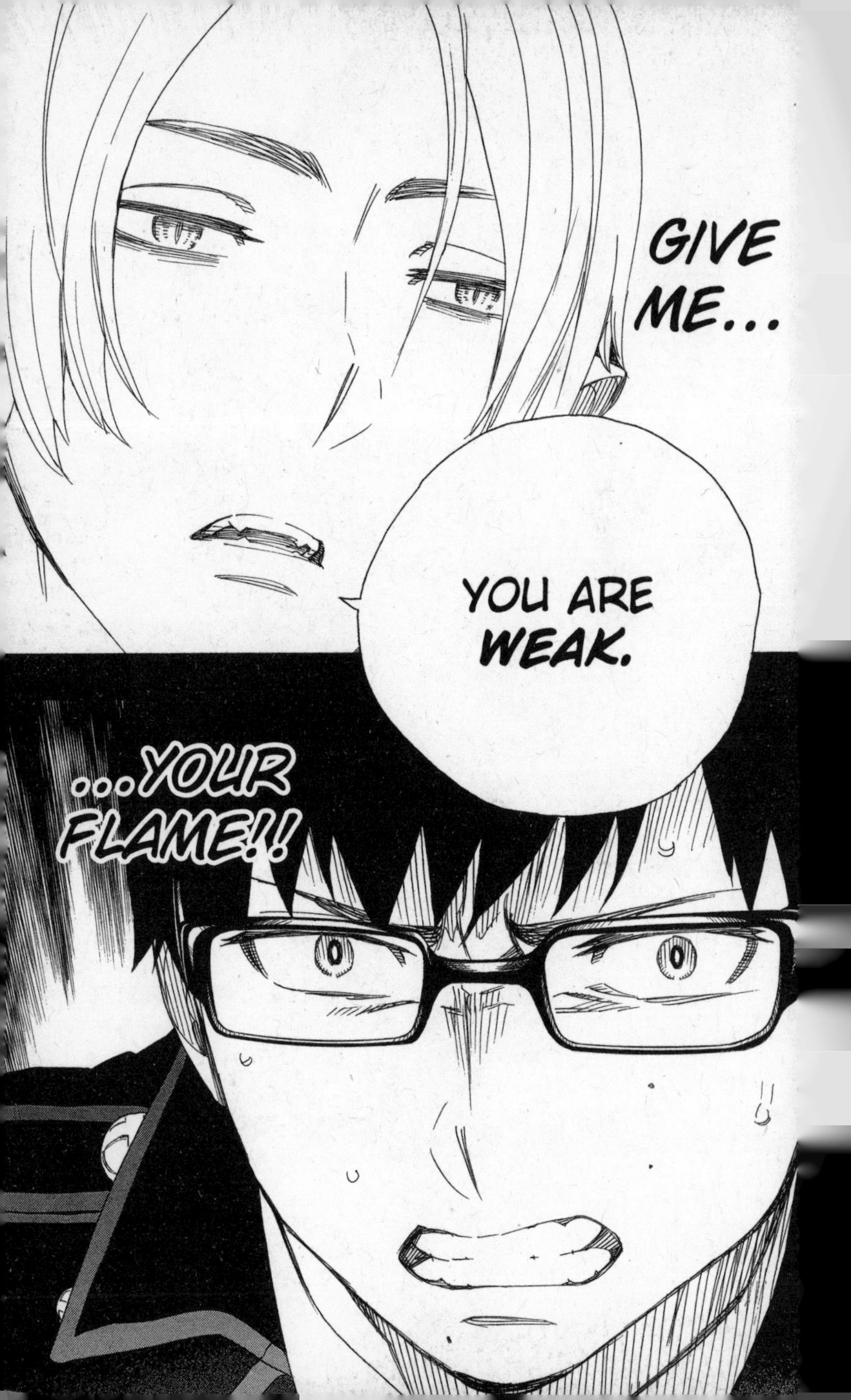
GIVE ME...
YOU ARE WEAK.
...YOUR FLAME!!

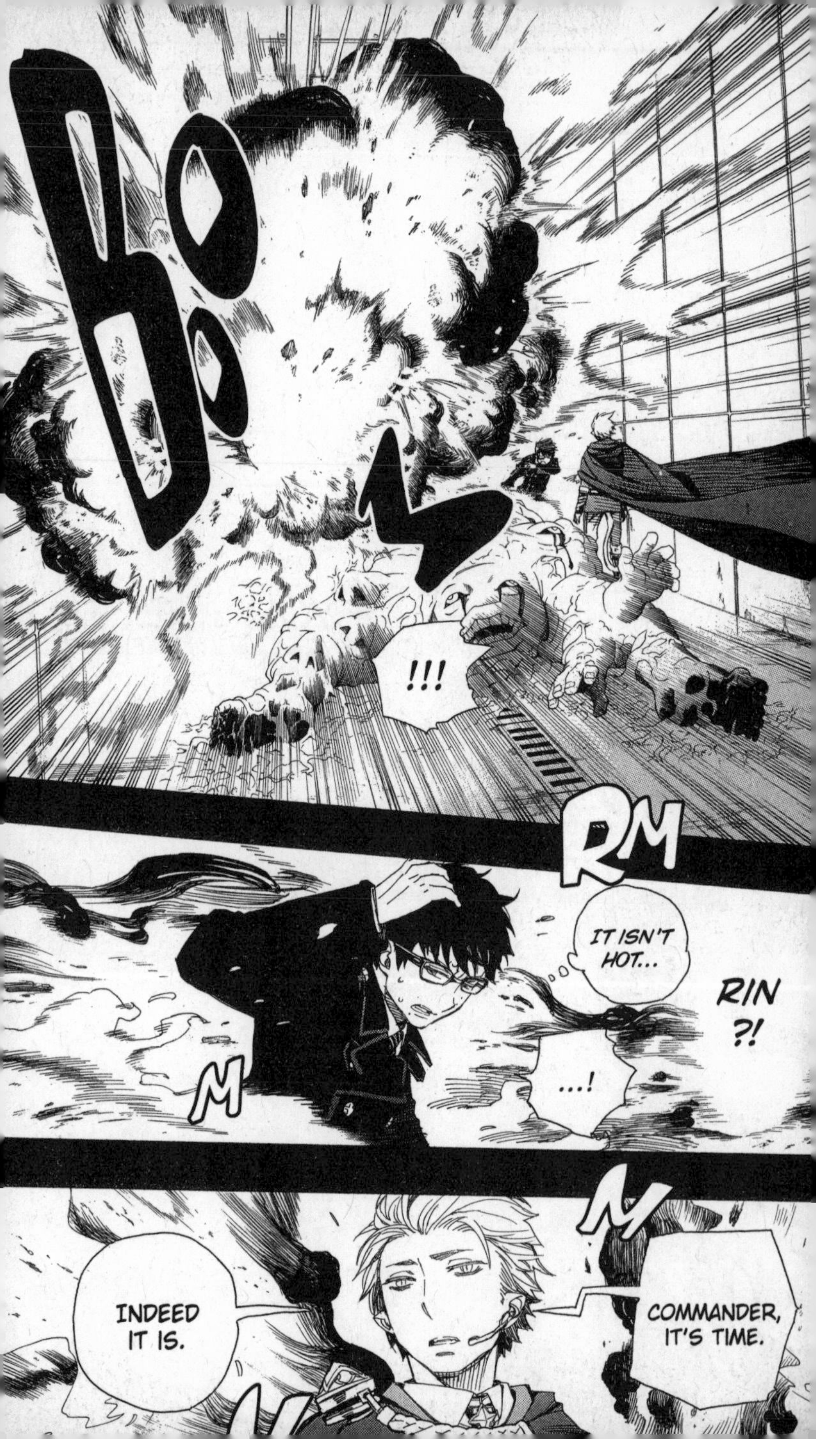
BOOM
!!!
RM
RIN ?!
IT ISN'T HOT...
...!
M
M
COMMANDER, IT'S TIME.
INDEED IT IS.

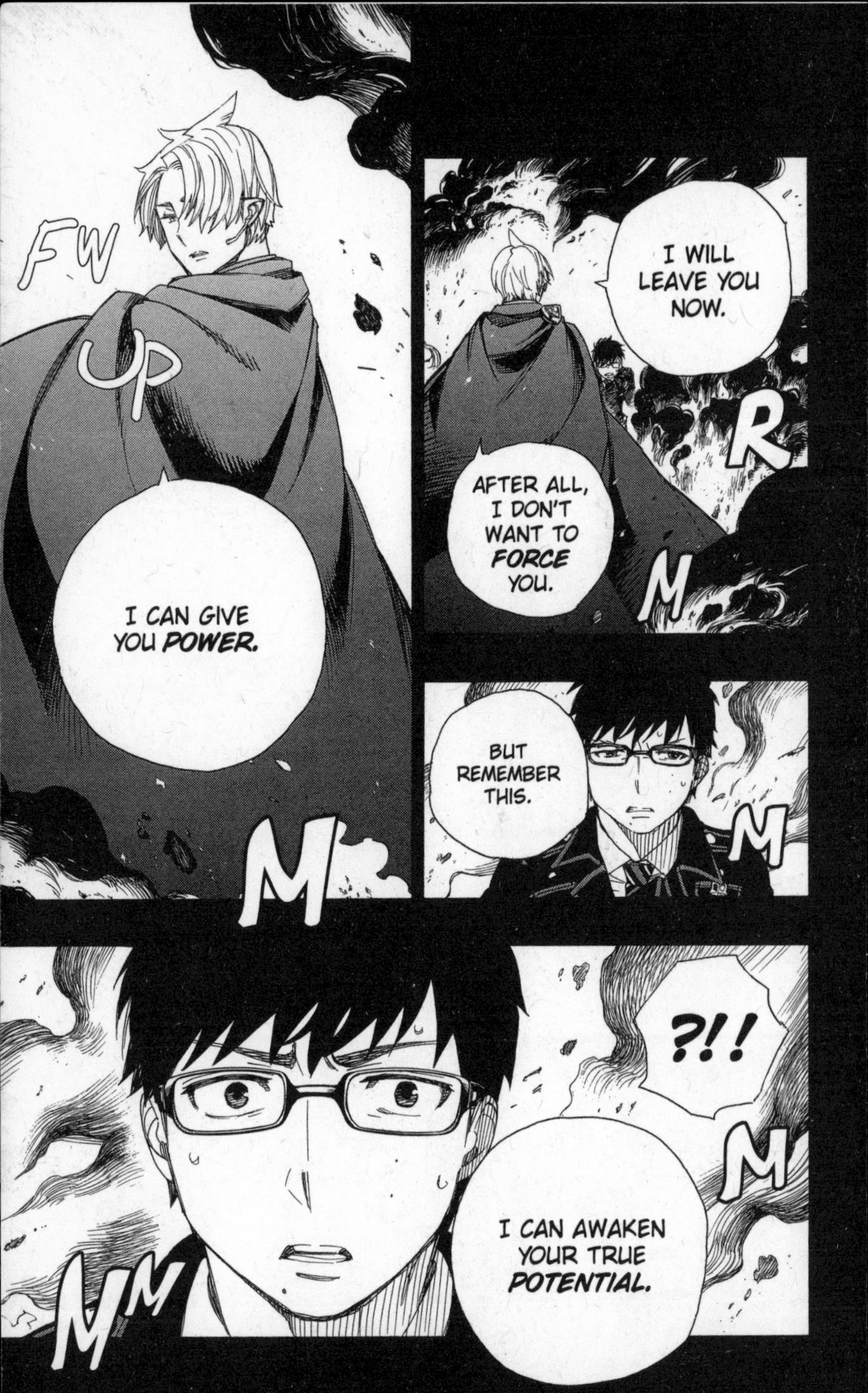
I WILL LEAVE YOU NOW.
AFTER ALL, I DON'T WANT TO FORCE YOU.
R
M
BUT REMEMBER THIS.
M
FWUP
I CAN GIVE YOU POWER.
M
?!!
M
I CAN AWAKEN YOUR TRUE POTENTIAL.
MMM

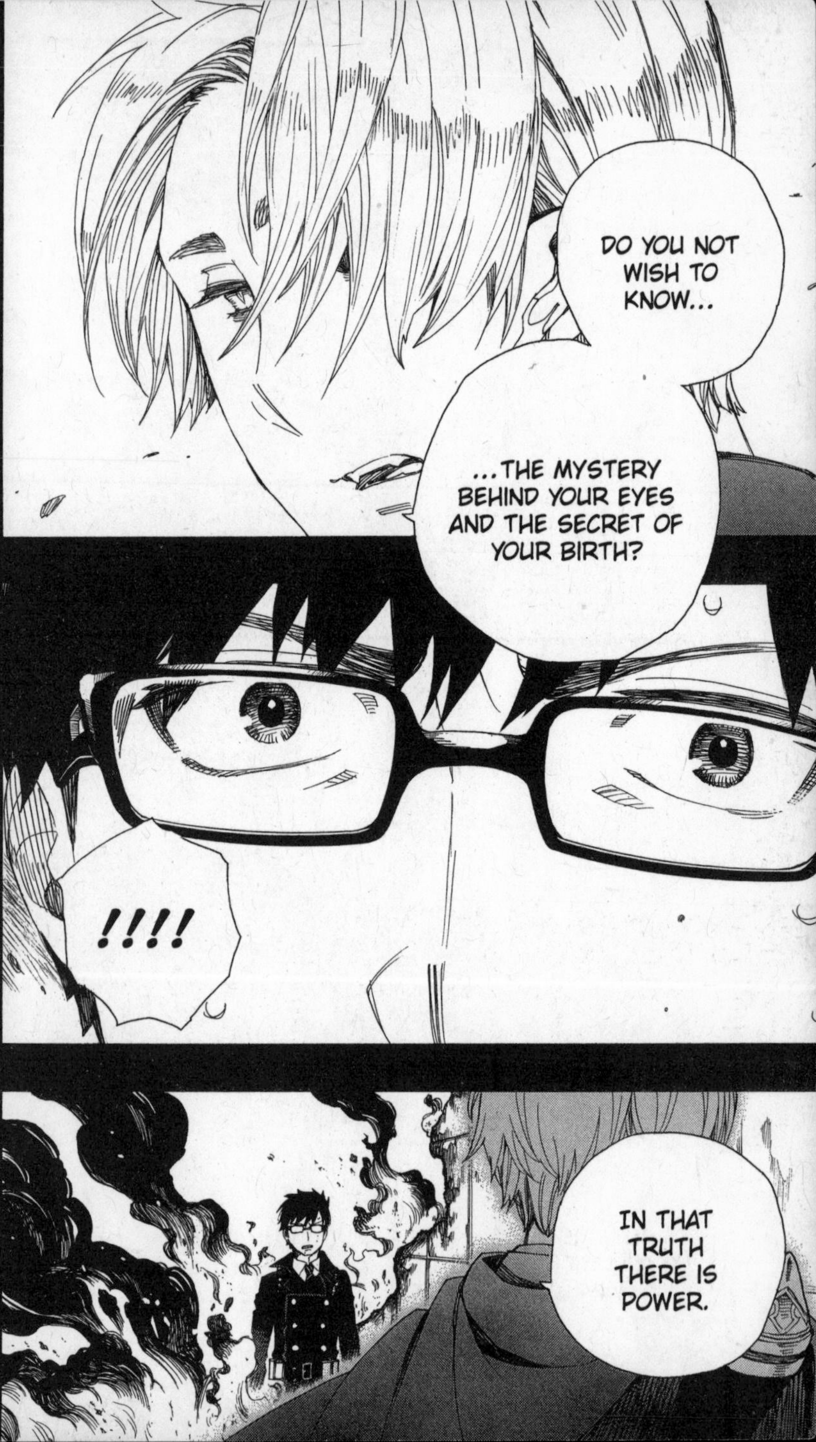
DO YOU NOT WISH TO KNOW...
...THE MYSTERY BEHIND YOUR EYES AND THE SECRET OF YOUR BIRTH?
!!!!
IN THAT TRUTH THERE IS POWER.

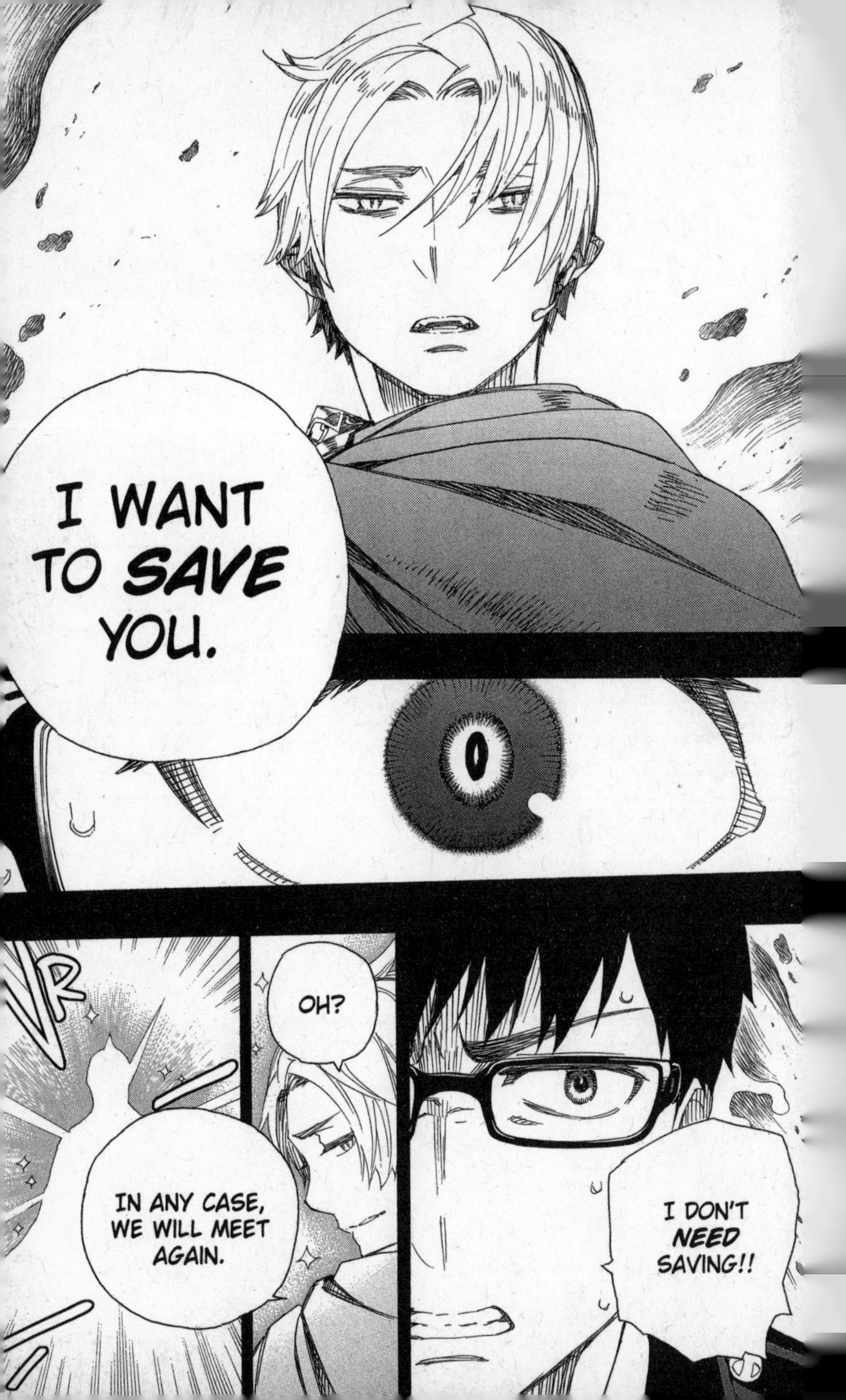
I WANT TO SAVE YOU.
I DON'T NEED SAVING!!
OH?
IN ANY CASE, WE WILL MEET AGAIN.

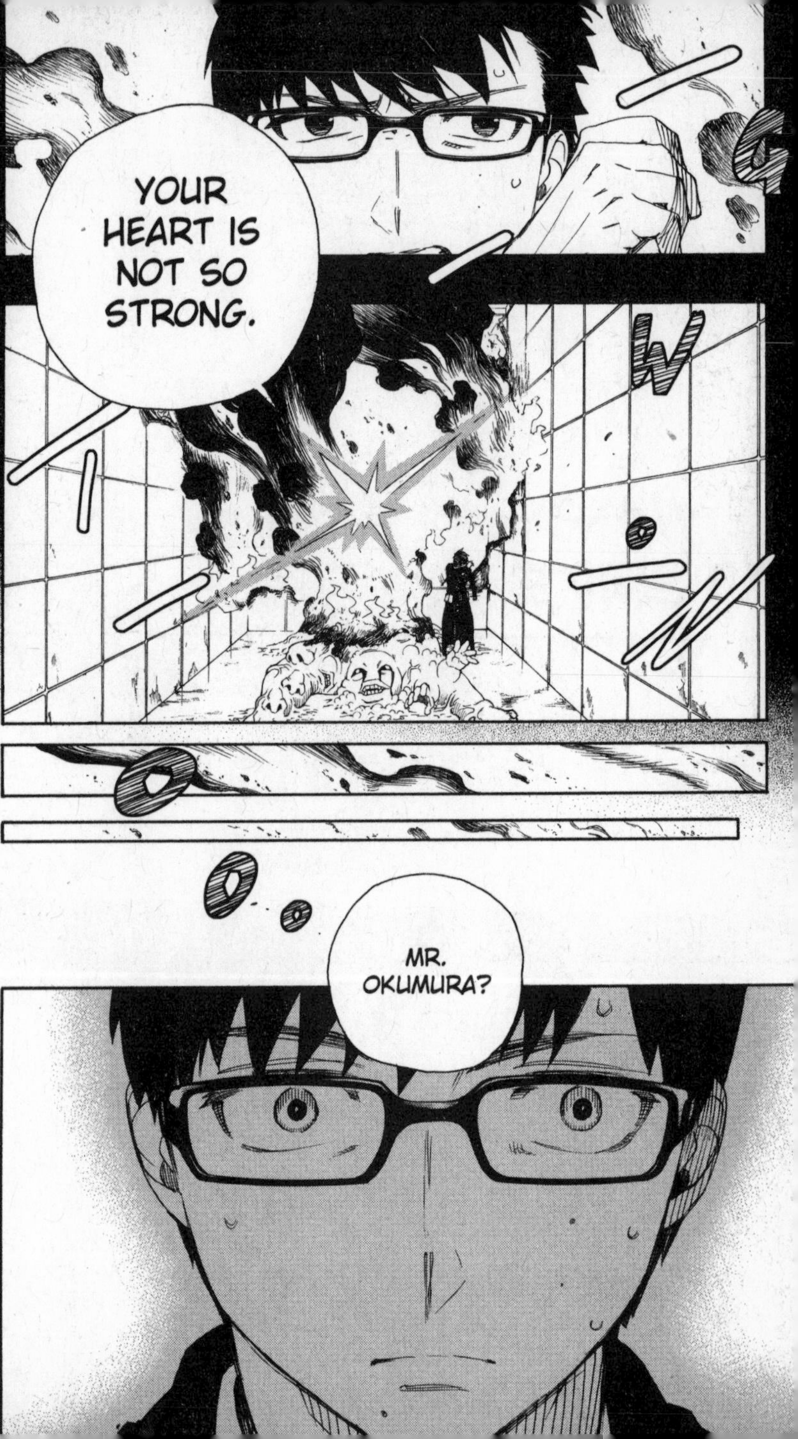
YOUR HEART IS NOT SO STRONG.
MR. OKUMURA?

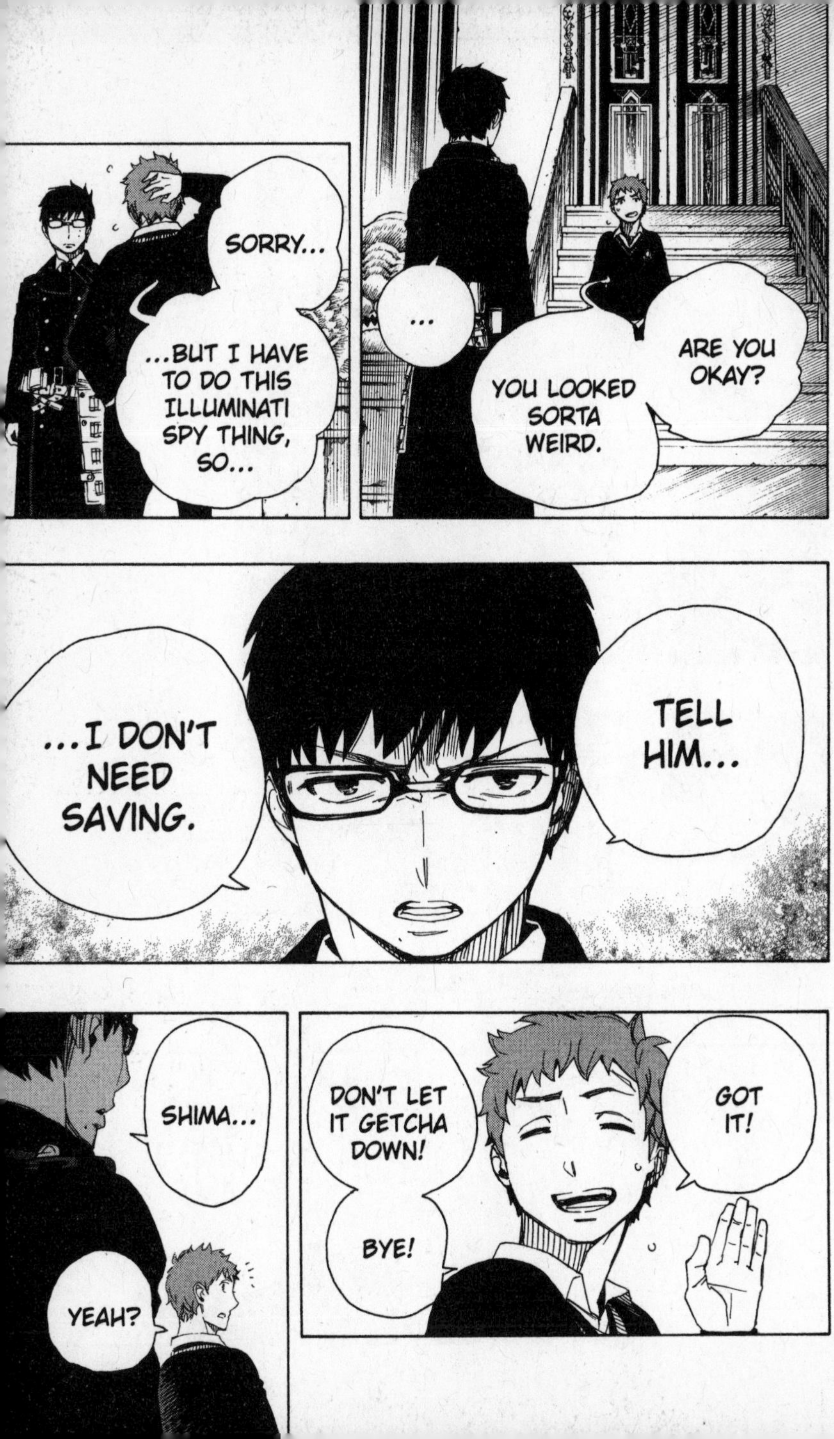
ARE YOU OKAY?
YOU LOOKED SORTA WEIRD.
...
SORRY...
...BUT I HAVE TO DO THIS ILLUMINATI SPY THING, SO...
TELL HIM...
...I DON'T NEED SAVING.
GOT IT!
DON'T LET IT GETCHA DOWN!
BYE!
SHIMA...
YEAH?

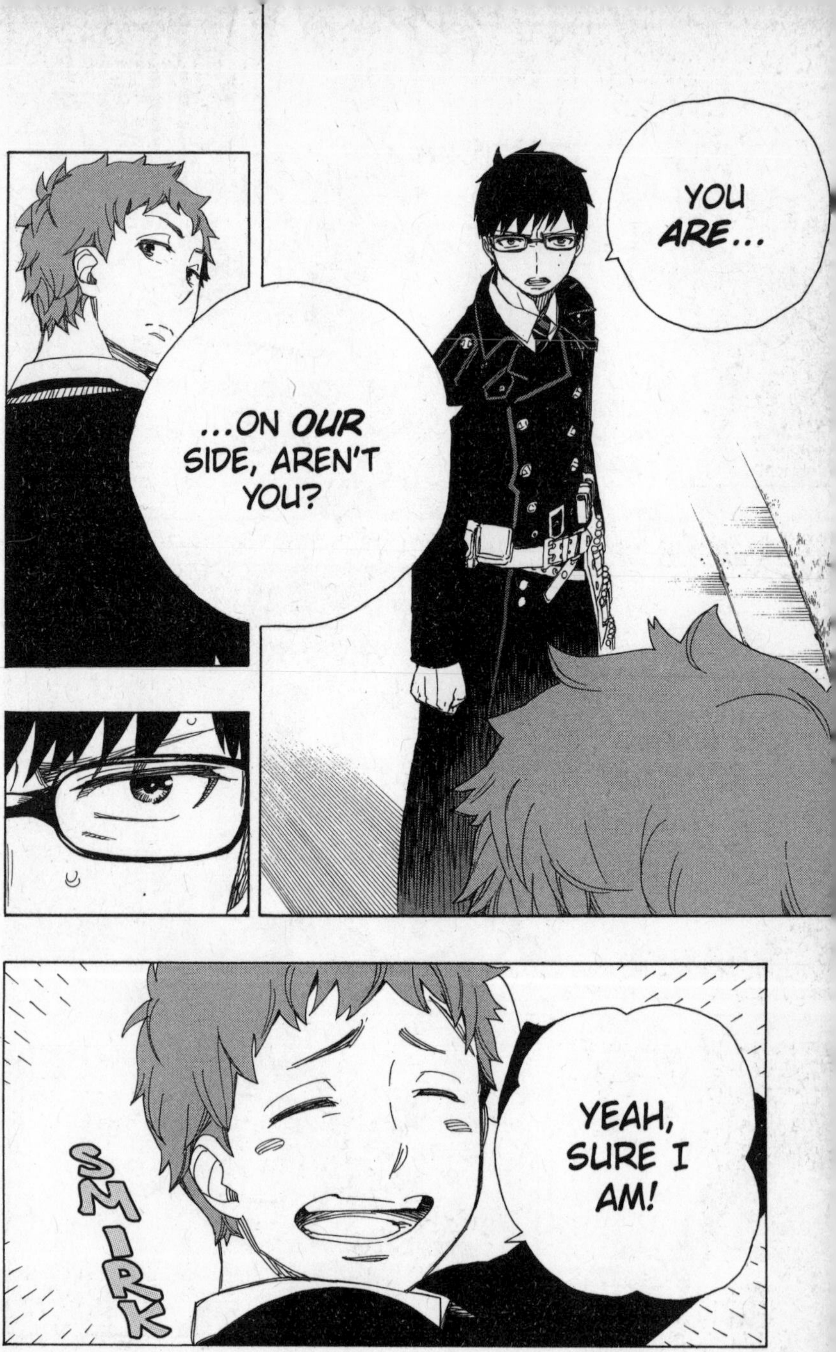
YOU ARE...
...ON OUR SIDE, AREN'T YOU?
YEAH, SURE I AM!
SMIRK

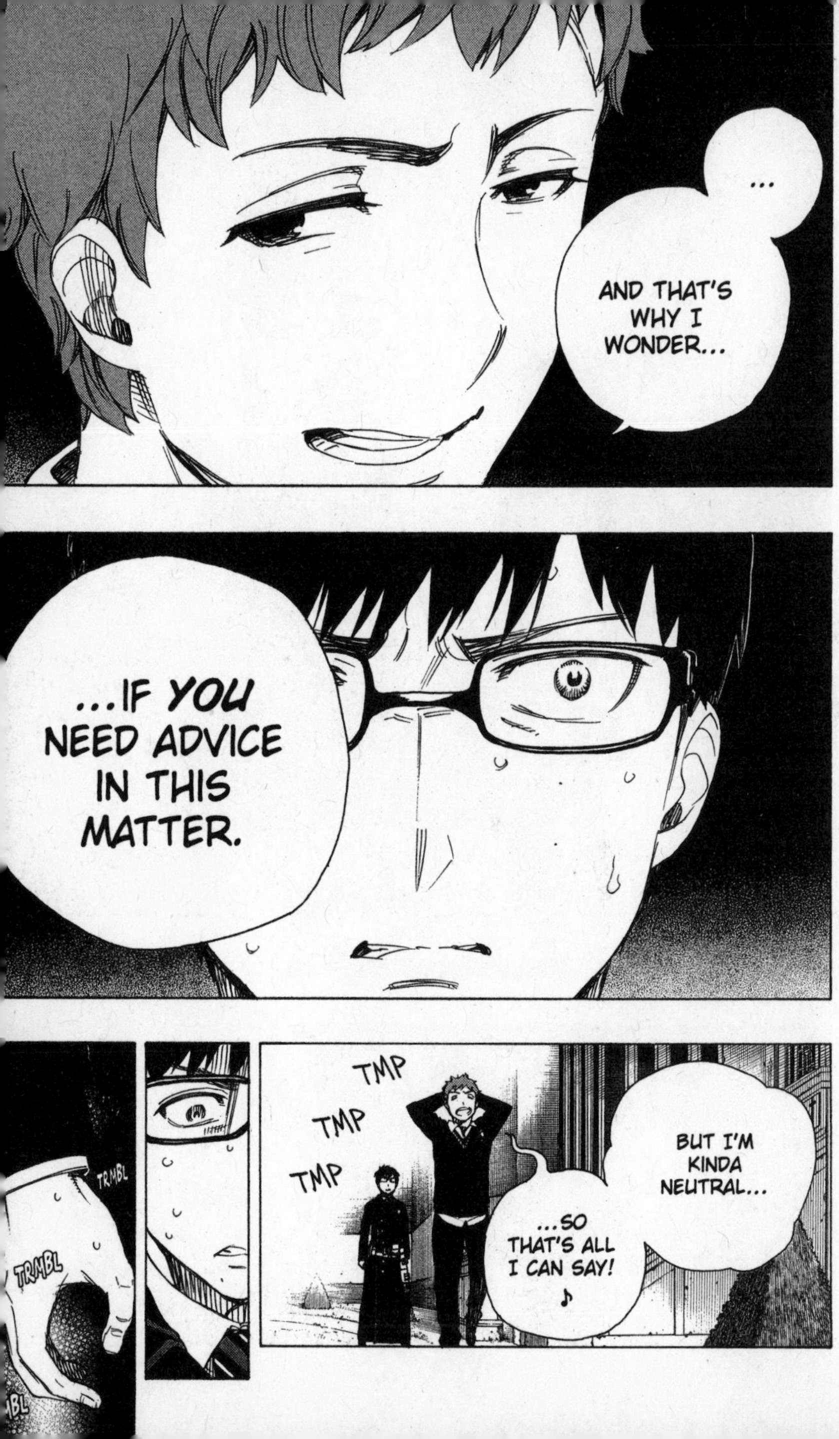
...
AND THAT'S WHY I WONDER...
...IF YOU NEED ADVICE IN THIS MATTER.
BUT I'M KINDA NEUTRAL...
...SO THAT'S ALL I CAN SAY! ♪
TMP
TMP
TMP
TRMBL
TRMBL

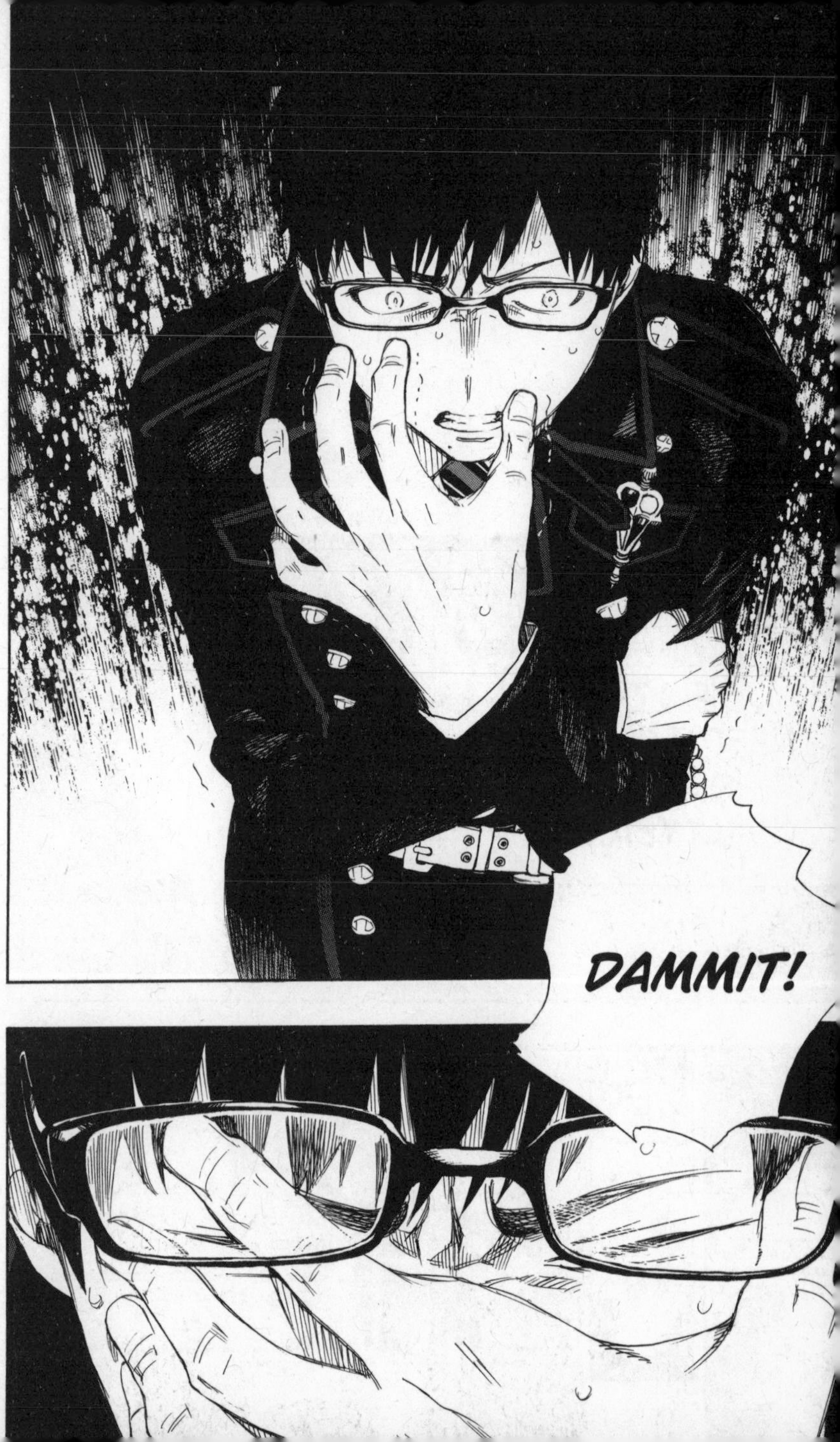
DAMMIT!

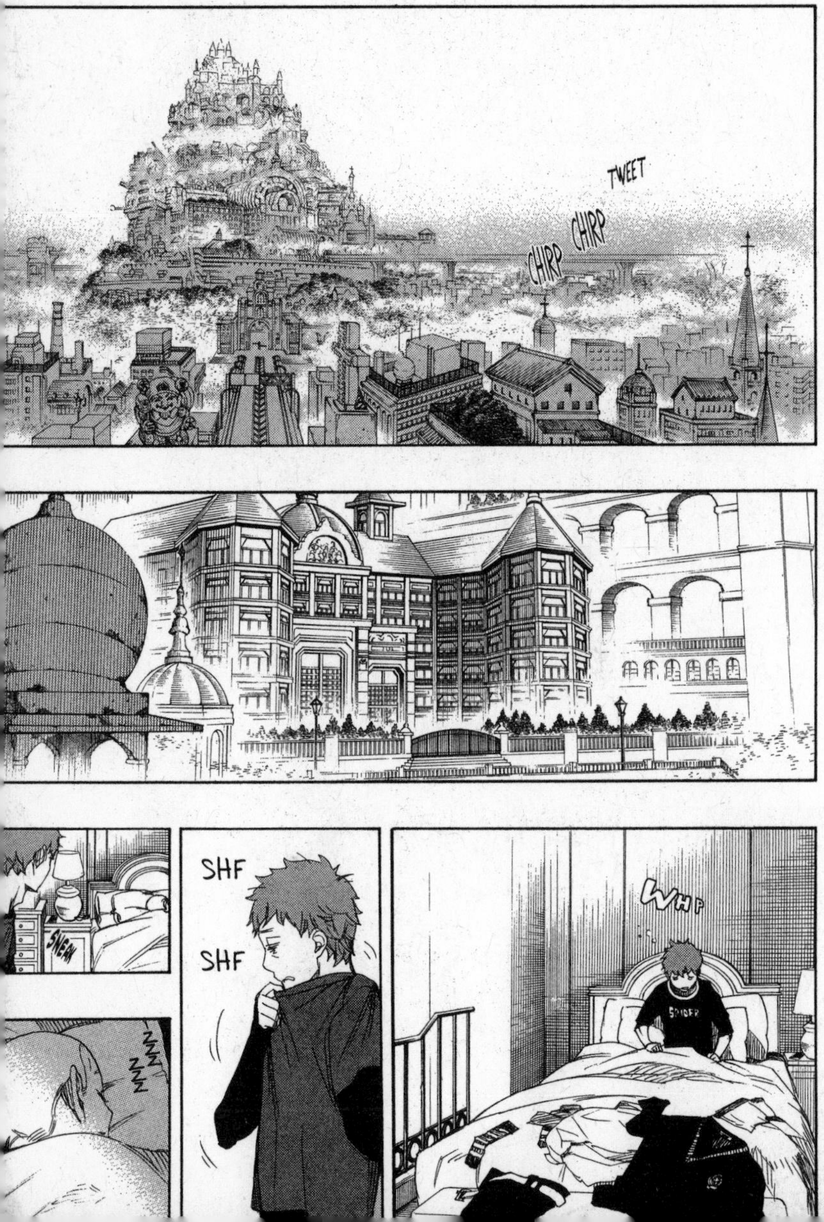
TWEET
CHIRP
CHIRP
WHP
SHF
SHF
SNEAK
ZZZ
ZZZ

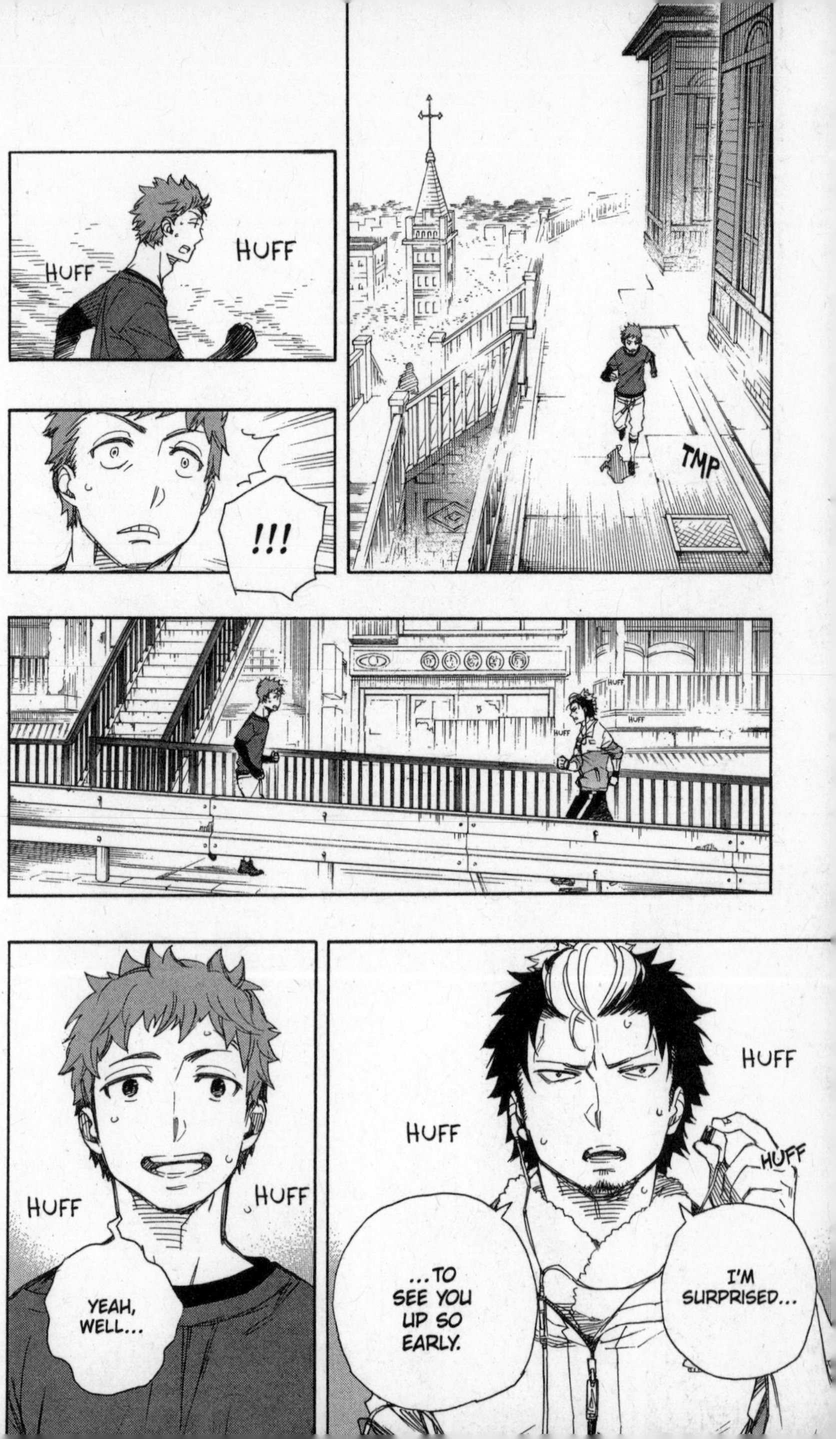
TMP
HUFF
HUFF
!!!
HUFF
HUFF
HUFF
HUFF
HUFF
HUFF
I'M SURPRISED...
...TO SEE YOU UP SO EARLY.
HUFF
HUFF
YEAH, WELL...

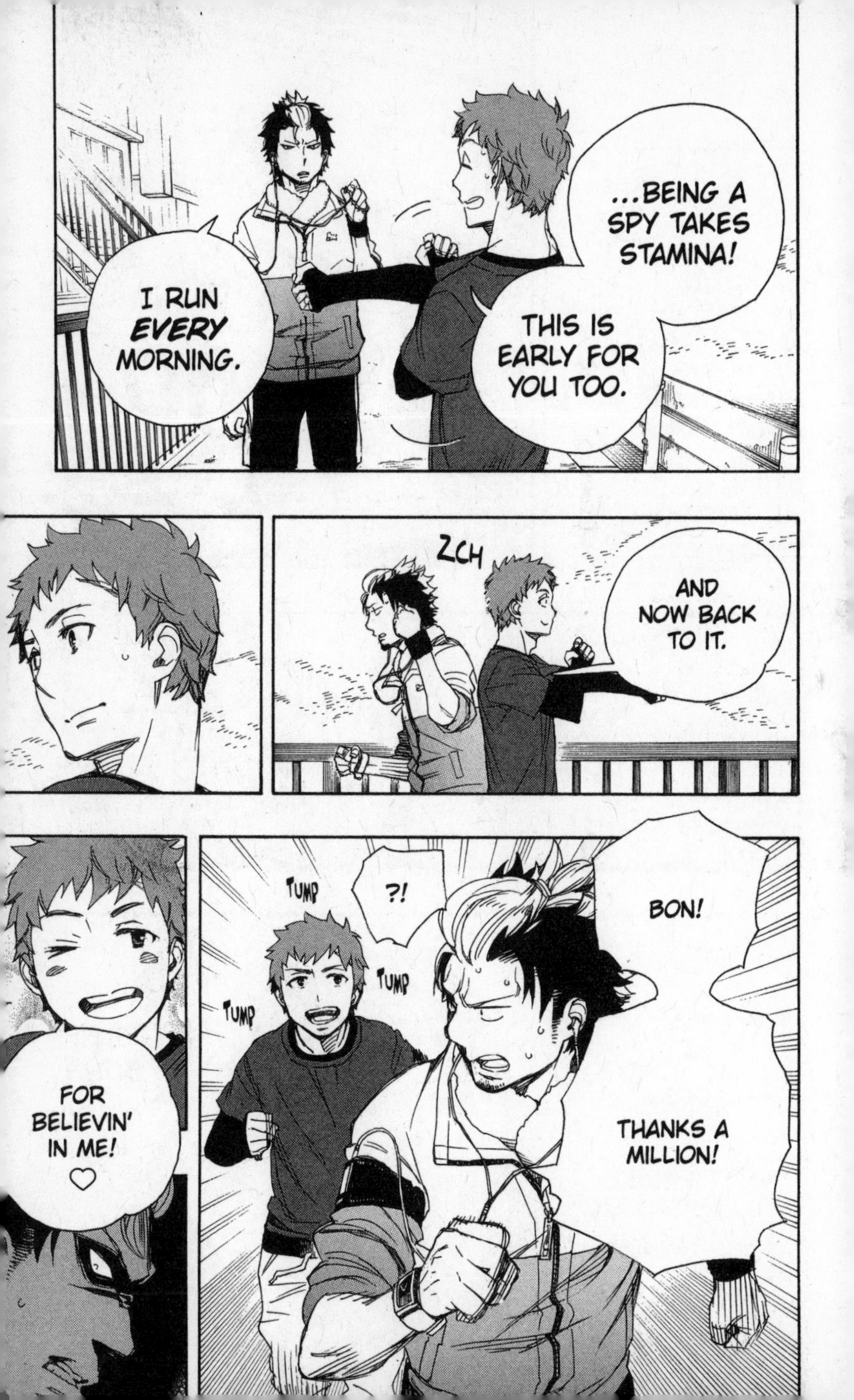
...BEING A SPY TAKES STAMINA!
THIS IS EARLY FOR YOU TOO.
I RUN EVERY MORNING.
ZCH
AND NOW BACK TO IT.
BON!
THANKS A MILLION!
?!
TUMP
TUMP
TUMP
FOR BELIEVIN' IN ME! ♡

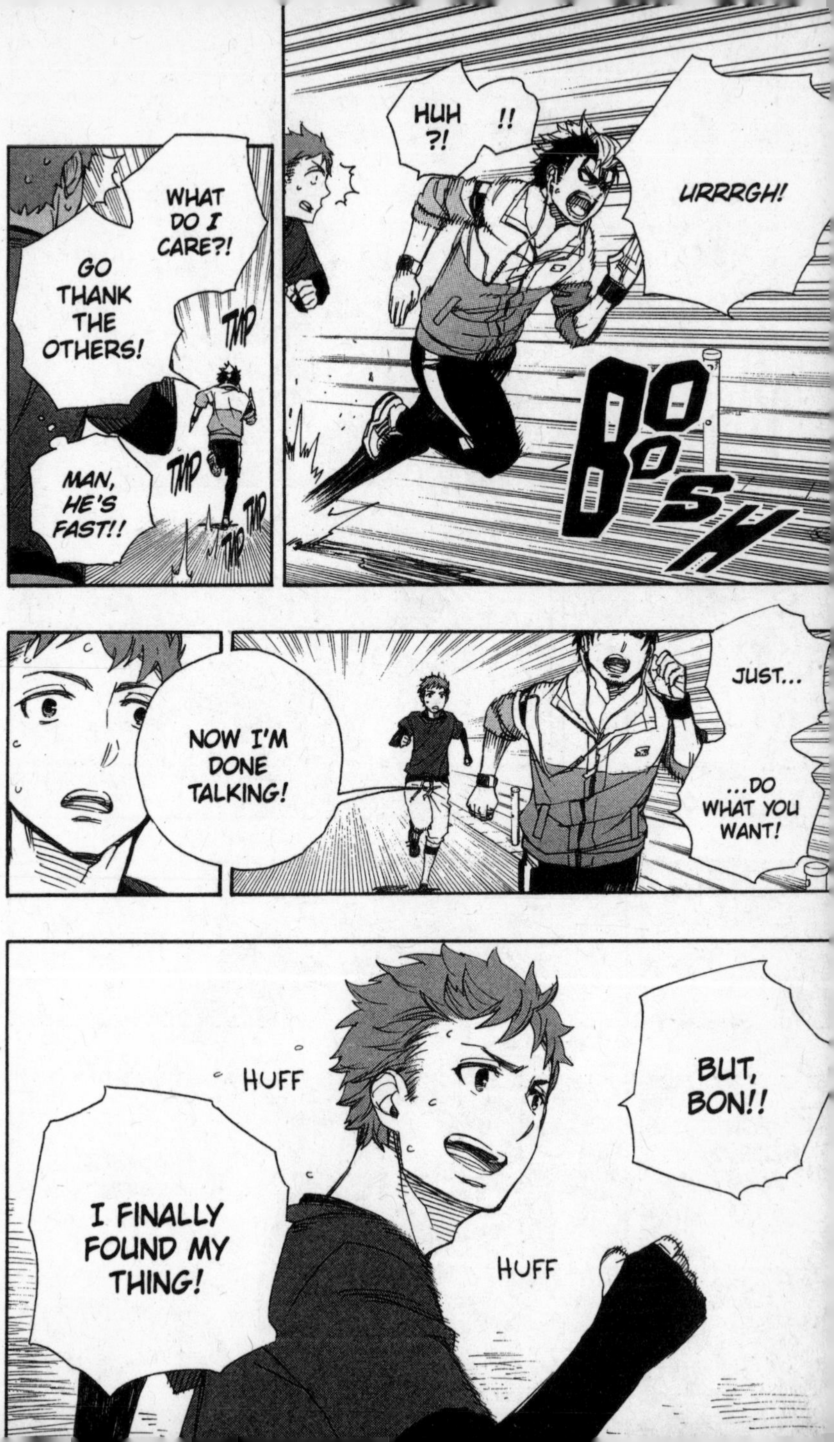
URRRGH!
!!
HUH ?!
BOOSH
WHAT DO I CARE?!
GO THANK THE OTHERS!
TMP
MAN, HE'S FAST!!
TMP
TMP
TMP
JUST...
...DO WHAT YOU WANT!
NOW I'M DONE TALKING!
BUT, BON!!
HUFF
HUFF
I FINALLY FOUND MY THING!

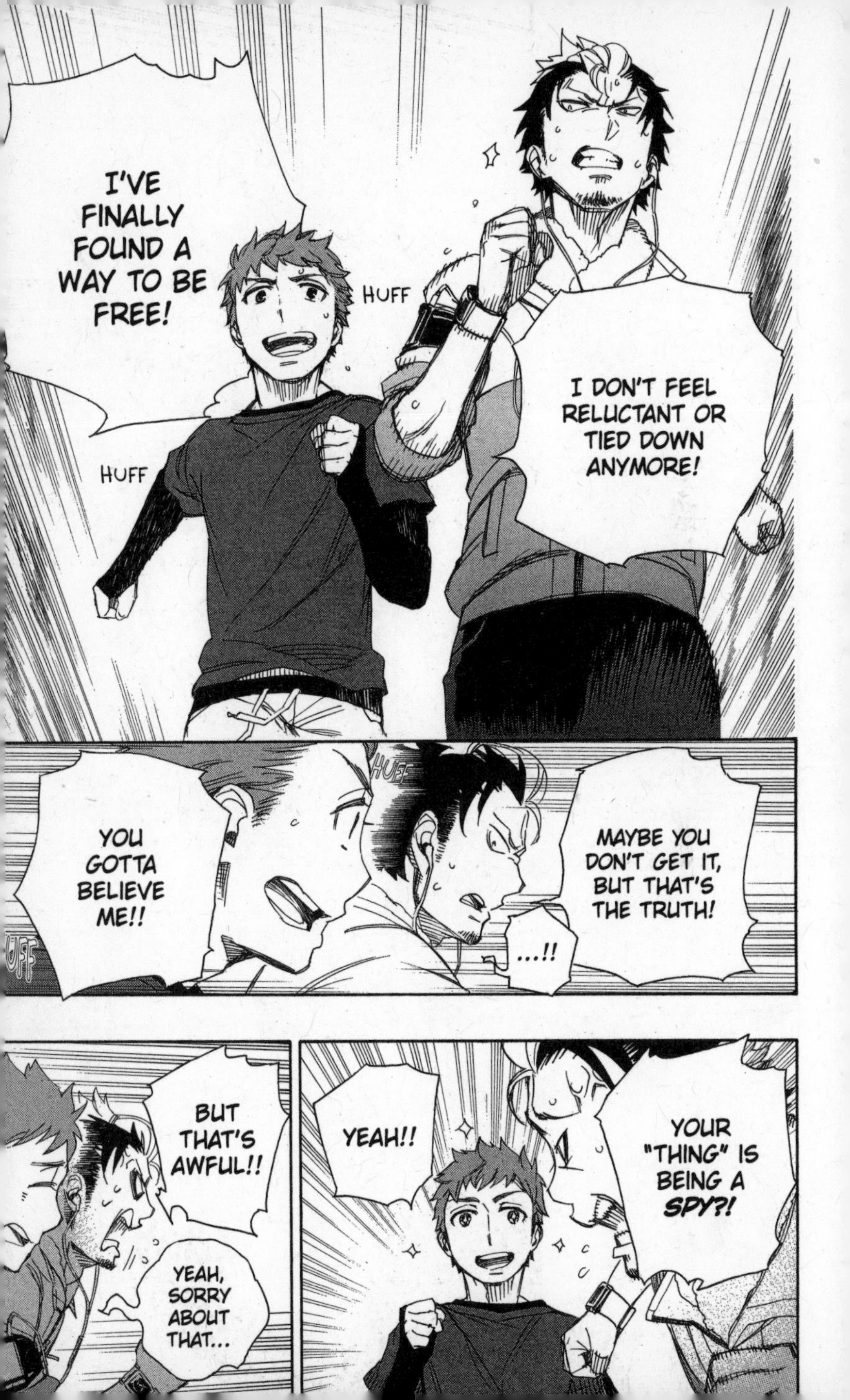
I'VE FINALLY FOUND A WAY TO BE FREE!
HUFF
HUFF
I DON'T FEEL RELUCTANT OR TIED DOWN ANYMORE!
MAYBE YOU DON'T GET IT, BUT THAT'S THE TRUTH!
HUFF
...!!
YOU GOTTA BELIEVE ME!!
UFF
YOUR "THING" IS BEING A *SPY*?!
YEAH!!
BUT THAT'S AWFUL!!
YEAH, SORRY ABOUT THAT...

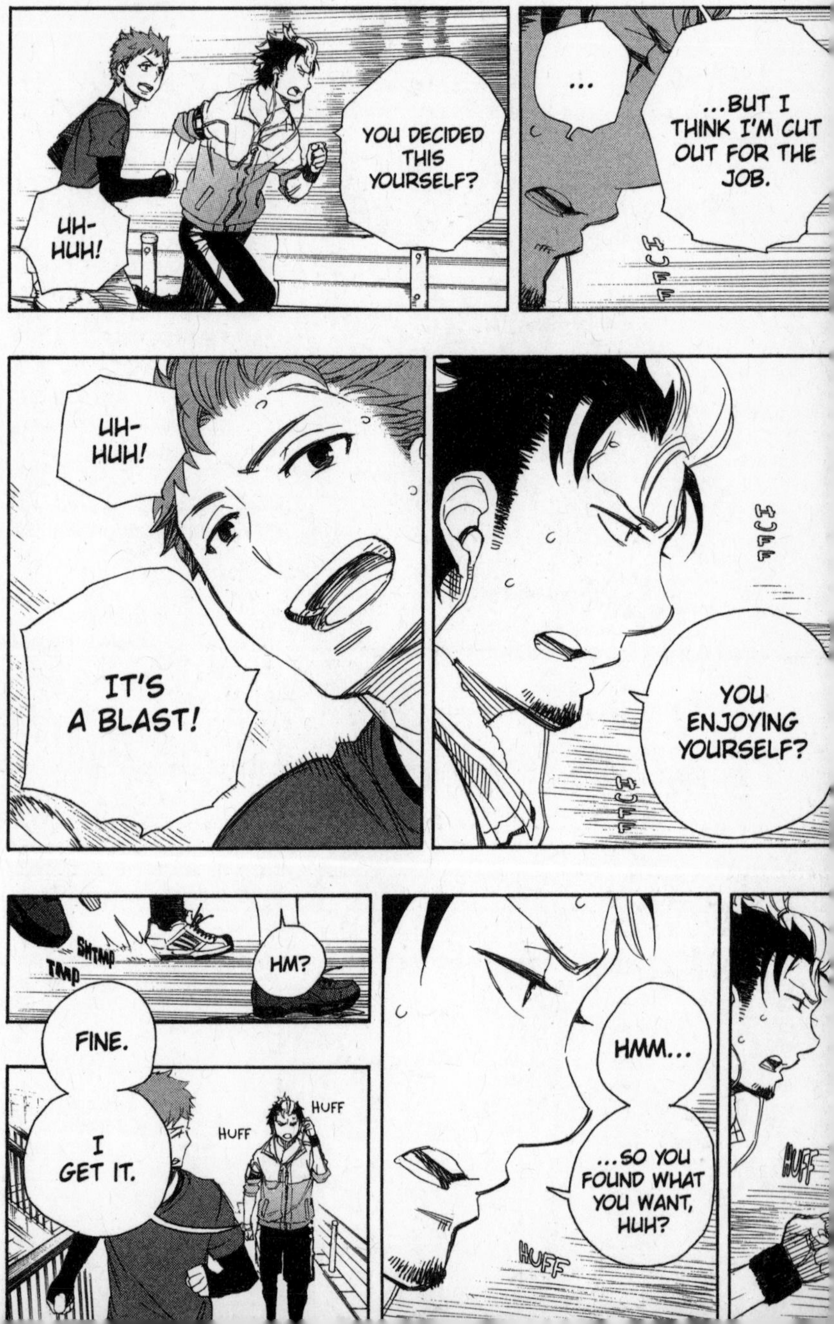
...
...BUT I THINK I'M CUT OUT FOR THE JOB.
HUFF
YOU DECIDED THIS YOURSELF?
UH-HUH!
HUFF
YOU ENJOYING YOURSELF?
HUFF
UH-HUH!
IT'S A BLAST!
HUFF
HMM...
...SO YOU FOUND WHAT YOU WANT, HUH?
HUFF
SHTMP
TMP
HM?
FINE.
I GET IT.
HUFF
HUFF

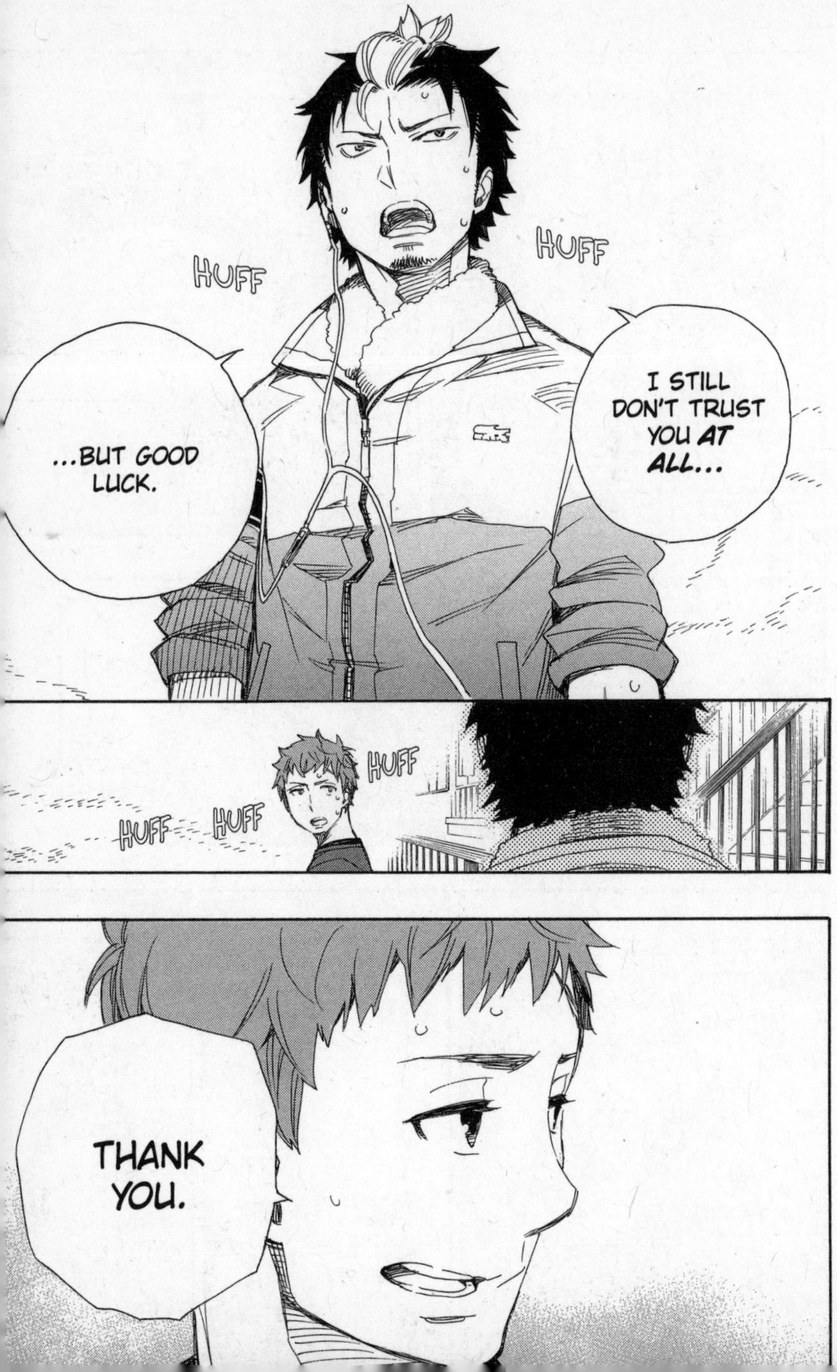
HUFF
HUFF
I STILL DON'T TRUST YOU AT ALL...
...BUT GOOD LUCK.
HUFF
HUFF
HUFF
THANK YOU.

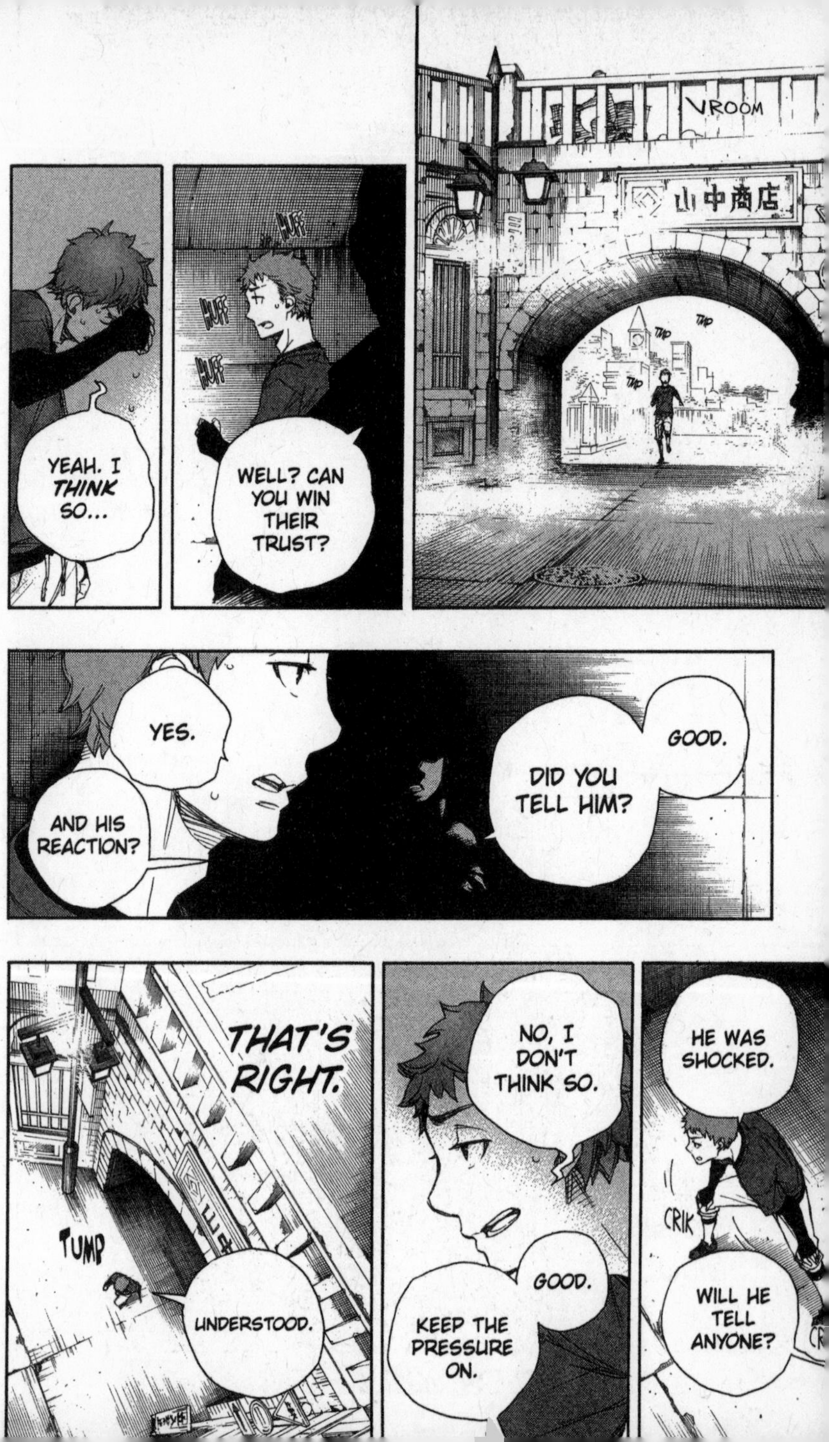
VROOM
山中商店
TMP
TMP
TMP
HUFF
HUFF
HUFF
WELL? CAN YOU WIN THEIR TRUST?
YEAH. I *THINK* SO...
GOOD.
DID YOU TELL HIM?
YES.
AND HIS REACTION?
HE WAS SHOCKED.
CRIK
WILL HE TELL ANYONE?
NO, I DON'T THINK SO.
GOOD.
KEEP THE PRESSURE ON.
THAT'S RIGHT.
TUMP
UNDERSTOOD.

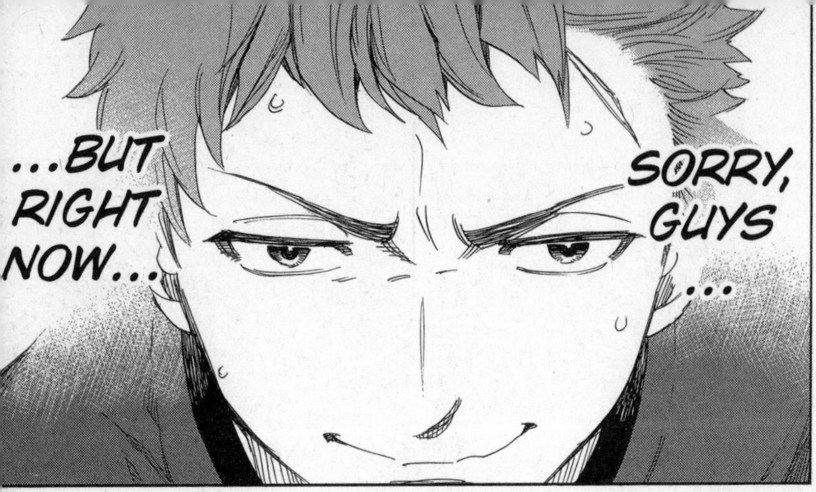
SORRY, GUYS...
...BUT RIGHT NOW...

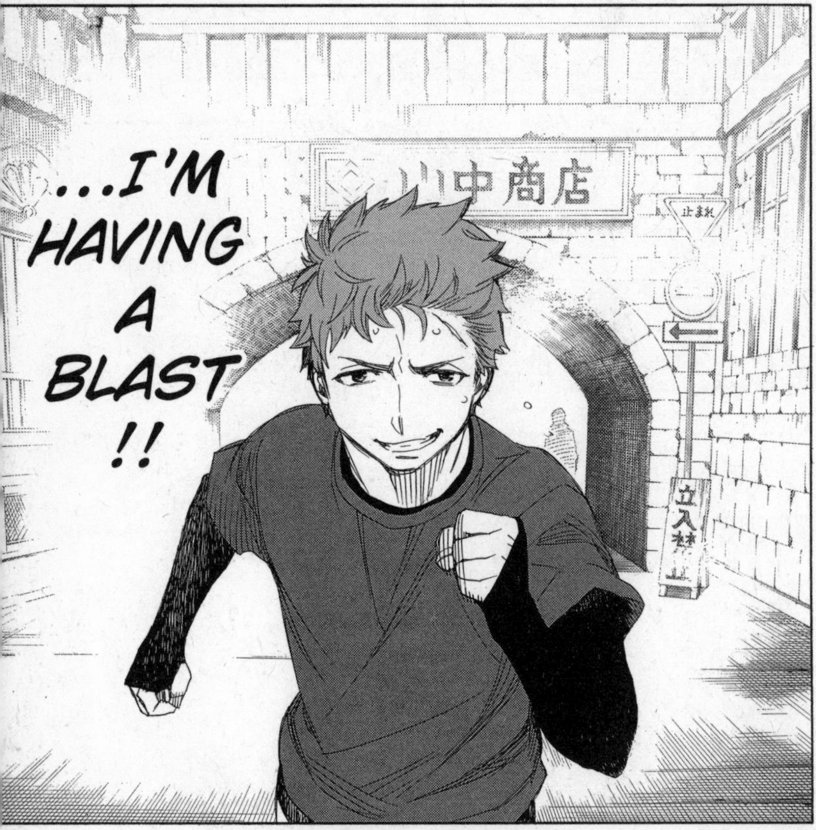
...I'M HAVING A BLAST!!

BLUE EXORCIST 15 - END -

Blue Exorcist Chapter 67: Pink Spider: Part 3

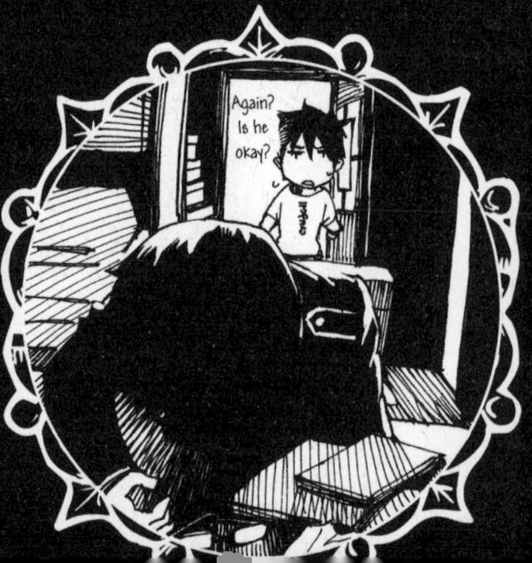
Again? Is he okay?

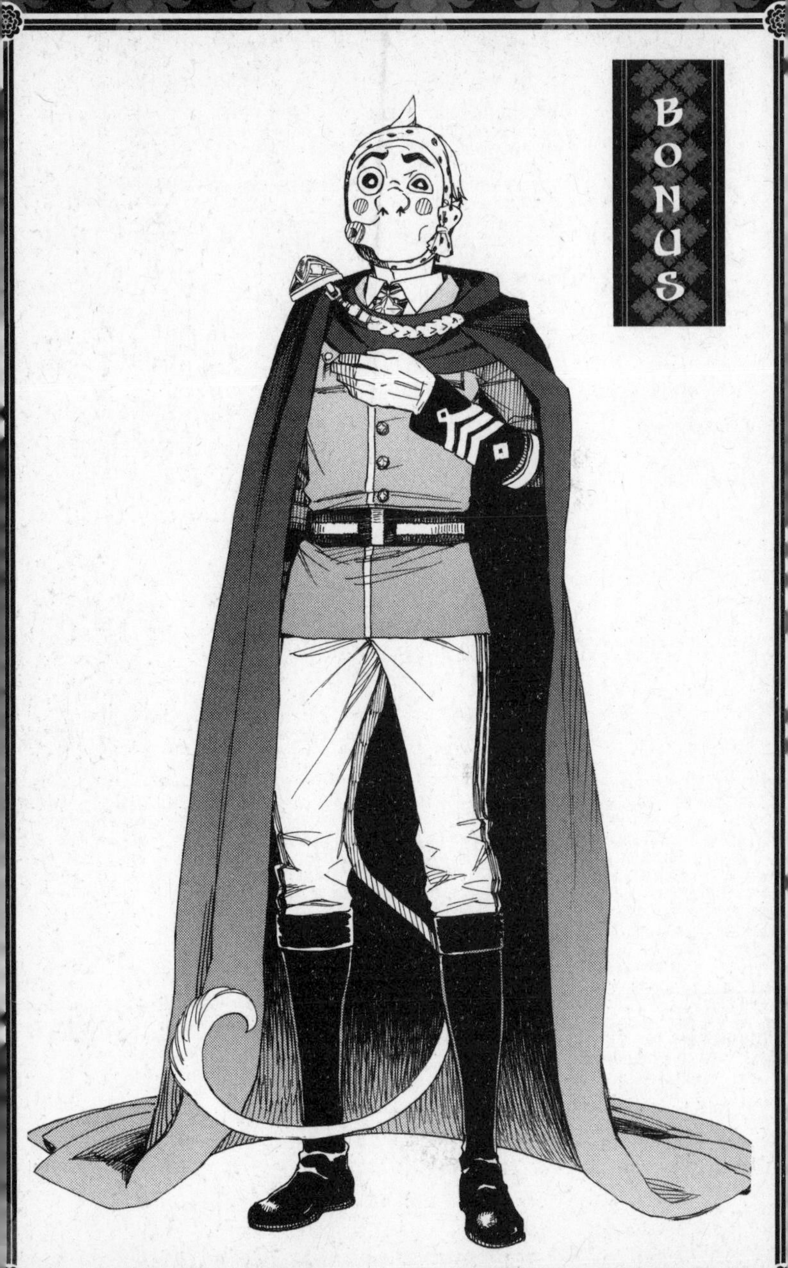
BONUS

BLUE EXORCIST BONUS

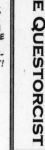

BLUE QUESTORCIST

ALL RIGHT, LET'S BEGIN VOLUME 15'S QUEST-ORCIST!

WHY DIDN'T IZUMO NEED HER PAPER WITH THE SEAL ON IT WHEN SUMMONING UKE AND MIKE IN CHAPTER 54? I'M SO CONCERNED ABOUT IT I CAN'T SLEEP AT NIGHT! *KAZUKI KATORI (14), TOKYO PREFECTURE*

HMM... GOOD QUESTION!

I DON'T REALLY KNOW MYSELF! AT THE TIME, I HAD SIMPLY ACCEPTED MY WEAKNESS, SO I WAS WILLING TO RELY ON OTHERS TO HELP ME. MAYBE UKE AND MIKE RESPONDED TO THAT FEELING. UNTIL THEN, WHEN I BORROWED THEIR POWER, I ARROGANTLY LOOKED DOWN ON THEM.

SEAL PAPERS ARE FOR FORCEFULLY SUMMONING DEMONS. IF YOU HAVE A CONTRACT BUT HAVEN'T ESTABLISHED A TRUSTING RELATIONSHIP, THEN YOU HAVE NO CHOICE BUT TO USE THEM. BUT A TAMER WHO HAS A GOOD RELATIONSHIP WITH DEMONS CAN SUMMON THEM WITHOUT ONE.

IN OTHER WORDS, YOU'VE LEVELED UP AS A TAMER!

HUH? L-LIGHTNING?!

HE JUST SUDDENLY SHOWED UP!

SO IF YOU WANT TO BE A TAMER, YOU SHOULD TRY TO GET ALONG WITH DEMONS. BUT IF ARTHUR AND OTHERS WHO ARE VEHEMENTLY AGAINST DEMONS HEARD THAT, THEY'D BLOW A FUSE! (LOL)

WHY DOESN'T LUCIFER HIDE HIS TAIL? AND DOESN'T SAMAEL EVER SHOW HIS? (WHAT'S IT LIKE?) WHEN I THINK ABOUT THIS, I CAN'T SLEEP! *TOKIMEKI-SAN (?), TOYAMA PREFECTURE*

SO MANY READERS ARE HAVING TROUBLE SLEEPING! QUESTIONS ABOUT LUCIFER SUDDENLY RAMPED UP FROM VOLUMES 12 THROUGH 14, AND THE MOST COMMON ONE IS ABOUT HIS TAIL. LET'S HAVE LUCIFER HIMSELF ANSWER!!

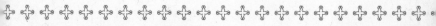

IT'S NICE TO MEET YOU, EVERYONE. I'M *KOFF CHOKE GAG!! BLEAGH HORK!*

L-LUCIFER?! ARE YOU ALL RIGHT?!

THE COMMANDER-IN-CHIEF ISN'T IN GOOD CONDITION, SO I'LL ANSWER FOR HIM.

OH, OKAY.

HE DOESN'T HIDE HIS TAIL BECAUSE HE DOESN'T WANT TO EXPEND EXTRA DEMONIC POWER. RIGHT NOW, HE USES MOST OF HIS STRENGTH TO MAINTAIN HIS HEALTH, SO HE CAN'T WORRY ABOUT HIS TAIL. BESIDES, ONLY WEAK DEMONS HIDE THEIR TAILS. THAT HE DOESN'T HIDE HIS IS A SIGN OF STRENGTH.

I SEE. SO WHY DOES SAMAEL HIDE HIS? IS HE WEAK?

IDIOT! SHOWING ONE'S TAIL IS LIKE BEING NAKED! SO BIG BRO IS ALWAYS NUDE, AND I'M TOO REFINED FOR THAT!

OH...I GUESS THAT MAKES YOU THE STRONGEST!!!

WHO PAYS IZUMO'S SCHOOL TUITION?

KIKU (29), TOKYO PREFECTURE

I TAKE IT FROM SAVINGS MY MOTHER LEFT TO ME.

YOUR MOM WAS REALLY THOUGHTFUL!

YEAH. I'M A LITTLE LATE RECOGNIZING IT, BUT SHE REALLY WAS.

GEDOIN WAS REALLY THIN IN HIS IMAGINATION, SO WHY IS HE CHUBBY IN REALITY? DID HE USED TO BE THIN?

SANCHO (14), MIYAGI PREFECTURE

A NUMBER OF PEOPLE ASKED ABOUT THIS TOO. UNFORTUNATELY, MR. GEDOIN IS NO LONGER ALIVE TO–

HEE HEE HEE! WHAT'S ALL THIS, YOU FILTHY PIGS?! WHAT A CRUMMY QUESTION! *GYA HA HA!*

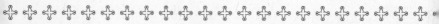

WHOA... HE CAME BACK AS A GHOST!! WELL, HURRY UP AND ANSWER! ARE YOU CHUBBY, PROFESSOR?

...? CHUBBY? WHAT DO YOU MEAN?

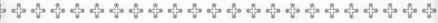

OH... THAT EXPLAINS IT.

IN CHAPTER 55, PROFESSOR GEDOIN MENTIONS "THE ONE IN A HUNDRED" AND "THE ONE IN A THOUSAND." HOW ARE THEY DIFFERENT? IS IT JUST A DIFFERENCE OF PROBABILITY? ALSO, I THINK PROFESSOR GEDOIN SHOULD GO ON A DIET.
TOHOJIN@AOZORA (13), OSAKA PREFECTURE

YOU DIDN'T UNDERSTAND THAT? KYA HA HA! I WAS RANKING ZOMBIE STRENGTH ACCORDING TO THEIR REGENERATIVE ABILITY AND NUMBER OF SURVIVORS. "ONE IN A HUNDRED" REFERS TO ANY SUBJECT WHO SURVIVES ELIXIR EXPERIMENTATION. SURVIVORS WITH PARTICULARLY HIGH REGENERATION—ONES THAT THE ORDER CALLS CHIMERA ZOMBIES CONSTITUTE THE "ONE IN A THOUSAND." GOT IT, YOU SCUMBAG?! *KYAAA HA HA HA HA HA!! KYAAA HA HA HA HA HA!!!* HM? DIET? WHAT DO YOU MEAN?

BEGONE, FOUL SPIRIT!!

?! *GYAA-AAAH !!!!!*

NEXT QUESTION!

I'D LIKE TO ASK YUKIO-SAMA A QUESTION. YOU SUMMON DEMONS AND LEAD MISSIONS, AND YOU'RE MAKING HUGE CONTRIBUTIONS, SO WHY DON'T YOU GET PROMOTED? I'M SURE YOU CAN DO IT!!
YUKIO-SAMA'S SELF-STYLED SERVANT (15), SHIGA PREFECTURE

"YUKIO-SAMA"?!

QUIET. DON'T POKE FUN.

WELL, ***EXCUUUSE ME,*** YUKIO-SAMA!

(IGNORING RIN) WHY DON'T I GET PROMOTED? EXORCIST TITLES DEPEND UPON THE STRENGTH OF THE DEMONS YOU CAN EXORCISE ALONE. IN MY EXORCIST CERTIFICATION EXAM, I FOUGHT UPPER-MID-LEVEL DEMONS, SO I BECAME AN INTERMEDIATE EXORCIST FIRST CLASS, BUT I'M STILL NOT CONFIDENT ABOUT FIGHTING A HIGH-LEVEL DEMON ALONE. OF COURSE, I DO WANT TO ADVANCE SOMEDAY. EXORCISTS USUALLY RECEIVE TITLES BY TAKING AN ADVANCEMENT EXAM, SO I'LL DO THAT TOO. BY THE WAY, MISSION LEADERS ARE GENERALLY CHOSEN FROM AMONG INTERMEDIATE FIRST CLASS EXORCISTS.

IN OTHER VORDS, SINCE I'VE ALREADY DEFEATED A HIGH-LEVEL DEMON ON MY OWN, I'M STRONGER THAN YUKIO!

THAT MEANS I'LL PROBABLY MAKE SENIOR EXORCIST FIRST CLASS IN MY CERTIFICATION EXAM!!

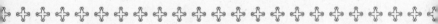

THERE'S ALSO A WRITTEN EXAM.

HUH? SERIOUSLY?!

IZUMO'S CHANT FOR REPOSE SPIRIT IN THE DECEMBER ISSUE OF *JUMP SQ* WAS DIFFERENT THAN IN VOLUME 14. WHICH ONE IS CORRECT?
AYAI (15), OKINAWA PREFECTURE

IT SEEMS LIKE YOU BOUGHT BOTH *JUMP SQ* AND THE GRAPHIC NOVEL! THANKS! I GOT THIS QUESTION A LOT TOO, SO I'LL GIVE A THOROUGH ANSWER. WHEN THERE ARE DIFFERENCES BETWEEN *JUMP SQ* AND THE GRAPHIC NOVEL, PLEASE VIEW THE GRAPHIC NOVEL AS CORRECT. THE MONTHLY CHAPTER IS THE ALPHA VERSION (TRIAL VERSION) AND THE GRAPHIC NOVEL IS THE IMPROVED BETA VERSION (FINAL).

BUT SHOULDN'T IT BE CORRECT FROM THE START?

YES, BUT THAT'S DIFFICULT! I'M ONLY HUMAN, YOU KNOW!

HOW CAN I JOIN THE ILLUMINATI?
SESAME TOFU (19), KYOTO PREFECTURE

YOU WANNA JOIN THE ILLUMINATI?! GASP

PLEASED TO MEET YOU. I AM LUCIGAG *KOFF! KOFF CHOKE!! GASP WHEEZ!!*

SOMEONE STRAP THIS GUY TO HIS SICKBED!!!

I'LL ANSWER FOR HIM.

I WISH YOU WOULD HAVE FROM THE START.

TO JOIN THE ILLUMINATI, EITHER A MEMBER HAS TO INVITE YOU OR WE HAVE TO HEADHUNT YOU. HEADHUNTING IS THE FASTEST WAY, I SUPPOSE. TRY TO ALWAYS FOLLOW THE TEACHINGS OF THE ILLUMINATI. WE'RE ALWAYS WATCHING AND INVESTIGATING PEOPLE. YOU HAVE TO CATCH OUR ATTENTION.

THAT'S ALL FOR NOW!

BLUE EXORCIST 15

Art Staff

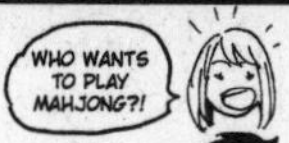
WHO WANTS TO PLAY MAHJONG?!

Miyuki Shibuya

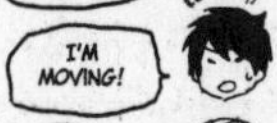
I'M MOVING!

Erika Uemura

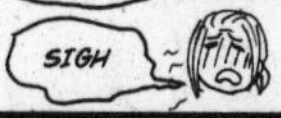
SIGH

Yoshino Kawamura

Art Assistants

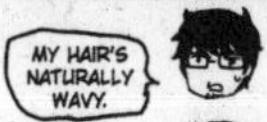
MY HAIR'S NATURALLY WAVY.

Hayashi-kun

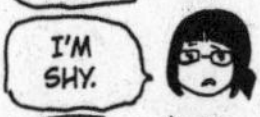
I'M SHY.

Yamanaka-san

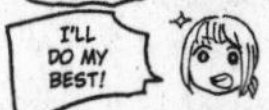
I'LL DO MY BEST!

Yanagimoto-san

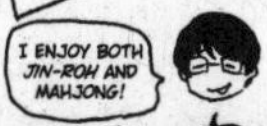
I ENJOY BOTH JIN-ROH AND MAHJONG!

Yamagishi-san

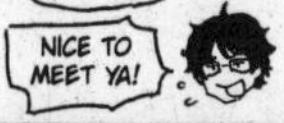
NICE TO MEET YA!

Yoshiyama-kun

Composition Assistant

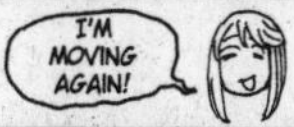
I'M MOVING AGAIN!

Minoru Sasaki

Kyoto Dialect Advisor

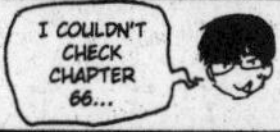
I COULDN'T CHECK CHAPTER 66...

Yosuke Takeda

Editor:

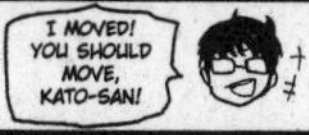
I MOVED! YOU SHOULD MOVE, KATO-SAN!

Shihei Rin

Graphic Novel Editor

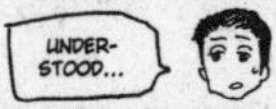
UNDER-STOOD...

Ryusuke Kuroki

Graphic Novel Design

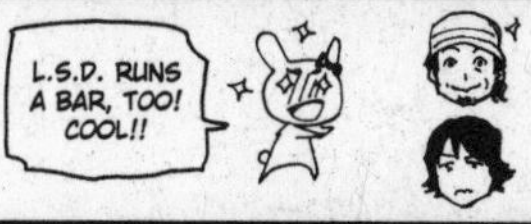
L.S.D. RUNS A BAR, TOO! COOL!!

Shimada Hideaki

Daiju Asami (L.S.D.)

Manga

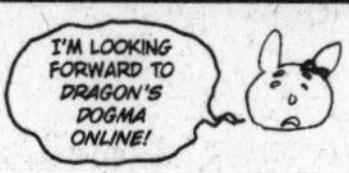
I'M LOOKING FORWARD TO DRAGON'S DOGMA ONLINE!

Kazue Kato

(in no particular order)
(Note: The caricatures and statements are from memory!)

Next is Volume 16! See you then!!

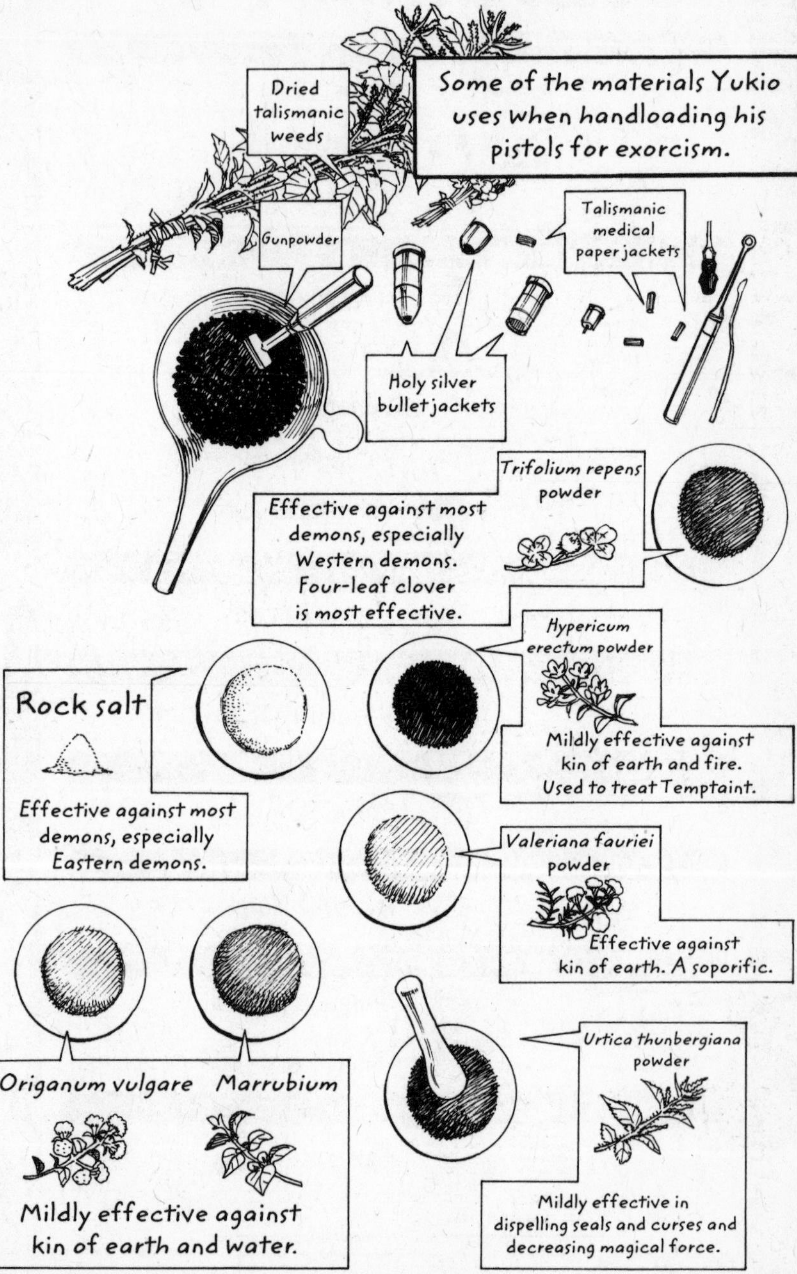

Some of the materials Yukio uses when handloading his pistols for exorcism.
Dried talismanic weeds
Talismanic medical paper jackets
Gunpowder
Holy silver bullet jackets
Trifolium repens powder
Effective against most demons, especially Western demons. Four-leaf clover is most effective.
Hypericum erectum powder
Mildly effective against kin of earth and fire. Used to treat Temptaint.
Rock salt
Effective against most demons, especially Eastern demons.
Valeriana fauriei powder
Effective against kin of earth. A soporific.
Origanum vulgare
Marrubium
Mildly effective against kin of earth and water.
Urtica thunbergiana powder
Mildly effective in dispelling seals and curses and decreasing magical force.

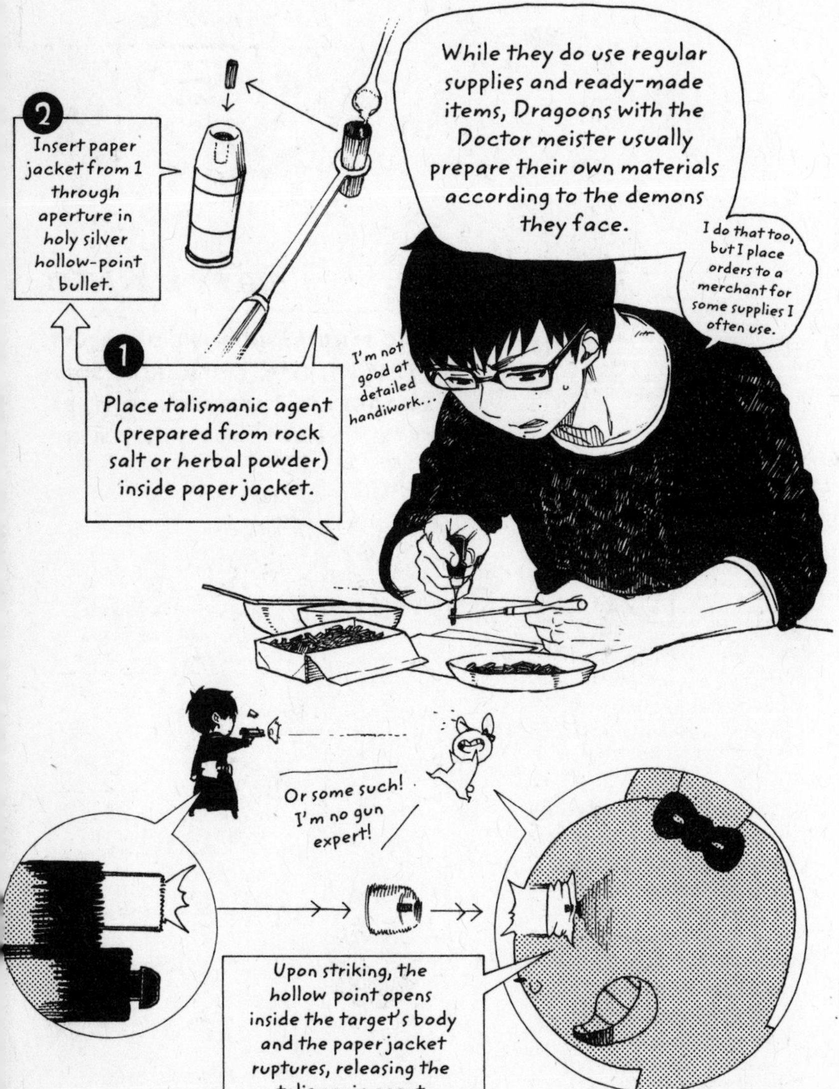

While they do use regular supplies and ready-made items, Dragoons with the Doctor meister usually prepare their own materials according to the demons they face.
I do that too, but I place orders to a merchant for some supplies I often use.
I'm not good at detailed handiwork...
1
Place talismanic agent (prepared from rock salt or herbal powder) inside paper jacket.
2
Insert paper jacket from 1 through aperture in holy silver hollow-point bullet.
Or some such! I'm no gun expert!
Upon striking, the hollow point opens inside the target's body and the paper jacket ruptures, releasing the talismanic agent.

KAZVE KATO

I'VE BEEN RAISING PLANTS...AND IT'S DIFFICULT!
BEGINNING THIS VOLUME, I'M MAKING SOME
CHANGES TO THE BONUS CONTENT.
I HOPE YOU DON'T MIND.

BLUE EXORCIST

BLUE EXORCIST VOL. 15
SHONEN JUMP ADVANCED Manga Edition

STORY & ART BY KAZUE KATO

Translation & English Adaptation/John Werry
Touch-up Art & Lettering/John Hunt, Primary Graphix
Cover & Interior Design/Sam Elzway
Editor/Mike Montesa

Printed in the U.S.A.

Published by VIZ Media, LLC
P.O. Box 77010
San Francisco, CA 94107

10 9 8 7 6 5 4 3 2 1
First printing, May 2016

In the next volume...

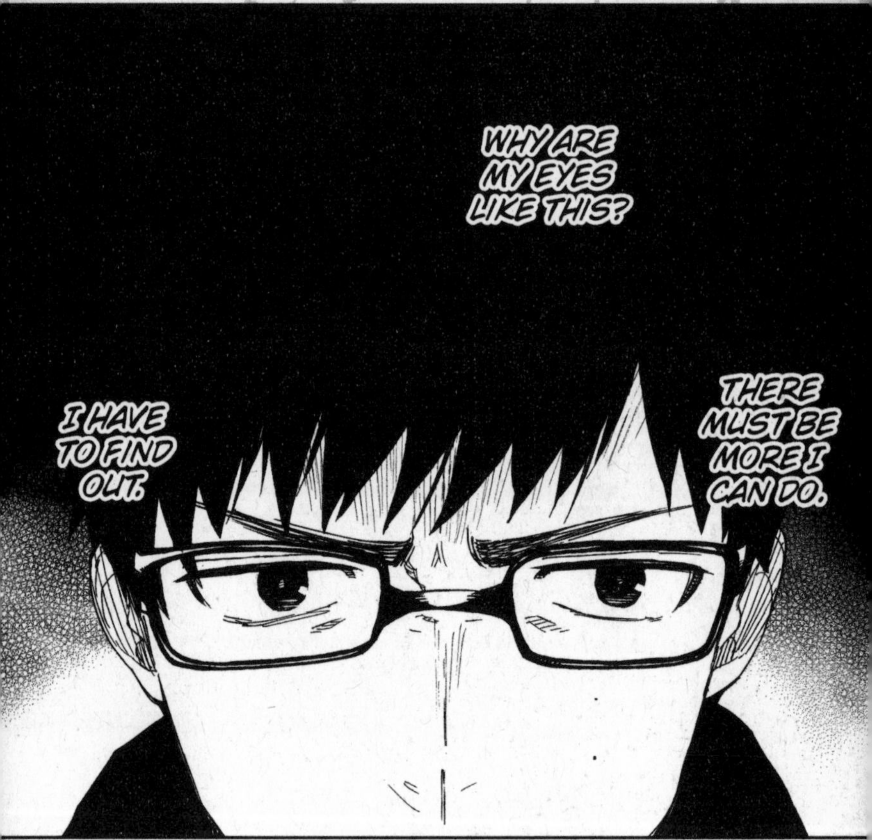
WHY ARE MY EYES LIKE THIS?
THERE MUST BE MORE I CAN DO.
I HAVE TO FIND OUT.

The surge of demonic activity around the world has the Knights of the True Cross worried at the highest levels. An important meeting at the Vatican will have serious effects on the lives of Rin and his Exwire friends. Back at True Cross Academy, the students get a sense that something is brewing with the arrival of an unexpected and definitely unconventional new instructor! Meanwhile, Yukio struggles to understand the strange fire in his eyes, a fire he has kept secret from everyone. Can he confront the flames inside him alone, or will they consume him?

Coming December 2016!

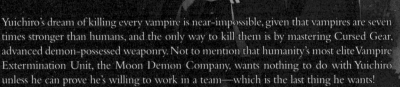

EYESHIELD 21

STORY BY RIICHIRO INAGAKI
ART BY YUSUKE MURATA

From the artist of *One-Punch Man!*

Wimpy Sena Kobayakawa has been running away from
bullies all his life. But when the football gear comes
on, things change—Sena's speed and uncanny ability
to elude big bullies just might give him what it takes to
become a great high school football hero! Catch all the
bone-crushing action and slapstick comedy of Japan's
hottest football manga!

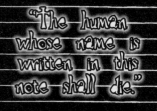

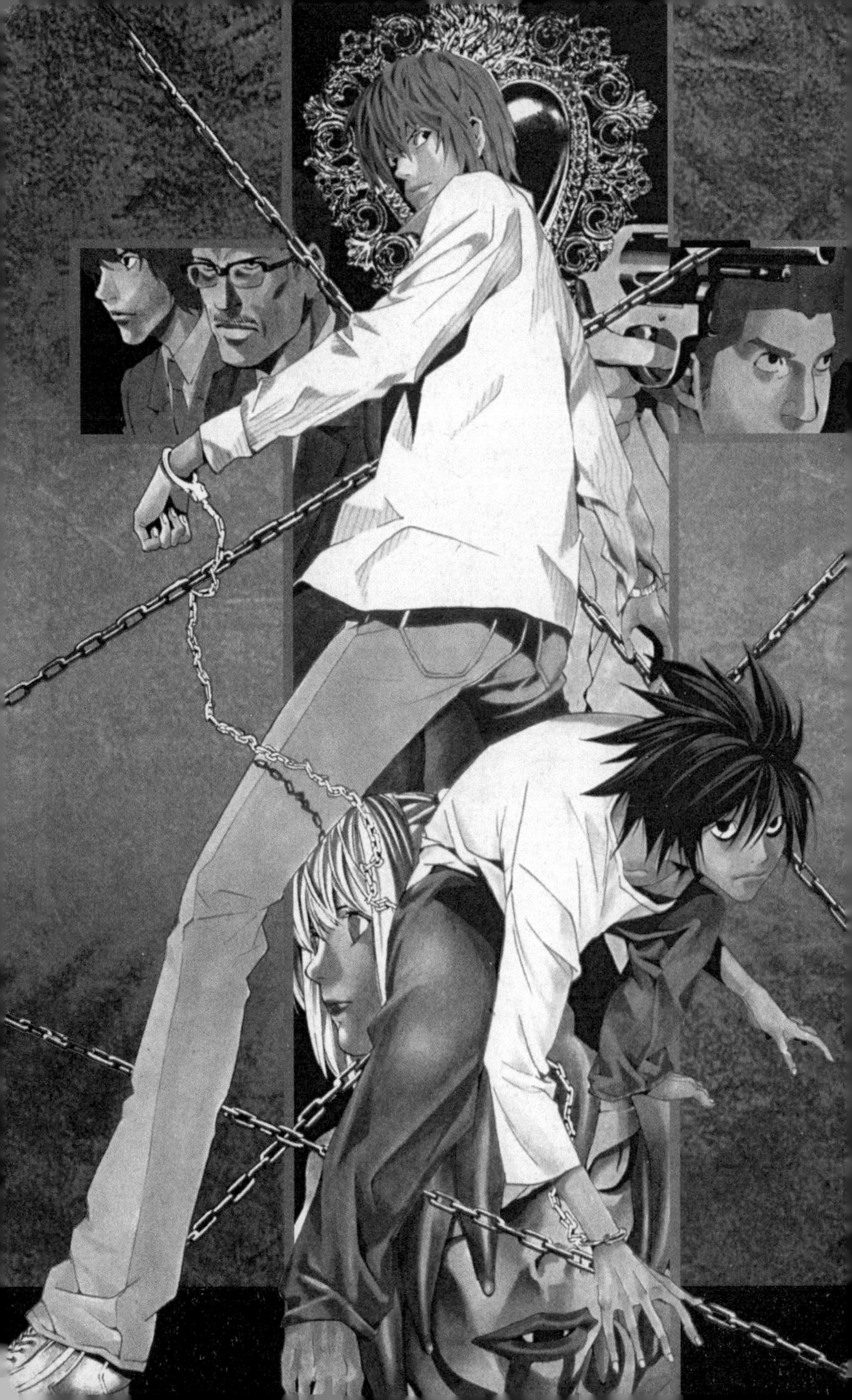

You're Reading in the Wrong Direction!!

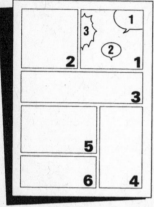

Whoops! Guess what? You're starting at the wrong end of the comic!

…It's true! In keeping with the original Japanese format, **Blue Exorcist** is meant to be read from right to left, starting in the upper-right corner.

Unlike English, which is read from left to right, Japanese is read from right to left, meaning that action, sound effects and word-balloon order are completely reversed… something which can make readers unfamiliar with Japanese feel pretty backwards themselves. For this reason, manga or Japanese comics published in the U.S. in English have sometimes been published "flopped"—that is, printed in exact reverse order, as though seen from the other side of a mirror.

By flopping pages, U.S. publishers can avoid confusing readers, but the compromise is not without its downside. For one thing, a character in a flopped manga series who once wore in the original Japanese version a T-shirt emblazoned with "M A Y" (as in "the merry month of") now wears one which reads "Y A M"! Additionally, many manga creators in Japan are themselves unhappy with the process, as some feel the mirror-imaging of their art skews their original intentions.

We are proud to bring you Kazue Kato's **Blue Exorcist** in the original unflopped format. For now, though, turn to the other side of the book and let the adventure begin…!

—Editor